Prussia and German History

An Enthralling Overview of the Holy Roman Empire, Habsburg Dynasty, and the Rise of Germany

Free limited time bonus

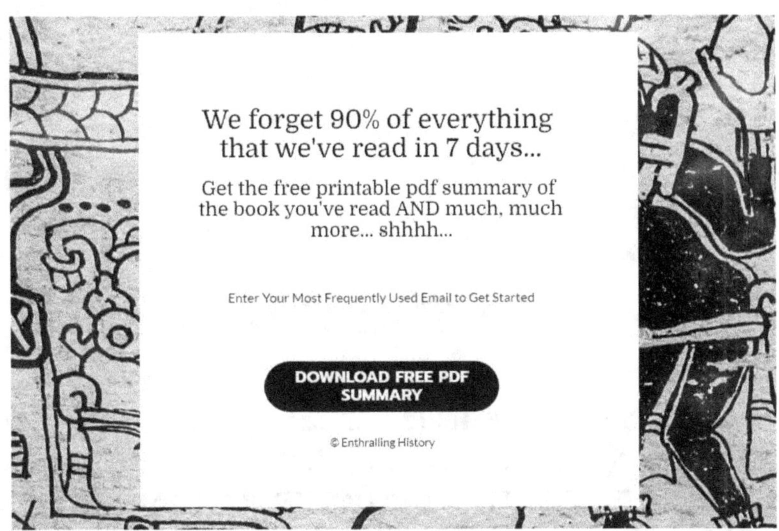

Stop for a moment. We have a free bonus set up for you. The problem is this: we forget 90% of everything that we read after 7 days. Crazy fact, right? Here's the solution: we've created a printable, 1-page pdf summary for this book that you're reading now. All you have to do to get your free pdf summary is to go to the following website:

https://livetolearn.lpages.co/enthrallinghistory/

Or, Scan the QR code!

Once you do, it will be intuitive. Enjoy, and thank you!

Table of Contents

Part 1: The Holy Roman Empire

An Enthralling Overview of One of the Most Powerful European States during the Middle Ages and Early Modern Period

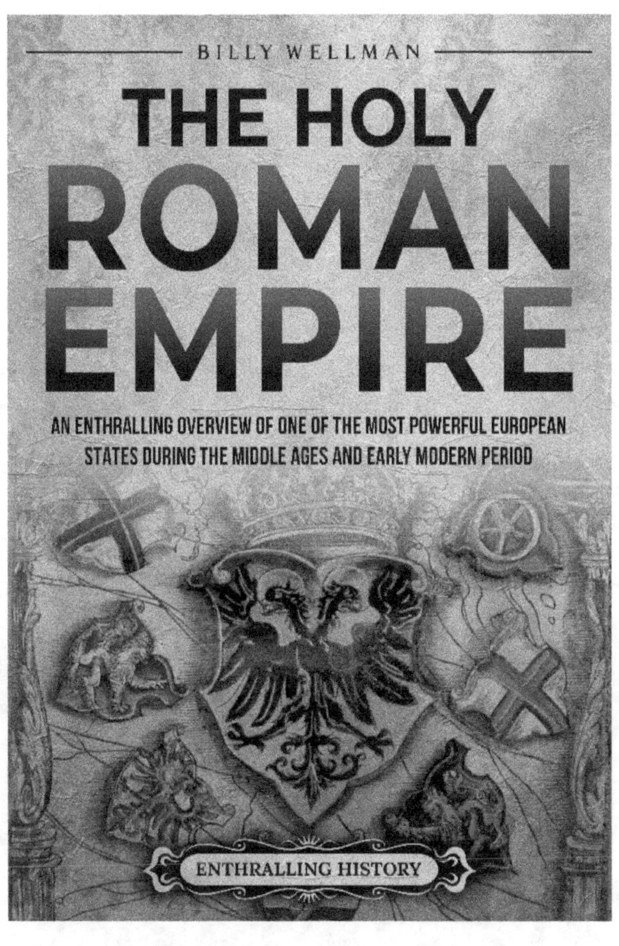

Introduction

The ascent and downfall of the Holy Roman Empire mark the seemingly universal oscillation of human societies between fragmentation and centralization and between unification and separation. Germanic peoples, who dealt the final blow that brought the Western Roman Empire to its knees, formed a number of new states, which were bound together at one point in the form of Charlemagne's empire. His empire soon perished, and from the ashes rose medieval France and the Holy Roman Empire, both of which were heavily fragmented and lacked central authority. In fact, these medieval states looked nothing like our modern nations.

Even during the most illustrious periods of the Holy Roman Empire, for instance, during the reign of Frederick Barbarossa, the emperor was much less in control of his empire in comparison to modern state administrations. The emperor, of course, almost always had a large army at his disposal, meaning that he could crush those who didn't go along with what he wanted. However, because concepts like nation, state administration, and centralization were virtually nonexistent at the time, it was impossible for the emperor to be in real control of his empire. Practically each emperor of the Holy Roman Empire had to renegotiate the basic terms of his authority with the nobility. The stability of the Holy Roman Empire was dependent on an emperor's ability to be on good terms with their nobles while not giving the nobles too much freedom.

Thus, the Holy Roman Empire, as was the case (and still is to a certain extent) with numerous other states, constantly shifted between periods of relative stability and periods of rebellion against the central authority. The emperor would quench rebellions in one corner of his empire while unrest sprung up elsewhere. So, each emperor had to wage multiple wars, lacking the means to keep his enormous empire fully together.

In a way, the Holy Roman Empire is a historical misnomer. The state was neither holy nor Roman. The adjective "holy" comes from the fact that German emperors were traditionally crowned in Rome. "Roman" comes from the fact that German emperors wanted the same sort of illustriousness enjoyed by the ancient Roman emperors. However, unlike the Roman Empire, the Holy Roman Empire never managed to establish the same centralized administration. During the times of the great Emperor Augustus, Rome had the same sort of state officials and administrative hierarchy across the whole empire, which was even bigger than the Holy Roman Empire. Frederick Barbarossa, on the other hand, arguably the most powerful of all the Holy Roman emperors, was more like a leader of autonomous states (even within modern-day Germany), each having its own laws and power structures. Barbarossa had his own lands and fiefs like his subordinates (vassals). In addition, the Roman Empire had a much more widespread and coherent cultural influence on vast non-Latin areas, whereas the Holy Roman Empire hardly managed to achieve even a fragment of the same kind of influence on non-Germanic areas of their own empire.

This is the main reason for the ultimate dissolution of the Holy Roman Empire after the Peace of Westphalia of 1648. France heralded the birth of a modern nation, while the Germans sank back to the fragmentation and disunity of the pre-empire days. It was only with Bismarck at the helm that Germans could form a single state led by a single, coherent administration.

In this book, we'll deal with the ups and downs of this strange empire. Starting with the fall of the Western Roman Empire, we'll show how Charlemagne's empire was slowly divided into smaller parts, with the Franks on the one hand and the Germans on the other. After describing the days of the first few dynasties that led to the creation of the Holy Roman Empire, we'll spend some time with Barbarossa, following him on his endless conquests and, most importantly, his two crusades. Moving on, we'll show how the Habsburgs gradually took over, leading the state into exceedingly turbulent periods of religious wars and pan-European conflicts.

This book, while being a meticulous collection of the most important facts about the Holy Roman Empire, also provides a deeper explanation of the pitfalls of this mighty and incredibly complex constellation of German states.

Chapter 1: The Genesis of the Holy Roman Empire

Prelude to an Empire

The Holy Roman Empire, like a phoenix, rose from the ashes of the Roman Empire.[i] When the "original" Roman Empire finally collapsed in 476 CE under the burden of barbaric invasions and internal strife, Europe became shrouded in a power vacuum, which was only filled with the gradual formation of the Holy Roman Empire with Charlemagne. But before talking about Charlemagne, one of the greatest emperors to ever live, we'll quickly dissect the fall of the Roman Empire and the power struggle that ensued.

The year 476 brought an end to a once great empire, the Roman Empire. Truth be told, it was only its western part that ceased to exist, as the Eastern Roman Empire continued to exist for another thousand years. However, the city of Rome itself was taken by barbarians, and the Western Roman Empire was dismembered. The invasion of the Huns in the 4th century, spearheaded by Attila, was the final blow to an opponent that was already struggling to stay on its feet. Quickly, over the course of the 5th century, the Western Roman Empire was dismembered by the Ostrogoths, Visigoths, Vandals, Franks, Angles, Saxons, and many others.

---

[i] Heather, Peter. Empires and Barbarians: The Fall of Rome and the Birth of Europe. Oxford University Press, 2010.

These Germanic tribes, which had been kept at bay for centuries by Roman might, spilled over the traditional borders of their states and ventured to new lands.

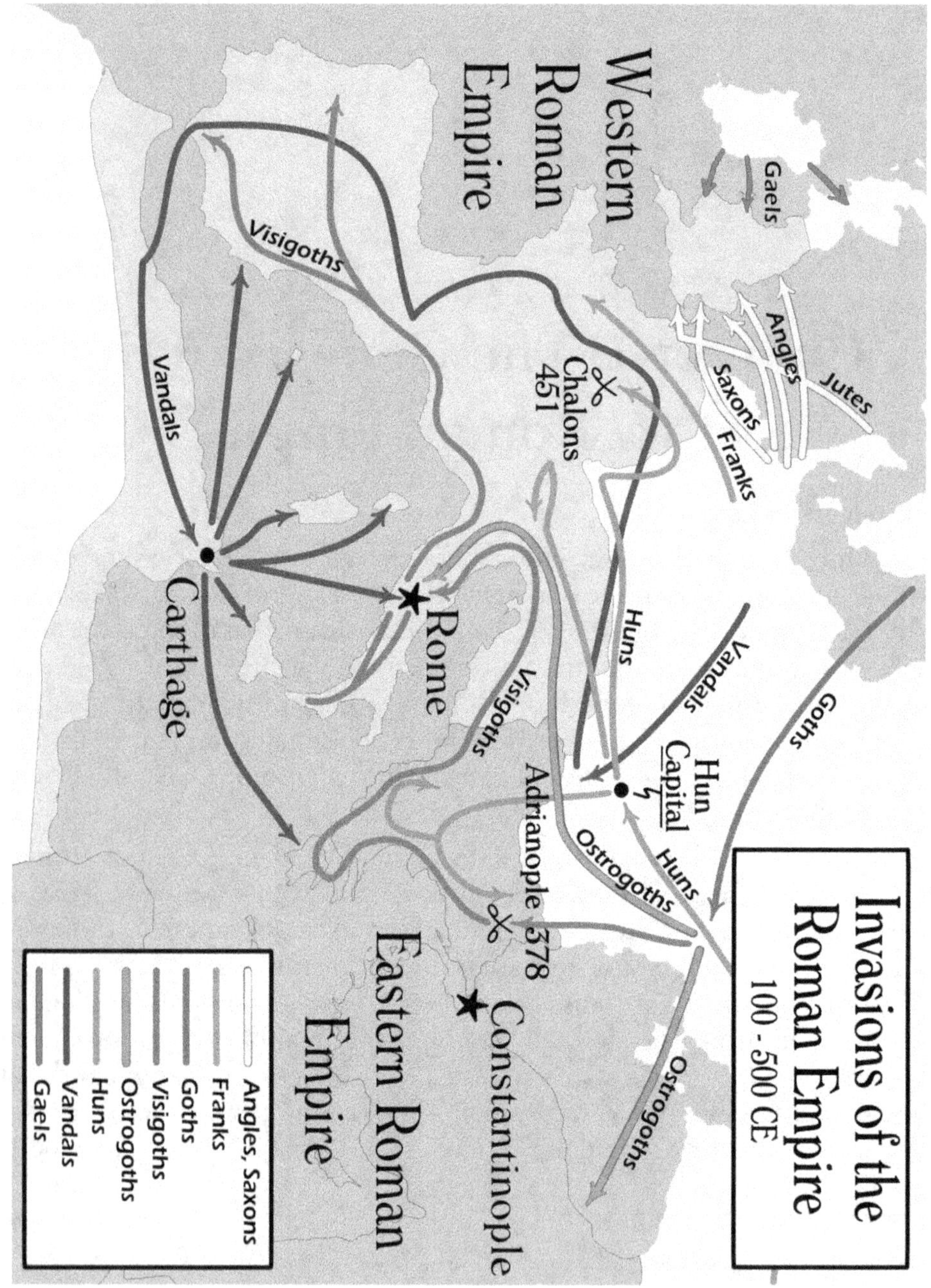

Dissolution of the Roman Empire due to the barbarian invasions[1]

The Great Migration sets the scene for the formation of the Holy Roman Empire. In fact, the modern landscape of Europe, for the most part, follows the line traced by the Great Migration. And much like our modern democracies draw upon the institutions of ancient Rome, so did the emerging Germanic states after the fall of the Western Roman Empire. Franks, or at least their leaders, believed they had procured their authority and legitimacy not only from God but also from old Roman emperors.

Speaking of God, the Germanic tribes fairly quickly accepted Christianity as their religion, and their successful incorporation of Christianity put them on the lucky side of history. The Eastern Roman Empire, partially thanks to Constantine the Great, who promoted Christianity, showed just how powerful Roman heritage was when coupled with the zeal of Christianity. The Western Roman Empire never seemed to be able to strike this balance.

However, the Germanic states that rose from the ruins of the Western Roman Empire were able to do this. The Franks, after whom modern-day France is named, conquered the old Roman province of Gaul (roughly speaking modern-day France), battling other Germanic tribes. The first Frankish dynasty was the Merovingian dynasty. We don't know too much about the early history of the Merovingian dynasty, but we do know that in the 5th century, they were led by Childeric I and fought other Germanic tribes in Gaul, such as the Visigoths, Burgundians, and others. Childeric I and his subordinates were still pagans. After Childeric I died around 481, his son, Clovis I, took over, finally uniting the Frankish sub-tribes and strengthening his dynasty's position against other Germanic states.

Clovis I married Clotilde, a Burgundian princess who was a Nicene Christian.[i] Eventually, Clovis I accepted the faith of his wife and propagated it to his subordinates, an important decision because most of the Germanic tribes, if baptized, were Arians. Clovis I at least had ideological support from the center of Orthodox Christianity, namely Constantinople. Clovis I chose Paris as the seat of his kingdom in a symbolic way by picking it as his place of burial.

---

[i] Nicene Christianity was the form of Christianity as defined by the First Council of Nicaea in 325 CE. It stood against Arianism (Arius was an Alexandrine presbyter who emphasized Christ's human nature, believing that Jesus Christ was more a man than a heavenly being and was actually created by God and thus had a beginning and an end).

The Merovingian kingdom wasn't stable, and after Clovis I died around 511, his successors vied for supremacy, successfully partitioning the kingdom. Clovis had four sons, so the kingdom was divided into four parts: Austrasia, Neustria, Burgundy, and Aquitaine.[i]

The Merovingian dynasty finally came to an end in the early 8th century. For quite some time, the Merovingian kings were only formally kings; the real power was in the hands of the mayor of the palace, who was, in a way, in charge of the Merovingian royal household. Charles Martel, a Frankish aristocrat, rose to this position in 718 and made way for a new dynasty: the Carolingians.

Charles Martel wasn't simply a court official. He was the de facto head of state and chief military commander. He protected the kingdom from other Germanic states and attempted to unite and enlarge the lands conquered by Clovis I. Charles Martel was also instrumental in the defense of Europe from the Umayyad Caliphate.[ii] In 732, a decisive battle was fought between the Muslim Umayyads and Germanic peoples: the Battle of Tours (sometimes referred to as the Battle of Poitiers). The Arabs managed to penetrate deep into modern-day France and were only stopped by the forces of Charles Martel and Odo of Aquitaine. From then on, the Muslims were confined to their Hispanic territories, where they stayed for centuries.

After Charles Martel died in 741, the kingdom was divided into two parts. The kingdom was left to his two sons (both de jure mayors of different palaces led by the Merovingians but also de facto rulers), Carloman and Pepin the Short (sometimes referred to as Pepin the Younger). By 747, Pepin the Short had assumed the sole and uncontested supremacy of the land of the Franks, as Carloman decided (or was forced) to become a monk, which was the most convenient way of disposing of unwanted competition. Pepin the Short also dealt with Childeric III, the last Merovingian "king," by sending him to a monastery, where he would spend the remainder of his days without posing a threat to Pepin the Short.

---

[i] Contreni, John J. "Introduction: The Merovingian Kingdoms, 450-751." French Historical Studies 19, no. 3 (1996): 755.

[ii] The Umayyad Caliphate is the second caliphate made after the death of Muhammad the Prophet. By 732, the Arabs had reached modern-day Spain and were threatening the Kingdom of the Franks. The Umayyad Caliphate is, territorially speaking, one of the largest empires ever.

Pepin the Short was the first king of the Carolingian dynasty, gaining support from the archbishop of Mainz, Boniface, in 751. Pepin was anointed by Pope Stephen II in 754. He received the title "Patricius Romanorum," which is an obvious reference to the continuity between the Roman Empire and the Kingdom of the Franks, which we often refer to as the start of the Holy Roman Empire.

Pepin the Short then went about assuring papal supremacy in northern Italy, which had recently been under threat by the Lombards. This is basically how the Papal States were established. The Papal States had an incredibly long lifespan, lasting from 756 all the way to 1870. Pepin also had to battle the Muslims once again, now in Narbonne (southern France), which was recaptured in 759. Pepin died in 768, leaving his kingdom to Charlemagne and Carloman I, with the kingdom once again being divided according to the old Frankish custom.

As was customary, the two brothers didn't really get along well. There were brief quarrels between Charlemagne's and Carloman's armies, but there wasn't enough time for an all-out war. Carloman I died in 771, and the Kingdom of the Franks was once again unified under one ruler.

Charles the Great

Charles the Great, better known as Charlemagne, was probably born in 742. He was the oldest son of Bertrada and Pepin the Short.[i] Charlemagne also had a younger sister named Gisela, as well as other siblings who probably didn't live long enough to be remembered well by chroniclers.

Charlemagne is well known for his conquests and restless attempts to enlarge his realm. Crucially, he continued the Frankish support of the Papal States, which, by the time of his succession to power in 771, were once again under threat from the Lombards.[ii] The Lombardian threat in Italy was silenced by 774, but Charlemagne had to return to Italy in 776 to quench another rebellion.

Charlemagne also continued his father's battle against the Andalusian Muslims. He was able to expand the Frankish realm into modern-day Spain across the Pyrenees. Charlemagne's first campaign here, in 778, almost turned out to be a catastrophe. After being forced to retreat,

---

[i] Barbero, Alessandro. Charlemagne: Father of a Continent. University of California Press, 2018.
[ii] The Lombards were Germanic people who lived in modern-day northern Italy.

Charlemagne's forces were ambushed in the Pyrenees, an event that is today known as the Battle of Roncevaux Pass. The Basques ambushed Charlemagne because the two had clashed before, with Charlemagne forcing the Basques into submission. So, the Basques retaliated, and they succeeded in seriously weakening the Frankish forces. Charlemagne got out alive, but many were killed, including people close to Charlemagne, such as a knight named Roland, whose death inspired the *Song of Roland*, one of the very first literary works of art written in French.

Over the next few decades, Charlemagne succeeded in conquering parts of Muslim Andalusia, and by 797, he was able to take Barcelona. Charlemagne was a careful diplomat and was able to make the most of the hostilities between the Umayyads and Abbasids.[i] He had many other conquests, virtually all of which were successful. For instance, Charlemagne pacified the Saxons in a war that lasted practically thirty years. The Saxons were a fierce, warlike Germanic tribe who were known by ancient Romans for their warcraft and zeal. Charlemagne successfully pacified the Saxons and managed to convert them to Christianity. Perhaps the most well-known war exploit of Charlemagne was his war against the Avars, who were Asiatic nomads who lived in modern-day Hungary. The campaign was particularly brutal. By 803, the Avars had been seriously weakened and had to accept Charlemagne as their supreme ruler.

Charlemagne also waged war on the Slavs in the north and south, further expanding his dominion. Thanks to all of these conquests, Charlemagne built an empire that spanned from Barcelona to modern-day Croatia and from modern-day Belgium all the way to Rome. This was an enormous empire, spanning across territories of modern-day Spain, France, Germany, Austria, Italy, Switzerland, Croatia, Hungary, Czechia, and Slovakia.

It was only natural for such a mighty individual to be coronated as the emperor of the Romans, Imperator Romanorum, in 800. Charlemagne ostensibly arrived in Rome to make peace between Pope Leo III and his adversaries. Humbled by Charlemagne's readiness to arrive and help, as well as by his conquests, Pope Leo III crowned Charlemagne and declared him to be Imperator Romanorum, a legitimate successor of

---

[i] In 750, the Umayyads were overthrown by the Abbasids, although Andalusia remained the stronghold of the Umayyads. However, the Umayyad authorities of Córdoba (the capital) were under constant threat from Muslims who supported the Abbasid Caliphate.

Constantine VI, who ruled the Eastern Roman Empire and had been deposed by his mother, Irene, who proclaimed herself to be the empress. Pope Leo III didn't consider her a legitimate successor to the Roman heritage and found a better candidate in Charlemagne.

Francia at the accession of Charles Martel (714). [2]

Although the coronation of Charlemagne legitimized his power in western and central Europe, it put him at odds with the Byzantine Empire, whose emperors considered themselves the only legitimate Roman emperors in Europe.[i] Western and eastern Europe were growing increasingly distant. Ultimately, the Byzantine Empire paid the highest

---

[i] Soon the political disunity would result in a religious split. In 1054, the Christian Church separated into two major currents, Catholic and Eastern Orthodox, an event today known as the Great Schism.

price, as it was unable to do anything against the impending Muslim invasion. However, that would happen about six hundred years later. For now, we're still deep in the early medieval age, a time that was dominated by the Franks and Byzantines.

After Charlemagne

As is always the case with great empires, the Carolingian Empire was doomed right from the start. Overextension and internal troubles plagued the Carolingian Empire. We've seen that even prior to Charlemagne, there were internal conflicts for supremacy within the Carolingian dynasty. Rebels in practically all corners of the kingdom, as well as external enemies, were just waiting for the right opportunity to arrive.

Charlemagne died in 814, leaving his empire to Louis the Pious. He was the last ruler of the Carolingian Empire to rule alone. After Louis the Pious died in 840, his sons quickly reintroduced the old Frankish custom of dividing the kingdom between all legitimate successors, so the empire was divided once again in 843 in the Treaty of Verdun.

The empire was divided into three parts: *Francia occidentalis* (West Francia), ruled by Charles II; *Francia media* (Middle Francia), ruled by Lothair I; and *Francia orientalis* (East Francia), led by Louis II. East Francia took a majority of today's France. Middle Francia encompassed previous Frankish conquests in Italy and parts of Germany, France, and Switzerland. East Francia encompassed, roughly speaking, modern-day Germany and Austria.

The consequences of the Treaty of Verdun, in a way, are felt today, as this treaty gave basic contours to two European states: Germany and France.[i] There was a handful of other important treaties that followed and further partitioned the empire. The Treaty of Prüm in 855 saw Middle Francia partitioned into three new states: Italy, Lotharingia, and Provence. Perhaps the most important and far-reaching effect of this treaty was the formation of Lotharingia, which encompassed the Alsace and Lorraine regions, which became some of the major points of animosity between France and Germany in the centuries to come. In further treaties, namely the Treaty of Meerssen or Mersen (870) and the Treaty of Ribemont (880), the once mighty empire was further partitioned, with various provinces changing hands repeatedly.

---

[i] Joranson, Einar. "The Dissolution of the Carolingian Fisc in the Ninth Century." (1936): 545-547.

There was, however, a brief period of unification under Charles the Fat from 881 to 888. The reunification of the empire and imperial coronation was rather haphazard. The Papal States, which had been under Frankish protection for years, were once again under threat from a regional warlord, and Pope John VIII sought help from Charles the Fat, who was the king of Frankish Italy and thus responsible for the security of the Papal States. Hoping for a revival of old power, the church coronated Charles the Fat, who, unfortunately, wasn't able to keep the empire unified.

Charles the Fat was unable to quench the rebellion rising in the eastern part of his empire. Arnulf of Carinthia, Charles's nephew, gathered a large army and defeated Charles the Fat, once again partitioning the empire.[i] This time, the division was much more long-lasting, with rare and relatively brief periods of reunification or mutual conquests. Arnulf of Carinthia ruled as the emperor until his death in 899.

In a similar vein, Louis the Blind, the adoptive son of Charles the Fat, tried to reunify the empire, but this was only a brief stint (901 to 905) that ended with him being blinded by the next big contender, Berengar I of Italy. This time, the interregnum period, the period between the death (or dethronement) of one ruler and the appointment of the new one, was even longer, with Berengar I of Italy becoming the emperor in 915.

Berengar I of Italy was in a good position to become the next emperor since he was the king of Italy and thus close to the pope. At the time (and more generally from the 9th to 11th century), Italy faced the so-called Saracen invasion in the south. Ancient Greeks and Romans sometimes referred, quite generally and indiscriminately, to Arabs as Saracens, and the name stuck for centuries. By the early 10th century, Arabs managed to gain a firm hold of Sicily, holding the island in its entirety and successfully repelling attacks from mainland Italy. Sicily served as a major Arab foothold in Italy, from where they could launch new invasions into mainland Italy and come dangerously close to Rome. A particular fortress built on the Garigliano River in central Italy was a thorn in the pope's side. Pope John X naturally didn't want Muslims on his doorstep and urged the noblemen of Christianized Europe to drive the Saracens away from Italy.

---

[i] Rosenberg, Harry. "Kingship and Politics in the Late Ninth Century: Charles the Fat and the End of the Carolingian Empire." The Historian 68, no. 3 (2006): 636-638.

Summoned by Pope John X, Berengar sent his troops and put them under the command of Alberic I. Others sent troops too, like the Byzantine Empire and powerful princes, dukes, and counts of Italy. The Garigliano Saracen fortress would be the last Saracen stronghold to fall in the Christian forces' sweeping attack, doing so in 915. Sicily, however, was still firmly in Muslim hands, and it would stay that way for some time. Berengar had to pull his forces so they could assist in repelling the Magyars (Hungarians) who threatened the borders of the empire. The Magyars were able to penetrate far into western Europe, much like the Huns some four hundred years prior. The Hungarians threatened not only East and West Francia but also Italy and even the Córdoban Caliphate in Spain.

In the same year as the Battle of Garigliano, Berengar was crowned Holy Roman emperor, but this was merely an act of goodwill from the pope, who wanted to thank Berengar for lending a hand in the battle.[i] At the time, the Holy Roman Empire was merely an abstract concept, so it was an empty title. Berengar seemed to have been unable or unwilling to even attempt to reunite the Holy Roman Empire; truth be told, the Arab, Magyar, and Viking invaders made such a thing a very challenging task. Throughout his short-lived "reign" (from 915 to 924), Berengar also faced internal strife. He was attacked by his own grandson (also named Berengar) and had to face the animosity of Rudolph II of Upper Burgundy. The Battle of Firenzuola, which was fought in 923, sealed Berengar's fate; after this battle, Berengar of Italy was murdered in the city of Verona.

However, a new dynasty would enter the scene: the Ottonian dynasty.

---

[i] Merlo, Brian. "Pope John X and the End of the Formosan Dispute in Rome." PhD diss., Saint Louis University, 2018.

Chapter 2: Feudalism and the State of Early German Politics

Medieval States

The medieval period, for a variety of reasons, is referred to as the Dark Ages. This was a very challenging period in the development of human beings and marked a fairly abrupt end of the Roman culture, at least in western Europe. We'd like to emphasize that a lot of good things happened during the so-called Dark Ages. It's likely that without this period, which seems to be much hated by many people today, we wouldn't have the modern age we enjoy today.

However, unlike the Roman administration, medieval states were fairly undeveloped, and it would take centuries for states like France or Austria-Hungary to reach the level of state administration set by the ancient Romans. As the Roman Empire stepped down, numerous Germanic tribes stepped to the forefront. Once victorious, the Germanic people started forming their own states in Europe, as we've seen in the case of the Kingdom of the Franks.

These states were rather different than the Romans in more ways than one. For instance, they didn't rely on slave labor, though they did rely on something very similar: serfdom.[1] It's likely that various Germanic aristocratic families appeared long before the fall of Rome, fighting for

---

[1] Ganshof, François Louis. Feudalism. Vol. 34. University of Toronto Press, 1996.

supremacy against ethnically related tribes, as well as battling everyone else. These families owed their influence to their war prowess, strength, and wealth. They likely gave birth to some incredibly strong warriors who proved themselves on the battlefield countless times. To summarize, the ruling class among Germans was a class of influential warriors who were able to muster strong groups of soldiers that could outpower rival groups.

The serfs were much more numerous but less powerful. Their livelihood was based on raising agriculture and livestock, and they were subjugated to a small minority of aristocrats. The warriors/aristocrats tried to exert as much influence as they could upon the masses. In exchange for military protection, the serfs worked the land ("given" to them by their master) and gave a portion of their products to their master.

This is a very simple description of the feudal system. As we can see, the authority of feudal lords lay entirely in their military power, depending completely on their personal authority and ability to settle problems within their own dominion. Although a feudal lord wasn't exactly a god on earth, he would, in a way, exert the common law of the period, and his word was final. The feudal system gradually grew more complex, finally resulting in the formation of kingdoms with a single king overseeing a network of vassals on multiple levels. A typical medieval king (or emperor) was a powerful man, controlling vast areas and keeping other areas under his control, thanks to a network of vassals. He also drew his authority from the church. The church was instrumental in the establishment of the feudal system, as it allowed for the centralization of power by investing a single man with spiritual power to rule. Thus, the feudal king wasn't simply a powerful man; he was also perceived as being predetermined to rule by God himself.

A typical feudal king or emperor always had to strike a balance between the nobility and the church, as he was highly dependent on their readiness to support his claims to the throne. Feudal vassals were relatively independent, cushioned in their castles, and they were often very hard to control. They owed a formal allegiance to the king since he granted them their lands, and they were obliged to pay the ruler a certain sum and provide armies when the king waged war. At times, instead of supporting their king, a handful of feudal lords teamed up against the king to increase their own influence. The king, in turn, would muster the forces of his true allies and pacify the rebels. The medieval age also saw endless conflicts between vassals themselves. For instance, the lowest vassal in the network, usually a local warlord of sorts, would attack his closest neighbor over some insignificant feud or territorial dispute.

If one refers to the medieval age as the "Dark Ages," it should be because of the inherent instability of the feudal system. Violence, war, and plunder were exceedingly common; in fact, they were too common for anything other than a very slow civilizational progress. Towns in Italy, which were among the most developed in Europe and the heralds of the Renaissance, were destroyed countless times in the medieval age. For centuries, German rulers descended south to pacify rebellious Italian towns and take the imperial crown. However, in Germany (and elsewhere in Europe), periods of peace and stability were separated by long years of internal strife, with high-ranking nobles rebelling against the emperor and against each other. Occasionally, a powerful leader emerged who was able to balance the demands of the nobility, the church, and the caste that often gets forgotten in discussions about the medieval age, the commoners, through the use of force and careful diplomacy. However, much more often, rulers didn't want or were unable to strike this balance, leading to chaos. Instability would often last for years without respite. Indeed, the feudal system brought forth the social state referred to by Thomas Hobbes as the "natural condition of mankind," in which only pure physical force determines one's outcome in life.

Keeping this in mind, it isn't surprising that it was exceedingly hard for medieval states, such as the Holy Roman Empire, to achieve any degree of centralization. There were many families vying for supremacy. One would prevail over another thanks to its military supremacy, but then another family would rise up and take everything by force. However, there was at least some kind of structure to the relationships between feudal lords, which was finally formalized in the Golden Bull of 1356.

It was customary among the most powerful Germans to periodically meet and choose the first amongst themselves. The Golden Bull defined the seven electors who would meet to choose the new king of the Romans (who would inevitably become the Holy Roman emperor once the pope approved): the duke of Saxony, the count palatine of Rhine, the margrave of Brandenburg, and the king of Bohemia. Three electors were ecclesiastical officials, the archbishops of Mainz, Cologne, and Trier. For centuries, Germans elected their king in a similar fashion, and they applied the same principle to the election of the new king of the Romans (Holy Roman emperor). More electors would be added as time went on, though the Habsburgs, in the end, managed to establish themselves as supreme rulers, nullifying the process of imperial elections completely.

The Golden Bull was the culmination of a long process that allowed Germans to elect the strongest feudal lord amongst themselves. It was a counterweight to the often brutal nature of relationships between families, tribes, and regions of Germany. Keeping this in mind, let's continue with our story and move toward our new stop, the Ottonian dynasty.

Chapter 3: The Ottonian Dynasty

The Rise of the Ottonian Dynasty: Setting the Stage for a New Era

After the transitory reunification under Charles the Fat, the Frankish-Carolingian Empire finally broke down under the burden of civil wars. In a sense, two major blocs formed, French and German, and they constantly vied for supremacy in the region.

The next crucial characters in our story come from the Ottonian line.[i] They were Germans but not Franks, and they were the first non-Frankish dynasty to take over the throne of the Holy Roman Empire. This dynasty was started by a regional warlord, Liudolf of Saxony, in the 9th century. The Ottonians played a major role in the history of the Holy Roman Empire. Liudolf's younger son, known as Otto the Illustrious, became the head of Saxony in 880, succeeding Bruno, his older brother, who died in combat fighting against the Vikings. It's likely that Otto the Illustrious was less crude in comparison to his brother, which earned him the nickname "Illustrious," although not much is known about his personal characteristics that earned him the nickname.

Henry the Fowler succeeded Otto the Illustrious when the latter died in 912. Initially the duke of Saxony, Henry the Fowler became king of East Francia in 919, a title he received from Conrad I. Soon enough,

---

[i] MacLean, Simon. "History and Politics in Late Carolingian and Ottonian Europe: The Chronicle of Regino of Prüm and Adalbert of Magdeburg." In History and Politics in Late Carolingian and Ottonian Europe. Manchester University Press, 2013.

Henry also received the Holy Lance from Rudolph II, King of Burgundy and Italy, around 922.[i] This version of the alleged Holy Lance is said to have been the lance once used by the mighty Emperor Constantine; its holiness was amplified since it supposedly encased the nails used to crucify Christ.

The Holy Lance wasn't simply a prestigious relic exuding mystical religious sentiments and symbolic power; it was also a political tool. Historians argue that the transfer of the Holy Lance in the 10th century was a political gesture, a finalization of a political pact. The exchange of a precious relic sealed deals between people who had been at war with each other. As we've seen and as we'll see, it wasn't unusual for the various kings, dukes, counts, and warlords of the ex-Carolingian Empire to wage war against one another. The predecessors of Rudolph II and Henry the Fowler are great examples of this precarious political situation. The transfer of the Holy Lance from Rudolph II to Henry the Fowler must have held a symbolic meaning of a peace treaty.

It's likely that Henry owes his nickname to his great love for hunting and bird-hunting since "fowler" essentially means "individual who hunts wildfowl." According to legend, Henry was so consumed by hunting that the news of him becoming a king reached him while he was hunting for birds (hence his nickname).

Henry the Fowler was perhaps more expansion-minded than his father. Even before becoming a king, Henry fought for Thuringia. After becoming a king, he set his eyes on Lotharingia, Bohemia, Schleswig, the northern Alps, and other regions. He also defended his territory from the Magyars (Hungarians), who were a major invading force in eastern and central Europe at the time. The Magyars were probably the most problematic for Henry. For a period, the Kingdom of Germany was even forced to pay annual tribute to the Magyars, who were able to inflict defeats upon Henry's forces. Eventually, however, Henry was able to strengthen his army (especially his heavy cavalry), build new fortifications, and repulse the Magyars once and for all.

---

[i] HAUFF, Andrea. The Kingdom of Upper Burgundy and the East Frankish Kingdom at the Beginning of the 10th Century. *History Compass*, 2017, 15.8: e12396.

Painting by Hermann Vogel (1854–1921), showing the legend of Henry receiving the news of his election. [8]

One of the strongest points of Henry's army and the Holy Roman Empire was most certainly the heavy cavalry. The heavy cavalry was made up of knights, skilled warriors who often wore heavy armor. They were a formidable force throughout the Middle Ages. It wasn't until cannons were introduced on a wider scale to European warfare that heavy cavalry became a thing of the past. During the reigns of Henry the Fowler and his immediate successors, the heavy cavalry was one of the most important military formations, as they were able to turn the tide of the battle and inflict heavy damage upon infantry and archers. This was why the people who constituted the heavy cavalry units were very important and much respected by their fellow countrymen and especially by their rulers.

We don't know for sure whether these early knights were noblemen from the start and thus able to procure the best equipment or whether they were simply skilled fighters who earned respect due to their merit. It's likely there was a mixture of both. In any case, knights quickly became noblemen and were instrumental in the feudal system of the Middle Ages.[i]

It is difficult to state how important the heavy cavalry was for the rise of both the Carolingians and the Holy Roman Empire. The heavy cavalry was the elite unit, the most modern and advanced for its age, much like tank divisions in the Second World War or drones in modern warfare.

Henry the Fowler, much like his predecessors and his successors, made good use of the heavy cavalry that was available to him. Moreover, he wasn't as interested in centralizing power and was happy to have worthy and honorable feudal lords in various regions he controlled. Those lords all had their own heavy cavalry units that could be called up to service when necessary. Feudal lords enjoyed a sort of autonomy and had absolute power within their fiefs, but they were ultimately subordinate to the king (or emperor). So, in times of war, they were tasked with levying armies in their respective provinces.

The Golden Age under the Ottonians

Henry the Fowler died in 936 and was succeeded by his son, Otto the Great, who was only around twenty-four at the time. He eventually became the first true Holy Roman emperor. Otto the Great, much like his father, worked hard to unify the Germans into a single nation. Unlike Henry, Otto the Great was more interested in centralizing power in the style of the Carolingian monarchs, which gave rise to internal strife that was quickly quenched by Otto.

Otto wanted to confirm the connection between the Carolingians and himself. He strove for that imperial allure that surrounded Charlemagne. That was why he wore a traditional Frankish robe for his coronation in 936.

---

[i] BACHRACH, David Stewart. Milites and Warfare in Pre-Crusade Germany. *War in History*, 2015, 22.3: 298-343.

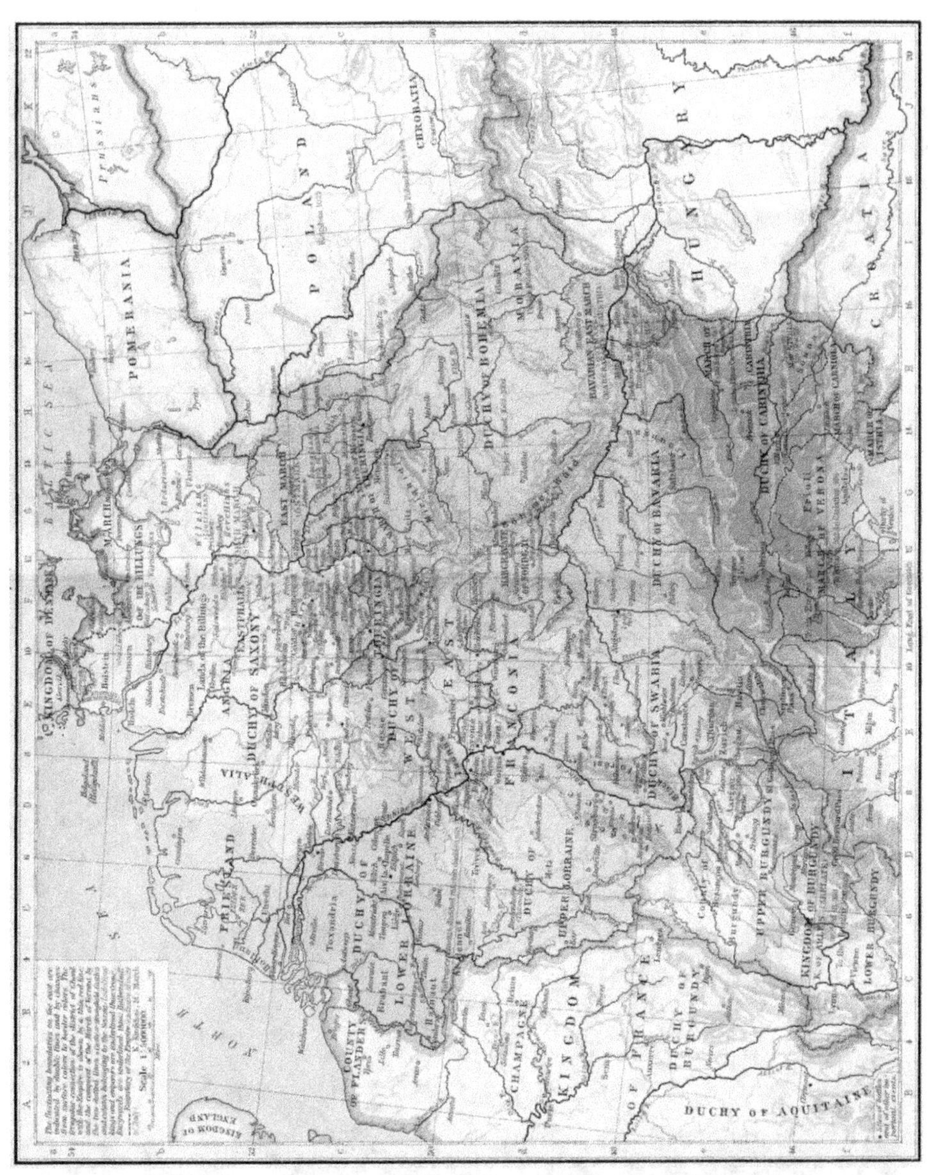

The Kingdom of Germany in the early 10th century.[4]

More importantly, Otto the Great laid the foundations of an intricate administration that would help disseminate royal power across the vast lands of the Holy Roman Empire.[i] Otto the Great, unlike, say, Louis the

BACHRACH, David. Exercise of royal power in early medieval Europe: the case of Otto the Great 936–73. *Early Medieval Europe*, 2009, 17.4: 389-419.

Blind or Berengar I of Italy, would hold his ground for many years and had a clear vision when it came to uniting the Holy Roman Empire. Otto the Great, as king of East Francia, slowly but surely weakened internal and external enemies. He formally became the Holy Roman emperor in 962.

Crown of the Holy Roman emperor.[5]

Before becoming emperor, Otto the Great faced a civil war in 938 and again in 953. He fought numerous enemies, such as Henry (his younger brother), Liudolf (his son), and the dukes of Franconia, Lotharingia, and Swabia. In 938, there was a local conflict in Saxony between Lord Bruning and Duke Eberhard of Franconia. Bruning wouldn't respond to

Eberhard's orders. So, Eberhard violently took Bruning's castle and killed all the inhabitants. Otto reprimanded Eberhard for this kind of behavior. Besides paying a large fine, Eberhard's men were publicly shamed and ordered to carry the carcasses of dogs in public.

This must have been outrageous to Eberhard, and he decided to start open hostilities with Otto. He sided with Thankmar, Otto's half-brother, and some other local lords. The rebellion was quickly quenched by Otto. Thankmar, in turn, was captured and executed in the Church of St. Peter in Eresburg.[i] Other conspirators, chiefly Eberhard, ostensibly proclaimed their submission to Otto, but in reality, they were planning a new rebellion.

Another conflict broke out in 939. Once again, Eberhard was in the midst of it. This time, Eberhard convinced Henry, who was the king of West Francia and Otto's younger brother, and they declared war on Otto. Others jumped onto the merry war bandwagon, like Gilbert, Duke of Lorraine. The decisive battle was fought near Andernach in 939, and Otto's forces crushed the enemy. Gilbert and Eberhard were both killed, with the former drowning in the Rhine and the latter being killed in action.[ii] Otto's brother Henry was spared, and the brothers reconciled by 940 due to their mother's mediation.

However, Henry wasn't satisfied with his new dukedom of Lorraine. He wanted the whole cake for himself, so he tried to defeat Otto through different means: assassination. The plot was discovered, and all the conspirators were swiftly arrested. Otto eventually pardoned the conspirators, though only after they formally and publicly sought penance for their crimes, in 941.

Otto the Great didn't kill his brother. He sought reconciliation again and tried to find a peaceful solution. This time, he was successful. Henry couldn't complain about receiving the dukedom of Bavaria around 948.[iii]

Otto the Great was a very active ruler and even traveled throughout his vast lands. It's likely he was rather tall and physically imposing, as well as charismatic and bold. He would stay in major cities for around a week,

---

[i] It is possible that Otto the Great ordered this execution.

[ii] BACHRACH, David S. Early Ottonian Warfare: The Perspective from Corvey. *Journal of Military History*, 2011, 75.2.

[iii] WILSON, Joseph. Holy Anointment and Realpolitik in the Age of Otto I. 2015.

where he would talk to locals, convincing them that he was "the chosen one." He must have been a good negotiator and communicator because he was able to make peace between noblemen who were often hostile to each other.

As we've seen in the cases of Eberhard and Henry, Otto the Great tried hard to avoid capital punishment. This wasn't simply an act of royal benevolence; it was also a very pragmatic move. Back in the day, blood feuds were still a tradition and something held in high esteem. If someone from your family was murdered, your task (provided you were a mature male) was to find and kill the murderer of your family member. Needless to say, blood feuds have a tendency to never end because someone always seeks revenge.

In other words, Otto was a wise ruler who knew how to disseminate his royal prestige across his kingdom. It isn't surprising that he was able to levy enormous armies that could stop the Magyar invaders. In 955, a decisive battle between the Magyars and Otto the Great's forces occurred. It was called the Battle of Lechfeld.

Similar to the Huns who came before them, the Magyars deployed thousands of agile horse archers who could cover large distances and inflict chaos across Europe. Before the Battle of Lechfeld, the Magyars invaded some lands in Bavaria and besieged Augsburg (the city is built around the Lech River, hence the name of the battle). Otto the Great was able to muster around eight thousand heavy cavalrymen, who rushed to relieve Augsburg.

The Magyars wanted to defeat Otto in an open battle and finally met Otto's army close to Augsburg. The Magyars' light cavalry and horse archers were no match for Otto's heavy cavalry, and the Magyars were soon forced to retreat. The Magyars also made some bad decisions. After successfully routing the Bohemian legion, they stopped to plunder the legion's cargo and provisions, which provided a great opportunity for the Germans to catch them off guard. One can only try to imagine the dread of being caught off guard by a heavy cavalry charge.

The bulk of Otto's forces then directly faced the Magyars, drawing them into close combat, which was somewhat more favorable for the Germans since they had better armor. With heavy casualties on both sides, the Magyars started to retreat in an orderly fashion, and Otto decided to call it a day. He didn't want to pursue the Magyars, probably because he knew that their cavalry was more agile and able to fire back during the retreat. Instead, Otto retreated to Augsburg and ordered all roads and river crossings in the region to be closed to impede further Magyar retreats. Over the next few days, the Magyars became encircled, making their retreat to eastern Europe made impossible. They were then hunted down and executed, one by one.

This was an illustrious victory, and it transformed Otto into an emperor, though Otto would have to wait a bit longer to be formally crowned as the Holy Roman emperor.

Even though Otto the Great was constantly on the move, he managed to lay the foundations for an efficient administration. By his time, the state had access to archives regarding property and lands of the aristocracy. We know this because Otto sometimes confiscated lands from certain counts, dukes, and lords, meaning he knew which lands to confiscate. He redistributed the lands to more docile members of the noblesse. For instance, after Count Guntram fell out of grace in 952, the court knew exactly what Guntram owned. He was quickly stripped of all his earthly belongings.

Otto depicted on a coin. '

Next, like some of his predecessors, namely Charlemagne and Louis the Pious, Otto the Great possessed a mobile library/archive, which was always available to him for consultation even when on the road.

Careful archiving (before and during the reign of Otto the Great) allowed for requisitions of land. Estates were taken away from disobedient members of the aristocracy, but Otto sometimes had designs and plans that necessitated land requisitioning from the church, which was an unpleasant but necessary practice. For instance, in 940, Otto the Great (at the time still just a king) authorized the return of Moosburg Monastery to its original owner (the Freising family), mentioning machinations and illegal practices as the primary means through which the church obtained the monastery in the first place.[i] There's a myriad of other similar court proceedings in which Otto was embroiled, and these stand as a testament to some of the more tedious but equally important activities of a medieval ruler.

Otto the Great managed to assert himself as a powerful king by defeating the Magyars in 955, even being hailed as *imperator* and *pater patriae* by his own troops after the Battle of Lechfeld, a custom that stems back to the times of ancient Rome. But there were still a few things to be done before he became an emperor.

Prior to defeating the Magyars, Otto the Great married Adelaide in 951. She had been the queen of Italy, so the marriage could be seen as an attempt to ease Otto's way to the Italian throne, which, in turn, would have allowed him to be crowned as the Holy Roman emperor.

Otto was careful about his relationship with the church. He managed to install relatives in high church offices, such as his brother Bruno, who became the archbishop of Cologne in 953. William, Otto's illegitimate son, became the archbishop of Meinz, and other high church officials were also all "Otto's men." Otto tried to present himself as the "holy anointed one," someone who was chosen by God to rule.

Otto managed to assert his position as the protector of the church when Berengar II, King of Italy, started becoming more rebellious. He attempted to take some territories he had been deprived of earlier by Otto. Berengar II also menaced the Papal States themselves, and Pope John XII's appeal ultimately pulled Otto into Italy. The trade-off was rather clear: the pope got back his security, while Otto became the Holy Roman emperor.

Otto levied his forces and entered Italy in 961. By 962, he was able to enter Italy and reach Rome. January 31st, 962, was the day Pope John XII anointed Otto as the emperor of the Holy Roman Empire in St. Peter's

---

[i] BACHRACH, David S. Early Ottonian Warfare: The Perspective from Corvey. *Journal of Military History*, 2011, 75.2.

Basilica. Early sources are surprisingly quiet about the details of the coronation, especially in comparison to Otto's previous coronation as the king of Germany in Aachen in 936.[i]

Lacking a contemporary description of the 962 coronation, let's turn briefly to the Aachen coronation. Otto was first lauded outside of the Aachen chapel by the most illustrious Franks and Saxons. This was repeated in the chapel itself, after which Otto was presented with the royal insignia. He was then anointed by the clergy, crowned, and finally allowed to sit on his throne in the Aachen Cathedral.

It's possible that the 962 coronation followed a similar pattern. Moreover, the relative silence of contemporary sources with respect to the coronation might be indicative of the future Investiture Controversy. Namely, why would Otto the Great need to accept his imperial crown from a pope? Isn't a Holy Roman emperor mightier than all the clergy combined? As far as Otto and the Germans were concerned, he had already been the emperor for about seven years in 962; he had been emperor since the Battle of Lechfeld in 955. The fact that the pope finally decided to proclaim Otto as emperor was, for all intents and purposes, insignificant.

It was obvious that Otto had the upper hand and more power in comparison to the pope. Otto also finally quenched Berengar's rebellion in 963, only doing so after receiving the imperial crown. That Pope John XII was, in a way, coerced into accepting Otto as the Holy Roman emperor might be supported by the fact that soon after the coronation, he attempted to weaken Otto's position and was subsequently deposed.[ii] It is interesting that Pope John XII is depicted as a "monster" and "traitor" by some of the early chroniclers of Otto's reign.[iii] The pope was accused of siding with Berengar's son, Adalbert. He was also reprimanded for his alleged sexual exploits, as well as for the wretched state of Rome's numerous churches. Otto the Great organized a large council in Rome in St. Peter's Basilica, which was attended by numerous archbishops,

---

[i] Robbie, Steven. "Can Silence Speak Volumes? Widukind's Res Gestae Saxonicae and the Coronation of Otto I Reconsidered." Early Medieval Europe 20, no. 3 (2012): 333-362.

[ii] Poole, Reginald L. "The Names and Numbers of Medieval Popes." The English Historical Review 32, no. 128 (1917): 465-478.

[iii] Grabowski, Antoni. "Liudprand of Cremona's papa monstrum: The Image of Pope John XII in the Historia Ottonis." Early Medieval Europe 23, no. 1 (2015): 67-92.

---

bishops, and members of the clergy and the Roman elite. This council quickly deposed Pope John XII in 963.

It is interesting how accusations against Pope John XII merged together to depict a person of wretched morale. He was not only a traitor but also a sexually promiscuous person. For instance, Pope John XII allegedly raped women in churches, had incestuous relations with his aunt, and held a brothel. Truth be told, in the 10th century, celibacy wasn't a necessary prerequisite for the Roman clergy. In fact, some priests were even married, and even more of them were widely known to be sexually active.[i] However, the crimes leveled against John XII were outrageous even in the somewhat lenient atmosphere of 10th-century Rome.

John XII never responded to these accusations; he ran away from Rome when he heard about the council being organized to depose him. The new pope was Leo VIII (chosen by Otto the Great), who must have had an even worse reputation because John XII managed to get back to Rome in 964 and cause Leo's own deposal with the help of the populace of Rome. Otto had disassembled his army and left Rome soon after deposing John XII. Upon hearing about the return of the ghastly John XII, Otto started planning a siege of Rome, but John's death was faster. In May 964, Pope John XII died, and Benedict V became the new pope, as he was desired by the Romans. Benedict V wasn't really Otto's favorite, so he, too, was exiled, and Leo VIII was brought back as the head of the church.

This short episode is one of numerous examples from the turbulent history of the Roman Church. As we can see, the Roman Church had its own scandals and affairs more than one thousand years ago. For now, though, let's focus on the end of Otto's reign and then quickly go through the reigns of his successors.

By 966, and after several more hiccups in Italy, Otto had decided to make Rome his permanent residence. Otto wanted to gradually subjugate the whole of Italy and once and for all crush the rebellion that had been fomenting in Italy for quite some time. Once again, Otto didn't allow for free elections of the new pope. After Leo VIII died in 965, another favorite of Otto became the new pope: John XIII. Pope John XIII continued what some authors call "pornocracy" in Rome, or at least that's how it appeared to be to the members of the Roman nobility.

Ibid. p. 76

(Pornocracy is when morally decadent, sexually promiscuous, and debauched individuals are allowed to govern.)[i] Like his predecessor, Leo VIII, John XIII was ousted from Rome and even held in captivity. And once again, Otto had to return to Italy with a large army. This time, he was more determined than ever to crush those who dared to bring John's and his own authority into question.[ii]

John XIII ordered a ruthless punishment of one of the rebellion's instigators, Peter, the Prefect of Rome, whose forces were instrumental in capturing and ousting John from Rome. Peter went through a whole ordeal of public shaming. First, he was left to hang from the statue of Marcus Aurelius. Then, he was stripped naked and placed on a donkey backward. Finally, he was adorned with feathers and taken for a ride through the whole city.

One of Otto the Great's final important political actions was his rapprochement with the Byzantine Empire. The conflict between the Holy Roman Empire and the Byzantine Empire was twofold. Both empires believed southern Italy was their exclusive dominion, and both empires wanted to be the sole successors of the great Roman Empire. Otto the Great was able to find a compromise. The Byzantines agreed to recognize him as the Holy Roman emperor without seriously undermining their own authority, and Otto the Great agreed to leave southern Italy (Apulia and Calabria) to the Byzantines. In addition, Emperor John I Tzimiskes agreed to have his niece Theophano (also spelled Theophanu) married to Otto's son, Otto II, with the marriage being completed in 972.[iii] For a brief period, the animosities between the East and West subsided, and the two empires were able to focus on other problems.

Otto the Great returned to Germany, where he celebrated Easter in 973. He died shortly after at the age of sixty. His youngest son, Otto II, who was seventeen at the time, rose to the imperial throne. Otto's older sons had all died, which made the youngest son the heir apparent.

---

[i] Brook, Lindsay. "Popes and Pornocrats: Rome in the Early Middle Ages." Foundations 1, no. 1 (2003): 5-21.

[ii] Roach, Levi. "The Ottonians and Italy." German History 36, no. 3 (2018): 349-364.

[iii] Osborne, John. "The Dower Charter of Otto II and Theophanu, and the Roman Scriptorium at Santi Apostoli." Papers of the British School at Rome 89 (2021): 137-157.

Decline and Transition

Otto II (Otto the Red) had the intention of furthering his father's plans for the Holy Roman Empire, though he wasn't able to do much. He died at the age of twenty-eight in 983, probably due to malaria, which was present in Europe at the time, especially in Italy, where Otto II died. Throughout the ten years of his reign, he managed to keep the Holy Roman Empire united, crushing rebellions and nurturing hopes of expanding his dominion into southern Italy. However, these hopes were ended by his premature death, which also plunged the precarious Holy Roman Empire into a state of chaos.[i] The son of Otto II, Otto III, was only three at the time, which, needless to say, sparked a succession crisis. A rift between Otto III's caregivers (his mother, Theophano, and his grandmother, Adelaide) and Henry II, Duke of Bavaria, appeared. Duke Henry II ("the Quarrelsome") was closely related to the imperial family; his father was Otto the Great's younger brother.

Initially, it looked as if Henry the Quarrelsome would take over the custody of Otto III because he was the first one to reach the young emperor after his father's death. Adelaide and Theophano were still in Italy when Henry reached young Otto III in Aachen. From 983 to 984, Henry, in a way, was hailed as a king throughout Germany. With the two empresses returning to Germany and garnering support from the nobility, Henry was forced to return Otto III to his mother and grandmother. In return, Henry was pardoned for treason.[ii]

Otto III remained under the custody of his mother and grandmother until 994, when he turned fourteen. The two empresses managed to keep the Holy Roman Empire together, at least ostensibly, leaving it to the young Otto III, who was supposed to silence the nobility that, in the absence of a firm ruler, started straying away from the unity Otto the Great had been able to achieve.

The young emperor suffered the same faith as his father. He died in 1002 in Italy, presumably from malaria. And like his father, Otto III was supposed to be married to a Byzantine princess. Princess Zoe Porphyrogenita, daughter of Emperor Constantine VIII, was on her way

---

[i] Welton, Megan, and Sarah Greer. "Establishing Just Rule: The Diplomatic Negotiations of the Dominae Imperiales in the Ottonian Succession Crisis of 983–985." Frühmittelalterliche Studien 55, no. 1 (2021): 315-342.
[ii] Ibid.

---

to Italy to marry Otto III, but his death was quicker. After his death, a new succession crisis emerged, which ended with the election of Henry the Exuberant, son of Henry II the Quarrelsome.

Henry II ("the Exuberant") formally became the emperor in 1014 when he was crowned by Pope Benedict VIII. Like his predecessor, Otto III, Henry II didn't have children, which produced another succession crisis when he died in 1024. This opened up space for the Salians to come onto the scene. A highly religious emperor, Henry the Exuberant was the only medieval German ruler canonized by the church; his wife was also canonized.

But for all his devout religiousness, Henry II was one of the sources of the Investiture Crisis (or Investiture Controversy), which will be discussed in the next chapter. Namely, Henry II strengthened the imperial grip of the church, making sure that everyone in the empire knew that the church was not only the responsibility of the ecclesiastical personnel (priests, bishops, archbishops, the pope, etc.) but also the responsibility of the Holy Roman Empire.[i] For instance, Henry II wanted to legalize the empire's right to intervene in church matters, such as choice of pope or archbishops, a practice that had already been in use for some time. Needless to say, the pope and the church didn't agree with this stance. However, during the reign of Henry II, possibly thanks to his charisma, animosities were put aside, only to resurface soon after during the reign of the Salians.

[i] ZELLER, Jules. *L'empire germanique et l'Eglise au Moyen-Age: les Henri.* Didier, 1876.

Chapter 4: Salian Rule and the Investiture Crisis

Prelude to the Investiture Crisis

As was customary among the Germans, after the ruler died without an heir apparent, elections were held among the nobility to choose the new ruler. Conrad II, whose great-grandmother Liutgarde was the daughter of Otto the Great, was chosen as the new German king thanks to his rich life experience and stable family life (Conrad II had a son who could inherit the throne).

The Ottonians had a somewhat ambiguous relationship with the church. Saint Henry (Henry II), the last Ottonian emperor, is a perfect example of this relationship. On the one hand, he was a highly religious man and contributed to the establishment and dissemination of the church hierarchy across the Holy Roman Empire. When the Salians marched onto the scene, the church had already become a powerful tool and was on equal terms with the secular nobility and feudal lords. The church, in a way, ensured the transition between rulers and dynasties. However, the first Salian German king, Conrad II, who had been elected by a council of nobles and religious authorities, still had some issues with rebels in Germany and Italy. After silencing the dissenting voices in Germany, he turned toward Italy, where he was crowned as the Holy Roman emperor in St. Peter's Basilica in 1027.

To understand the conflict between the Salians and the Roman Church, we first have to understand how the church became such a crucial instrument in the hands of the Ottonians, especially Henry II. Church officials, priests, bishops, and archbishops became, in a way, more important than feudal lords. They were responsible not only for otherworldly matters but also for the arrangement of worldly matters. For instance, in Lorsch Abbey, there was a monastery, and the church officials there were responsible for gathering a force of ten thousand men by Henry II.[i] There was a sort of balance between the church's own powers (conferred to them by the emperor) and its submission to the emperor.

However, when the Salians came to power, this balance was brought into question. Conrad II and his successors relied more on the secular nobility to ensure the submission of vast areas of the Holy Roman Empire. The Salians were a very old family; they were able to track their ancestry way back to the early days of the first Frankish states (even before the Carolingians came to power).[ii] They owed their ascent to power to this illustrious heritage.

It is interesting, though, that the first Salian ruler, Conrad II, was mostly illiterate, much like other German medieval leaders who would come after him. However, Conrad's incomplete grasp of reading and writing didn't really make him unable to rule. In any case, medieval leaders owed their authority to their war prowess and the amount of force they could muster; their education was secondary.

Conrad II inherited a very peculiar empire. In spite of carrying the name of the ancient Roman Empire, the Holy Roman Empire had a much weaker administration (it was virtually nonexistent, in fact) in comparison to the Roman Empire. Although the Ottonians were fond of warfare, they tried to usher in at least some sort of administration with the help of the church, which would become, in a way, the right hand of the imperial family. But for all intents and purposes, the Holy Roman Empire was just an idea, a sort of prestige that numerous rulers tried to attain without really managing to establish a permanent government over the vast areas they allegedly possessed. This was why each ruler in the Ottonian dynasty literally had to reconquer some of "his" lands immediately after rising to power. When the Ottonians pacified Italy, problems would break out elsewhere.

---

[i] Zeller, Jules. L'empire germanique et l'Eglise au Moyen-Age: les Henri. Vol. 3. Didier, 1876.
[ii] Ibid.

It was up to the Salians to attempt to solve this big issue of governing such a vast territory. Conrad II faced all the usual troubles. As soon as he took over the title of king of the Germans, he faced rebellious nobles, such as Rudolf III, King of Burgundy; Ernest II, Duke of Swabia; and Odo, Count of Champagne. They felt they were only subordinate to the Ottonians, not to the newly elected Salian dynasty. As we will see, the idea of subordination was largely personal. It's not that a nation was a part of a larger nation or state; it's just that two leaders agreed on something between them. The concept of power was personal and also concrete, as it could be expressed through the very real force a ruler could exert.

Conrad II reaffirmed the heredity of singular fiefs, making it harder for them to be alienated from the families that traditionally governed them. By doing this, he cast light on the perennial rift between worldly and spiritual powers.

Conrad II faced considerable resistance in Italy. The Roman Church planned to proclaim Prince Guillaume (William) of Aquitaine as emperor. He refused, knowing he would only be a pawn in the game of chess played by Italian popes, archbishops, and bishops. In 1026, Conrad II arrived in Italy with a fairly large army, making sure everyone in Italy knew what could happen if they decided to disobey him. Conrad's arrival and stay in Italy sometimes seemed more like a brutal invasion than a visit to one of the parts of his vast empire. Some towns dared not open their doors to the German king, and they paid dearly for their disobedience. The town of Pavia was spared, but its routes and vineyards weren't. Ravenna suffered even more. Conrad II's soldiers were let in, but scuffles between them and confused inhabitants started to break out. The gates of Ravenna were then closed, and those soldiers who made their way into the city were chased through the streets and slaughtered. Upon hearing of this, Conrad II let his soldiers enter the city in order to avenge their fallen brethren.[i]

This sort of scenario was more a rule than an exception for the German conquests in Italy. Each German king (to-be-emperor or already the Holy Roman emperor) arrived with a large army. As the proverb goes, "A large army is always disorderly." A large army has to be fed, clothed, and sheltered, and over time, this becomes an incredible burden for the nation that receives the army. Moreover, Italian towns, culturally

---

Ibid. p. 39

speaking, were much more advanced than towns in Germany. The people were somewhat less crude and warlike than the Germans. People in Italy didn't really like seeing endless masses of German warriors ravaging their fields and towns. This was the deeper reason why each German king had to essentially reconquer Italy in order to be proclaimed the Holy Roman emperor.

Conrad II reached Rome by March 1027. The pope at the time was John XIX, who wasn't really on friendly terms with Conrad II. The coronation didn't go well. While the ceremony was still being performed, a fight broke out between the Germans and the Romans. A German soldier allegedly tried to steal some leather from a Roman. In the scuffle that broke out, an aristocrat from Sweden was killed. He was then brutally avenged by the German soldiers. Those who participated in the combat were punished the following day, with the punishment being accomplished with the very weapons they used to hurt others the day before.

Conrad II stayed in Italy for almost two years. While he was busy pacifying Italy, nobles in Germany, profiting from the absence of their emperor, started to rebel. Ernest, Count of Swabia, was the most important figure in this new rebellion, although he was joined by many others. The main reason for this rebellion was the conflict between the old nobility and the new church elite. The high nobles felt their power was being diluted while the church became ever more powerful.

But here, Conrad's clairvoyance came to the forefront. Earlier, he demanded an oath, not only from the high nobles but also from the lower nobles who were traditionally directly responsible to dukes and counts but not necessarily to the emperor. Now, they all had a feeling of direct obedience to the emperor, so they would regularly abandon their dukes and counts when they rebelled against Conrad II.

After quenching this rebellion, Conrad appointed his oldest son as his heir apparent. He didn't leave anything to chance. All the other sons of Conrad were eventually sent to monasteries, where they could do little to endanger the authority of their oldest brother. This nicely shows the position of the church during Conrad II's reign. The church was an instrument of power and was ultimately subordinate to the emperor.

While Conrad II took great care to be on good terms with the low nobility, ensuring the hereditary status of their lands, he did the exact opposite with the high nobility. Whenever he could, Conrad II would take away the hereditary status of important dukedoms and feuds so that he could gradually, through strategic marriages, bring more and more land into his own family. He started to remove all the intermediaries between the lower nobility and himself, eradicating the vain ambition of dukes, counts, and princes. The lower nobility, however, was fragmented, as it was fairly hard for them to join their strengths and come to terms: there were simply too many of them. On the other hand, a few dukes and counts could easily meet and decide whether they wanted to rebel or not. In a way, this was a start, however timid and slow, of the formation of the modern German identity. The "small" German nations of Swabia and Bavaria were stripped of their leaders and slowly began melting into one universal German identity.

But at the same time, this was the root of the Investiture Crisis. Conrad II weakened the position of the church and, in a way, functioned like a pagan leader who was only on good terms with the church as long as it served his interests. He dealt with ecclesiastical matters as long as he could draw profit and gain something for himself and his family. Everything else (perhaps the more spiritual and idealistic things admired by Henry II) was of secondary importance.

The ruling German dynasty supported whoever would ensure the church's subservience. Conrad II even allowed for the ascension of a very young man to the papacy, who owed this ascent to his father's bribery.[i] In 1032, Benedict IX was proclaimed the new pope. It's not certain just how old he was at the time, but according to some sources, he might have been as young as twelve. Most historians believe he was around twenty years of age, which still makes him the youngest person to ever sit in St. Peter's chair. He is also the only pope to serve more than once. Benedict's age and way of attaining the papacy would have been disgraceful for the more pious Henry II, but for the pragmatic Conrad II, this wasn't an issue at all.

It isn't surprising that rebellion started to foment in Italy as early as 1035. A number of nobles, vassals, and rich townspeople united in northern Italy and rebelled against Archbishop Heribert, who was basically the personification of imperial power in Italy. By 1036, Conrad II had reached Italy with a large army to personally quench this rebellion. He tried to introduce similar changes to the ones he already applied in

---

[i] Ibid.

Germany. Namely, Conrad II tried to reduce the powers of the high nobility by demanding personal subservience from the lesser nobles.

During the last few years of his life, Conrad II spent most of his time in Italy, trying to once and for all destroy any power that dared question his own. In 1039, he returned to Germany, but he fell ill and soon died. He laid the foundations for a different sort of Holy Roman Empire, one that was proud of its terrestrial power and endlessly thirsty to enlarge itself. Henry III logically continued the work started by Conrad II.

Henry III ("the Dark") was much better educated than his father. His nickname comes from his dark beard, which might have been fairly unusual in 11th-century Germany. He was described as pious, humble, beautiful, courageous, and a lover of peace.[i] However, being a lover of peace had a different meaning in the medieval age, a time when war was more of a standard part of life. Henry III engaged in numerous wars across Europe; it was as if he was driven by an irresistible compulsion. First came Bohemian Prince Bretislav, who conquered Poland, which had fallen into a sort of anarchy and experienced a revival of pagan traditions. Bretislav, a major defender of Christianity, invaded Poland, possibly with the pretext of bringing back much-needed order and the Christian religion. Henry III didn't really like this territorial expansion by Bretislav, and he wanted Bretislav to retreat from Poland, to which the latter simply said no. In 1040, there was an attempted conquest of Bohemia, which was ultimately unsuccessful since the invading German forces were constantly ambushed from the thick Polish forests. The next year, Henry returned with an even larger army, this time attacking Bretislav's center of power, Prague.

Next came Hungary, which had also been recently Christianized. King Stephen, Hungary's first Christian king, left a highly educated and civilized son, Peter, to rule the country. However, Peter was unable to placate the still very much uncivilized Hungarians and was ousted by Samuel Aba, a prominent Hungarian noble. Samuel went on to destroy some German settlements, which attracted Henry's attention. Henry's first Hungarian expedition in 1042 was partially successful, as his army got stuck in the pestilent swamps of the Danube River. The second expedition in 1043 was more successful, and Hungary was completely subjugated to the Holy Roman Empire.

---

[i] Ibid. p. 83.

Conflicts broke out, even within Germany itself, for the most insignificant reasons: a stolen cow, fields run over by hunters, sheltering a runaway serf, etc. All of these were perfect occasions for inciting violence within Germany. Low nobles would unite against their seniors, while senior nobles would do everything they could to ensure the subservience of their vassals.

Parish officials often came into conflict with neighboring feudal lords, who they believed took away their power and authority. This sort of atmosphere gave rise to the typical medieval landscape, consisting of small, highly fortified towns. Each monastery and each town had to fend for itself, often at the expense of its neighbors. Germany slipped into a sort of perennial war. Whole villages were burned down to punish their feudal lord while the lord sat within his fortifications. Neighbors became potential enemies, which impeded free trade and stifled the economy. It's likely that numerous famines stemmed from this state of anarchy, which made the transfer of information and goods between settlements nearly impossible.[i] At points, the famine was so drastic that it compelled people to resort to cannibalism. People were forced to eat bread made from infested grains, which resulted in epidemics of diseases, such as ergotism.[ii] Other diseases also set foot in Europe, such as the black plague or leprosy

The cultural, social, and economic landscape of Henry's country was abysmal. Death was everywhere, and death came in the worst possible forms. It isn't surprising that people from all walks of life searched for a way out. They needed consolation, something that would convince them that their terrestrial suffering wasn't for nothing. Fortunately for them, the church was able to do this. By interpreting all these evils as punishments from above, the church gave people hope that they could improve things if they became good and pious people. Even though the Salians focused on the secular value of the church, the people recognized the spiritual value of the church. This revivified status of the church is another reason for the Investiture Crisis.

---

[i] Ibid.

[ii] Ergot is a species of fungi that grows on grain, especially rye. The drug LSD is made from ergot. Up until recently, it wasn't uncommon for whole villages or even regions of a country to suffer from ergotism, which is characterized by gastrointestinal issues, gangrene, hallucinations, and psychosis.

The church was perhaps the only institution to preach peace on Earth. While everything screamed war, the church murmured words of peace to the ears of the population. From this stemmed the church's Peace and Truce of God initiatives, not only in Germany but in all of Europe. People should not engage in warfare activities during certain periods of the year (such as important Christian holidays). In some regions, people abstained from warfare activities from Wednesday to Monday. Henry III, who understood the momentum of this collective movement, accepted it in 1043.

Perhaps the people of Europe didn't observe the Peace and Truce of God diligently enough, as the winter between 1045 and 1046 was exceedingly bitter, followed by famine and plague. Henry III fell ill, and it seemed as if Germany would have to seek a new emperor since Henry III only had a female child. However, Henry soon got better and continued with his ambitious plans for his empire. One of the things he did was ramp up simony and implicitly allow marriage among priests.[1] By doing this, he went against two important canons of the church. Marriage among priests wasn't unheard of, but this practice became even more frequent in the early 11th century. Positions in the church were bought and sold like any other commodity on the market. In Germany, elections within the church became insignificant and meaningless because someone could always make a good bid and take a certain post, often leaving it to his successors. Thus, simony and marriage among priests combined to make an absurd situation in which people would buy positions in the church hierarchy and then attempt to bequeath them to their children.

Coronation of Henry III and the Perpetuation of the Investiture Crisis

Henry III crossed the Alps in 1046, leading a sort of ecclesiastical army into Italy. He was welcomed by Pope Gregory VI, who had done a few things that angered Henry III, such as not appointing bishops liked by the imperial court. A council was held, which resulted in Gregory's dismissal. He was accused of simony, publicly shamed, and forced to step down from the papacy. The whimsical quality of Henry's ethical reasoning is obvious. In Germany, simony was rampant and somewhat encouraged by the court. In Italy, it was used to depose Pope Gregory VI.

---

[1] Simony is the practice of selling positions in the church hierarchy. Henry III was not the first nor the last German ruler to do this, but during his reign, simony reached new heights.

A sort of mock papal elections were held. Ostensibly, the people of Rome were allowed to choose their new pope. However, they renounced this right and shifted it to none other than Henry III, who proclaimed the bishop of Bamberg, who was on very friendly terms with his court, as the new pope. He was named Pope Clement II. The new pope crowned Henry III and proclaimed him to be the Holy Roman emperor in 1046.[i]

In the next few days, it became clear that Henry III had amassed terrestrial and total spiritual power. He had the power to choose and depose important authorities within the hierarchy of the Roman Church. He could depose any pope he wanted and put his own German pope on the throne.

Returning to Germany, where a plethora of problems awaited him, he left Clement II in Rome, bringing the old pope, Gregory VI, with him. Gregory VI was put into a prison/castle situated on the banks of the Rhine. Clement II died in 1047, poisoned by the Romans (at least some speculated). The Holy Roman emperor chose a Bavarian named Poppo, Bishop of Brixen, to be the new pope. Poppo became Damasus II, but his stay in the chair of Saint Peter was exceedingly short; he died twenty-three days after being proclaimed as pope in 1048. He was likely poisoned by the anti-imperial party, whose members were still rather numerous in Rome.

Emperor Henry III then chose Bruno, Bishop of Toul, to be the next pope. Bruno took the name Leo IX. He knew that his personal power in Rome would be slight and that he had to come to some sort of agreement with the people and priests of Rome. He met and talked with the most important people of Rome before he even entered the city, and he took the position granted to him by the emperor. This placated the Romans, who accepted Leo IX.

Leo IX's papacy signified a sort of truce between Henry III and the church. However, the conflict wasn't fully solved, as the Investiture Crisis was simply moved to the side. Henry III returned to the main craft of the Salians: warfare. Conflicts with Hungarians, Slavs, Flemish, Italians, and Poles kept Henry III busy. He fell ill and died in 1056, leaving the throne to his son, Henry IV.

---

[i] Zeller, Jules. L'empire germanique et l'Eglise au Moyen-Age: les Henri

Henry III was an extremely powerful ruler, possibly more powerful than Charlemagne and Otto the Great. He dominated numerous nations without really governing them. His power and influence depended on his personal energy and ability to quickly solve complex political issues, often thanks to his use of force. However, the problems he left to his successors were too heavy for them to bear. The Investiture Crisis, which became somewhat dormant during his reign, would reignite as soon as he died.

Henry IV was six years old when Henry III died, so he naturally needed a regent. His mother, Agnes, implored Pope Victor II to support her son and herself until Henry became mature enough to follow in his father's footsteps. In spite of receiving support from the church, Agnes couldn't maintain the same level of order within the empire. As soon as Henry III died, various nobles started to rebel. Agnes felt obliged to return numerous dukedoms to the high nobility, increasing their power and influence.

The increasing autonomy of the Italians shouldn't come as too much of a surprise. In 1058, Stephen IX was elected pope after the death of Victor II. The election happened without the knowledge of the imperial family. With a lot of reforms in mind (for instance, he foresaw the future choice of popes led by the cardinals, not by the emperor, the people, or the nobles of Rome), Stephen IX was deemed dangerous by numerous important players in Rome. He was assassinated soon after he rose to the papacy. In the chaos that ensued after the assassination, Benedict X became the new head of the Roman Church (he was actually an antipope, as his ascension wasn't legitimate). He rose to power thanks to intrigue and powerful connections; Benedict X was the brother of the much-hated but influential ex-Pope Benedict IX. The next pope, Nicholas II, was brought in by the supporters of the assassinated Stephen IX, who removed Antipope Benedict X in 1059. Benedict X could only cling to the papal throne for a short while; despite having powerful connections, the clergy simply wouldn't tolerate an antipope on the throne for a long time.[i]

Nicholas II was of immense importance for separating the church from the influence of the Holy Roman emperors. Pope Nicholas II confirmed the reforms initiated by Stephen IX, moving on to once and

---

[i] The antipope was essentially a pope who was later rejected by the Catholic Church as illegitimate. Benedict X was one such pope who was rejected by the Catholic Church.

for all ban marriage among priests. He also incited people to reject priests known for their simony and licentious behavior. During the time of Nicholas II, it became clear that the pope could only be chosen by a council of cardinals and that the opinions of people, nobility, and the emperor himself could only come after the cardinals made their candidate known.

By this time, the numerous priests became so much like the commoners that they started carrying arms and amassing material possessions. Nicholas II reinstated the ban on weapons among priests and sought to limit private possession among church personnel. The communal spirit was enhanced by an obligation of group meals of all religious personnel serving within the same church. All these and many other obligations were proclaimed formally by the Council of Melfi in 1059.

Meanwhile, young Henry IV was growing up, with his responsibilities as the head of state being fulfilled by his mother. A group of influential aristocrats decided that young Henry should be guided and educated by serious church authorities, such as Bishop Anno. In 1062, Henry IV was kidnapped by Bishop Anno while he was staying with his mother in Kaiserswerth. As the story goes, the bishop visited Henry and Agnes in their palace at Kaiserswerth (modern-day Düsseldorf) and invited Henry for a boat ride on the Rhine. The boat ride turned out to be a kidnapping, and Henry IV came under the custody of Bishop Anno.

Anno was a different sort of pedagogue for the young Henry. While his mother ostensibly allowed for numerous indulgences, Anno was sterner and would often drive Henry to the brink of mental collapse with his disciplinary methods.[i] This sort of upbringing was too unstable and contributed to Henry IV becoming unstable. He was less than prepared to deal with the challenges of the Investiture Crisis and the internal strife in Germany.

In 1065, Henry IV reached the age of majority and started to rule the empire on his own. Henry IV wanted to revive the power of his father, which had been lost during the years of regency under his mother Agnes. He set about attempting to obtain the control of large fiefs and suppress the power of the high nobility, relying heavily on the low nobility, much

---

Ibid. p. 236

like his father had. However, Henry IV had to face a much stronger church, which was led by a very important figure: Hildebrand.

You may recall that we talked about how Henry III exiled Pope Gregory VI, sending him to Germany. Hildebrand was one of the people who followed Gregory VI to Germany. Hildebrand slowly made his way up the ranks, thanks to his religious zeal, honesty, and tact. Hildebrand's efforts were recognized when he was appointed the archdeacon of the church around 1058. He led the administration of the church from then on and through the reigns of numerous popes.

By 1073, Hildebrand's popularity and influence were such that it almost allowed him to bypass the papal election laws that he himself set forth! As Pope Alexander II was being mourned by the people and clergy of Rome, the crowd started to shout Hildebrand's name, offering him up as the new pope. Hildebrand didn't want to be elected in this way. In fact, he fled the scene to avoid any irregularities. He was quickly found and elected by a council of cardinals and promptly hailed by the people of Rome. He became Pope Gregory VII, the name being chosen as an homage to his teacher, Pope Gregory VI. Gregory VII immediately set about reissuing bans of simony and marriage among priests, which were now serious offenses punishable by excommunication. Gregory VII also reaffirmed the exclusive papal right to elect bishops and move them across dioceses.

Needless to say, this wasn't really welcomed back in Germany. Henry IV wanted to do the exact opposite; he wanted the church to completely submit to him, and he wanted to control the elections of popes and bishops. But right about the time of Hildebrand's ascension to the chair of Saint Peter, the so-called Saxon rebellion broke out in Germany. Saxony had many powerful lords who felt threatened by the young and rash Henry IV, and they rebelled against their king around 1073. The conflict lasted for several years, seriously weakening Henry's power. By 1075, it had become clear that Henry's forces would prevail, and the young king could finally turn to the rebellious Italians. He then went blatantly against the laws promulgated by Gregory VII by appointing Tedald as the archbishop of Milan.

In 1076, the animosities between the Holy Roman Empire and the church reached new heights. Gregory VII was formally "deposed" by the Synod of Worms, which consisted mainly of imperial-friendly German priests. In turn, Henry IV was excommunicated by Pope Gregory VII, which seriously endangered his status in the Holy Roman Empire. The rebellious counts and dukes (especially in Saxony) now had another argument against Henry IV. Seriously weakened and shaken by the excommunication, Henry was forced to seek penance from Gregory VII. In 1077, Henry IV journeyed to Canossa, where Gregory VII awaited him.[i] According to an old story, Henry kneeled for three days in front of Canossa Castle before being let in. By performing such a deed, Henry managed to wash away his previous sins, forcing Pope Gregory VII to forgive him for his previous wrongdoings.

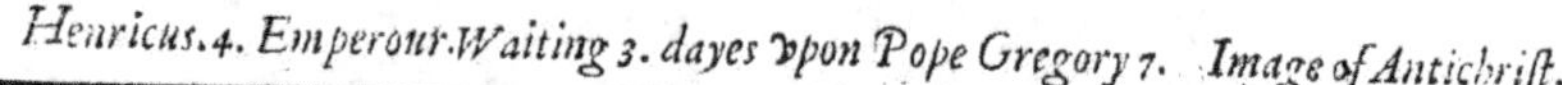

Henry IV at Canossa.[7]

Generally speaking, Gregory VII was ready to negotiate with Henry IV, even after Henry's subsequent and numerous breaches of agreements he made with the church. Henry did not openly or formally accept the new German king (or anti-king) Rudolf, who was chosen by the German nobility and supported by the church. By 1078, Gregory was regularly receiving angry letters from the Saxons, who renewed their rebellion, spurred by Henry's recent problems with the church. They were perplexed by Gregory's ambiguous stance toward Henry and the new

---

[i] Morrison, Karl F. "Canossa: a revision." Traditio 18 (1962): 121-148.

king, Rudolf, and didn't understand why Gregory continued to recognize Henry as the king of the Germans. The hesitancy continued well into 1080 when it became clear that Henry would prevail over Rudolf. Only then did Gregory express his support for Rudolf. He also renewed his excommunication of Henry, something that was not necessarily driven by military concerns. Henry continued to work with people who had already been excommunicated by the church. He tried to bribe a papal legate and continued behaving in a flagrant and impudent way.

Henry, in turn, deposed the pope via the Synod of Brexen, which was attended exclusively by bishops friendly to the Holy Roman Empire. The new pope was proclaimed as well. Archbishop Guibert became Antipope Clement III.

Henry managed to reach Rome by 1084, and Clement III was finally and formally proclaimed as the new pope. Gregory VII had no other choice but to flee the city. The same year, Clement III proclaimed Henry as the Holy Roman emperor. Both were soon forced to flee Rome due to the threat posed by the Norman forces that were friendly to Gregory VII. However, the old pope wasn't allowed to sit in the chair of Saint Peter, largely due to the disorder the Norman troops caused in Rome. Gregory VII was held responsible for this and was forced to flee once again.

Over the next twenty years or so, two lines of popes would be elected, one pro-imperial and the other anti-imperial. For the most part, the pro-imperials weren't really influential in Rome, but they sporadically made themselves known, even in Rome proper. The Investiture Crisis continued until the ascent of Henry V, the son of Henry IV, in 1105.

Henry IV returned to Germany, where he had a multitude of unsettled matters with aristocrats. These internal quarrels kept him busy in the last twenty years of his reign. The influence of Henry's son, Henry V, increased in the last few years of Henry IV's reign. Ultimately, Henry V obtained support from the nobility and forced his father to abdicate in 1105.

Henry V initially gave people the impression of a young man who wanted to resolve the conflict between the church and the empire. However, that opinion changed in 1111 when he imprisoned Pope Paschal II, compelling the pope to give him the imperial crown. This started a conflict between the nobility and the church, which ended in the Concordat of Worms in 1121, which once and for all ended the Investiture Crisis.

The Concordat of Worms affirmed the pope's supremacy in the realm of the church, setting the scene for an unprecedented rise in the pope's power.[i] Henry V died at a fairly young age in 1125, and his death also ended the Salian dynasty.

De Mesquita, Bruce Bueno. "Popes, Kings, and Endogenous Institutions: The Concordat of Worms and the Origins of Sovereignty." International Studies Review 2, no. 2 (2000): 93-118.

Chapter 5: The Hohenstaufen Emperors

With the dusk of Salian rule came the dawn of the Hohenstaufen dynasty. Progenitors of the Hohenstaufen dynasty had already come to prominence during the Ottonian dynasty. The Hohenstaufen family came from Swabia, and the heads of the family served as counts of the palace in Swabia. Frederick Hohenstaufen was one such count of the palace. In the 11th century, he managed to prepare the ground for his family's future rise to power. Count Frederick's son, Frederick of Büren, married a cousin of Pope Leo IX, which immensely improved the status of his family. Frederick of Büren had a son who ultimately became Frederick I, Duke of Swabia, in 1079 on the orders of Holy Roman Emperor Henry IV.

Frederick I, Duke of Swabia, married the daughter of Henry IV, Agnes, fostering the bonds between the rising Hohenstaufen family and the ruling Salian dynasty. Frederick I helped the Salians in their struggle within the province of Swabia. At the time, there were a number of powerful warlords (such as Rudolf of Rheinfelden, the anti-king) in Swabia who contested the authority of Salians. These warlords might have understood that the downfall of the Salians had already started, but they didn't get the timing right. Their revolt came too soon.

Frederick was succeeded, unsurprisingly, by another Frederick around 1105. Much like his father, Frederick II also closely followed the orders of the Salians.

With the death of Emperor Henry V in 1125, the Salian dynasty made its final appearance in the great historical drama. The power void had to be filled as soon as possible, and the choice ultimately fell to either Frederick II, Duke of Swabia, or Lothair of Supplinburg, Duke of Saxony. Frederick II must have pointed out that his mother, Agnes, was the daughter of Henry IV, which meant he had the imperial blood necessary for rising to the throne of the Holy Roman Empire. Lothair of Supplinburg, on the other hand, had the aristocracy on his side; all the imperial blood in the world didn't mean anything if one wasn't supported by the aristocracy.

Lothair was chosen by the members of the nobility in the elections that came immediately after Henry V's death in 1125. As was customary at the time, the new ruler had to assert his dominance within Germany itself. Lothair had the Hohenstaufens against him. Frederick II lost to Lothair in the royal elections and also faced the prospect of losing some of his lands due to Lothair's policies. It was only natural for armed conflict to break out due to such issues.

Another civil war ensued, in which Lothair's side prevailed, making Lothair of Supplinburg not only the new German king but also the new Holy Roman emperor in 1133. Lothair's tenure was a sort of interregnum, a short span that came in between two dynasties (in this case, the Salians and Hohenstaufens).

Although Lothair didn't really rule for a long time, he was instrumental in one of the schisms that happened within the Catholic Church. In 1130, Innocent II and Anacletus II both claimed to be legitimately chosen heads of the church, and neither would back down. Innocent II was driven away from Rome by supporters of Anacletus II, but he managed to obtain the support of major European rulers, including Lothair.

Perhaps one of the clauses of Lothair's support for Innocent II was the latter crowning him as the Holy Roman emperor in 1131. Some five years later, Lothair succeeded in finding an agreement with the German aristocrats, but he died shortly after, in 1137, leaving the succession question open since he had no direct male successors.

Conrad III Hohenstaufen

At this historical moment, Conrad III Hohenstaufen stepped onto the scene after being elected as the new German king in 1138. In the first few years of his reign, Conrad III had to face rivals, such as Lothair's cousins, Henry the Proud and Henry the Lion, with the matter being settled by 1142.

Conrad III was a typical German ruler. He was rugged, warlike, ambitious, and energetic. He was taken aback when he heard priests preaching in favor of the Second Crusade. After extensive preparations, he set the course for the Holy Land in 1147, bringing a large army with him. The future Holy Roman emperor, Frederick Barbarossa, followed his uncle Conrad III on this crusade.

The Germans were led through Hungary, the Balkans, and the Byzantine Empire before finally reaching the Holy Land.[i] Although the Germans encountered mainly Christians, there are many testimonies of their less-than-laudable behavior. For instance, it is said that German troops regularly stole food and other products from the local populations and engaged in numerous small skirmishes and street fights with angry sellers. Word about the Crusaders' barbaric behavior soon spread throughout the Byzantine Empire, with market deals between local populations and Crusaders being completed over thick town walls. Philippopolis, a city in Thrace (modern-day Bulgaria and, at the time, a settlement within the Byzantine Empire), saw similar scenes. The German army was stationed outside of the city, and some soldiers found their way to a tavern, where they proceeded to drink large quantities of alcohol and get into a scuffle with a snake charmer, who they believed tried to poison them.[ii]

In Adrianople, the situation was similar. Prior to the arrival of the main group of German armies, a German noble stopped to rest and

King Conrad III. [*]

---

[i] Roche, Jason T. "King Conrad III in the Byzantine Empire: A Foil for Native Imperial Virtue." (2015).

[ii] Roche, Jason T. "King Conrad III in the Byzantine Empire: A Foil for Native Imperial Virtue."

recuperate in a monastery close to Adrianople, only to be murdered by robbers or soldiers who happened to be there. When the main group of German forces arrived, King Conrad ordered his nephew Frederick to sack the monastery and find the culprits. The excessive force with which Frederick's troops inflicted revenge called for the intervention of the Byzantine Empire, though the Germans soon continued their march toward the Holy Land.

The Germans faced other events as well. At one point, while camping in the plain called Choirobacchoi, the whole army was surprised by a flash flood. Numerous soldiers died in this incident, and many more lost their equipment and provisions. The Byzantines considered this to be a divine intervention, similar to that of the drowning of the Egyptian army in the Red Sea.

However, the Germans continued marching, soon reaching Constantinople. The people in the city, including Byzantine Emperor Manuel, were wary about the intentions of the Germans and made the necessary preparations for a potential attack. The city's garrison was fostered, and the famous walls of Constantinople were strengthened.

Battle of Inab, Second Crusade.[9]

The Germans didn't attempt to conquer Constantinople, and they were able to cross the Bosphorus in relative peace and order. However, the Second Crusade was a general failure, with the Germans and French being defeated by the Seljuk Turks and failing to capture Damascus. The Second Crusade ended in 1149, with the major protagonists returning home. Fairly soon after returning, in 1152, Frederick was crowned king of the Germans in Aachen, shortly after the death of King Conrad III. King Conrad had recognized Frederick's potential and also acknowledged that his own son, Conrad, was still too young to become king. Conrad sought to avoid some of the mistakes of past kings and emperors. He didn't leave any space for the regent period, where the royal power was usually diluted.

The young King Frederick was immediately put in a position to assert his royal authority and administer justice impartially. As the story goes, a knight, accused of some criminal acts that seriously endangered his reputation, came to Frederick during the celebration of his coronation and started imploring the new king to pardon him for his misdeeds. The young king remained unmoved by the knight's plight and decided that justice should not be bent to suit individual whims.[i] This is a perfect example of medieval royal justice, which was quite often delivered personally and publicly by the king himself.

Barbarossa excelled in these matters, often participating in disputes between dukes, counts, and princes and settling feuds that had been going on for a long time. This proved instrumental in establishing his reputation and granted him the title of *pater patriae* ("father of the fatherland"). Barbarossa wasn't simply a powerful German leader. He was also a fairly wise man, someone who would gladly try to settle disputes between local lords to foster the growth of the kingdom.

Frederick Barbarossa

One of Frederick's initial moves was to sign the Treaty of Constance in 1153, which was, in a way, his show of respect for the pope. As was the case with many other German leaders, Frederick Barbarossa vowed to defend the pope's interest in Italy in case anyone tried to go against it, such as the Byzantine Empire, which still wanted a piece of southern Italy.

---

[i] Weiler, B. (2009). The King as Judge: Henry II and Frederick Barbarossa as Seen by Their Contemporaries. In Challenging the Boundaries of Medieval History: The Legacy of Timothy Reuter (pp. 115-140).

Frederick also went through the usual ordeal of having to reconquer Italy. On the wings of the Treaty of Constance and a renewed respect for the pope, Frederick marched into Italy with his army in 1154, sacking and looting a few cities, such as Tortona. The aim of this Italian expedition was to finally bring Sicily within the pope's sphere of influence.

As you may remember, Sicily had been under the command of the Saracens (Muslim Arabs) who dared to cross into mainland Italy. By the time of Frederick Barbarossa, the Muslims had been pushed out of Sicily, only to be replaced with insubordinate Normans, who were avid adventurers and incredibly good soldiers. The aim of Frederick's first Italian expedition was to push the Normans out. In this respect, Frederick's first Italian expedition was a failure because he was forced to return to Germany in 1155 due to unrest that started to unravel there.

Barbarossa (middle) with his two children. [10]

Frederick's first Italian expedition also resulted in him being crowned as the Holy Roman emperor, something that was, of course, part of the inevitable tit for tat between him and the pope. As mentioned, Frederick's job in Italy was far from complete, so he was forced to cut his military expedition short and return to Italy. The Normans were still a threat, which was why Pope Adrian IV sought negotiations with the Normans. This left Barbarossa very displeased and strained his relationship with the pope. Moreover, word reached Frederick Barbarossa that somewhere in Rome hung a picture of Emperor Lothair receiving the imperial crown from the pope. It was obvious in this picture that the pope had the upper hand and that Lothair was merely receiving the pope's divine wisdom and power. This picture remained in place despite Frederick's orders to remove it.

The stage was thus set for another Italian campaign. By 1158, Frederick was once again in Italy with his army. This didn't go well with the cities in northern Italy, which were used to being plundered with each German campaign in Italy. The revolt, this time, came to a tipping point in Milan, which sought to assert itself in the region of Lombardy. Milan and other cities in Lombardy took matters into their own hands, executing power that Frederick believed was rightfully reserved only for him.[i]

Frederick felt obliged to punish Milan for such behavior and started by besieging a close ally of Milan, Crema. The siege of Crema lasted from 1159 to 1160 and ended with excessive violence and the sacking of the city. During the long siege of Crema, a lot of prisoners were killed on both sides in an endless stream of retributions. Frederick even tied some hostages to his siege equipment so they wouldn't be targeted by the defenders from Crema. Whether this tactic worked or not, Frederick ultimately burst into Crema, destroying it completely while sparing the citizens.

A similar fate awaited Milan. First, Frederick sent a special envoy to Milan. He took one of the Milanese hostages he had at his disposal and pulled out one of his eyes. The hostage was then sent to Milan just so that

<hr>

[i]Velov, Ivana. Literary And Historical Interpretation Of Frederick Barbarossa's Conquest Of The Italian Communes: Analysis Of The Events And Personalities Described In The Novel" Baudolino" By Umberto Eco. *Дипломатија И Безбедност*, 249.

the people knew what was waiting for them around the corner.[i] The subsequent siege of Milan in 1161 was particularly bitter. During the winter of 1161/62, Frederick cut all roads leading to Milan and barred anyone from entering or exiting the city. Eventually, the starved population gave in and surrendered. The citizens were brought out, and the city was razed.

It goes without saying that Frederick Barbarossa experienced the same sort of troubles in Italy as his predecessors had. In the 12th century, a number of Italian cities experienced major social shifts, moving away from the feudal system. Italian cities, which were culturally and technologically advanced, provided opportunities relatively unavailable to the average German serf. Commerce and quality craftsmanship made for bustling city markets, and some people started amassing serious capital. Artisans made high-quality products, with prices dictated by associations of artisans, which grew increasingly influential, not only in Italian cities but also throughout Europe.

Such cities demanded freedom and would never fully accept any of the German kings who entered Italy. Perhaps they might have accepted him if he had been Italian. But during this period, the Germans had the military advantage, so the Italians were doomed to being constantly conquered by what they perceived to be barbaric Germans. And they were right in recognizing that the Germans were bringing an entirely different culture and system with them.

The conflicts with Italy would continue for quite some time. In 1176, the hostilities temporarily stopped. The Italians managed to inflict a decisive defeat and repel Frederick Barbarossa in the Battle of Legnano.[ii] By this time, Frederick was facing a highly organized revolt, which had materialized in the form of the Lombard League, heralded by the rebuilt Milan. This time, Frederick's forces were fairly weak and scattered throughout Italy. The previous Italian expeditions didn't go well, and the nobles were increasingly reluctant to participate in another pointless Italian expedition. Epidemics would often break out in the army during these expeditions, decimating the already weakened morale of the troops. This was the major reason why Frederick arrived with a somewhat smaller body of men in comparison to his earlier exploits.

---

[i] Ibid.

[ii] FRANKE, Daniel. From Defeat to Victory in Northern Italy: Comparing Staufen Strategy and Operations at Legnano and Cortenuova, 1176-1237. *Nuova Antologia Militare*, 2021, 2.5: 27.

His forces throughout Italy attempted to achieve subordination to his rule. In 1176, Barbarossa was waiting for his reinforcements, led by Philip of Cologne, to arrive. Barbarossa was stationed in Pavia (near Milan) and was moving north to Como to meet the arriving reinforcements. This was a risky move since all these maneuvers were well within the range of the forces stationed in Milan and its environs. It is likely that, together with his reinforcements, Barbarossa had around three thousand men. His forces were made up almost exclusively of cavalry units.

Barbarossa left Pavia with around one thousand cavalrymen, leaving a small regiment in Pavia itself. He headed north to meet Philip of Cologne in Como. The Italians might have numbered up to fifteen thousand men, mostly infantry. After merging with the reinforcements, Barbarossa headed back to Pavia. His path was blocked by a large force of the Lombard League. Imperial forces were drawn by Lombardian cavalry into battle, with the main body of Barbarossa's forces being gradually surrounded by the much larger Lombardian army. Carnage ensued, and Barbarossa just barely made it back to Pavia. It's said that Empress Beatrice had already started mourning him when Barbarossa arrived in Pavia.

The defeat at Legnano practically drove Barbarossa out of Italy, though he did have some pockets of support. He was forced to accept the Peace of Venice in 1177, as well as the Peace of Constance in 1183, both of which were favorable to the Lombard League. The Germans had lost the upper hand in Italy, but they were free to focus on other conquests. The Third Crusade, Frederick's second, would turn out to be his last military endeavor.

Barbarossa's Policies

Unlike some of his predecessors, namely the Ottonians and Salians, Frederick Barbarossa was on much better terms with the nobility, or at least he knew how to manage the nobles so that they didn't question his power in a violent way.[i] He was, as mentioned, a fair judge in resolving disputes, for instance, between Henry the Lion and Henry Jasomirgott, very early on in his career. Another important early move was the destruction of the castles of nobles who dared to try and make the most out of Barbarossa's absence in 1154 and 1155.

Friederich A. Warlord or Financial Strategist: Frederick Barbarossa. Johns Hopkins University. 2022 Nov 10;3(1).

The economy also saw some improvements during Frederick Barbarossa's reign. Prior to his rule, there were only around twenty-five mints across Germany. Barbarossa left a total of 215 mints in Germany after his death.[i] He was a skilled businessman and a great negotiator. At one point, the people of Cologne came into a dispute with the archbishop of Cologne. The people of Cologne wanted to make some changes to the public spaces, but they found a powerful opponent in the form of Philip von Heinsberg. The emperor had to step in and settle the dispute. Barbarossa decided that the people were right in wanting to change their public space, but they had to pay a certain sum to their local church. In turn, the church couldn't just spend this money; it was obliged to invest it in some lucrative business endeavors with high rates of return.

Barbarossa was no stranger to debt and would sometimes even pawn off royal property so that he could obtain money as fast as possible. However, he was also very good at obtaining money. For instance, he insisted on taxing imperial churches and claimed the properties of dead clergymen. This gave rise to some funny scenes; instead of letting their money go automatically to Barbarossa after their death, some clergymen preferred to give it away. Customs and tolls were another important source of income for Barbarossa's administration.

Occasionally, other less laudable ways of obtaining money were employed. The Jews in Germany were accused of numerous crimes for which they were fined. Funnily enough, Barbarossa fined another gentleman, Philip, Archbishop of Cologne, for extorting the Jews. Barbarossa recognized the power of fines. There were hefty fines for not showing up at the councils he organized, and the fines were especially high for the nobility.

Barbarossa would also sometimes sell his exclusive right to govern certain areas, the so-called regalia. Regalia included things like the right to levy different kinds of taxes, such as market tolls, wagon tolls, forage taxes, gate tolls, and transit tolls. Regalia also included the right to control mills, bridges, and fisheries. Finally, those who were ready to pay good money to Barbarossa for their regalia could levy the standard annual tax on property, as well as an interesting and a bit frightening "tax on persons."[ii]

---

[i] Ibid.
[ii] Ibid.

Depending on the political situation and the need for money, Barbarossa would sometimes accept large payments instead of besieging and occupying a city. This was especially prevalent in Italy's wealthy north, where Genoa and Pisa paid good money to Barbarossa, who, in turn, had to grant them ownership of Sardinia.

Barbarossa's numerous conquests and military victories can only be understood by looking at his careful money management and strong business sense.

Third Crusade, Barbarossa Death, and the Decline of the Hohenstaufen Dynasty

The Muslims managed to take over Jerusalem in 1187, sending shockwaves through the whole of Europe. The Second Crusade, as we've seen, has left a number of questions unanswered. The Arabs weren't in any way defeated, and the Christian regions in the Middle East were doomed to be slowly ground down by the Arabs. One of the major successes of the Crusaders, namely the capture of Jerusalem, was negated by Sultan Saladin and his forces. Three European leaders—Richard I the Lionheart, Philip II of France, and Frederick Barbarossa—agreed to embark on the Third Crusade. Richard the Lionheart and Philip II preferred the naval route, while Barbarossa took the land route, which ultimately cost him his life.

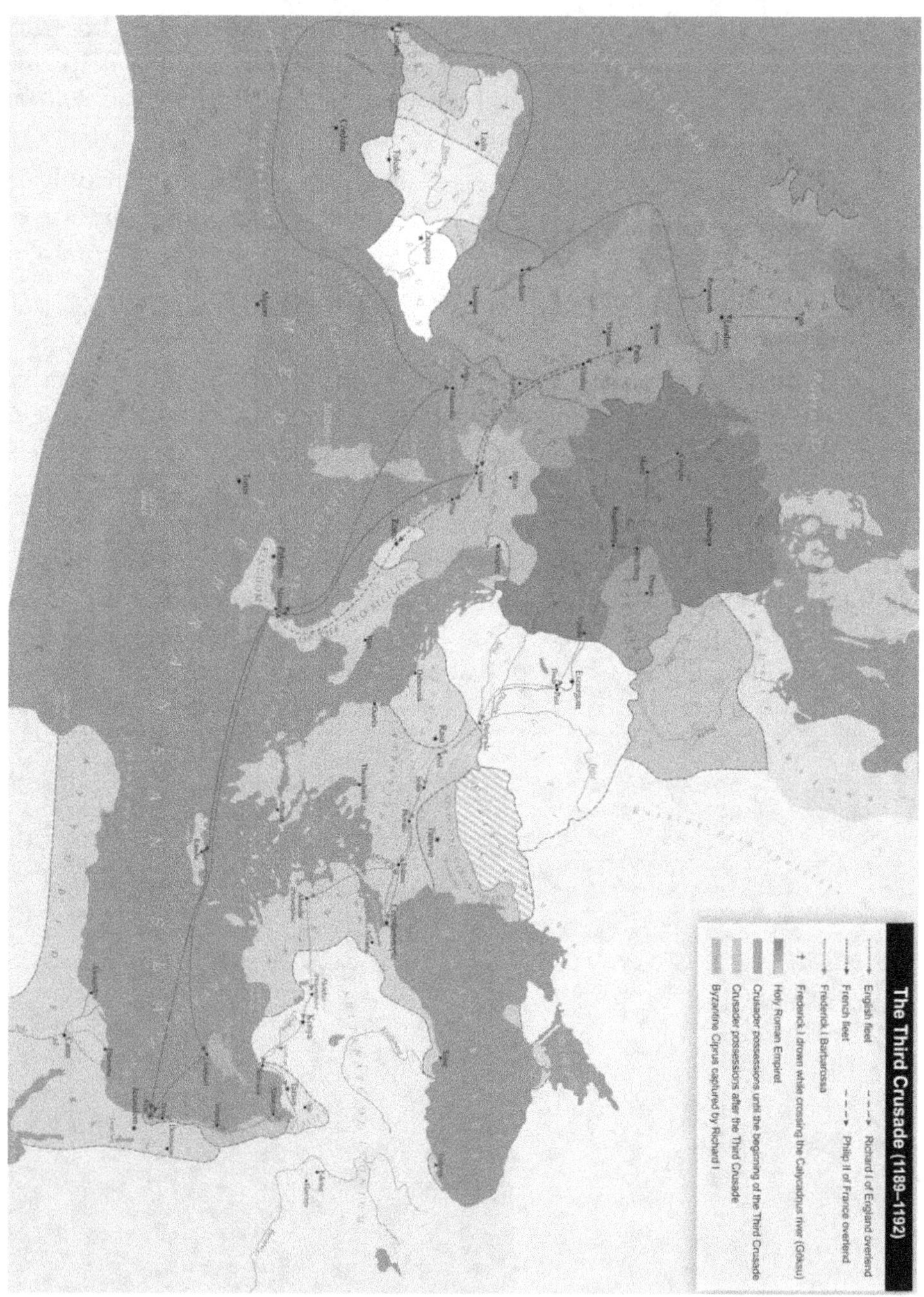

Holy Roman Empire in the late reign of Barbarossa, as well as Barbarossa's path toward the Holy Land. [11]

It is interesting that already in the 12th century, there was a sort of separation between England, France, and the Holy Roman Empire with respect to their naval actions. Namely, England and France were starting to use the sea to their advantage more and more, while the Germans preferred to stay on land. This separation remained in the centuries to come, and the Germans never really became a "naval nation" like the French and especially the English.

Barbarossa first had to ensure the safe passage of his army through Hungary and the Byzantine Empire. King Bela III of Hungary granted safe passage, as did Byzantine Emperor Isaac II Angelos. Money was always a source of worry for Barbarossa, and this was certainly true in the case of the Third Crusade. His soldiers were forced to help themselves along the way, and Barbarossa even managed to strike a deal with Isaac II, who allowed Barbarossa's forces to gather fruit and vegetables they came across in the Byzantine Empire. This deal wasn't really welcomed by the populations who directly encountered the Germans, though, so numerous skirmishes and scuffles broke out along the way.

Sometimes, the locals tried to profit from the Crusaders by offering criminally bad exchange rates. Currency exchange back in the day was still a novel thing, and it was very challenging to come up with a fixed, fair rate. The exchange rate was thus left to chance and the whims of the locals, who sometimes took advantage of the fact the Crusaders often had no other choice but to buy their products. This further complicated the already tense relationship between the Germans and the Byzantines.

Also, the Byzantines didn't look favorably upon the military presence of Germans in the Balkans. The Serbs and Bulgarians already had their own states in the Balkans and were trying to expand their sphere of influence. Barbarossa was in contact with the Serbian zupan (supreme leader or grand prince) Stefan Nemanja. Barbarossa's army was warmly welcomed by Stefan Nemanja. The Germans received food, such as grain, livestock, and wine. The nobles were lavished with luxurious gifts.[i]

---

[i] Frederick I. The Crusade of Frederick Barbarossa: The History of the Expedition of the Emperor Frederick and Related Texts. Ashgate Publishing, Ltd.; 2010.
This manuscript is a collection of works written immediately after the Third Crusade and later copies of these early works. Its authorship is a fairly complicated issue, especially due to the fact that only portions of the early texts remain; for the rest, we have to rely on much later copies of early works.

After passing through Bulgaria and a long stay in Philippopolis, the Germans reached the region of Constantinople. After a lot of back and forth and a lot of drama, the Byzantine emperor agreed to ferry the Germans from Europe to Asia Minor (modern-day western Turkey). As they traveled eastward, the Germans encountered numerous unpleasant scenes. Besides the cultural differences, there were also religious differences, all of which gave rise to animosities between the Germans and their unwelcoming hosts.[i]

Once in the area held by the Muslims, the Germans encountered the Seljuk Turks, one of the many ethnic groups roaming the regions of the Middle East and allies of the Arabs, who were gaining the upper hand in the Middle East. The Turks occasionally harassed the German army, setting up ambushes and skirmishes, even though the Germans expected a peaceful reception since the Turks previously agreed to let the Germans pass through their lands.

The Germans were exhausted, having passed through a fairly arid region with little food. On April 30th, 1190, the Germans left their camp, and Turks quickly captured it in the hopes of gaining good loot. However, the Germans turned back and crushed the unsuspecting Turks. Two days later, there was another battle between the Germans and Turks. This time, the dukes of Swabia and Merania, as well as the counts of Kyburg and Oettingen, distinguished themselves by showcasing admirable valor on the battlefield. Count Kyburg is said to have killed seventeen men, a deed worthy of Homer's Achilles.

The Bohemians also proved to be worthy soldiers of Christ. Low on provisions, the Bohemians had to go out of the camp and forage. The Turks were diligently waiting for small groups of Germans to exit the camp in search of food. So, six Bohemian nobles put their armor on and then some servants' clothes. From afar, they might have looked like fairly large servants. In any case, they fooled the Turks, who rushed to attack them. The Bohemians quickly drew their concealed weapons and slashed the six opportunistic Turks.[ii]

---

[i] The cultural difference between Greeks and Germans moves along the same lines as the difference between Italians and Germans.

[ii] Frederick I. The Crusade of Frederick Barbarossa: The History of the Expedition of the Emperor Frederick and Related Texts. Ashgate Publishing, Ltd.; 2010. P. 102

On May 3rd, the Germans were faced with a difficult situation. A Turkish prisoner was coerced into helping the Germans choose the best option. Either they would continue their passage through the desert or take a detour through a mountainous but more favorable region. The Germans started their climb in the mountains of Pisidia (the Taurus Mountains). The Turks knew the terrain better and would strategically place themselves above the Germans and shower them with stones and arrows. The heavy German armor came in handy here, though many were injured. Even the duke of Swabia was injured by a stone, and a knight named Werner was killed.[i] The Germans nevertheless managed to climb up to the Turks and eliminate them.

Just how perilous and dangerous the Crusades were is nicely showcased by the difficulties the Germans encountered along their way. They hadn't even arrived in the Holy Land yet; in fact, they had a long way to go, but they already participated in numerous small battles, their forces slowly being ground down. A few days after the events in the Pisidia mountains, on May 6th, 1190, another distinguished knight, Frederick of Hausen, died, not in battle but after falling off a horse.

Early depiction of Barbarossa during the Third Crusade. [12]

About a month following this event, on June 10th, another tragedy struck the German army. Barbarossa was marching with his army through the region of Seleucia (modern-day southern Turkey). A major part of the army took a mountain pass to find a safe passage across the Saleph River.

---

[i] Ibid. p. 102

Barbarossa, tired of the endless Turkish mountains and drained by the heat, decided to swim across the Saleph in spite of warnings from his entourage that the river had a very strong flow. It should also be mentioned that Barbarossa was around sixty-seven years old at the time. He entered the river and soon drowned, although scholars don't know how exactly that happened.

The duke of Swabia, Barbarossa's own son, immediately became the head of the German army. Although seriously shaken by the death of their emperor, the Germans marched on toward the Holy Land. Ultimately, this crusade saw some successes, with Saladin's forces being pushed on several fronts. However, Jerusalem remained in Saladin's hands. The European armies finally returned home in 1192.

Barbarossa was succeeded by his second oldest son, Henry VI, who formally was the king of Germany for some time before his father's death. Henry was careful to first negotiate peace with the Italians, who were happy enough to crown him the Holy Roman emperor in 1191. Henry was known to be a highly educated man, much more so than his father, but he wasn't less cruel or warlike. He continued to hamper relationships with the Byzantine Empire and managed to extort a lot of money from the Byzantine emperor, threatening to invade it unless Germany received a hefty payment.

Henry VI died in 1197 at a fairly young age while preparing for the next crusade. In spite of trying hard to do so, Henry VI never managed to legitimize the hereditary monarchy. So, after his death, there was another interregnum period, which ultimately ended the short rule of the Hohenstaufen dynasty.

Chapter 6: The Great Interregnum Period

The unsolvable conundrum of succession has led to periods of disorganization and struggles for supremacy in many cases throughout history. The same scenario, combined with the prevarications of the Roman clergy, resulted in a period of instability and conflict in the Holy Roman Empire in the 13th century. The beginning of the Hohenstaufen dynasty's decline started to become evident with Emperor Henry VI's death in 1197. Before his passing, Henry designated his son Frederick as the heir to the Kingdom of Sicily and bequeathed the imperial throne to him as well. Frederick II was only three years old at the time of his father's death, and the fact that such a young heir was about to ascend to the throne emboldened aristocrats who were hostile to the Hohenstaufen dynasty.

One of the most influential popes of the Middle Ages, Innocent III, was drawn into these political events as soon as he ascended the papal throne in 1198. The late Emperor Henry came into possession of vast territories in Sicily that the pope considered to be his own. Pope Innocent took young Frederick under his protection and supported his claim to the Kingdom of Sicily, hoping that the youngster would hand these territories back to the church.

Amid the uproar in Germany that followed the death of Emperor Henry, Henry's brother, Philip of Swabia, issued a charter declaring that he would act on behalf of the newly appointed King Frederick to quell the impending conflict.[i] In the meantime, reluctant nobles took the opportunity to elect Otto IV, known by historians as an anti-king. Otto was the son of a former Saxon and Bavarian duke, and he was the nephew of Richard the Lionheart. Therefore, he enjoyed the support of John, the reigning king of England. Philip, on the other hand, had the support of Philip II of France, which further aggravated the impending conflict between France and England. A division in the Holy Roman Empire, created by the emergence of the two candidates, triggered a civil war that would last a decade.

Pope Innocent exerted a wide influence, claiming supremacy over all of Europe's kings. He successfully organized the Fourth Crusade in 1202, which resulted in the sack of Constantinople. He played an important role in the dispute between the two kings. He was originally sympathetic to Otto IV, but the German anti-king was not as enthusiastic about an alliance with the pope. Half-heartedly, Innocent III sought an alliance with Otto's rival, Philip. It seemed that this alliance would put an end to the conflict, but Philip's assassination in 1208 in Bamberg turned out to end the war.[ii] The circumstances of Philip's death led to controversies and various theories. It is believed by some that Otto of Wittelsbach, who assassinated him, acted on behalf of the supporters of Otto IV. It is important to note that there is no agreement among experts regarding these assertions.

After Philip's death, Otto was determined to destroy Italy in case he didn't receive the imperial crown. As he remained the only candidate, Pope Innocent III had no choice but to crown him a year later. As all this was happening, Frederick II came to maturity and started to spread his influence in Sicily. Since the pope could not rely on an alliance with Otto, against whom he had only recently fought, young Frederick was the only viable option for him to try and achieve his interests.[iii] Otto himself felt safer on the throne and did not feel the need to yield to the pope's entreaties. At the Battle of Bouvines in 1214, Otto faced a major defeat against a coalition of forces from France, Flanders, and parts of the Holy Roman Empire. Otto's influence and position were weakened after this battle, and he was eventually deposed in 1215. He withdrew to his

---

[i] Bryce, James, *The Holy Roman Empire*, MacMillan and Company, 1866. 232

[ii] Painter, Sidney, *A History of the Middle Ages 284-1500*, The MacMillan Press LTD, 1973. 326

[iii] Holmes, George, *The Oxford History of Medieval Europe*, Oxford University Press, 1988. 225

hereditary lands of Brunswick, where he died in 1218. The throne was left for Frederick to claim, and he was eventually crowned emperor.[i] Pope Innocent's plan to reunite Sicily with the rest of the Papal States didn't go as he had hoped, though. By supporting a Hohenstaufen claimant, he achieved the opposite: Sicily was united with the rest of the Holy Roman Empire, further cementing Hohenstaufen authority in the city and surrounding lands.

Frederick remained in Germany for about five years but only in order to organize the kingdom so that he only had to intervene in internal affairs as little as possible. On two occasions, in 1220 and 1232, he granted bishops and nobles some customary rights and gave them legal sovereignty in their own territories. He gave princes, dukes, and counts almost everything they asked for. He even went as far as to imprison his own son for trying to establish stricter governance by resisting the demands of the nobles.[ii]

Frederick could have become one of the more capable rulers of his time, which he proved by consolidating his power and influence in Sicily. However, he did not seem to have the enthusiasm to extend this to the rest of the empire, thus laying the foundation for the rise of local rulers. He spent the rest of his reign traveling and did not concern himself much with the empire's internal affairs. His jurisdiction was limited to cities that were directly dependent on the imperial crown.

Hohenstaufen coat of arms. [18]

Frederick promised the pope his participation in the Fifth Crusade (1217–1221) and vowed to aid Andrew II of Hungary and Leopold VI of Austria in their quest. In return for this promise, he expected to be granted imperial rights over certain cities in Italy. These imperialistic attempts led to the renewal of the Lombard League.[iii]

---

[i] Painter, Sidney, *A History of the Middle Ages 284-1500*, The MacMillan Press LTD, 1973. 326
[ii] Ibid. 327
[iii] The Lombard League was an alliance between the acting pope and certain noblemen against the emperor, which proved to be efficient in the conflict against Frederick's grandfather Barbarossa a few decades prior.

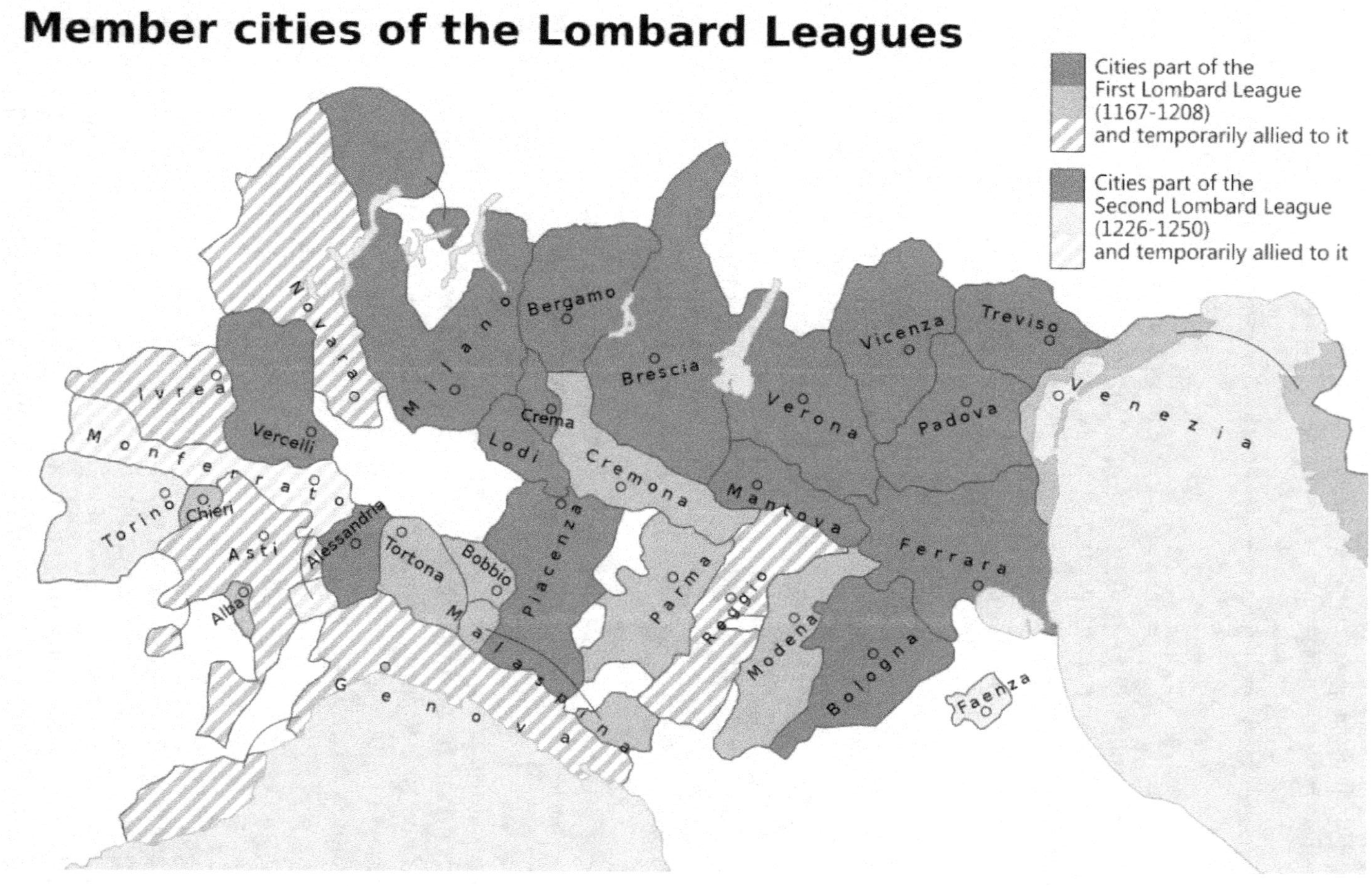

Map of the cities that were members of the Lombard League. [14]

Frederick withdrew his claims, realizing the power of the Lombard League. Because of his mixed heritage (he had Norman and Flemish roots) and his frequent travels, Frederick considered himself a cosmopolite. His ties to the Muslim community, whom he welcomed in Rome, weren't welcomed by the clergy. Frederick tried to impose his worldview in Sicily and other parts of Italy and the Holy Roman Empire. These tendencies were in direct contrast with the church, which led to a rather unpleasant relationship between the emperor and the popes, most notably Pope Gregory IX. Although Frederick eventually fulfilled his promise and launched what he considered to be a successful crusade (1228–1229), Pope Gregory IX wasn't satisfied with Frederick's ideas and his disinterest in the matters of the church. Frederick set a precedent, having achieved a successful crusade without the pope's involvement.[i] Pope Gregory IX excommunicated the unfavorable emperor, and this rivalry extended to both of their successors.

After a long and eventful reign, Frederick's death in 1250 marked the end of the rule of the Hohenstaufen dynasty. After his death, Frederick's supporters recognized the late sovereign's son, Conrad IV, as the rightful heir to the German throne, but other electors did not give their acquiescence. Due to Frederick's excommunication, which extended to his successor, the power in the Holy Roman Empire transitioned to rival kings of Germany who supported the pope. The first to be backed up by Pope Innocent IV was Henry Raspe, who died a few months after his election, leaving William, Count of Holland, to succeed him.

Despite Conrad's attempts to reconcile with the pope, no agreement was reached, and Conrad was excommunicated. He sought to assert control over the Kingdom of Sicily, ultimately planning to develop his influence from there as his father did before him. Conrad's four-year-long reign came to an end with his death during a military campaign in Italy. Frederick II's illegitimate son, Manfred, and Conrad's son, Conradin, replaced the late king and continued the struggle with the papacy, although they were unsuccessful. Manfred and Pope Urban IV negotiated for over two years. The pope offered Manfred recognition of his kingdom in exchange for his support in regaining Constantinople.

The results of the Sixth Crusade are not universally acclaimed, although Frederick proclaimed its success to Henry III of England.

In 1263, Pope Urban IV issued an official regulation stating that the right to elect a king, although an age-old custom among the Germans, now officially belonged to the seven electors. The three archbishops of Mentz, Trier, and Cologne, the pastors of the oldest and richest dioceses in Germany, represented the German Church and had, for centuries, played a leading role in the elections. The other four electors were the dukes of Franconia, Swabia, Saxony, and Bavaria.[i]

Seven prince-electors, Balduineum picture chronicle. [16]

Pope Urban IV's successor, Pope Clement IV, provided continuity in the negotiations with Manfred when he became king of Sicily, where most of the Hohenstaufen influence still remained. Dissatisfied with Manfred's leadership in Sicily, Pope Clement IV sought help outside of Germany and Italy. First, he tried to gain support from King Henry III of England. The pope offered the Sicilian throne to Henry's son, Edmund of Lancaster, but some English nobles openly opposed this offer. King Henry's planned expedition to Sicily was thwarted by rebellious barons and required Pope Clement to seek alternatives. He sought help from King Louis IX of France, specifically from his brother, Charles I, Count of Anjou and Provence. Charles proved to be a competent leader; he defeated Manfred's army in the Battle of Benevento in 1266. Manfred himself refused to flee and died on the battlefield. Charles took control of Sicily, where he was crowned king by the pope.[ii]

[i] Bryce, James, *The Holy Roman Empire,* MacMillan and Company, 1866. 241
[ii] Painter, Sidney, *A History of the Middle Ages 284-1500,* The MacMillan Press LTD, 1973. 329

The imperial rule had largely declined by this time. The Holy Roman Empire looked more like an interwoven network of small territories ruled by kings, princes, dukes, counts, and other nobles. They all attempted to dominate certain areas, increase their sphere of influence, and make life harder for their rivals.

As the Norman Kingdom of Sicily became independent again and was subject to the House of Anjou, the pope fostered his control within the Papal States. Aside from the Papal States, the rest of Italy was without a centralized leadership, and there was constant conflict between local nobles and leaders. Burgundy and the surrounding provinces came under the overwhelming influence of France.

The greatest unrest in the Holy Roman Empire was mainly concentrated in Germany. The first to be elected as anti-king in Germany after the fall of the Hohenstaufens was William of Holland, who was crowned at Aachen, although he faced opposition from the Swabian party. The count palatine of the Rhine was excluded from taking part in the election on the grounds that he was under sentence of excommunication as a supporter of Conrad IV. A few of the remaining Hohenstaufen supporters claimed that William lacked courage and chivalrous qualities. Despite this, William managed to enjoy an unchallenged reign from 1254 to 1256.[i]

The electors eventually deemed him unfit, and a new foreign candidate emerged. In a sort of double election, the son of English King John, Richard of Cornwall, became the king of the Romans in 1257, receiving four out of seven votes from the electors. Richard was viewed as a compromise candidate, as he was seen as being capable enough to reconcile internal divisions within the empire. Soon, the electors found out that Richard had offered an unequal bribe to some of them before the election. So, their allegiance shifted to Alfonso X of Castile, who claimed succession to the Hohenstaufen dynasty through his mother, one of the daughters of Philip of Swabia.[ii]

Richard had to return to England due to deteriorating relations between his brother, King Henry II, and the English barons. King Henry attempted to reform the legal and judicial systems and demanded

[i] Wilson, Peter H. *Heart of Europe: A History of the Holy Roman Empire.* Harvard University Press, 2016. 548

[ii] Bryce, James, *The Holy Roman Empire*, MacMillan and Company, 1866, 214

increased taxes, which was the primary source of discontent among the barons. During his absence, Richard's supporters succeeded in expelling Conradin, the grandson of Frederick II and the last true Hohenstaufen, from Italy. Conradin was captured by Charles, who was king of Italy, at the Battle of Tagliacozzo in 1268. The battle that took place was the final display of power by the Hohenstaufen family. Conradin was held captive for three months in Naples until Charles decreed his fate: beheading.

While there are reports claiming that the pope disapproved of the atrocious treatment of Conradin committed during Conradin's imprisonment, there are also statements suggesting that Pope Clement IV might have given his approval or even suggested Conradin's execution in 1268.[i] Judges wouldn't concur with the sentence, but being backed by the pope, Charles went through with the public beheading in the marketplace of the town square of Naples. After Conradin's death, the situation in Germany changed in such a way that it became more favorable for Richard to return. He ruled for a short time before being forced to return to England, where he died in 1272.

Conradin's death as the last Hohenstaufen claimant secured the pope's main goal of maintaining his domain over Sicily and Naples, keeping them separate from the Holy Roman Empire.[ii] In short, the popes, aided by the electors, triumphed over the Holy Roman emperors, and the empire lost its power.[iii]

The conditions in Germany during that time were extremely poor and unpleasant. The German nobility was constantly appointing two opposing representatives with no real power for either side. The conflicts and power struggles between these candidates and their supporters contributed to the instability of the period. This was the height of the disarray and chaos in Germany during the Great Interregnum (named this way to distinguish it from the shorter period between 924 and 962). Disgruntled and power-thirsty dukes and barons attempted to expand their dominions through wars. Robbers swarmed the rivers and roads, and violence was the order of the day everywhere in the empire. There was a tendency for German society to return to this "natural condition of

[i] Bryce, James, *The Holy Roman Empire*, MacMillan and Company, 1866. 212

[ii] Wilson, Peter H. *Heart of Europe: A History of the Holy Roman Empire*. Harvard University Press, 2016. 144

[iii] Painter, Sidney, *A History of the Middle Ages 284-1500*, The MacMillan Press LTD, 1973. 331

mankind" characterized by chronic war, to use the much later expression of Thomas Hobbes. Trade and commerce were disrupted, and the lack of a stable political environment made it challenging to establish consistent economic policies. Occasionally, some cities benefited economically from this arrangement, but the lack of public law, courts of justice, and, most importantly, an emperor meant that the empire was headed toward a massive catastrophe.

These turbulent times also saw another "smaller" interregnum. The church was not immune to the constant feuds between the noblemen, and the conflicts transferred to the clergy. After Pope Clement IV's death, there were internal conflicts between the more notable cardinals and bishops. The temporary governance of the Catholic Church was collectively taken up by the College of Cardinals. This body was split equally between French and Italian representatives, leading to a deadlock between rival cardinals. There was no pope for almost three years, between 1268 and 1271. This was the longest *sede vacante* in history.[i] The extended duration of the conclave even resulted in the deaths of several cardinals. This further complicated the situation since the number of electors had decreased. In August 1271, the cardinals appointed a committee consisting of three representatives from each side to negotiate a settlement. However, the committee was unable to come to an agreement. As a result, one of the cardinals suggested looking outside their ranks for a solution. The elector-cardinals eventually agreed upon Teobaldo Visconti, Archdeacon of Liege, who had ties to France.

Although the decision was ratified by all the cardinals, it was more of a victory for the French faction. The church was experiencing a lot of disorder, and this encouraged Teobaldo, now known as Pope Gregory X, to act quickly to try to solve the problem. Although he himself could have benefited from the disorderly state the Holy Roman Empire was in, he found the disorganization generally unconstructive and realized the threat this chaos imposed. He instructed his subordinates and threatened the electoral princes to choose an emperor; otherwise, he would have to do it himself. Pope Gregory X also issued the papal decree *Ubi periculum* during the Second Council of Lyon in 1274, establishing regulations for

---

[i] Latin for "with the chair [being] vacant," *sede vacante* is a term for the state without an acting pope upon his death or resignation.

the papal election, including measures to expedite the election process.[i]

With the growing power of King Ottokar II of Bohemia and under the threat of Pope Gregory X, the electors realized that the chaotic state of affairs could not last much longer. King Ottokar II was a relative of Philip of Swabia and, therefore, posed a threat with his claim to the imperial throne through his Hohenstaufen roots. His intentions of expanding his jurisdiction into Babenberg lands (the eastern borders of the empire) alarmed the elector-princes. They swiftly went into action and appointed Rudolf, Count of Habsburg, as the new king of the Romans, ending the twenty-year-long period of unrest.

Rudolf's family gained prominence in the Alpine region, where he proved his military and diplomatic skills. His reputation contributed to his appeal as a candidate for the throne. The contested territories in Austria became a focal point of tension between Ottokar and Rudolf. The conflict culminated in the Battle of Marchfeld in 1278, where Ottokar suffered a decisive defeat, leading to his death.

Three men standing at the grave of an emperor; this depiction of the Interregnum can be found in *Chronicon pontificum et imperatorum*, written by Bishop Martin of Opava. [16]

The title of the decree is taken from the opening words of the text, as is traditional for such documents. *Ubi periculum maius intenditur* can be translated to "where greater danger lies."

Rudolf didn't do much to improve the power of the German crown, although he successfully paved the way for a new great dynasty by marrying his son to the heir of Austria. He started his reign by reclaiming Hohenstaufen land that had been lost during the previous turbulent decades. During the course of his reign, he managed to recover the majority of the Hohenstaufen estates. His policy met some opposition in 1274 when a Diet in Nuremberg decreed Count Palatine of Rhine would be the judge in blood feud cases, diluting Rudolf's power in a way.

One of the main consequences of the crisis of the Great Interregnum was the official establishment of prince-electors as a legal entity that chose the next sovereign. The total number of cities grew tenfold, and they gained a certain degree of independence under the decisive interest of the local hegemon. Cities that managed to achieve more independence from the Holy Roman Empire emerged as new centers of economic power. Despite the political chaos, the increase of the empire's population was remarkable, as it almost doubled within a hundred years. Little did people know that the bubonic plague would soon wreak havoc across the whole of Europe.

Chapter 7: The Habsburgs Rise

The Habsburgs, a powerful German family, can trace their origins back to the 11th century. Their family name is derived from their ancestral seat at Habsburg Castle in Aargau (modern-day Switzerland). Initially holding minor titles, they gradually gained resources, and by the mid-13th century, they became serious contenders for the royal title. Through strategic marriages and alliances with other noble houses, such as the House of Luxembourg and the House of Burgundy, the Habsburgs expanded their influence and acquired vast territories across present-day France, Spain, the Netherlands, and the Holy Roman Empire.

Following the tumultuous and destructive events of the Great Interregnum (1254–1273), Pope Gregory X, who had recently been elected after a long period of instability in the church, urged the electors to choose a legitimate emperor to end the chaos in the empire.[i] Finally, after two decades of unrest, in 1273, it was agreed that Rudolf I, Count of Habsburg, would be elected as the king of the Germans. The second choice in the election was Ottokar II, King of Bohemia, but the electors preferred to choose a candidate who seemed to be a figure of mediocre power and influence in contrast to Ottokar II, who was fairly powerful and wealthy.

There are some claims that the Great Interregnum started immediately after Emperor Frederick II's death in 1250, although it is generally described as following the death of his son Conrad IV in 1254.

During Frederick II's reign in the first half of the 13th century, the domestic power of the German king and the supremacy of the emperor suffered greatly.[i] During the turbulent times of the Great Interregnum, the German nobles seized power and prevented the restoration of the previous system of governance. The number of nobles who held almost complete control over their territories increased rapidly. Even a lord who held a small piece of land along the Rhine was often considered an independent prince.[ii] Potential uprisings and unification among princes posed a great threat to the already reduced imperial authority.

Rudolf's election marked the beginning of a new era in European history. Known for his military expertise, Rudolf represented order and legitimacy in the empire, which helped calm tensions. His reign was, like Frederick II's, marked by issues and conflicts with the Papal States. Securing recognition from the pope was difficult due to the tarnished reputation of imperial rule in the preceding decades. Therefore, Rudolf's ability to exercise his imperial authority was somewhat affected.

Holy Roman Emperor Rudolf I as depicted in a 19th-century statue.[17]

---

[i] Painter, Sidney, *A History of the Middle Ages 284-1500*, The MacMillan Press LTD, 1973. 332-3
[ii] Bryce, James, *The Holy Roman Empire*, MacMillan and Company, 1866. 229

The election of Rudolf as the king of Germany did not immediately lead to widespread uprisings, but it did have implications for the political landscape of the empire. Rudolf was able to consolidate Habsburg control in Austria by acquiring various lands and rights, which became the core of the Habsburg dynasty's power. However, he faced pressure from powerful nobles and bishops. During his time as ruler, he focused on taking advantage of his position to raise wealth by selling crown privileges for the benefit of his family. Despite this, the combined value of crown possessions increased thanks to the empire's successful economic development. Rudolf's success was fairly swift and surprising, indicating that the value of the positions of German king and Holy Roman emperor wasn't completely lost by the time Rudolf came to power.[i,ii]

The main changes during this period were the expansion of crown-owned lands and the response to the continuing emancipation of the ministeriales, who were granted full knight status and further immunities for royal monasteries.[iii,iv] Monasteries were required to provide food and accommodation to royal representatives in the early 12th century, and this taxation was extended to royal towns as well. Rudolf developed on the structures initiated by Richard of Cornwall during the Great Interregnum and established bailiwicks to recover Austria, Carinthia, Styria, and Thuringia, which he claimed were vacant imperial fiefs.[v] The bailiffs relied on entrusting minor lords with the supervision of royal assets, shifting the basis of true imperial rule to rest on the king's direct possession of immediate fiefs as hereditary family lands.

Before his ascension to the throne, Rudolf's only rival was Ottokar II of Bohemia, who, despite losing the imperial election, still had claims to the Babenberg inheritance. Rudolf used his imperial powers to forcefully

---

[i] Bryce, James, *The Holy Roman Empire*, MacMillan and Company, 1866. 230

[ii] It must be noted that Rudolf I was never crowned Holy Roman emperor, although he played a significant rule in reviving it.

[iii] Ministeriales were unfree individuals who held military or administrative positions within the feudal system. They were not fully free knights and were bound to the service of a lord. Rudolf granted many of them the status of knights, allowing them to bear arms, thus expanding his influence over their positions.

[iv] Wilson, Peter H. *Heart of Europe: A History of the Holy Roman Empire*. Harvard University Press, 2016. 555

[v] A bailiwick is usually the territory of a town or a monastery; it is under the jurisdiction of a bailiff, a legal officer responsible for overseeing the designated area.

resolve the issue in his favor in 1276, although Ottokar had certain princes backing him up and supporting his claim. Fortunately for the reigning emperor, Ottokar II died in the Battle of Marchfeld in 1278, and Rudolf continued to reign uncontested.[i]

Four years later, Rudolf assigned the Duchy of Austria to his sons at the Diet of Augsburg. The electors eventually agreed that Rudolf could employ his sons as dukes of Austria and Styria. There were still princes who supported Ottokar's family's claims and were wary of a king who was acquiring fiefs as personal property.

From that moment, the Habsburg dynasty was also known as the House of Austria. Nobles in other parts of the Holy Roman Empire still used lands that belonged to the emperor, but they also took advantage of their royal office to secure vacant fiefs for themselves.

After an eventful reign, Rudolf died of natural causes in 1291. Although he tried his best, he couldn't secure the succession to the German throne for his son Albert, largely due to the objections raised by Ottokar's son, King Wenceslaus II of Bohemia, as well as some other nobles.

Albert was known as Albert the One-Eyed, and there are various stories about how he lost his eye. One story claims he lost it in a battle, but some of his contemporaries believed that it could have been caused by an attempted poisoning, which he narrowly survived. Albert was not elected due to his poor attitude toward the electors and because of his "undignified looks." Despite this, Albert continued his father's efforts and tried to expand Habsburg influence and control in the Holy Roman Empire.

The prince-electors eventually chose Count Adolf of Nassau-Weilburg as the king of the Romans in 1292. Adolf's refusal to compromise with nobles over land disputes, which had reduced their support for him, led to a decline in his popularity. The electors did not plan to depose the king, but Adolf's policy toward Thuringia and his involvement in conflicts against nobles and electors made them join together to enforce their own interests. This occurrence was the first deposal of a sovereign by electors without papal involvement.[ii]

---

[i] Wilson, Peter H. *Heart of Europe: A History of the Holy Roman Empire.* Harvard University Press, 2016. 557

[ii] Wilson, Peter H. *Heart of Europe: A History of the Holy Roman Empire.* Harvard University

It is interesting to note that Adolf was not even excommunicated by the pope prior to being deposed. The reason behind this is that there was no convincing proof against Adolf since his election and coronation went uncontested. Despite this, the decision to let him remain in power remained highly controversial. Everything was eventually settled when Albert defeated Adolf in the Battle of Gollheim in 1298. By doing so, Albert regained the throne and immediately consolidated his possessions in Thuringia while also securing Bohemia, which had been left vacant after the death of Ottokar II.

Albert proved to be a competent ruler and gained more support from the imperial cities through effective economic measures. However, Albert was murdered by his own nephew, John, Duke of Swabia, in 1308. John was motivated by a desire for power and the inheritance of Albert's territories. After this event, John's name went down in history as John the Parricide. With the death of Albert, the House of Habsburg lost one of its most dynamic representatives, and his sudden death put an end to the efforts to keep the imperial crown in the family.

Albert's son, Frederick III of Austria, was supposed to succeed him, but the electors rejected the Habsburg heir. Also known as Frederick the Fair, he held the Austrian and Styrian duchies, but he couldn't manage to acquire the royal title.[i] Instead, Count Henry VII emerged as a better choice since he came from the affluent House of Luxembourg. Henry was voted by six of seven electors and was crowned by Pope Clement V in 1312. He unexpectedly died from malaria in 1313.

Henry's short reign and sudden death resulted in yet another tempestuous election. This was the first double election since the one that took place during the Great Interregnum. Henry's son, John of Bohemia, seemed too powerful for the electors, and the electors again neglected Frederick to become a candidate for the crown. The Habsburgs and Luxembourgs were evenly matched before the Habsburgs took the chance to proclaim Frederick the Fair as king in 1314 on the grounds that he was the legitimate heir. The very next day, the Luxembourgs elected their candidate as an anti-king, Louis IV of Bavaria, who was also supported by the powerful John of Bohemia. Frederick, however, still remained the first and right choice.

Press, 2016. 557

This distinction helps differentiate him from Emperor Frederick III (1452–1493).

Louis was crowned at Aachen, while Frederick was forced to travel to Bonn for his coronation. Both tried to achieve the support of the imperial states, engaging in several years of bloody warfare for hegemony. Victory initially seemed to be within Frederick's grasp. The war for leadership ended in 1322 near the town of Mühldorf. Frederick was captured along with over one thousand nobles, but Louis didn't execute him.

In 1325, after a few years of imprisonment and due to the stubbornness of Frederick's brother, Leopold, Louis agreed to release Frederick under the Treaty of Rausnitz. With this act, Louis defused the unrest in the country caused by the war. He even recognized Frederick as a nominal co-king, while Frederick recognized him as a legitimate ruler. Strongly objected by the pope and prince-electors, Louis and Frederick ruled jointly.

With the Habsburgs' claim now weakened, a new rival emerged to counter Louis: Charles IV of Bohemia. Louis tried to acquire new territories, which inspired opposition from the Luxembourg elector, who foresaw Charles as the new king. Although the Habsburgs were displaced as kings by the Luxembourgs in 1308 and the Wittelsbachs of Bavaria in 1314, they were now in the front rank and were able to consolidate and expand their possessions in return for cooperating with the current monarch.[i]

Under the rule of the Wittelsbachs and Luxembourgs, the Habsburgs mostly ruled as dukes, primarily in Austria. The Habsburg dukes stayed loyal to Louis, while Pope Clement VI showed his support for Charles. Louis, in turn, remained politically powerful until his death in 1347. Louis's death occurred during a time of significant changes imposed by the devastating bubonic plague known as the Black Death. The death of an emperor coinciding with one of the deadliest pandemics in human history posed a great threat to the empire's stability.

Louis IV's sons supported Günther von Schwarzburg as a new rival king to Charles IV. Günther held the title briefly but faced difficulties in establishing widespread recognition. Just a few months after the election, Günther died, further complicating the political situation. Elector-princes eventually recognized Charles IV as the legitimate emperor.

---

[i] Wilson, Peter H. *Heart of Europe: A History of the Holy Roman Empire.* Harvard University Press, 2016. 610

Map depicting territories under different jurisdictions

- Land of the Luxembourgs
- Duchy of Austria under Habsburg rule
- Territory of Wittelsbach[18]

The brothers of Frederick the Fair and their sons succeeded one another or ruled jointly throughout the next few decades. Rudolf I (not to be confused with Emperor Rudolf I) became the king of Bohemia but died at a relatively young age. Leopold I was, for a time, a co-ruler with his brother Frederick in the Duchy of Austria. Otto the Merry (sometimes referred to as Otto the Jolly), nicknamed like this in reference to the festive atmosphere of his court, took the title of duke of Austria. His focus shifted toward Bavaria after he married the daughter of Bavarian Duke Stephen. Albert II was a duke of Austria, Styria, and Tirol at one point and was the closest to being crowned Holy Roman emperor. His sons, Albert III and Leopold II, ruled the Habsburg possessions together until 1379. Although always leaning toward it, none of the heirs to the Habsburg possessions reclaimed the imperial throne until the election of Frederick III in 1452.

Frederick was the son of Ernest, Duke of Austria. His father died in 1424, which made him the duke of Inner Austria. His uncle, Frederick IV, Duke of Tyrol, acted as regent since Frederick was only nine years old at the time of his father's passing. When Frederick was able to rule in his own stead, his younger brother, Albert, immediately asserted his rights as co-ruler, starting a long rivalry between the two. Frederick had to ward off the claims of his brother but eventually prevailed with the support of the Tirolean aristocracy.

Albert II (not Frederick's brother) became the Holy Roman emperor over a decade after marrying the duchess of Luxembourg, Elizabeth. She was the daughter of Holy Roman Emperor Sigismund, who died in 1437. Upon the death of Frederick IV, Frederick's uncle, in 1439, Frederick III became the regent for the duke's young heir, Sigismund.[i] In the same year, Albert II unexpectedly died of an illness, leaving Frederick to become the regent for his young heir, Ladislaus the Posthumous.

Ladislaus died at the age of seventeen in 1457, allowing Frederick to take over his inheritance. By this point, Frederick had already crowned himself king of the Romans, doing so in 1440. This coronation faced opposition from some electors who were dissatisfied with certain aspects of his rule. As a result, Frederick delayed his formal coronation and wasn't present at his own election in 1452. His regency in the lands under the jurisdiction of the Albertinian line was still viewed with suspicion.

Between the years 1444 and 1471, Frederick mostly stayed in his own lands, except in 1452 when he traveled to Rome to be crowned emperor. He would become the last Holy Roman emperor to be crowned in Rome.[ii] Criticism arose after the emperor referred to himself as Frederick III, the successor to Hohenstaufen rather than a successor to Frederick the Fair. In Vienna, during the year 1448, Frederick III signed an agreement recognizing Pope Nicholas V as the legitimate pope. In exchange, the pope restored the archbishop-electors of Trier and Mainz.

---

[i] He is known for becoming the king of Hungary at only three months old since he was born after his father Albert II's death, which granted him the nickname "Posthumous."

[ii] His great-grandson Charles V was the last emperor to be crowned, although this was done in Bologna.

The pope also confirmed the emperor's role in maintaining peace and order. The concordat was part of a broader effort by Frederick to stabilize the relationship between the Holy Roman Empire and the papacy. This concordat remained in force until 1806 and regulated the relationship between the Habsburgs and the Holy See.

Frederick also created an improved and centralized administrative institution known as the Imperial Chancery. This office was responsible for managing the Habsburg lands and records. The chancery played a central role in maintaining diplomatic relations with other European powers. It was responsible for treaties and agreements. This entity helped centralize power in the hands of the emperor and his advisors. Despite being known for his cautious and conservative approach to governance, Frederick did not actively pursue comprehensive reforms, instead focusing mainly on maintaining stability rather than implementing changes.

Tapestry depicting the coronation of Frederick III, wrongly attributing the pope in attendance as Pius II instead of Pope Nicholas V.[19]

Frederick secured his own lands before turning his attention to the rest of the empire. However, he faced significant opposition from Austrian and Bohemian nobles. He abandoned his claims to disputed lands in 1458 but was soon embroiled in a dispute with his brother, Albert VI, over Austria between 1461 and 1463. In 1462, Albert raised an insurrection against Frederick in Vienna, and the emperor was besieged in his own residence. These conflicts forced him to move his court between various parts of the empire over the years. He lived in Graz, Linz, and Wiener Neustadt, where he is credited with the construction of a castle and a monastery.

Frederick opposed certain reforms proposed by Count Berthold of Henneberg, who emerged as a profound spokesman after becoming elector of Mainz in 1484. Henneberg wanted to exploit Frederick's desire to secure recognition of his son Maximilian as a successor. Frederick avoided direct conflict and held numerous discussions until electors accepted Maximilian I as king of the Romans in 1486. This was the first time in 110 years that a successor had been chosen during an emperor's lifetime. This was a positive sign that Henneberg and others genuinely wanted to work together with the Habsburgs after all.

Frederick retired to Linz in 1488 and left his son to manage the Holy Roman Empire. Since Maximilian could act as a mediator between princes and his father, the door to compromise was finally open. Maximilian continued this policy after Frederick's death in 1493.

The House of Habsburg was one of the most significant and longest-lasting royal families in European history. Over the course of centuries, they accomplished great feats and expanded their territories through strategic marriages and diplomatic prowess. For example, Maximilian I's union with Mary of Burgundy brought the Burgundian Netherlands under Habsburg control. The marriage of their son, Philip the Handsome, to Joanna of Castile further solidified Habsburg influence and united the Spanish and Burgundian territories.

Unfortunately, after Philip's death in 1506, Joanna began to suffer from mental health issues, earning her the nickname Joanna the Mad. Their son, Charles V, inherited all the lands from both sides of the family. From 1519 to 1556, during Charles's reign, the Habsburg Empire included the Holy Roman Empire, the Spanish Empire, the Austrian Empire, the Kingdom of Hungary, and many other territories. Charles V was fluent in Dutch, French, German, Italian, and Spanish, covering the most widespread languages of the empire. The Habsburg possessions were so vast that Charles had to appoint deputies and regents throughout his dominions.

In 1556, Charles shocked everyone when he decided to step down from his position as ruler and retire to the Monastery of Yuste in Spain. He divided his territory into two separate branches, each governed by representatives of the House of Habsburg. He officially abdicated the Holy Roman Empire and handed over the imperial scepter to his brother Ferdinand I, as appointed in the Diet of Worms back in 1521. During this period, Spain established a global empire through the colonization of the Americas. Charles V gave up the Spanish crown to his son, Philip II. The resources and wealth obtained from the Americas contributed to the rise of European global dominance and economic power.

The Habsburgs also played a significant role in the development of culture since they were major patrons of the arts. Vienna, as the capital of the Habsburg territories, became an important cultural center that attracted musicians, artists, and intellectuals. Notable figures, such as Wolfgang Amadeus Mozart, Ludwig van Beethoven, and Franz Schubert, found patronage and support from the royals. Charles V was known for his support of Titian, who painted several portraits of the emperor. The Habsburg Empire facilitated diverse cultural exchange, encompassing various ethnicities and cultures, which had a lasting influence on the regions involved.

The House of Habsburg's division was a momentous event in European history, leading to the formation of distinct branches that would shape the destinies of Spain and Austria in the forthcoming centuries.

Chapter 8: The Empire during the Reformation

Let's first focus a bit on the societal and cultural context in which the Reformation came about. During the late 15th and early 16th centuries, the Catholic Church experienced a significant increase in corruption. The church was characterized by moral decay, simony (the buying and selling of church offices), and the sale of indulgences (certificates that promised remission of sins).[i] Numerous clergymen were focused on wealth and political power. Rising interest in classical learning led scholars to explore ancient texts and the Bible in their original languages. The Renaissance resulted in questioning the official interpretation of the Bible. In addition, great discoveries, most notably the advancement of the printing press by German inventor Johannes Gutenberg in the mid-15th century, played a crucial role in the spread of new ideas.

Around 1500, the Holy Roman Empire underwent significant institutional changes known as "imperial reforms." However, these changes were not fully implemented, which led to a decline in both imperial and papal authority. These reforms also became closely intertwined with the problems within the church. As a result, the regulations were either rejected, accepted, or adapted by different

---

[i] Simonies were named after Simon Magnus, who is described in the Acts of the Apostles as having offered payment to two disciples of Jesus.

national and local communities, which ultimately led to a reduction of respect toward the emperor.

The political situation in Germany during this time foretold disaster. Unlike France or England, Germany was not a unified country but rather a collection of semi-independent states with similar dialects and cultural backgrounds, which all formed an empire, not a nation in the modern sense of the word. The emperor's influence was at an all-time low, which led to tensions and hostility toward the church, which was always allied with the Holy Roman Empire. As mentioned, the clergy managed to destroy its status and reputation via simony and the selling of indulgences. Despite some efforts made by Frederick III and his son Maximilian I, the situation remained unchanged throughout the first two decades of the 16th century.[i] Not only did the political arrangement look more anarchistic than monarchistic, but there was also chaos and disarray within societal norms and moral beliefs.

Maximilian I had an extremely strong character and was known for his bravery, strictness, and self-discipline. One of the last Holy Roman emperors to go by the example of his medieval predecessors, Maximilian I fought wars personally and even was deemed a bit reckless and over the top. On one occasion, he is said to have climbed to the top of the Cathedral of Ulm and walked to the very edge of the building, going around so that the frightened onlookers could see his reckless feat. Indeed, he is a personality worthy of a much more in-depth investigation that surpasses the narrow confines of this book.

Although Maximilian was a fairly fascinating character, he had his faults. He contributed to the accumulation of debt due to his unscrupulous, lavish, and irrational spending. His spending was so bad that the Italians referred to him as "Massimiliano di pochi denari" ("Broke Maximilian"). He was also unable to break the Venetian blockade and force his way to Rome, where he should have been crowned Holy Roman emperor. Although Pope Julius II granted Maximilian I the title of Elected Roman Emperor, Maximilian was the first Holy Roman emperor not to be crowned in Rome, which put an end to centuries of tradition.

---

[i] Maximilian had a plan to hold both the title of the pope and the Holy Roman emperor in 1511 but didn't succeed. This further emphasized the descending imperial and papal authority.

In 1515, Pope Leo X was determined to complete the construction of the new St. Peter's Basilica in Rome. Indulgences were already a well-established method of funding, and he introduced new and more expensive ones in the papal bull issued the same year. According to the church's statement in the *Collectio de Judiciorum de Novis Erroribus*, published a few decades prior, "Every soul from Purgatory immediately goes to Heaven and is immediately released from any sin from the moment a believer puts six silver coins in the box to build the Church of St. Peter."[i]

Vatican obelisk and Saint Peter's Basilica in reconstruction, drawn shortly after 1523 by Marteen van Heemskerck. [20]

Although he was greatly opposed in Rome, Pope Leo X appointed Cardinal Albert of Brandenburg as the archbishop of Mainz, Magdeburg, and Halberstadt. Even though he was young and unqualified, Albert achieved supremacy over the three bishoprics with the help of a "self-willed agreement."[ii] This act introduced the German public to the obvious

---

[i] *Collectio de Judiciorum de Novis Erroribus* is a collection of decisions of the Catholic Church over rising beliefs considered heretical; it was dismissed in Sorbonne as far as 1482 by an unnamed priest but continued to exist despite the censorship. Febvre, Lucien, *Martin Luther: A Destiny*, LDI, 1996. 75.

[ii] Albert obliged himself to pay a fee in order to keep his claim to the bishoprics; he then borrowed the funds from a banker and paid off his title. Febvre, Lucien, *Martin Luther: A Destiny*, LDI, 1996. 72

abuse of positions achieved through simonies and indulgences. In the papal bull, Leo appointed Albert's bishoprics to give away half of their income for the construction of St. Peter's Basilica. The level of organization in this economic manipulation is nicely showcased in Pope Leo's alliance with Jakob Fugger, a successful banker who served as the pope's advisor. The pope recommended appointing Albert of Brandenburg to supervise the sale of indulgences in Germany. This campaign was led by Friar Johann Tetzel, who was notorious for his aggressive methods. Tetzel proposed a full remission of all sins to those who visited seven respected churches and paid a designated sum of silver after saying prayers. The abuse of position and the campaign in Germany shocked serious-minded believers, including Martin Luther, a theology professor at the University of Wittenberg in Saxony.

A few years prior, in 1510, Luther went on a pilgrimage to Rome. He walked for more than one thousand kilometers (seven hundred miles) over the snowy Alps, only to be dispirited by what he saw upon reaching his destination. This journey had a somewhat positive impact on Luther, allowing him to visit many holy sites and deepen his beliefs. However, the scenes he witnessed in Rome exposed the misuse of religious practices within the Catholic Church. In contrast to his native country, where the monks were known for their humility and modesty, he found wealthy priests indulging in drinking and gambling and engaging in relationships with women. These priests were found to be enriching themselves and living in luxury through the sale of indulgences.[i]

This had a profound effect on Luther. Upon his return to Wittenberg, he began sharing his thoughts with students during his lectures. He continued to preach to ordinary citizens, other theology professors, his superiors at the university, and even his foes. Gradually, he became a leader of a school of thought that challenged many of the Catholic Church's practices.

In response to the campaigns of Tetzel and Albert, a debate called *Disputatio contra scolasticam theologiam* was held under the auspices of Martin Luther. During the debate, Martin Luther presented ninety-seven theses, rejecting Scotistic doctrines, as well as Aristotelian metaphysics, logic, and ethics.[ii,iii] Copies of the theses were sent to Luther's friends, but

---

[i] Grand Larousse Encyclopedia, Vuk Karadzic, 1971-1973. 372

[ii] Scotists were followers of Duns Scotus, a Scottish theology professor who tried to separate theology and philosophy in the 13th century.

he did not allow his students or other affiliates to print them for almost two years. In October 1517, Luther wrote better-structured theses and reduced the number to ninety-five. He attached the theses to a letter addressed directly to Archbishop Albert.

The calm and well-mannered tone of the letter and Luther's sincere intentions didn't mean this wasn't a bold move that could have bigger consequences. Luther's move became the first spark that started a fire that would soon take over Europe. The case was forwarded to the Roman Curia for judgment, although Pope Leo X remained uninterested in the matter at the time. On All Saints' Day, which falls on October 31st, many pilgrims came to Wittenberg to be granted forgiveness and to donate money to the church and crown. Luther saw this as a perfect opportunity to share his ideas. He posted his *Ninety-five Theses* on the gates of Wittenberg church.[i]

Wittenberg Castle Church as depicted in an illustration by Lucas Cranach the Elder in 1509. [ii]

[ii]Febvre, Lucien, *Martin Luther: A Destiny*, LDI, 1996. 77
[i]Luther titled the announcement *Disputatio pro declaratione virtutis indulgentiarum*—a disputation on the power and efficacy of indulgences.

The tensions between the pope and Luther rose as the papal nuncio (a diplomatic representative of the Holy See), Girolamo Aleandro, ordered the burning of Luther's books. In response, Luther, accompanied by his supporters, publicly burned the papal bull. The most significant challenge to imperial and Catholic goals came after the year 1517. The Reformation proved to be not only a religious movement but also a cause of political change. The uneven outcome of reformations and the already growing political and cultural differences led to the growth of more distinct national churches across Europe. This included the drift of some territories toward independence, such as Switzerland and the Netherlands.[i]

The decline in papal and imperial authority meant there was no single authority influential enough to judge Luther's beliefs. This resulted in acceptance, rejection, and adaptation of his beliefs by various local communities and clergies. It wasn't clear whether the emperor, princes, magistrates or the people should decide which version of Christianity was correct.

Luther's protest came at a very unpleasant moment for Maximilian I, who was in the middle of appointing his grandson, Charles V, as king of Spain and successor to the imperial throne. Charles won the election against the likes of King Francis I of France and King Henry VIII of England in 1519. Other circumstances ensured that Charles couldn't come to the Holy Roman Empire for two years after his coronation. Emperor Charles V was never a favorite among the Germans and was very attracted to the old faith. Two firm blocs began to form, and they were poised to start a bitter fight.

Luther wrote a grim letter to Pope Leo X in 1520 in which he expressed his anger and disappointment about what he had witnessed while in Rome. He showed sincere emotions, and he did not hesitate to tell his truth. "The Church of Rome, formerly the holiest of all Churches, has become the most lawless den of thieves, the most shameless of all brothels, the very Kingdom of sin, death, and hell; so that not even antichrist if he were to come, could devise any addition to its wickedness."[ii]

---

[i] Wilson, Peter H. *Heart of Europe: A History of the Holy Roman Empire.* Harvard University Press, 2016. 200

[ii] He wrote the letter in September 1520 as a response to Pope Leo's demand to renounce all of his writings.

Holy Roman Emperor Charles V's alliance with Pope Leo X was proven in the Diet of Worms in 1521.[1] Charles V called Luther and summoned him to the city of Worms, asking him to renounce his beliefs and accept the pope as a central figure within the church. Luther showed up and stubbornly disputed the old beliefs in front of the pope. As a result, he was proclaimed a heretic and excommunicated, along with everyone who supported him. Preaching these heretical beliefs was forbidden.

Luther survived only by the protection of Frederick the Wise, a Saxon prince who was hostile toward the church. Frederick escorted Luther to the security of Wartburg Castle in Eisenach, where Luther spent ten months translating the Bible into the German language. This work enabled a new perspective on the church to spread throughout Germany. Frederick had earlier forbidden the campaign of Friar Tetzel and Archbishop Albert in his territory. This was due to their role in lowering his revenues and depriving him of his income.

Luther's fallout resulted in the diversification of the initial movement in Germany. Soon, other reformers arose in other parts of Europe, most notably Ulrich Zwingli in Switzerland and John Calvin in France. The official excommunication of Martin Luther was published in January 1521 by Pope Leo X. Although the Reformation is usually considered to have started with the publication of the *Ninety-five Theses*, Luther's excommunication marked the definitive split between him and the church. Only a year after his expulsion, Luther returned to Wittenberg, where he asked Saxon elector-prince Frederick to title him as a servant of Christ and an Evangelist.

Contrary to Luther, who was surrounded by princes, noblemen, and scholars, some preachers found support among the poorer townspeople and peasants between 1521 and 1525. There were revolts by the peasantry in Franconia, Swabia, and Thuringia, known collectively as the German Peasants' War. These uprisings didn't receive approval from Luther, and many rebels laid down their weapons, feeling betrayed by him. Some preachers were executed at the Battle of Frankenhausen in 1525. This battle brought the revolution to a close, although radicalism continued to live on in the Anabaptist movement.

---

[1] Wilson, Peter H. *Heart of Europe: A History of the Holy Roman Empire.* Harvard University Press, 2016, 202

Around 1526, a league of Protestant princes rose up against the Catholic Church. This league marked a period of tensions and conflicts with Charles V. The emperor had problems fighting with Francis I of France while also holding off the advance of Sultan Suleiman of the mighty Ottoman Empire.

This league was succeeded by the Schmalkaldic League, a league of Protestant princes focused on opposing the Holy Roman emperor. The league got its name from the town of Schmalkalden in Thuringia, where the Protestant princes met. Unlike previous formations, this league had a vastly better military to defend its interests. It was officially established by Philip I of Hesse in 1531. However, the Schmalkaldic League was weakened by internal divisions and scandals among its leadership.

The threats from outside of the empire, namely attacks by Sultan Suleiman and King Francis I of France, combined with the unification of his enemies inside the empire, forced Charles to conclude peace at Nuremberg in 1532. The Schmalkaldic League existed for fifteen years after that because Charles was too busy fighting wars with the French and the Ottomans. Inferior in military force and organization, the Protestant princes initially provided for their safety by forming leagues among themselves. Nevertheless, they began to look beyond their domain and found out that France was willing to join them in their fight against their common enemy, the Holy Roman emperor.[i] Francis I was a Catholic, and he even violently persecuted the Protestants at home, but he was smart enough to take advantage of the situation to further destabilize Charles's power and influence.

Charles was struggling, and he had to make peace with Francis, which was done with the Treaty of Crèpy in 1544. He also signed the Truce of Adrianople with Suleiman, allowing him to then focus on suppressing the Protestant resistance within the empire. Internal conflicts and scandals weakened the Protestants' position in Germany in the early 1540s. In 1542, Philip of Hessen and John Frederick I of Saxony invaded the Duchy of Brunswick, which earned them disapproval from the other princes. During this period of rising disagreements between the Protestants, sixty-two-year-old Martin Luther succumbed to illness and died in 1546.

---

[i] Bryce, James, *The Holy Roman Empire,* MacMillan and Company, 1866. 376

Charles built a coalition of princes against Philip of Hesse and John Frederick of Saxony, the most notable of whom was Prince Maurice of Saxony. Charles and his allies won a decisive victory in the Battle of Mühlberg in 1547. The triumphant emperor regulated religious issues with an imperial edict known as the Augsburg Interim in 1548. These regulations were only implemented in the southern German Protestant cities, proving that Protestantism was rooted deeper than Charles thought. It was agreed that if John Frederick surrendered, his life would be spared if he handed over his territory and electoral rights to Maurice. Charles didn't respect the agreement and imprisoned John Frederick and Philip of Hesse. This interim ended the Schmalkaldic War for a few years, but the Protestant princes, supported by Francis's successor, Henry II, were dissatisfied with the interim regulations. John Frederick was soon released from captivity, but Philip remained captive until 1552. The princes' main goal was to liberate him.

Since the league was dissolved and its leaders were captured, Charles rested and enjoyed his success. The North Germans, however, were still not giving up. They rose to arms and hurried through the Alps to surprise Charles and reach the imprisoned Philip.

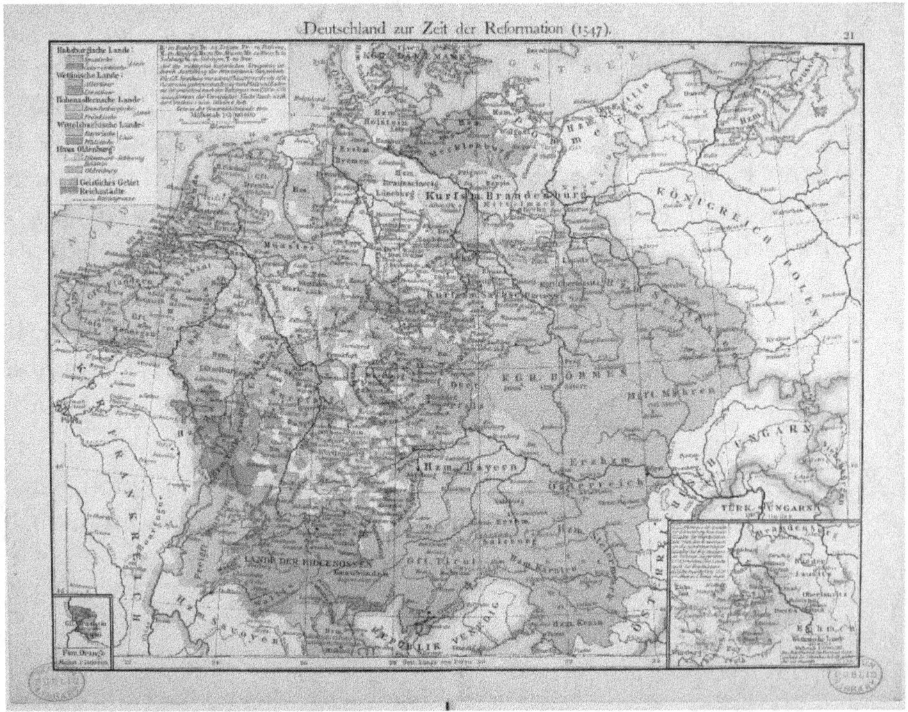

Map of the Holy Roman Empire in 1547 after the Augsburg Interim. [22]

The imprisonment of his father-in-law and the emperor's disregard of the Augsburg Interim estranged Maurice of Saxony from his imperial ally. As a result, Maurice went against the Augsburg Interim and landed on the side of the Protestants. In a momentary lapse of reason, Emperor Charles V sent Maurice to lead an army against Magdeburg, where Protestant princes were unifying. Maurice surprised the emperor when he switched sides to unite with the princes in the city. Their unified power was too great to defend against. The southern German cities that were still loyal to the emperor were quickly conquered in 1552. This victory forced Charles to flee to avoid capture. He appointed his brother, Ferdinand, King of the Romans, to sign a peace treaty and end the Second Schmalkaldic War. Because of Maurice's role in it, this war is also known as the Princes' Revolt.

In the city of Passau, King Ferdinand persuaded and coerced his opponents into agreeing with his proposals. The Peace of Passau in 1552 granted some freedoms to Protestants and ended Charles's hopes of religious unity. This treaty became the basis for the future Peace of Augsburg.

The Peace of Passau covered three main principles:

1. Ferdinand made an agreement on *cuius regio, eius religio.*[i] Though the phrase "he who rules decides the religion" was absent in the peace (it was coined by a professor in 1586), this was the basic underlying principle of both the Peace of Passau and the later Peace of Augsburg.[ii] The principle provided for internal religious unity within the state. A prince's religion would become the religion of the state and its inhabitants, allowing other non-believers to leave freely.

2. The second principle covered the status of ecclesiastical states. If a prince-bishop changed his religion, he would have to relinquish his rule, allowing the state to, for example, elect a Catholic successor.

3. The third principle is known as Ferdinand's Declaration, and it exempted princes and some cities from the requirement of

---

[i] *Cuius regio, eius religio* is Latin for "whose realm, their religion."

[ii] Wilson, Peter H. *Heart of Europe: A History of the Holy Roman Empire.* Harvard University Press, 2016, 212

religious uniformity.[i] This was a concession aimed at a few imperial cities where Lutherans and Catholics coexisted.

The Peace of Passau led to the religious division of Germany between Catholic and Protestant princes. Since Charles's interim solution didn't satisfy anyone, he ordered a general diet in Augsburg in 1555, at which various states would meet to discuss religious problems.

Since the last effort to produce religious uniformity by violence had failed, an armistice was agreed upon in 1555 in Augsburg. It lasted for more than sixty years, but there was still mutual fear and suspicion. This agreement entered history as the Peace of Augsburg.

Representatives of the German estates negotiating the religious peace at the Augsburg conference. [28]

Between 1554 and 1556, Charles gradually divided the Habsburg Empire and the House of Habsburg between a senior Spanish line and a German-Austrian line. He gave more sovereignty in Spain and the Indies to his only surviving son, Philip II, as well as Flanders and Naples. Charles completed his abdication in 1556 and passed the imperial scepter in favor of his brother Ferdinand. The succession was recognized in 1558 by the electors and by the pope in 1559.

---

[i] Ferdinand implemented it at the last minute; Emperor Charles didn't order it.

Ferdinand ruled the Holy Roman Empire capably and managed to leave things as he found them. His son, Maximilian II, who was personally inclined toward Protestantism, was unable to quench the flame of political and religious hatred still present within the empire and the church. Germany remained divided into two factions and was further away than ever from unification. There was no recognized center of authority.

Although a period of coexistence and peace was achieved, the slow but gradual expansion of Protestantism beyond the boundaries of Lutheran and Catholic cities destabilized the settlement. The Peace of Augsburg, in a way, presented opportunities for those who sought to weaken central authority that had already been weakened. The peace was far from perfect and only attempted to address the immediate consequence of the rift between Protestants and Catholics. In the end, the religious conflicts of the 16th century contributed to the devastating Thirty Years' War, which saw further religious and territorial divisions within the Holy Roman Empire. During the fifty years of forced respect between factions, the underlying unrest expanded to a war of grand proportions. This war became one of Europe's deadliest conflicts.

Chapter 9: The Thirty Years' War and the Peace of Westphalia

The Thirty Years' War was a major European war, its consequences projecting far into the future and even influencing our modern lives. In a way, the Thirty Years' War was a war of religion, one of many that happened in Europe around that time, but it was also fought because of economic, political, and ethnic reasons.[i] However, the religious nature of the war was certainly prevalent. As we've seen, early on in the Holy Roman Empire, there was a sort of oscillation between the church as the holder of the empire and the church being the enemy of the empire. For hundreds of years, popes and emperors were able to find solutions to the never-ending struggle between the spiritual and worldly realms.

However, once the authority of the Catholic Church came into question via the Protestant Reformation, even more serious problems started to emerge. The authority of the Habsburgs, who were allied with the Catholic Church, was also undermined.

It all started in Bohemia, where Protestantism had already set foot. In 1618, open conflicts between Bohemian Protestants and the Catholic Habsburg monarchy started. But there is a whole historical introduction to the war in Bohemia. Around 1606, in Donauwörth (in Bavaria, though

---

[i] Wilson PH. The Causes of the Thirty Years' War 1618–48. The English Historical Review. 2008 Jun 1;123(502):554-86.

at the time Donauwörth was a free imperial city),[i] a city populated by mostly Protestants, the city council refused to allow Catholic processions in the city.[ii] Minor scuffles broke out, and each time, the Catholics were refused access to the city. Finally, Emperor Rudolf II ordered an armed takeover of Donauwörth, which was carried out by the head of Bavaria, Maximilian. Donauwörth lost its status as a free imperial city and was gradually integrated into the Bavarian administration. Protestants were refused the right to worship.

This event alarmed normal citizens and the Protestant aristocrats, who faced the prospect of losing some territories that had recently been taken away from the Catholic Church and given to them. The heads of Palatinate, Brandenburg, Kulmbach, Baden-Durlach, Hessen-Kassel, Württemberg, and Ansbach were all Protestant and decided to form a sort of union to counter the atrocities against the Protestants in the Holy Roman Empire. Soon enough, the Catholics formed their own league, vowing to defend the interests of their religion.

The next important precipitator of the Thirty Years' War happened when the head of the Jülich-Cleves-Berg region died without an apparent heir. The two main claimants were both Protestants and had temporarily entered into a sort of alliance because the emperor wanted to give the region to another contender due to political reasons. The two Protestant claimants started rallying their forces to repel the forceful retake of what both of them perceived to be their own territory. The emperor, in turn, sent his cousin, Leopold, to take over the region and bring it under direct imperial control. However, Leopold's forces were too few, and his progress into the region was blocked. The two Protestant contenders were soon supported by some very powerful people, such as King Henry IV of France. Leopold, on the other hand, expected support from the Spanish Crown. A hereditary conflict threatened to turn into a real all-out European war.

Tensions were building between Protestants and Catholics. In 1610, King Henry IV of France was killed by an assassin. This event quelled the tension around the hereditary question of Jülich-Cleves-Berg, as the

---

[i] Free imperial cities were directly responsible to the court; they weren't governed by regional authorities.
[ii] Mortimer G. The Origins of the Thirty Years' War and the Revolt in Bohemia, 1618. Springer; 2015 Aug 11.

Protestant side saw its support dwindle. However, the animosities between Protestants and Catholics were such that they were bound to spring up elsewhere.

In Bohemia, the Catholics started suppressing the rights of Protestants, pressuring them to convert to Catholicism. Distinguished Protestants lost their positions in the administration in spite of assurances made by the Habsburgs. In 1618, the most notable Protestants of Bohemia were scheduled to meet with the imperial delegation and discuss their precarious position. The meeting between Protestants and imperial envoys was strained and tense at best. Not happy with the answers, one of the Protestants drew out his pistol and fired in the air. Two of the four imperial envoys were particularly despised by the Bohemian Protestants, William Slavata and Jaroslav Martinic. The other two were expelled from the negotiation room, and the Protestants were alone with what they perceived to be their arch-enemies.

The Protestants recounted all the misdeeds committed by Slavata and Martinic against the Protestants. The crowd became angrier and angrier, and people soon started shouting and calling for punishment. The two, as well as a secretary, were thrown out of the window. In spite of falling down around fifteen meters, they survived. Martinic and the secretary suffered minor injuries, and Slavata earned himself an injured head. All three managed to escape the assailants.

Defenestration of Prague by Johann Philipp Abelinus.[24]

Martinic returned to Germany, where he told everyone about the violence he and his colleagues had been subjected to. Back in Bohemia, people were arming themselves against the imperial army, quickly amassing around four thousand men.[i] Now the tables had turned, and the Protestants started pressuring the Catholics in Bohemia.

The Habsburg government wasn't exactly in the position to quickly suffocate this rebellion. The government was almost always in heavy debt, and its forces were guarding the borders of the vast empire. The Bohemian rebels had some time to establish their rule. In 1618, Frederick of Palatine, a German Calvinist, accepted the Bohemian crown, becoming the most hated person among German Catholics. In 1619, the leader of the revolt, Thurn, ordered the Bohemian forces to enter Moravia, a Czech region that vacillated between the imperialists and the Protestants. Thurn then turned toward Vienna, besieging it in 1619. However, the Spanish reinforcements aiding the Holy Roman Empire stopped this siege. Another army friendly to the Bohemian Protestants, Mansfield's mercenary army, was defeated by the imperialists, which prompted Thurn to retreat to Bohemia. The Bohemians once again besieged Vienna in 1620 but to no avail. The military actions, coupled with the approaching winter and general neglect of the army, exhausted the Bohemian soldiers, who had been decimated by illnesses, the cold, and a lack of basic necessities.

This set the stage for the ultimate and decisive breakdown of the rebellion in Bohemia. In 1620, the imperialists finally crushed the revolt, though seeds of dissent were already sown across Europe. It wouldn't take too long before conflicts sprang up elsewhere.

Thirty Years' War: The Belligerents

It has to be emphasized right from the start that the Thirty Years' War was neither a purely religious nor purely political war. On the one hand, we had France, the Netherlands, Scandinavian kingdoms, Bohemia, Swiss cantons, German Protestant princes, Venice, and Hungary. This was a very diverse bunch. France, for instance, was, strictly speaking, a Catholic country, and Venice was as well, at least to a certain extent, but they chose to side with the Protestants due to their animosities with the Catholic Habsburgs of Germany and Spain.

-----

[i] Mortimer G. The Origins of the Thirty Years War and the Revolt in Bohemia, 1618. Springer; 2015 Aug 11.

On the other hand, we had the Catholic Holy Roman Empire, Spain, the Italian states, and Poland.[i] The Thirty Years' War also had economic and constitutional roots. The modern age had begun, and feudalism was on its deathbed. However, Europe didn't simply go from the medieval age to modernism in a fortnight. This was a gradual process unevenly spread throughout Europe. There were centers of all kinds of reforms, and there were centers of conservatism. Generally speaking, in the Thirty Years' War, one side (Bohemia, the Netherlands, Scandinavia, etc.) sought more political, religious, and economic changes, while the other side (the Holy Roman Empire, Spain, Poland, etc.) sought to minimize these changes and go back to the feudal system as much as possible. In a way, religion was in the midst of this whole process. Protestantism was the religion of wealthy, educated middle-class citizens, who incidentally were the most likely to seek profound changes to the nations they lived in.

However, things weren't so simple. France, a Catholic kingdom with a significant Protestant minority, sided with the Protestants due to its animosities toward Spain and Germany. The Italian states, arguably among the most developed in Europe at the time, sided with Spain and Germany, helping them to maintain a political system far from that which was enjoyed by the many semi-independent Italian states. Venice is a good example. It was on very bad terms with Spain and the Holy Roman Empire during the Thirty Years' War despite sharing the same Catholic faith.

The Thirty Years' War: Delving Deep into the Chaos

After the defeat of Bohemia, the Catholics in Germany were emboldened and threatened to repress the liberties enjoyed by Protestants in regions like Saxony and Brandenburg. Denmark's king, Christian IV, had interests in these regions since he was closely tied with the aristocrats who were holding these areas. Even though Christian IV was a Protestant, he wasn't really interested in joining the conflict until he realized his lands in Saxony and Brandenburg were in danger because the Catholic League wanted to get a hold of them.[ii]

The Danes attempted to take control of what they perceived to be their land in Germany in 1625. However, they were soon overpowered by

---

[i] POLIŠENSKÝ, Josef V. The Thirty Years' War. Past & Present, 1954, 6: 31-43.
[ii] Lockhart, Paul Douglas. Political Language and Wartime Propaganda in Denmark, 1625–1629. European History Quarterly, 2001, 31.1: 5-42.

the imperial army and were forced to retreat. Danish pride was salvaged thanks to the fierce resistance of their troops, but Christian IV never managed to salvage his own reputation despite signing a fairly favorable peace with the Holy Roman Empire in 1629.

Sweden's intervention in Germany was much more successful than the Danish intervention. This addition to the Thirty Years' War came about thanks to the diligent diplomatic work of the French. Heralded by the devious and covetous Cardinal Richelieu, the French were able to quell the animosities between Poland and Sweden and then convince Sweden to join the war against the Holy Roman Empire. In a little bit, we'll deal with the French side and the incredibly interesting Cardinal Richelieu.

The Swedes were pushed to act due to their expansionist territorial interests. They were also sincerely worried about their religious freedoms if the Holy Roman Empire succeeded in completely suppressing the Protestants. The Swedes were frightened seeing the Danes almost completely crushed by the Germans.[i]

With the entrance of Sweden, the conflict that started in Bohemia and moved toward the northern part of Germany, close to the Baltic Sea and Denmark, was becoming more and more international. The war was drawing France further into conflict with both Spain and the Holy Roman Empire. Sweden managed to sway the city of Magdeburg to join its cause in 1631 and took important positions in Pomerania.

The siege of Magdeburg was an important event in the Thirty Years' War. The Swedes were en route to Magdeburg, where a friendly politician was installed. However, the Swedish forces weren't quick enough to capture Magdeburg, and the city fell to the imperial forces on May 20th, 1631. The imperialists proceeded to sack the town, which only furthered the Swedish cause within the Holy Roman Empire. Numerous princes were persuaded to join the Swedish side.

The head of the region of Saxony, John George, immediately allied with King Gustavus Adolphus of Sweden. The two men combined their armies to form a formidable force that was able to face imperial might. The combined armies of Saxony and Sweden faced the imperialists near the village of Breitenfeld. Interestingly, the Swedes were able to defeat the

---

[i] Davis TM. The Swedish Intervention: How the Thirty Years' War Became International. The Alexandrian. 2017;6(1).

imperialists despite the Saxons fleeing the battlefield shortly after the battle began. This win drew even more support for the Swedish cause within the Holy Roman Empire. In 1632, the Swedish forces were able to take vast areas in the north of Germany largely unopposed.

Gustavus Adolphus by Johann Jakob Walter.[25]

The Battle of Lützen shows just how fierce the battles during the Thirty Years' War were. The Swedes narrowly won, but their king, Gustavus Adolphus, was killed in the battle. A mass grave from this battle has been recently found, and it was filled with skeletons of those who were presumably killed during the battle. It provided a good opportunity to learn about the type of people who participated in the battle, such as how old they were.[i] It was found that the youngest victim in this pit was around fifteen years old, while the oldest was around fifty. Most had died due to trauma inflicted by projectile-based weapons (artillery or guns), but there were some signs of injuries inflicted by blades, which were still widely used in the 17th century. The Swedish Army was somewhat more numerous than the Germans, though only slightly.

Prior to the fighting, the forces of Gustavus Adolphus, aided by the Saxons, faced the German forces led by Albrecht von Wallenstein on a

---

[i] Nicklisch N, Ramsthaler F, Meller H, Friederich S, Alt KW. The face of war: Trauma analysis of a mass grave from the Battle of Lützen (1632). PLoS One. 2017 May 22;12(5):e0178252.

foggy evening, which made navigation almost impossible and forced the two armies to wait a bit before attacking each other. Around noon, German reinforcements arrived in the form of cavalry units, which managed to push the Swedes back and inflict heavy damage. From then on, the battle degraded into a sort of free-for-all. Visibility was once again impaired due to the heavy smoke caused by gunfire, making any attempt to gain control over the armies futile. We can only imagine how hard it was to establish control over different units of a large army in the 17th century, let alone doing so with low visibility.

Gustavus Adolphus virtually lost his way on the battlefield and ran into enemy cavalry. He was promptly killed. Curiously, the death of Gustavus Adolphus didn't completely destroy morale among the Swedish troops, and the Germans didn't even believe that the Swedish king had been killed. The German reinforcements were also late to the battlefield, arriving late at night and only having the option of covering the retreat of their comrades, who were going back to Leipzig. The Swedes remained on the battlefield and were able to recover the body of their king.

The losses were heavy on both sides, with both armies losing around five thousand or six thousand troops. The Swedes, however, took the moral victory, proving to the whole of Europe that the Holy Roman Empire and the Catholic Church were far from invincible.

This precipitated the final entrance of France onto the scene of the Thirty Years' War. Seeing the fruits of its previous endeavors, France, led by Cardinal Richelieu, entered the war in 1635. Let's focus for a while on this great personality since he was so important for the developments of the Thirty Years' War and long ago entered European popular culture through works such as *The Three Musketeers.*

Richelieu's beginnings were fairly modest. Although a minor noble by birth, Armand Jean du Plessis (later 1st Duke of Richelieu) saw many hardships in his early life in the French region of Poitou. The region and indeed a majority of France at the time of his birth (1585) had been ravaged by years of conflict between Protestant Huguenots and French Catholics.[i]

Rehman I. Raison d'Etat: Richelieu's Grand Strategy during the Thirty Years' War (May 2019). Texas National Security Review. 2019.

Violence wasn't only around Richelieu; it was also deep within his family. Richelieu's father, François, had been drawn into a blood feud when he was only seventeen years old. Following an age-old feud between Richelieu's family (du Plessis) and their neighbors, the Maussons, over who was going to control their local church, François's uncle was murdered. François then carefully prepared a vendetta on the head of the Mausson family, murdering him in an ambush. François made his way up the French royal hierarchy thanks to his ruthlessness and discipline, becoming an important commander and executioner to French Kings Henry III and Henry IV.

Cardinal Richelieu by Philippe de Champaigne. [26]

However, François died when Richelieu was only five years old, leaving his wife to attend to the family in exceedingly bitter times. Richelieu vacillated between a military or ecclesiastical career before finally settling on a career in the church when he gained control over the Bishopric of Luçon. Richelieu's older brother became a monk within the Order of Carthusians, giving up the ecclesiastical position in Luçon, which the family originally designated for him.

Thanks to Richelieu's cunning, self-discipline, and superior intellect, he slowly rose through the ranks. Inspired more by the strategy of Machiavelli than classical works (Richelieu was proficient in Greek and Latin), he knew who to side with. For instance, he made his way in the entourage of Concino Concini (the king's minister), who was much admired by the queen-mother, Marie de' Medici. Concino promoted Richelieu to the position of secretary of state in 1616, but he wasn't able to do much else for Richelieu as he was assassinated the year after. Assassination was a very frequently utilized instrument at the time. In the decades leading to Richelieu's ascension, four French kings were assassinated, which greatly contributed to the general chaos in the state, something that plagued Richelieu's conscience and pride as a Frenchman.[i]

France's chaos and perception of overall decline, especially in comparison to the Habsburgs, who managed to almost completely surround France, precipitated Richelieu's rise and his use of devious tactics. Unlike what's been painted in the works of popular culture, Richelieu wasn't necessarily or exclusively a power-hungry man who would do anything to increase his influence and dominance. Richelieu was, first and foremost, a nationalist. He wanted to bring France back to its glory. This desire to reinvigorate the already-hurt French national pride nicely explains Richelieu's "the ends justify the means" tactics. Richelieu, for instance, knew that France was too weak to directly confront either Spain or the Holy Roman Empire at the time of his ascension to the post of chief minister (the king's closest advisor and second-in-command). So, he labored against the Habsburgs by inciting other kingdoms to fight them and succeeded by drawing Sweden into the conflict. This not only gave France more time to recover from decades of calamity and internal strife, but it also weakened France's main adversary.

While Sweden was battling Germany, France was busy building a powerful navy that could pose a significant threat to the Spanish. Richelieu also built a powerful diplomatic force. Numerous French emissaries crossed Europe, seeking to draw new players into the conflict against the Habsburgs and plant seeds of disunion within Spain and Germany. Secessionist movements within Catalonia and Portugal received significant backing from France, as did rebellious German princes.

---

[i] Ibid.

In France, Richelieu managed to suppress the Huguenots, a large Calvinist-Protestant group in France, with a combination of reason and ruthlessness. Initially moderate toward Huguenots and supporting their conversion to Catholicism via rational persuasion, as the years went on, Richelieu became a supporter of more direct military confrontation with the Huguenots, which resulted in the final victory of French Catholics in 1627 when the Huguenot-held city of La Rochelle was taken over. Richelieu was also a far-sighted policy-maker. In 1626, the destruction of most French fortresses (other than those situated on the frontiers) was ordered in an attempt to unify the French nobility by discouraging internal strife. Counts, princes, and dukes were less likely to fight one another if they didn't have a safe place to withdraw to. Also, in 1627, Richelieu ordered a ban on duels, which decimated the elite and complicated the question of succession and inheritance.

The cardinal constantly persuaded people within France that a war against Spain, implicit or explicit, was more favorable to France than an alliance. Those who wanted to side with France and put an end to its alliance with Protestant nations were swayed by a powerful propaganda machine. Numerous writers cried out against Spain's inhumane treatment of indigenous populations. Richelieu himself was a proponent of the more humane and enlightened approach to assimilating indigenous peoples to the French way of life in the French colonies. The Spaniards' Catholicism, one of the few ties between Spain and France, was thus undermined. Anyone who favored an alliance with Spain on the pretext of Catholicism received this strong counterargument.

Finally, Richelieu opened Académie Française and Imprimerie Royale, two institutions that were under the careful control of the royal court.

These and other sophisticated methods covered the period of France's involvement in the Thirty Years' War known as the *guerre couverte* ("covert war"). In 1635, Sweden had significantly weakened the Holy Roman Empire. Richelieu recognized it was high time to turn the *guerre couverte* into *guerre ouverte* ("open war").[i] The Swedes couldn't face the Habsburgs on their own. In spite of fighting valiantly, they suffered several defeats. Now, the Swedes and the Dutch were pushing France to come out of the shadows and face the Spaniards and Germans out in the open.

---

[i] Ibid.

By this time, France had amassed up to 200,000 men, a formidable army in comparison to what the French had been able to put out just a few decades prior.

However, the *guerre ouverte* wasn't simply a war of arms. It was also a war of propaganda. Just prior to the breakout of hostilities, Richelieu sent numerous envoys across Europe, hoping to shape the narrative about the impending conflict. France, of course, was displayed as a protector of the most noble virtues. Spain was an evil colonialist kingdom that was only superficially Christian. In 1625, the "barbaric" Spanish troops attacked the French town of Trier, slaughtering anyone who was found within. The Spaniards were painted as a people who constantly vied for supremacy in Europe, threatening the basic liberties of European populations.

In 1635, France was somewhat successful, defeating the Spaniards at Les Avins. A year later, the Holy Roman Empire was drawn into the conflict, and France faced a war on two fronts. This proved to be disastrous for France, as its enemies managed to penetrate deep into its territory, coming to around sixty kilometers of Paris. This was probably the lowest point in Richelieu's career. He plunged into a deep depression. He seemed to give up and even attempted to resign. However, this wasn't allowed, and Richelieu was quite literally forced to move on and get back to work. General mobilization was ordered in France, led by the fiery and warlike King Louis XIII. Luckily for the French, the invading forces in the north of France were dangerously overextended, and pushing the forces back to Germany wasn't as hard as it might have initially seemed.

A protracted war favored the French, who had more people than Spain or the Holy Roman Empire. The French managed to gradually push the Spaniards and Germans back and even crossed into their territories. However, the unseasoned French troops weren't used to fighting in foreign territory. Richelieu solved this problem by hiring mercenaries to fight abroad and keeping the bulk of domestic forces in France.

We chose to focus on France's role in the Thirty Years' War because it decidedly shifted the balance of power away from the Habsburgs and toward the French-Protestant bloc. Although the Germans finally managed to bring religious peace to their empire in 1635 via the Peace of Prague, they weren't able to provide significant backup to their Spanish allies and mostly dealt with constant Swedish incursions into northern Germany. France kept the Spaniards busy and also caused some problems for the imperial army. The French provided enough space for the Dutch to harness a powerful fleet and constantly harass the Spaniards, whether in Europe or in faraway colonies. The Dutch were able to slow down Spanish naval actions in the colonies, constantly breaking their supply chain.

Although the power of the Swedes was very much weakened by 1634, prompting France to enter the war, in a few years' time, the Swedes managed to recover and got back on the road to victory. In 1639, the Swedes were once again in Germany, penetrating deep into enemy territory from their Baltic Sea bases in northern Germany. After reaching Saxony, their advance was halted near Chemnitz by Saxon forces led by Rodolfo von Marzin. The Swedes inflicted a crushing defeat on the Saxons in 1639, opening the way to Bohemia.

The Dutch naval victory at Downs (the English Channel) over the Spanish navy in 1639 and another victory close to the Brazilian coast of Pernambuco in 1640 contributed to the breakdown of Spanish naval dominance and marked a symbolic breakdown of Spanish power. These losses heralded Spanish problems back home; Portugal and Catalonia both started to revolt over harsh living conditions and heavy taxation.

For several years, there was heavy fighting, and the German and Spanish forces were slowly ground down. Swedish intervention was once again crucial. Lennart Torstensson led the Swedish Army to multiple victories in 1642, most importantly in the Second Battle of Breitenfeld, where around ten thousand imperial soldiers perished. Leipzig soon fell under Swedish pressure.

By now, it had become clear that the Habsburgs, for all intents and purposes, had lost the war. The only question was how much territory they would lose. Not even the war between Sweden and its neighbors, Norway and Denmark, could seriously slow down the Habsburgs' breakdown. In 1646, the French and Swedes were able to further grind down the imperialists, with Saxony deciding to exit the war.

The end of the war didn't come without some surprises. Richelieu's successor, Cardinal Mazarin, sought to strike a secret agreement with Spain in which Spain would completely withdraw its claims to Catalonia, now occupied by the French. In return, the French would give up the Netherlands to Spain. This secret offer went public, angering the French and prompting the Dutch to seek a separate peace with the Spaniards in 1647.

In 1648, understanding that the end of the war was near, the Swedes tried to take over Prague, hoping for bountiful loot and an even more favorable position for the peace talks that were going on at the time. They were unable to capture the whole of Prague, but they did raid numerous castles, monasteries, and buildings, taking historical documents and works of art.

The peace talks that were going on during the siege of Prague in 1648 are now known as the Peace of Westphalia. The war that started in 1618 in Prague ended with the siege of Prague in 1648. The Dutch negotiated a peace separately with Spain in what is today known as the Treaty of Münster; the peace between France and the Holy Roman Empire was also achieved in Münster. The Swedes settled matters with the Holy Roman Empire in the Treaty of Osnabrück.

The most important consequences of the Peace of Westphalia are the following:

1. The Netherlands gained de facto independence, though some areas, such as Antwerp, would still remain under Spanish command.

2. The Holy Roman Empire vowed to grant religious freedom to its subjects; more specifically, Lutherans gained virtually the same rights as Catholics. Calvinism was officially recognized as a legal religion.

3. The *cuius regio, eius religio* of the Passau and Augsburg talks from one hundred years before was reaffirmed with an important addition: subjects didn't have to follow their leaders' religious denominations.

4. The defining date for the division of ecclesiastical property was January 1st, 1624. All changes that had been made after this date had to be reverted.

5. France received territories around Toul, Verdun, and Metz, as well as Pignerol in Italy and Decapole in Alsace.

6. Sweden received Western Pomerania, a region in northern Germany.

7. The Swiss received formal independence.[i]

The Peace of Westphalia marked the final end of the Holy Roman Empire. The German states became heavily fragmented, just as they had been during the end of the Roman Empire. The Habsburgs still enjoyed

---

[i] GROSS, Leo. The Peace of Westphalia, 1648–1948. *American Journal of International Law*, 1948, 42.1: 20-41.

power in Spain and Austria. They managed to cross into the modern age, although the same cannot be said for the Holy Roman Empire.

It cannot be emphasized enough that the Holy Roman Empire never managed to get out of the medieval age. It was a medieval state *par excellence*. Because the leaders were unwilling or unable to transform the Holy Roman Empire into a modern empire, it failed under the burden of religious, political, and economic conflicts brought about by the modern age. The Germans, divided across a multitude of smaller or bigger states led by quasi-feudal lords and divided by religion, with varying dialects and different traditions, had to wait a bit longer to be unified under the banner of one nation, one language, and one culture.

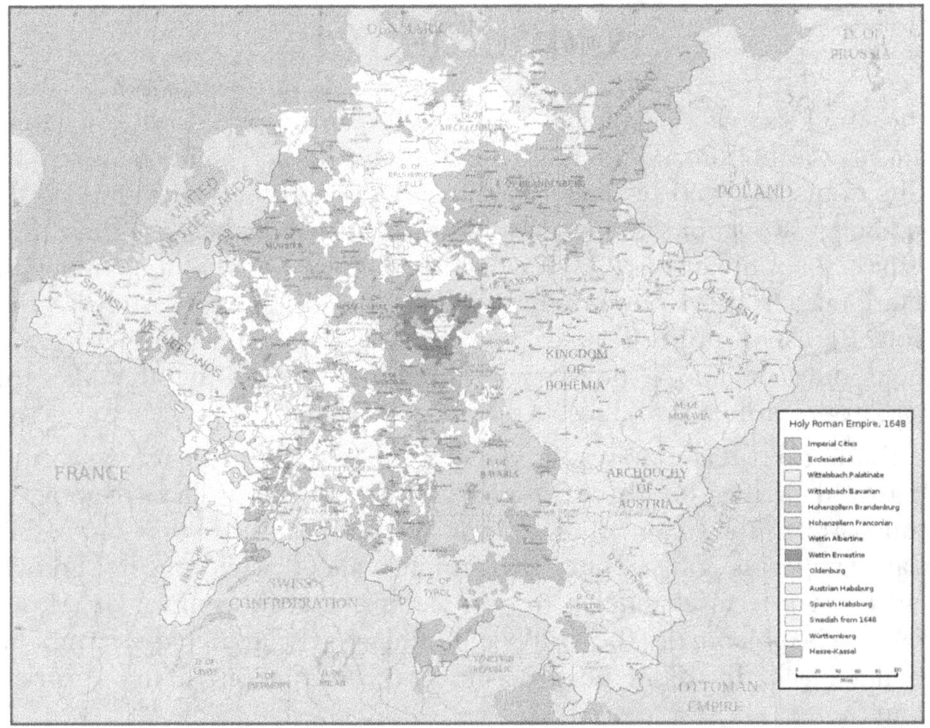

The Holy Roman Empire after the Peace of Westphalia. [27]

Conclusion

After the Peace of Westphalia, the Holy Roman Empire slowly but surely sank to the bottom. With France gaining the upper hand, heralded by King Louis XIV and his incredibly long reign, and the Habsburgs slowly building a stronghold in Austria that would eventually become their next empire, the remnants of the Holy Roman Empire were left to continue to deteriorate. In the 150 years that followed the Peace of Westphalia, the Holy Roman Empire formally and symbolically had an emperor who could only dream of power and influence enjoyed by the likes of Barbarossa or the early Habsburgs.

But like all great empires, the Holy Roman Empire met its end. It was destroyed by the short-lived French Empire and the brilliant Napoleon Bonaparte. Holy Roman Emperor Francis II had the incredibly challenging task of keeping the empire afloat while facing French revolutionary zeal channeled by Napoleon's strategic genius.[i] Unable to counter Napoleon on the battlefield, Francis II attempted a symbolic counterattack. In 1804, he proclaimed the formation of the Austrian Empire.

It's hardly a coincidence that earlier in 1804, Napoleon proclaimed himself the first French emperor. It became clear to Francis II that the days of the Holy Roman Empire were numbered after seeing Napoleon's initial successes. By forming the Austrian Empire, where the Habsburg

---

[i] EVANS, Robert; WILSON, Peter (ed.). The Holy Roman Empire, 1495-1806: A European Perspective. Brill, 2012.

dynasty would have the strongest foothold, Francis II ensured that his family would continue enjoying imperial might even after the dissolution of the Holy Roman Empire. Moreover, the Austrian Empire, in a way, inherited the allure and pride of the Holy Roman Empire, becoming the most powerful German state in the 19th century, at least before the formation of the German Empire in the late 19th century.

In the aftermath of the Battle of Austerlitz in 1806, Francis II formally dissolved the Holy Roman Empire. It's likely that Francis II was afraid that Napoleon would crown himself the Holy Roman emperor and take this opportunity away from him. The Confederation of the Rhine (West Germany, roughly speaking) was established by Napoleon, who was the confederation's protector.

The Holy Roman Empire, always oscillating between fragmentation and unity, finally ceased to exist. However, the German people's desire to unite under a single banner would live on. The breakdown of the French Empire would leave enough space for the Germans to regroup and regain their strength, culminating in the proclamation of the German Empire in 1871.

It is hard to describe the importance of the Holy Roman Empire in history. With the decline of the Byzantine Empire in the late medieval age, the Holy Roman Empire took the banner and led Europe, allowing for the slow but progressive rise of Western Christianity and cultures. The Holy Roman emperors acted as protectors of the church, without which there wouldn't have been such things as the Renaissance or the modern age. It may sound a bit surprising that we're establishing a sort of continuity between the modern period and the Holy Roman Empire by pointing out the empire's role in protecting the church. After all, the church did many bad things during the medieval age. However, the church also allowed for cultural endeavors and ensured at least some kind of education.

The Roman Church provided much-needed structure in a world riddled by war, disease, and famine. It also provided a structure against which to rebel. New kinds of people emerged from deep within the Holy Roman Empire, people willing to criticize the church and make the world a better place. Without the Holy Roman Empire, we likely wouldn't have had the Reformation, and without the Reformation, Europe and the world would be totally different. The Protestant ethic, according to German sociologist Max Weber, resulted in a special kind of economic system that we refer to today as capitalism.

The Holy Roman Empire was also, in a way, a reflection of the German people's desire to unite under a single state. However, the very idea of the Holy Roman Empire was supra-ethnic and supra-national; it's much older than the idea of nations, which is the basis of the modern world order. The Holy Roman Empire was, strictly speaking, a medieval empire based on much older Roman ideals, and for that reason, it was deemed to fail as Europe reached modernity. This meant that other nations that were quicker to grasp the power behind nation-states and adopt republican constitutions, such as France and the United Kingdom, took primacy in Europe and the whole world in the 19th century.

When the Germans finally awoke from their sleep and unified in 1871, they realized they had to fight with an increasingly powerful France and the UK. What the Germans perceived as a lack of balance within Europe ultimately led to World War I in 1914. Although some believe this war was caused by the assassination of Archduke Franz Ferdinand in Sarajevo, it was, in fact, an extremely long process that started with the dissolution of the Holy Roman Empire.

The Holy Roman Empire, therefore, is instrumental in understanding some of the events that happened relatively recently, such as the Great War. It's also well known that Hitler referred to his state as the Third Reich, a successor of the Holy Roman Empire (the First Reich) and the short-lived German Empire (the Second Reich). Hitler's obsession with German history and the events of the 19th and early 20th centuries that saw German influence in Europe dwindle prompted him to promote a radical ideology meant to bring Germany back into the spotlight of history. It's not a coincidence that one of the greatest military offensives in history was called Operation Barbarossa.

Fortunately, the German nation outlived Hitler's perverted vision of the Third Reich, and it continues to exist today, leading Europe into a new age.

Part 2: The Habsburgs

An Enthralling Overview of One of The Most Important Dynasties in European History

Introduction

The history of Europe is intertwined with the story of the Habsburgs, one of the oldest and most powerful families in Europe for centuries. Originating from the Austrian territories of Tyrol in the late medieval period, the Habsburg dynasty quickly expanded its reach across central and eastern Europe, eventually becoming the most significant political dynasty on the continent. Throughout their long reigns, the Habsburgs faced numerous challenges, yet they persisted and became one of the most significant and influential dynasties in European history.

The Habsburg dynasty came to power at a time when Europe was undergoing massive transformations. The 15th and 16th centuries, in particular, were characterized by religious, political, and social upheaval. It was during this period that the Habsburgs rose to imperial power, bolstering their position through marriages and military conquests. Their most significant triumph was the acquisition of the Duchy of Burgundy in 1477, which gave them access to resources that they used to expand their power base.

In the mid-16th century, the Habsburgs established one of the most significant territorial empires in Europe. Their provinces included the Spanish Empire, Austria, Hungary, and various territories in the Balkans. The Habsburg Empire became a dominant force in Europe thanks to its vast resources, talented leadership, and military might. The Habsburgs waged wars against the Ottoman Turks, which helped to preserve Christianity in Europe. They also engaged in political alliances that helped them to maintain their position.

However, like all dynasties, the Habsburgs faced significant challenges. One of their most significant adversaries was the Reformation movement, which was gaining ground in Europe during the 16th and 17th centuries. The Habsburgs, being devout Catholics, tried to stamp out the movement, which led to a series of religious wars across Europe. The Thirty Years' War, which started in 1618, saw the Habsburgs fighting against various Protestant states and almost led to the demise of their dynasty. However, the war ended in 1648 with the signing of the Treaty of Westphalia, which marked the end of major religious wars in Europe and saw the Habsburgs maintain their position.

The Habsburgs faced another significant challenge in the 18th and 19th centuries, as they lost territories to rising powers such as Prussia and France. The loss of their power base significantly weakened the dynasty, and it eventually collapsed in 1918 following the First World War.

Despite this, the impact of the Habsburgs on Europe remains significant to this day, making them one of the most significant and notable dynasties in European history.

Chapter 1: The House of Habsburg Rises

It all started in the Alps. The road that led the Habsburgs to the heights of incredible glory and power began in the Swiss canton of Aargau. The dynasty's founding father is Guntram the Rich, who lived in the 10th century. The dynastic momentum started to build in the 11th century.

The European political landscape at that time was a tapestry of feudal kingdoms and principalities. The Habsburgs were a part of it, and they were not the most notable family. Nevertheless, they flourished and grew as other noble families died out. Radbot of Klettgau is a noteworthy member of the family's early history because he built Habsburg Castle in the early 11th century.[i]

The Habsburgs' holdings were modest at the beginning. Other families, such as the Hohenstaufen noble family, held more power and influence. Yet, the Habsburgs developed a strategy that served them well in the years to come. It was marriage.

The sacrament of matrimony was not a festival of love in those days. Instead, it was a means by which families would enter into strategic alliances, and dowries could be gifts of land. Territorial acquisitions

---

[i] The World of the Habsburgs. (2023, October 21). The Habsburgs' Origins as a Swiss Noble Family. Retrieved from The World of the Habsburgs: https://www.habsburger.net/en/chapter/habsburgs-origins-swiss-noble-family.

increased the size of the Habsburgs' domain so that by the 13th century, they were the most important family between the Upper Rhine and the Alps. The family was ready for a great leap forward. That happened in 1273.

In that year, Rudolf Habsburg was elected the king of the Romans and Germany. This election was no doubt a compromise among the empire's electors, who were looking for stability after the collapse of the Hohenstaufen dynasty. Rudolf was a very shrewd and astute politician. In the words of Otto of Freising, "Through his wit and God's grace, Rudolf rose from the shadows, and all were awed by his ascent."[i]

Rudolf was no longer a poor count but the most powerful man in central Europe.[ii]

<u>Gaining Respectability</u>

Rudolf was aware that he had to move quickly and decisively to cement his control. King Ottokar of Bohemia was his biggest rival. Ottokar opposed Rudolf's election, and Rudolf reciprocated by declaring Ottokar's land forfeit. In the Battle of Marchfeld in 1278, Rudolf won a victory, and Ottokar was killed in the fight.

Rudolf capitalized on this by claiming Austria and Styria. He then gifted the territories to his sons Albert and Rudolf, giving the Habsburgs a land base that would be in the family's hands for centuries.

Rudolf used marriage as a means of diplomacy. He married his daughter Judith to Wenceslaus of Bohemia, which permitted him to neutralize a possible threat while forging an alliance with a very powerful neighbor.

Rudolf would continue to work on gaining positive recognition. He followed policies that favored the Roman Catholic Church and reestablished imperial authority in German regions that had grown too independent. He used political and military maneuvering to make his family the preeminent noble house in Germany.

---

[i] The World of the Habsburgs. (2023, October 21). Rudolf I of Habsburgs: From "Poor Count" to King of the Romans. Retrieved from The World of the Habsburgs: https://www.habsburger.net/en/chapter/rudolf-i-habsburg-poor-count-king-romans.

[ii] The World of the Habsburgs. (2023, October 21). Rudolf I of Habsburgs: From "Poor Count" to King of the Romans. Retrieved from The World of the Habsburgs: https://www.habsburger.net/en/chapter/rudolf-i-habsburg-poor-count-king-romans.

Adolf of Nassau succeeded Rudolf because the electors were concerned about the dynastic aspirations of the Habsburgs and did not want a hereditary monarchy. Adolf was unpopular, though, and was killed in the Battle of Göllheim. He was then succeeded by Rudolf's son Albert, who was elected the German king on July 27th, 1298.

Albert I

Albert Habsburg was a very intelligent man and continued his father's legacy of astute statesmanship. He had a firm understanding of the politics of the time. Albert would use military force if he had to, but he mainly relied on his ability to govern.

Albert had a well-rounded education that gave him a broad worldview and allowed him to approach governing with a combination of pragmatism and innovation. He was a reader and was intellectually curious. Albert maintained close ties with scholars and fostered the development of the University of Vienna. His intellectual talents helped him enormously in the areas of diplomacy.

King Albert I recognized how fractional disputes destabilized central Europe. Consequently, he worked to centralize administrative functions, and he promoted legal justice. His understanding of Roman canon law helped him initiate necessary legal reforms.

Albert was an interesting figure. His sense of justice was not limited to how much he might benefit from it. He offered protection to the Jews, and serfs found a friend in this stern man. He understood the importance of cities and how these urban centers were good for the economy. Albert gave privileges to various cities, and these concessions enabled them to become trade hubs. However, Albert was assassinated in 1308 by his nephew, who had been denied his right of inheritance by Albert.

The 14th century was a crucial time for the Habsburgs in regard to their future trajectory in European

King Albert I. [28]

politics. The principal Habsburgs were Duke Frederick I of Austria and Leopold I, who was the co-ruler of Austria with his brother.

The family used its time to consolidate its power and increase its territory. Bohemia was a strategic target that would enhance Habsburg influence in central Europe. After an attempt to seize the crown of Bohemia failed, the Habsburgs turned their attention to the south, where they were very successful. In 1311, they secured Savinja in modern-day Slovenia. Next, they took control of Carniola and Carinthia in 1335 and then took the Tyrol in 1369. Additional territories in the following years included Pazia (1374) and Trieste (1382). What is noteworthy about these acquisitions is that they were not taken in battle but after the death of the existing rulers.

They did pay a price for their successes. The original home territories of the Habsburgs in Switzerland, including Habsburg Castle, were swallowed up by the Swiss Confederacy. By the end of the 14th century, the Habsburgs' land was primarily in what is now modern Austria. Numerous members of the family held royal titles in central Europe, including Frederick III (King of Germany, r. 1314–1330) and Albert V (Duke of Austria, r. 1404–1439; King of Hungary and Croatia, r. 1437–1439; King of the Romans as Albert II, r. 1438–1439; and King of Bohemia, r. 1438–1439).

Albert II

Albert II's life is remarkable since his marriage put him in a position to gain titles without having to lead armies. He became king of Hungary and Bohemia because he was the husband to the daughter and heiress of Sigismund, who was king of both countries. Although Albert was pronounced king of the Romans, he was never crowned Holy Roman emperor.

Albert II was also known for his harassment of the Jews. He established new taxes on the Jewish community to finance military campaigns and accused them of collaborating with his enemies. Albert

Albert II, King of the Romans. [29]

used the accusation of Jews desecrating the Host in 1420 to finally destroy the Jewish community in Austria.

Albert used the accusation to force Jews to either convert or face imprisonment. Jews were deported and tortured. The forced baptism of Jewish children was stopped only by the intervention of Pope Martin V. Albert's final act of persecution happened on March 12th, 1421. Ninety-two men and 120 women were burned at the stake south of the city walls of Vienna. Jews were then placed under an eternal ban, and their synagogue was demolished.

Albert II was succeeded by his son, Ladislaus. He is known to history as Ladislaus the Posthumous because he was born a few months after his father's death. The passing of Albert II allowed Ladislaus to become duke of Austria and the king of Hungary, Croatia, and eventually Bohemia. Ladislaus died in 1457 when he was only seventeen years old. His death caused the Habsburg territories to be divided.

<u>Frederick III</u>

There was another Habsburg on the scene at this time. Frederick became the duke of Styria, Carinthia, and Carniola in 1424 when he was nine years old. He became a principal player in European history when he was elected and crowned the king of Germany in 1440. Frederick was formally crowned Holy Roman emperor in 1452. He was the longest-reigning Holy Roman emperor, holding the title for fifty-three years.

Frederick was not a great military man and was criticized by some historians for being too passive. However, he achieved his objectives without spilling a lot of blood. Frederick was patient and was able to sit out various political situations. He was more of a diplomat and strategic thinker. Frederick triumphed in certain situations simply because he outlived his opponents and inherited their land. He also used dynastic marriage as a means of achieving goals. His most significant success was to compel Charles the Bold of Burgundy to give his daughter, Mary of Burgundy, to his son Maximilian.

Frederick had a personal motto, "A.E.I.O.U.," which was imprinted on all his belongings. He never explained to anybody what it meant, but historians have suggested that it stood for "Alles Erdreich ist Österreich Untertan" ("All the world is subject to Austria").[i]

---

[i] Holy Roman Empire Association. (2023, October 21). Holy Roman Emperor Frederick III-1440-1493. Retrieved from Holy Roman Empire Association:

Frederick and Maximilian ruled jointly for the last ten years of Frederick's life. He died in 1493 and was succeeded by Maximilian.

Maximilian's succession was a significant turning point in the history of the Habsburg family. They were no longer regional aristocrats or insignificant monarchs. The twenty-six years following Frederick's death would see the Habsburgs vault over the Tudor and Valois families to become the primary dynastic family of Europe.

The years to come were heady for the family that had started in Switzerland and gradually moved to the imperial court. As the century progressed, the Habsburgs' prestige and power grew. Their territories sprawled, their coffers swelled, and their influence began to reverberate throughout the European courts. Such was the clout they wielded that when Charles IV, Holy Roman Emperor, needed allies, he turned to the Habsburgs, sealing the pact with the marriage of his daughter to Albert II.

It is evident that the foundations of the Habsburg dynasty were intricately laid with a blend of ambition, shrewd alliances, and fortuitous events. With Austria and surrounding territories firmly under their control, the stage was set for a dynamic future. The consolidation of Habsburg power, which had been carefully and methodically achieved, laid the groundwork for the dynasty's future successes and their pivotal role in shaping history. Next, we will delve deeper into the labyrinth of Habsburg power, exploring how the family's foundational strength paved the way for an empire on which the sun never set.

---

http://www.holyromanempireassociation.com/holy-roman-emperor-frederick-iii-.html.

Chapter 2: The Royal Marriages

Marrying for love is a romantic notion that gained popularity in the Victorian era. It was more of a business decision before that time; a couple got married and hopefully discovered love later on. Marriage was a sacrament in the church, but it was also a contract and a diplomatic tool in the eyes of the 15th-century aristocracy.

In the medieval and early modern periods of European history, matrimony was not just a personal matter but was pivotal to the political, territorial, and diplomatic strategies of dynasties. Among the intricate tapestry of European royals, few played the matrimonial game as adeptly as the Habsburgs.

<u>Understanding the Sacrament/Contract</u>

Before delving into the Habsburgs, it is crucial to understand the broader European tradition of marriage as a political tool. During the medieval and early modern eras, royal weddings aimed to secure political alliances, end hostilities, or guarantee inheritances. Unlike today, these unions were rarely about love; instead, they served as strategic instruments wielded by ruling families to cement their influence and expand territories.

Territory and lineage were deeply interwoven, and feudal practices and customs reinforced this pattern. Powerful lords, for instance, might marry off their daughters to secure an alliance or a vassal's loyalty. For monarchs, the stakes were even higher. A suitable marriage could mean the acquisition of entire kingdoms or critical buffer zones.

The status of a marriage could also spell the difference between peace in the land or civil war. For instance, the validity of a royal wedding and the children produced played a significant role in the Wars of the Roses and the eventual success of the Tudor family.

There were several critical dynastic marriages in the 15th century:

- John II of Aragon and Juana Enríquez (1444)

This union was significant in consolidating the Trastámara dynasty's rule in Aragon. Their son, Ferdinand II, would go on to marry Isabella I of Castile, marking the beginning of a united Spain.

- Ferdinand II of Aragon and Isabella I of Castile (1469)

Known as the "Catholic Monarchs," their union effectively unified Spain. Together, they completed the Reconquista, expelling the Muslims from Granada, sponsored Christopher Columbus's 1492 voyage, and initiated the Spanish Inquisition.

- Richard III of England and Anne Neville (1472)

This marriage closely tied Richard to the Warwick inheritance and the northern estates. It consolidated his power and further complicated the intricate family and political dynamics of the Wars of the Roses.

- Henry VII of England and Elizabeth of York (1486)

This marriage united the warring houses of Lancaster and York, symbolically ending the Wars of the Roses. It laid the foundation for the Tudor dynasty, with their son, Henry VIII, and granddaughter, Elizabeth I, becoming two of the most notable monarchs in English history.

These marriages demonstrate the intricate interplay of power dynamics, alliances, and territorial ambitions in 15th-century Europe. Let's take a look at how the Habsburgs utilized political marriages to their advantage.

<u>The Burgundian Union</u>

The Burgundian union was arguably the most significant marriage of the century, and it underscores the genius of the Habsburg matrimonial strategy. The marriage of Frederick III's son, Maximilian I of Austria, to Mary of Burgundy epitomizes how marriages were leveraged to secure vast swathes of land and power. It was a drama with incredible consequences.

The opening scene of this high-energy play is on a battlefield near the city of Nancy in Lorraine. Charles the Bold, Duke of Burgundy, was engaged in a campaign to take the Duchy of Savoy, and things were not going well for him. Against the advice of his generals, Charles led a small force against a larger army on January 5th, 1477, and was routed. The duke's frozen corpse was found in a pool of water on January 7th.[i]

In the 15th century, the Burgundian territories represented a significant portion of western Europe, comprising much of present-day eastern France, Belgium, and parts of the Netherlands. Economically, the Burgundian state was one of Europe's wealthiest due to its robust textile industry, trade routes, and the bustling cities of Ghent, Bruges, and Antwerp. Moreover, the geopolitical location of Burgundy as a buffer between France and the Holy Roman Empire magnified its strategic importance.

Mary of Burgundy was Europe's most sought-after bride, as she was the sole heir to Charles the Bold, Duke of Burgundy. Her inheritance included the Burgundian Netherlands, a patchwork of territories stretching from modern-day France to the Netherlands. With Charles's unexpected death in 1477, Mary became a key figure in European politics. Recognizing the immense geopolitical ramifications of controlling Burgundy, Louis XI of France sought to annex parts of the duchy and, if possible, align Mary with a French prince.

Frederick III, Holy Roman Emperor and Maximilian's father, was acutely aware of the value of a Burgundian alliance. In a Europe dominated by matrimonial politics, securing Mary's hand for Maximilian was both a defensive and an offensive move. There had been earlier attempts to broker a marriage in 1473 that failed. Mary, who was now the duchess of Burgundy, was worried about the intentions of Louis XI to absorb Burgundy and reopened marriage negotiations with Frederick III.[ii]

Frederick III moved quickly to bring the negotiations to a successful conclusion. The emperor promptly dispatched envoys to negotiate with Mary and her advisors. Frederick signaled a willingness to provide military support to protect Mary against possible French aggression. He also helped financially to make all the negotiations successful. Frederick

---

[i] Abernethy, S. (2013, May 3). Charles the Bold, Duke of Burgundy. Retrieved from The Freelance History Writer: https://thefreelancehistorywriter.com/2013/05/03/charles-the-bold-duke-of-burgundy/.

[ii] Flantzer, S. (2023, May 29). Mary, Duchess of Burgundy, Archduchess of Austria. Retrieved from Unofficial Royalty: https://www.unofficialroyalty.com/mary-duchess-of-burgundy-archduchess-of-austria/.

was not wealthy and had to secure a loan to pay for all the expenses. He, therefore, approached the most influential financiers of the time.

<u>Understanding Renaissance Loan Management</u>

Marriage alliances required a substantial amount of money right away. Monarchs could not wait for taxes to be collected; if they waited, someone with the available funds could make an offer. The finances of Renaissance banking could be the topic of a whole book, but it is worthwhile to know how bankers moved the money into the hands of debtors.

The Renaissance witnessed a surge in the need for credit and financial services to fund dynamic economic expansion. The Roman Catholic Church created an obstacle: the practice of usury. The church condemned charging any amount of interest on loans.

This prohibition stems from Thomas Aquinas's opinions on usury. This Doctor of the Church argued that money was a sterile medium and could not by itself breed money, making interest on loans unnatural. According to Aquinas, money was created for the purpose of exchange, not to increase wealth through charged interest. Earnings did not come from economic activity but from the money itself. And that, in the opinion of Aquinas, was morally reprehensible.

Aquinas believed that people who took out loans were people who really needed money to take care of themselves and their families. The lender did not need the money since he had the necessary resources to cover the loan. If they charged interest, then they would be taking advantage of those in need.[i]

He was not the only one who thought that usury was wrong. In the *Divine Comedy*, Dante places those who practice usury in a particular part of hell. They are in the seventh circle and are condemned for a form of violence that is against both natural and moral order. Dante has usurers roasting in hell with heavy purses hung around their necks.

Bankers had to find a way to justify what they were doing, and they used several means. The *contractum trinius* was a way of going around

---

[i] Munoz, J. A. (2019, September 20). Profit vs. Usury: Difference from the Point of View of Saint Thomas Aquinas. Retrieved from The Tseconomist: https://thetseconomist.wordpress.com/2019/09/20/profit-vs-usury-difference-from-the-point-of-view-of-saint-thomas-aquinas/.

the usury laws. The *contractum trinius* was a set of three contracts: an investment, a profit sale, and an insurance contract. These were offered to those seeking a loan.

The lending banker would invest an amount equal to the financing needed by the borrower for a year. The lender would then purchase insurance on the investment from the borrower and sell the borrower the right to any profit made over a prearranged percentage from the investment. The lender was protected from default, and the law protected the borrower from any attempt to collect money by force.

Rent charges and bills of exchange were also used to charge interest without actually charging interest. There would come a day when the Catholic Church withdrew its opposition to interest, and monarchs who were in need of money protected the bankers.

When considering the financial world of the Renaissance, the Medici family of Florence often comes to mind first. They were the bankers of popes and great patrons of the arts. Nevertheless, there was another banking dynasty that was arguably just as powerful as the House of Medici. This other family was the Fuggers, and they were headquartered in Augsburg. Both families were willing to work with the Holy Roman emperor.

Significant financial resources were required to ensure the marriage between Maximilian and Mary. We do not have comprehensive records of the exact terms of the loans made to Frederick. This is probably due to the complex arrangements and agreements that were sometimes verbal and had non-standardized contracts. The loans from the Medici family typically involved high-interest rates for sovereigns. Collateral in the form of revenue from taxes, customs duties, or possibly territorial holdings was what the Medici wanted in return for their cash.

The Fuggers were known for securing trade privileges, mining rights, or other concessions in return for their financial services. Both banking houses were known to drive hard bargains, and Frederick had to be willing to deal.

Bankers had a good reason to be firm. Loaning money to a monarch was very risky. Edward III of England defaulted on his debts to the Badi and Peruzzi banking houses of Florence, causing both to collapse. A ruler's death could cause a succession crisis, which might result in policy changes that would increase financial risk to a lender. In addition, there was no clear legal framework for international lending and debt enforcement. Bankers were vulnerable to defaults.

Cost-benefit analysis indicates that whatever Frederick had to promise, it had to be worth it. After all, the Habsburgs would have a connection with Burgundy that would strengthen the family's position against France and expand Habsburg territory. The economic vitality of Burgundy would add tremendous value to the Habsburg name. Burgundy proved to be a major asset.

<u>A Power Couple</u>

Frederick III's diplomacy and political efforts ultimately succeeded. Maximilian and Mary were married in Ghent on August 19th, 1477. The nuptials had immediate and profound implications.

- Halting French expansion: Louis XI was able to annex Burgundy and other Burgundian territories, but with the marriage, French aspirations for additional annexation were thwarted.

- Territorial acquisitions for the Habsburgs: The marriage paved the way for the Habsburgs to lay claim to the vast Burgundian territories, including what is modern-day Belgium, the Netherlands, and Luxembourg, significantly enhancing their stature in Europe.

- Tensions with France: The union sowed the seeds for heightened tensions and future conflicts between the Habsburgs and the Valois and later Bourbon monarchs of France. Habsburg possessions were now pressing on French borders, and land disputes would surface constantly during the next few centuries.

The marriage was a foundational moment in the rise of the Habsburg dynasty as a dominant European power. Their descendants would go on to control vast territories across Europe and even claim the Spanish throne.

The union also shifted the balance of power in Europe, setting the stage for centuries of conflicts, alliances, and rivalries, particularly involving the French and the Habsburgs. It would be nearly three hundred years before France and the Habsburg Empire ceased being bitter enemies.

Contemporary records paint Maximilian as a dynamic and savvy politician. Similarly, Mary's character emerged from the pages of history as both steadfast and politically astute.

Best of all, the marriage was a love match. Maximilian and Mary were devoted to each other. Their correspondence hints at a partnership based on mutual respect, a rarity in politically arranged marriages.

The Maximilian-Mary union bore fruit both literally and politically. Their offspring, Philip the Handsome and Margaret of Austria, would go on to make their own pivotal matrimonial alliances. Philip married Joanna of Castile, leading to the Habsburgs inheriting Spain and its vast colonial empire.

The Habsburgs' marital strategy undoubtedly shaped the map of Europe. Their dynasty, at its zenith, controlled Spain, Austria, parts of Germany, the Low Countries, and vast colonial territories. However, this strategy also sowed the seeds of their decline. The intricate web of alliances and intermarriages led to genetic complications (most notably, the Habsburg jaw) and intricate political quagmires.

The intertwining of so many royal houses meant that succession issues frequently arose. By marrying within a limited pool of royal families (sometimes resorting to intermarriage within their own family), the Habsburgs occasionally faced challenges and even wars of succession.

Nonetheless, their strategy also provided stability, fostering a period of artistic and scientific revival in territories under their rule.

The Habsburgs exemplified the potential and the pitfalls of using marriage as a tool of geopolitical strategy. Their rise to power through marital alliances underscores the importance of matrimony in medieval and early modern Europe. At the same time, their eventual challenges serve as a cautionary tale about the complexities such alliances can introduce.

Chapter 3: Charles and the Global Habsburg Empire

Maximilian became the Holy Roman emperor in 1493 and reigned until his death in 1519. His reign symbolizes a period of significant transition, marked by the waning influence of feudalism, the rise of centralized nation-states, and the burgeoning tension between emergent Renaissance humanism and enduring medieval chivalric ideals.

<u>The Burgundian Inheritance</u>

The original marriage contract between Maximilian and Mary gave the Habsburgs an enormous prize with consequences.

This inheritance was a double-edged sword. While it significantly expanded the Habsburgs' territorial and economic power, it also plunged Maximilian into the complex politics of the Low Countries and a protracted struggle with France, which contested the Burgundian legacy. Maximilian's reign was marked by near-constant military campaigns, most notably against the French and the Ottoman Empire. His struggles with France, ignited by the Burgundian inheritance, were characterized by shifting alliances and sporadic warfare, culminating in the Treaty of Senlis of 1493, which solidified Habsburg control over the Low Countries.

In the east, Maximilian faced the advancing Ottomans, who threatened Habsburg territories in Austria and Hungary. While not as directly involved as his successor would be, Maximilian's diplomatic and military efforts laid the groundwork for the Habsburg-Ottoman rivalry that would dominate European politics for centuries.

<u>The Dawn of a New Era</u>

Perhaps Maximilian's most enduring legacy is his administrative reforms and patronage of the arts and sciences, which deeply influenced the reign of his grandson, Charles V. Maximilian recognized the importance of a centralized administration to maintain his disparate territories. He reformed the existing institutions and laid the foundation for the Spanish Council of State and the Council of Finance in the Netherlands, which played crucial roles in Habsburg governance under Charles V.

Culturally, Maximilian was a key figure of the Northern Renaissance. His court was a haven for artists, musicians, and humanists. He commissioned works from Albrecht Dürer and Hans Burgkmair, among others, who created enduring visual representations of the emperor and his court. Maximilian's own writings, including his autobiographical *Der Weisskunig*, reflect both his chivalric ideals and his keen interest in the new humanist teachings.

Though Maximilian is often overshadowed by his grandson, Charles V, his legacy is evident in the realms of administrative reform, patronage of the arts, and the complex web of Habsburg territories that Charles would inherit.

Maximilian's era was one of both continuity and change, and his policies and actions left an indelible mark on the trajectory of European history. His efforts to maintain the autonomy of his territories while respecting local privileges and customs set a precedent for the delicate balance of centralized authority and regional autonomy that would characterize the reign of Charles V and the broader scope of European governance for centuries to come.

<u>The Giant of the Era</u>

In the annals of history, few figures loom as large as Holy Roman Emperor Charles V, ruler of the Spanish Empire and archduke of Austria. He was born in 1500 in Ghent, a thriving city within the Burgundian Netherlands. His life, fraught with incessant conflict, religious upheaval, and monumental responsibility, encapsulates the grandeur and complexity of the Habsburgs' global empire at its zenith.

Charles stood out in an age that produced Henry VIII of England, Francis I of France, and Suleman the Magnificent of the Ottoman Empire. The canvas of Charles's rule was vast and varied. He inherited an empire where, famously, the sun never set. His patrimony included the kingdoms of Castile, Aragon, and Navarre in Spain; the Burgundian territories in the Low Countries; vast Italian dominions, including Naples, Sicily, and Sardinia; and the burgeoning colonial realms in the Americas and the Philippines.

Yet, these were not peaceful realms dutifully passed from a dying father to a waiting son. Charles's inheritance was a patchwork of territories, each with its own distinct laws, traditions, and loyalties, stitched together by the dynastic marriages of his grandparents, Maximilian I and Mary of Burgundy and Ferdinand and Isabella, the famed Catholic Monarchs of Spain.

One of the greatest challenges Charles faced was the religious schism that threatened to tear Christendom asunder: the Protestant Reformation. Initiated by Martin Luther's *Ninety-five Theses* in 1517, the Reformation spread quickly due to the printing press and burgeoning nationalist sentiments. Charles's response was nuanced. While he summoned Luther to the Diet of Worms and later outlawed him, his focus on the larger political chessboard sometimes necessitated a more pragmatic approach. For instance, despite his Catholic fervor, he allied with Protestant princes against the Schmalkaldic League when political expediency demanded it.

<u>Inheritance Acquisitions</u>

Charles did not use the sword to acquire large tracts of land. He didn't have to; he inherited an enormous legacy. Charles was the son of Archduke Philip the Handsome, son of Holy Roman Emperor Maximilian I, and Joanna of Castile, daughter of Isabella I of Castile and Ferdinand II of Aragon. Charles gained the Habsburg Netherlands when his father died and was named co-ruler of Spain with his mother. When Joanna was declared mentally unfit to rule, Charles assumed the sole rule of Spain. By 1516, he was lord of the Netherlands and king of Spain and its New World possessions, as well as the monarch of Naples, Sicily, and Sardinia. He was only sixteen years old. When his paternal grandfather died, Charles was proclaimed the archduke of Austria.

A portrait of Charles V. [80]

The Game of Imperial Succession

The death of Maximilian I in 1519 left the imperial throne of the Holy Roman Empire vacant. A new emperor had to be elected. Charles wanted to succeed his grandfather, but there were two others who also wanted to be the Holy Roman emperor: Francis I of France and Henry VIII of England. Henry's candidacy was not considered serious, but Francis was definitely interested in the imperial crown.

The French king was concerned about France being encircled by Habsburg possessions and wanted to disrupt any Habsburg schemes to dominate French borders. The French had an interest in Italy, and Francis briefly held Milan after his victory at Marignano in 1515. Francis wanted to extend French influence in the Italian Peninsula, particularly northern Italy. He could do that as Holy Roman emperor.

Charles had considerable resources at his disposal, thanks to his inheritances. However, getting the imperial crown was going to be a difficult challenge. The emperor was elected by the seven electors, but this was not democracy as we may think. It was an election based on bribery. The one who was able to make the right number of assurances and back those up with considerable sums of money was going to be the one to wear the crown.

France was a unified and wealthy country. King Francis I was going to be hard to beat, and Charles knew it. He had to summon extraordinary financial resources. So, he turned to an old ally.

<u>A Modest Man of Incredible Wealth</u>

A portrait of Jakob Fugger exists. It shows a man who dressed simply. There are no fabulous furs wrapped around his shoulders, nor are there eye-catching jewels on his fingers. Jakob Fugger did not have to impress anyone. Like Cosimo de Medici, who dressed modestly and did not try to draw attention, Fugger, who was the son of German merchants, had enormous amounts of money instead of fancy titles. He was a kingmaker who did not have to draw his sword.

Jakob Fugger was a businessman who knew the value of money and how to invest it. Fugger helped Archduke Sigmund of Austria pay

Portrait of Jakob Fugger.[81]

his exorbitant debts when no other bankers would. Fugger was a reliable lender, but he was also a tough banker. The collateral for the debts was ownership of the Austrian silver mines, and Fugger was repaid for his loans with large amounts of silver. He eventually gained control of the state treasury.

Fugger became the banker of choice for the Habsburg family, and he loaned money to Maximilian I when the emperor needed it. Fugger would also become a significant lender to the popes.[i]

Fugger did a lot of business with the Habsburgs and wanted to continue his association with the dynasty. It would serve his own interests to have a client on the imperial throne.

Fugger's primary support was financial, as Charles did not have the liquid assets required to secure the votes of the electors. The German bankers supplied Charles with enormous sums of money to gain the support of the electors. The money would be used for financial incentives and gifts to the electors. The amount of money was staggering. Fugger's estimated financial support was approximately 850,000 florins.

This ally of Charles went even further. Jakob Fugger loaned money to very important people in Europe. His contacts and connections were considerable, so he could get the attention of the right people. Fugger pulled strings and used his contacts to gather support for Charles. He maneuvered vigorously, knowing that if Charles won, there would be huge prizes for him and his banking family.[ii]

<u>The Concessions Charles Made</u>

Charles had to be willing to put up substantial collateral to gain the help of Jakob Fugger. These included the following:

- Territorial revenues: Charles was required to agree to offer revenues from lands within his possession as collateral.

- Mining rights and monopolies: Charles granted Fugger mining rights within Habsburg possessions, particularly the copper and silver mines. The Fuggers would be allowed to operate mines and also have trade monopolies, such as the right to be the sole trader of certain commodities.

[i] Getlen, L. (2015, July 26). Meet the World's Richest Man Who Changed Christianity. Retrieved from New York Post.com: https://nypost.com/2015/07/26/meet-historys-richest-man-who-changed-christianity/.

[ii] Sorkin, A. D. (2015, September 11). How to Finance an Emperor's Election. Retrieved from The New Yorker: https://www.newyorker.com/news/amy-davidson/how-to-finance-an-emperors-election.

- Repayment with favorable terms: Charles was willing to repay the debts with more than just revenue from territories. The Fuggers would be allowed to collect taxes in certain cases and receive payments from imperial incomes. The interest rates on the loans were guaranteed.

- Protection: The Fuggers would become the primary creditor of the Holy Roman emperor. This also meant the Fuggers could rely on Charles for help if they ever got in trouble. These bankers could exert considerable influence because of their association with the emperor.[i]

The price for the support of the richest man in Europe was worth it. Charles won the election and became the Holy Roman emperor. He was the ruler of nearly all of central Europe. The title carried tremendous prestige but also great responsibilities. Charles was only nineteen when he was elected in 1519. He would be forced to deal with the greatest force of change Europe had experienced since the Roman Empire.

<u>The Monk Who Shook the World.</u>

Charles was elected Holy Roman emperor on June 28th, 1519; he would be formally crowned by Pope Clement V on February 24th, 1530. He emerged from the election as the most powerful man in Europe, master of the largest European empire of the last one thousand years.

Charles had little time to celebrate this success. An event that happened on October 15th, 1517, would cast a long shadow on his reign.

There was nothing remarkable about Martin Luther. He was an Augustinian monk and a theologian who taught at the University of Wittenberg. He was a man of deep thoughts and concern about his salvation. Luther was also very alert to the corruption and abuses of the Roman Catholic Church. He was horrified by the sale of plenary indulgences that Johann Tetzel was using to raise money for the construction of the new St. Peter's Basilica. Tetzel's marketing slogan, "As soon as the coin in the coffer rings, the soul from purgatory springs," was very offensive to Luther.

Martin Luther was brave enough to speak out. He opposed the sale of indulgences and other contemporary church practices. To him, only God

---

[i] Heath, R. (2023, October 21). Emperor Charles V and the Fugger Family. Retrieved from Emperor Charles V: https://www.emperorcharlesv.com/charles-v-fugger-family/.

could forgive sins; indulgences had no effect on a person's salvation. While it is not certain whether Luther physically nailed the *Ninety-five Theses* expressing his views on the door of All Saints' Church in Wittenberg, he did write to the local bishop in October 1517. He included his work, *Disputation of the Power and Efficacy of Indulgences*, which were to become known as the *Ninety-five Theses*.

Portrait of Martin Luther.[83]

A normal reaction of the authorities to Martin Luther would be to shrug their shoulders. After all, the church had dealt with self-proclaimed reformers before. If things got out of hand, these people would be excommunicated and, like Jan Hus, executed and their followers persecuted.

Martin Luther was different. Unlike earlier dissidents, Luther had a powerful weapon at his disposal, which he was going to use. It was the printing press.

<u>The Power of the Printed Word</u>

The invention of Johannes Gutenberg, the printing press, transformed Europe. The printing press could produce printed works faster than ever before. Thus, Luther could spread multiple copies of his work without having to wait months for someone to painstakingly do it by hand. Martin Luther and other Protestant reformers exploited the capabilities of the printing press to get their arguments and new religious beliefs to thousands.

Messages like Martin Luther's insistence on salvation by faith alone or John Calvin's predestination could be spread easily and in multiple places, allowing these men to gain thousands of followers among the common people and the nobility alike. The printing press allowed the reformers to communicate directly with the populace, bypassing the traditional authority structures of the Catholic Church and the Holy Roman Empire. This direct line to the masses provided a platform for dissent and allowed for the questioning of long-established doctrines and practices. The old order was in serious trouble.

<u>A Serious Challenge to the Status Quo</u>

The Roman Catholic Church's power was heavily predicated on its control over religious knowledge and interpretation. The printing press enabled the laity to access religious texts, including vernacular Bibles, thereby undermining the church's monopoly on religious matters. The spread of Protestant ideas contributed to the fragmentation of Christendom. This was a direct threat to the Catholic Church's claim of being the universal church, diminishing its spiritual authority and temporal power.

Charles V ruled over lands that were held together tenuously by custom and the Catholic Church. Protestant dissent threatened the political stability of the empire and challenged his ability to govern a diverse and increasingly divided populace. The printing press was used not only for religious texts but also for pamphlets and broadsheets that criticized imperial governance. A surge in anti-clerical and anti-imperial sentiment, readily visible in printed materials, stoked public dissent.

Charles tried to find some amicable way to bring both sides of the religious contest together. He allowed Martin Luther the opportunity in 1521 to defend his ideas at the Diet of Worms. Luther did not recant his writings, so Charles had to do something. What he did was issue the Edict of Worms, which rejected Luther's doctrines and placed the Habsburgs firmly against the forces of Protestantism.[i]

Charles made another effort to try to reach conciliation. He summoned German princes in 1530 to the Diet of Augsburg to end the religious struggles. Instead, something more radical, the Confession of Augsburg, was submitted to Charles. The Confession of Augsburg was a profession of the Protestant faith that clarified the Protestants' position on various religious topics. The document was rejected by Charles. On November 19th, 1530, the Diet issued a verdict that gave Protestant princes six months to renounce their new religion. That did not happen.[ii]

Charles viewed the Protestant Reformation as a threat and worked tirelessly to bring it to an end. He tried political maneuvering, and then he decided to use military campaigns to force upstart Protestant princes back into the church. His most significant enemy was the Schmalkaldic League, an alliance of Protestant princes. The league was dedicated to defending the Reformation. Charles defeated the league at the Battle of Mühlberg in 1547, but it was an expensive victory. Charles was facing major threats from the Ottoman Empire and France. He could not fight religious wars and secular disputes at the same time. Ultimately, he had to compromise.

The Peace of Augsburg of 1555 allowed the coexistence of Catholicism and Lutheranism in the Holy Roman Empire. It created an interesting legal term, "cuius regio, eius religio" ("whose land, his religion"). It means that the religion of the local ruler would dictate the religion of those whom he ruled.

The Peace of Augsburg provided an end to the religious conflict and also acknowledged the permanent religious division in Europe. The days of the Roman Catholic Church as the sole arbiter of theological matters were over. It was hard for Charles to accept this, but he had other matters to face that were more troublesome. His borders were not very secure.

---

[i] Ferdinand, M. d. (2023, September 17). Charles V Holy Roman Emperor. Retrieved from Britannica.com: https://www.britannica.com/biography/Charles-V-Holy-Roman-emperor.
[ii] Musee Protestant. (2023, October 21). The Augsburg Confession (1530). Retrieved from Museeprotestant.org: https://museeprotestant.org/en/notice/the-augsburg-confession-1530/.

<u>The French and Ottoman Threats</u>

Francis I was an implacable enemy of Charles. The French king was constantly probing for a way to checkmate the Habsburgs and increase the influence of France. The Habsburg-Valois Wars against France were particularly draining, both financially and personally. These conflicts, which spanned Charles's entire reign, were a chess game for control of Italy and preeminence in Europe.

Italy was a testing ground for the two nations. France made incursions into Italy with the hopes of challenging the hegemony of the Habsburgs. The Battle of Pavia in 1525 was a decisive victory for Charles. The French were defeated, and Francis was captured. He became a prisoner and signed the Treaty of Madrid in 1526, in which he renounced all his claims in Italy.

The threat of the Ottoman Empire was another constant preoccupation. The advances of Suleiman the Magnificent in central Europe culminated in the siege of Vienna in 1529. Though the siege was unsuccessful, it marked the beginning of a protracted struggle between the Habsburgs and the Ottomans. Charles's response was a mix of military opposition and pragmatic diplomacy, as seen in his correspondence, where he weighed the costs of war against the benefits of temporary peace.

<u>The Twilight</u>

Exhausted by decades of warfare and diplomacy and suffering from severe gout, Charles abdicated in a series of steps from 1554 to 1556, dividing his empire between his son, Philip II, King of Spain, and his brother, Ferdinand I, Holy Roman Emperor. His abdication letters evoke a man weary of the burden of power and who sought solace in faith. He retired to the Monastery of Yuste in Spain, where he died in 1558.

<u>The Final Word on a Significant Reign</u>

Charles ruled over a far-flung empire. It could months to go from one place to another. The Habsburgs had possessions on five continents: Europe, Africa, Asia, South America, and North America.

To administer these vast dominions, Charles employed a mix of traditional Habsburg dynastic strategies and innovative bureaucratic mechanisms. He frequently traveled, understanding the importance of presence as a means of asserting authority. His itinerary, as recorded in letters and court documents, was grueling, yet it reflects his commitment to direct oversight. His personal correspondence reveals a keen intellect and a detail-oriented ruler. He often delved into minutiae that would seem below the notice of an emperor.

Those letters also show how Charles marveled at the quantities of gold and silver in the Americas, as these precious metals offered him the financial means to maintain his far-flung territories and fund his numerous military campaigns. Managing distant colonies required a delicate balancing act. In his correspondence with colonial administrators, Charles emphasized the conversion of indigenous peoples to Christianity, though these missives also betray a ruthless pragmatism, as he condoned harsh measures to ensure the colonies' profitability.

<u>Charles V's Legacy</u>

Charles V's reign represents the Habsburg dynasty's high watermark. Under his stewardship, the disparate lands under Habsburg rule were, for the first time, united under a single ruler. However, his reign also sowed the seeds of future challenges. The financial strains of constant warfare and the difficulties in governing diverse territories foreshadowed troubles that would plague his successors.

His legacy is complex. To his detractors, he was an autocrat whose staunch defense of Catholicism led to decades of religious warfare. To his supporters, he was a visionary ruler who sought to maintain Christian unity and imperial stability amid unprecedented challenges.

Whatever view you take, Charles V was a colossus, straddling the worlds of the Middle Ages and the Renaissance, of feudal lordships and nation-states, of regional kingships and global empires. His reign, marked by both triumph and tragedy, encapsulates the grandeur, complexity, and, ultimately, the fragility of the Habsburg global empire.

Chapter 4: The Wealth of the New World

The sun never set on the lands held by the Habsburgs. That is not poetic license but an actual fact. It took centuries for the Habsburgs to acquire the territories they owned in 1510. It took less than a century to assume sovereignty over possessions that spanned the globe. It was an international empire and the first of its kind.

Traditional empires covered landmasses. For example, the Roman Empire controlled land in Europe, Asia, and Africa, but land connections enabled relatively easy access to all the provinces. What the Habsburgs held by the end of the 16th century was thousands of miles apart. Manila was more than ten thousand miles away from Madrid. Traveling from Mexico City to Lima, Peru, would take months. However, the colonial empire included staggering wealth to be exploited.

<u>Conquistadors</u>

Much of the Habsburg Empire was in the New World. The expansion began when Christopher Columbus landed in the Bahamas. Hernán Cortés then landed in Mexico and defeated the Aztecs by the time Charles V was crowned Holy Roman emperor (remember, he was also the king of Spain and the ruler of various other territories). This remarkable accomplishment was performed by a special breed of men known as conquistadors.

These soldiers of fortune were drawn primarily from the Iberian Peninsula and were adventurers looking for considerable wealth and everlasting fame. They were military types who had seen action in the European wars. It is wrong to think they were illiterate because many had classical educations in Latin and Greek, as well as specialized studies in mathematics. They came from all classes of society. The conquistadors were not knights in shining armor nor valiant warriors made famous by the songs of troubadours. Instead, these men were, by and large, violent and ruthless individuals who did not hesitate to use extreme means to get what they wanted. Greed was one of their greatest motivators.

<u>Cortés and Pizarro</u>

The two best-known conquistadors were Hernán Cortés and Francisco Pizarro. Both men were able to conquer significant empires in the New World with relatively few men. People are amazed at how these two men were able to do so much when the odds were definitely not in their favor. The best explanation is that Cortés and Pizarro were in the right place at the right time.

For instance, there is the claim that the Aztecs thought Cortés was the god Quetzalcoatl, whose return had been the stuff of legends in central Mexico. Pizzaro arrived in Peru after the Inca Empire had been exhausted by internal disputes and civil war. The two men took advantage of the military technology they had, which the natives did not, but that was not the only method they employed.

The Aztecs and the Incas had been tyrants who could be incredibly cruel to their subjects. Cortés was aided in his final assault of the Aztec capital, Tenochtitlan, by thousands of indigenous allies who saw an opportunity to destroy their Aztec overlords. Pizarro made strategic alliances with South American tribes, including the Huancas, Chankas, Cañaris, and Chacahpoyas. These tribes furnished troops for the conquistadors. When these indigenous tribes realized they had supplanted one tyrant for another, it was too late.

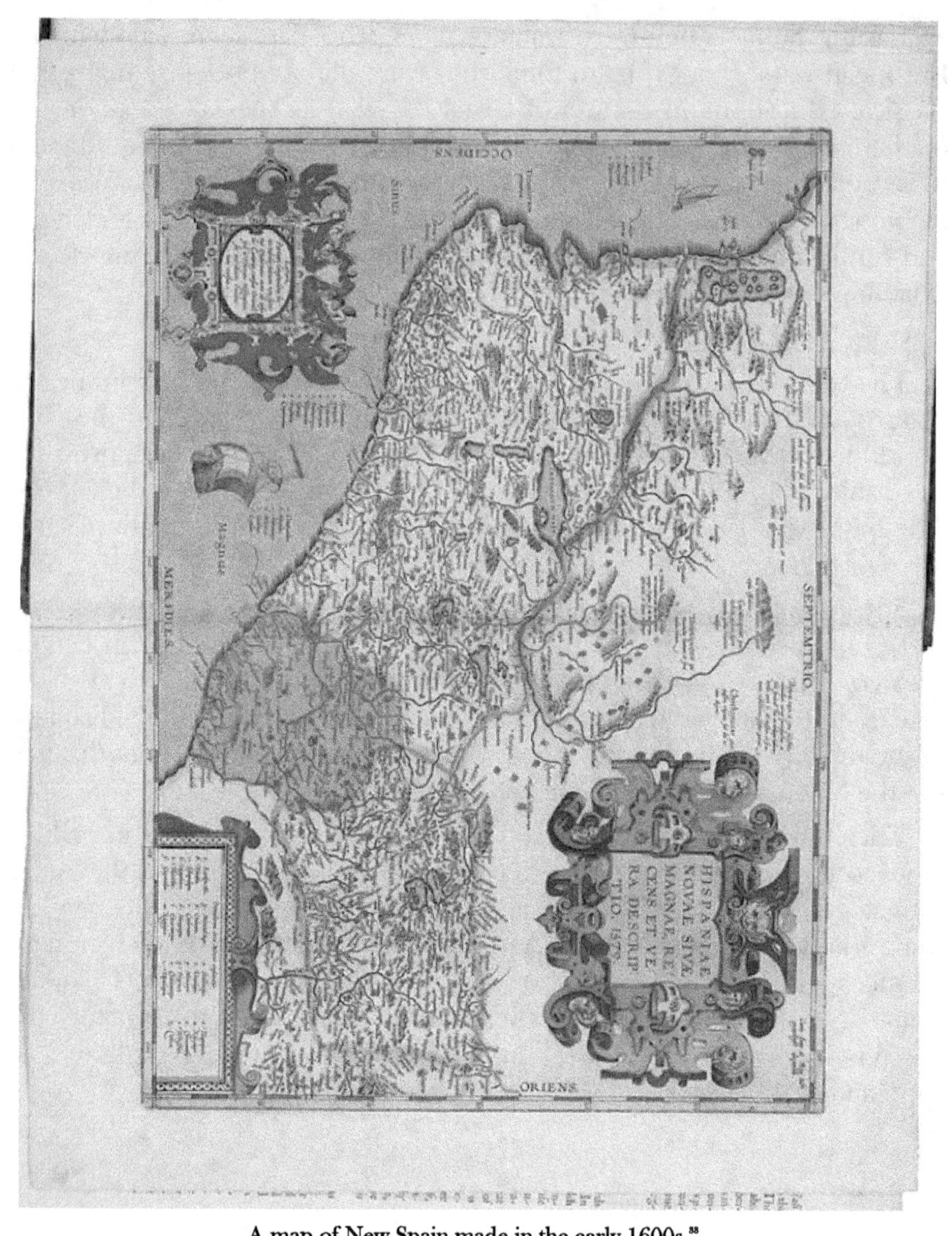

A map of New Spain made in the early 1600s.[88]

While Hernán Cortés and Francisco Pizarro are among the most well-known conquistadors, there were others who made significant contributions to Spanish colonization efforts. In addition to being conquerors, these men were explorers who discovered lands and cultures unknown to Europeans. Here are some of the most famous conquistadors and the lands they conquered:

• Hernando de Soto

Hernando de Soto led an expedition through what is now the southeastern United States between 1539 and 1542. His journey took him through regions such as Florida, Georgia, Alabama, and Mississippi, adding to Europe's knowledge of North America. His expedition was significant in opening up the interior of the continent.

• Pedro de Alvarado

Pedro de Alvarado was a key lieutenant of Cortés during the conquest of Mexico. He would lead his own expedition into Central America, where he played a primary role in the conquest of what is now Guatemala, Honduras, and El Salvador.

• Vasco Núñez de Balboa

Vasco Núñez de Balboa is best known for being the first European to cross the Isthmus of Panama. He discovered the Pacific Ocean in 1513.

• Álvar Núñez Cabeza de Vaca

Cabeza de Vaca was a member of an ill-fated expedition to Florida led by Pánfilo de Narváez. After surviving shipwrecks and hardship, he embarked on an epic journey across the Gulf Coast and into the American Southwest. He was one of the first Europeans to explore those regions.

These conquistadors and others played vital roles in expanding the Spanish Empire across a vast portion of the Americas, leaving a lasting legacy that included cultural exchange, colonization, and the exchange of goods and ideas between the Old World and the New World.

In the Sign of the Cross

Charles V insisted that any conquered people in the New World were to be brought to Christ and baptized as Christians. Dominicans and Franciscans went to the Americas just for this purpose. Their objective was to evangelize the new subjects. That appears to be a noble idea, but conversion was unfortunately mingled with suppression. Many indigenous people were forced into Christianity.

The subjugation in the name of Christ was not ignored even back then. Priests and monks noticed the savagery of the conquistadors and the avarice of those who governed the native population. The chief critic was Bartolomé de las Casas. He reported back to Spain about the treatment of these new subjects. Those letters, combined with those of other observers, were shocking. Charles V was among those who were disgusted by what they read.

An outcome of the outrage was the Valladolid debate. These took place in Valladolid, Spain, on August 15th, 1550, and centered on the abuse of the indigenous people who lived in New Spain. The result of the debate was a decision that the natives deserved the same rights and privileges enjoyed by Europeans. De las Casas published a book, *A Short Account of the Destruction of the Indies*, that shed light on the terrible treatment of the native peoples. The conquistadors could not hide behind the cross anymore.[i]

Philip II, who succeeded Charles, would define future Spanish discoveries as pacifications, not conquests. Still, considerable damage had been done, and many indigenous people suffered. Their treatment remains a sad legacy to this day.

<u>Governing the New World</u>

Governing the immense possessions of the New World with its numerous nationalities was a challenge. The Council of the Indies was created in 1524 to oversee the new colonies. The Spanish Habsburgs divided up the territory of New Spain into viceroyalties. Viceroys governed these administrative units. They represented the Spanish Crown and were answerable to the Spanish king. However, given the distance between the Americas and Madrid, the viceroys had considerable autonomy in daily affairs. Maintaining order in the colony was their primary responsibility.

Beneath them was an administrative system that was intended to guarantee that the colonies were productive. The encomienda system was initially used to keep the land and its inhabitants productive for the sake of the Crown. It was a method of land distribution where Spanish settlers, encomenderos, were given land grants. They gave the settlers control over the local indigenous people. The encomenderos were given the responsibility of providing religious instruction, protection, and fair treatment to the native people, who were expected to provide free labor as tribute. As you may have already guessed, what usually happened was that the indigenous people were exploited.

---

[i] History Skills. (2023, September 14). The Valladolid Debate: When Europeans Argued About Whether Indigenous People Were Human. Retrieved from Historyskills.com: https://www.historyskills.com/classroom/year-8/valladolid-debate/.

De las Casas and his associates showcased the abuses of this system. The Spanish government tried to reform it. The repartimiento system was created to take the place of the encomienda system. This system was intended to regulate the use of the native population so they could be treated more fairly. It required an indigenous person to work a set number of days per year on assignments such as mining. The repartimiento system did provide a certain amount of protection.

The Roman Catholic Church played a significant role in the Americas. Its basic mission was to convert the native population to Christianity. Missions were established throughout the Spanish New World. They were both religious centers and agricultural hubs. The treatment of native peoples was more humane under the guidance of the church. Other efforts to moderate the treatment of the native populations included the Laws of the Indies and the New Laws.

This did not mean that the indigenous populations were free from all abuse or exploitation. The Americas were a rich territory, and the Spanish were intent on exploiting all of it. The populations of the indigenous people suffered as a result. Many succumbed to either European diseases or the backbreaking labor they were forced to provide for the sake of their overlords.

An enduring legacy of the Spanish Habsburgs in the New World was the gift of language. Spanish was the lingua franca of New Spain, and it supplanted the various languages spoken in the Americas. It was not long before a person could travel from the Rio Grande to Tierra del Fuego, a distance of over six thousand miles, and be understood most of the way. Spanish was a valuable commercial tool.

<u>The Trade Routes</u>

The wealth the Spanish extracted from the New World was staggering. The amount of mined gold and silver bullion had no comparable figures in European history. It is hard to pinpoint precisely how much was taken from the ground during the days of the Spanish Empire. It is known from the registered trade accounts that between 1500 and 1650, 181 tons of gold and 16,000 tons of silver went from the Americas to Spain. The need to safely export these precious commodities to Europe created various trade routes.[i]

---

[i] Encyclopedia.com. (2023, October 25). Mining, The Americas. Retrieved from

The Voyage of the Flotas

Single vessels were prey to pirates, so a system was developed that would permit convoys to cross the Atlantic. These were the Spanish treasure fleets known as flotas. The best-known flota was the Flota de Indias, supervised by the Casa de Contratación (House of Trade of the Indies), which would sail from Veracruz in Mexico to Seville. Many ships arrived safely, but there were instances where the flotas were caught in hurricanes and sunk. Archaeologists and treasure hunters have been dredging up cargoes from these lost ships, and the value of what was carried in them is in the millions of dollars. The findings represent only a fraction of what was in the holds of treasure ships that left port and headed to Spain.

The Camino Real and the Inca Roads

Most mines were located in remote areas, such as the mountains of northern Mexico. Gold bullion had to be transported to the coast, so the Spanish created a network of commercial roads. The Camino Real was one that connected mines in Zacatecas to Mexico City. From there, the gold would be sent to Veracruz.

The Spanish also made use of the existing Inca road system in South America. These paths were expanded to allow the transportation of resources. The roads not only permitted treasure to be sent to Europe. They also helped economic development in Spanish America, with goods going back and forth along the trails.

There is a story about the movement of precious metals in the New World that is not very well known but is fascinating nonetheless. It is not a legend but a fact that the silver extracted by the Spanish was in extraordinary quantities. Modern visitors to Mexico and South America can see for themselves that the amount of silver was so enormous that it was used for ordinary decorations in numerous churches and holy places. The intriguing story of silver from the New World is that the metal did not always flow east to Europe. Large quantities also sailed west.

The Spanish discovered deposits of silver in Mexico, but the motherlode was not in North America; it was in South America. In 1545, an indigenous person named Diego Gualpa discovered a vein of silver in

Encyclopedia.com: https://www.encyclopedia.com/history/encyclopedias-almanacs-transcripts-and-maps/mining-americas.

the Bolivian Andes. It was the purest quality of silver ever seen. Gualpa made his discovery in a mountain that was over fifteen thousand feet high. Further explorations confirmed that what Gualpa uncovered was the stuff of legends and fairy tales. It was more than just one trace of silver: the Andean native had discovered a mountain of silver.

It is the stuff of fairy tales, but the silver mountain was real. The Spanish named it Cerro Rico ("Rich Mountain"), and Potosí was the name of the mining town established to dig the silver out of the mountainside. The find was beyond words to describe accurately. Charles V came close by calling Potosí the "treasury of the world." Between 1545 and 1810, Potosí produced almost 20 percent of the silver in the world. Its production effectively ended any lack of silver in Europe.[i]

So, why did any of it go west instead of east? An imperial decree caused that to happen.

China had relied for centuries on an in-kind form of taxation (taxes paid with goods or services rather than money), and the government relied on grain and labor to secure needed revenue. It was inefficient, and changes needed to be made. In 1581, the Ming dynasty decreed that all taxes would be paid in silver. That was a more effective way of getting the money for needed public projects. However, the difficulty was that China itself did not have large deposits of silver. It had to be imported from someplace else.

Potosí was the solution to that problem. South American silver could be exported to China, and a westward trade route was born out of the Chinese demand for silver bullion.

A fleet of silver-bearing ships left Acapulco, Mexico, twice a year to sail across the Pacific Ocean until it reached Manila in the Spanish-held Philippines. Manila became the contact point for exchanging silver for Chinese products, such as silk and ceramics. The trade route operated from 1565 to 1815, gathering momentum as the years passed.[ii]

---

[i] Maxwell, K. (2020, December 30). The Beginnings of Globalization: The Spanish Silver Trade Routes. Retrieved from Defense.info: https://defense.info/global-dynamics/2020/12/the-beginnings-of-globalization-the-spanish-silver-trade-routes/.

[ii] Sun, L. (2020, Fall). Late Imperial China, Silver, and Global Trade Routes. Retrieved from Association for Asian Studies: https://www.asianstudies.org/publications/eaa/archives/late-imperial-china-silver-and-global-trade-routes/.

China received silver imports from Japan, but these fell off in the 17th century. Potosí became the primary source of what the Ming dynasty needed. Manila became the permanent trade link between the Americas and Asia.

The Habsburgs extracted ore from their colonies in the New World, and the wealth they achieved was staggering. However, there was a dark side to the picture. The Habsburgs faced problems in Europe and were required to be proactive in defending their territory and ambitions. Some of the issues might have been quickly resolved if diplomacy were used.

However, the Habsburg New World riches made the dynasty overconfident. They believed they could settle their problems with military force. They had the money to afford large armadas and armies and felt they could overcome obstacles with pure force. It was a terrible mistake. The Habsburgs would discover that all the silver mined in South America could not sufficiently cover the expense of conducting military campaigns that produced few positive results and assured only destruction and death.

Chapter 5: The Ottoman-Habsburg War

Charles V divided his empire in 1556 when he abdicated. Spain and the western Habsburg territories went to his son Philip. His brother Ferdinand received Austria and the Holy Roman Empire. Ferdinand had already been elected king of the Romans in 1531 and was formally recognized as the Holy Roman emperor in 1558. He had ruled the Austrian lands of the Habsburgs in his brother's name and had the additional titles of archduke of Austria and king of Hungary, Croatia, and Bohemia.

Charles's decision was a pragmatic one based on his own experiences. He felt it was not possible for one man to rule over all the Habsburg possessions. This division permitted his two successors to focus their attention on their areas while keeping everything within the dynasty. It was a smart move. Ferdinand was able to provide close attention to a formidable enemy who was threatening Europe from the southeast.

The Ottomans were a force to be reckoned with. They steadily chipped away at what was left of the Byzantine Empire until, in 1453, they seized Constantinople. Their aggression did not stop there. The Ottomans gradually worked their way through the Balkans and, on August 29th, 1526, decisively defeated the Hungarians at the Battle of Mohács. These Muslim imperialists were now on the border of Habsburg land.

<u>The Magnificent One</u>

The Habsburgs faced the most extraordinary sultan of the Ottoman Empire: Suleiman the Magnificent. Suleiman ruled the Ottoman Empire when it was at its zenith, and he stretched the borders to its furthest point. He was devoted to spreading Islam through conquest, and he intended to confront and eventually defeat his Christian rivals. Suleman's victory at Mohács gave him control over Hungary and Transylvania. He then decided to campaign against Archduke Ferdinand.

Suleiman marched an army of more than 100,000 men into Austria in May 1529. He was at a disadvantage because of the rainy weather, and the mud forced him to leave behind heavy artillery pieces. The Ottoman army was able to reach Vienna by September, but the weather still caused problems. The heavy rains dampened the Ottomans' gunpowder. Suleiman was forced to retreat and lost thousands of men by withdrawing in the winter. A second attempt to seize Vienna failed in 1532.[i]

The reversals in Vienna were the first time European opposition had effectively stymied the Ottomans. It proved there were logistical challenges that the Ottomans had to confront when invading deep into Europe; extending supply lines beyond the Ottoman core territories was a problem for the empire.

Wars on the eastern front with Persia forced Suleiman to draw his attention away from Europe, but it did not mean he had lost interest. The Ottomans and the Habsburgs would fight another day.

Charles V tested the Ottoman Empire's might in North Africa and came away disappointed. He intended to fulfill the dream of his grandfather, Ferdinand of Aragon, to conquer North Africa and defeat the Ottoman corsair Barbarossa. Charles captured Tunis in 1535 and commanded an expedition against Algiers in 1541. It was a disaster, and over twelve thousand Habsburg soldiers and sailors were killed. Charles's ventures in North Africa did not accomplish any lasting results, and Ottoman pirates were able to continue raiding European coasts and disrupting maritime commerce.

---

[i] Parry, V. (2023, October 25). Suleyman the Magnificent. Retrieved from Britannica.com: https://www.britannica.com/biography/Suleyman-the-Magnificent.

The Siege of Malta

The Ottomans wanted control of the western Mediterranean, and the island of Malta stood in their way. Sulieman had a personal interest in taking Malta that went beyond imperial designs. The military order that controlled Malta was originally the Knights Hospitaller. The sultan had defeated this Christian order in the siege of Rhodes in 1523 and permitted the surviving Christian knights to leave without harm. Charles gave Malta and the neighboring islands to the order, and they changed their name to the Knights of Malta. They then began harassing Ottoman shipping. Suleman was determined to settle old scores at long last. He sailed with a force of 40,000 men and a fleet of 250 ships to take Malta.

Malta was more than an island; it was a floating fortress. The harbor was fortified, and the city of Valletta had high walls and substantial fortifications. It was a tremendous challenge, and the Knights of Malta were determined to resist the Ottoman invaders. The attack would prove costly.

The siege began on May 18th, 1565. The knights were outnumbered by more than five to one, but they held on for four months until a Spanish relief force landed on September 7th, 1565, and forced the Ottomans to abandon the siege. Objectively, the siege of Malta was a waste of time for Suleiman and his Ottoman troops. The sultan could have considered far more critical areas for assault and conquest, such as Sardinia. Precious time and troops had been wasted.

The siege of Malta.[54]

<u>New Rulers, New Approaches</u>

Charles V was dead and gone by the time of the siege of Malta. Suleiman himself lived only for a few more years after the siege. The son of Charles, Philip II, was now leading the Spanish Habsburgs. Holy Roman Emperor Ferdinand I had died in 1564. His successor, Maximilian II, was crowned Holy Roman emperor that year. Maximilian was more tolerant than other Habsburgs. He permitted some degree of tolerance to Lutherans without granting all their demands, which was still a welcome change from earlier years.

Maximilian did not hesitate to protect his borders from Ottoman incursions, but he was also open to negotiation. He concluded the Austrian-Turkish War (1566–1568) by negotiating a peace treaty with Suleiman's successor, Selim II. The Treaty of Adrianople was signed on February 17th, 1568. Maximilian agreed to give the sultan an annual gift of thirty thousand ducats and recognized Ottoman authority in Transylvania, Moldavia, and Wallachia. What Maximilian received in return was relative peace for the next twenty-five years. This allowed both sides to concentrate on other matters, including internal difficulties. The peace may have been one of the reasons why Maximilian was not involved in the greatest naval battle of the 16th century.

<u>The Battle of Lepanto</u>

The Battle of Lepanto was the most significant naval engagement of its time. It pitted Christian Europe against the Ottoman Empire at a time when the Ottomans were at the height of their power. It was also the last battle where the galleys played a significant role.

The Christian Holy League was led by Spain under Philip II. Philips's nephew, Don Juan of Austria, commanded the Christian fleet. The Christians and the Ottomans met in combat on October 7th, 1571. The Christians used superior military technology and tactics to defeat the larger Ottoman fleet.

Although the victory did not mean that the Ottomans were no longer a power to be reckoned with in military affairs, the win was a significant morale boost for western Europe. It marked the beginning of the slow decline of the Ottoman Empire. The legacy of Lepanto can be found in the art, poetry, and theater of the 16th century. It was seen as a decisive Habsburg victory.

The contest between the Habsburgs and the Ottomans showcased the military technology and diplomacy of the 16th century. It was a classic struggle between two opposing religions and ideologies, and the consequences shaped the history of central and eastern Europe for the next three centuries and into the modern era. We can better understand the struggle by examining the military innovations, treaties, and political changes that resulted from these two opposing forces colliding.

It was a see-saw relationship. One side would have the upper hand for some time, and then the other side would come out on top. It created a unique situation where, at one point, Christian France entered into an alliance with Ottoman Turkey to check the aspirations of the Habsburgs.

Peace treaties were often signed to give both sides some breathing room and the opportunity to address other more pressing issues within their borders. Such interludes were temporary. A few years might pass, and then the armies were on the march against each other. Lands would change hands as the strategic chess game went back and forth.

Siege warfare was prominent in the wars of the 16th century. Major cities and locations would be heavily defended and attacked by superior forces. Starving out the garrison or using diplomacy combined with treachery were often the means of ending these encounters, which would usually last for months or even years. The Ottomans developed a siege war strategy that enabled them to overcome defenses and end a siege within a reasonable period of time.

The siege of Constantinople in 1453 introduced western Europe to Ottoman siege tactics. Constantinople's walls permitted it to resist repeated attempts to take the city. These were massive bastions with walls that were several feet thick and towered above opposing forces.

The Ottomans used siege artillery to batter the walls of the Byzantine capital. These war machines eventually helped create a breach in the wall that led to the capture of the city. The Ottomans would continue to use specialized artillery in siege warfare.

The siege cannons were known as the Ottoman bombards. These monsters could be anywhere from six to seventeen tons in weight and hurl cannonballs weighing as much as seven hundred pounds. The Ottomans became highly proficient in gunpowder strategy, and the Balkans were their testing grounds.

Bombards were larger than contemporary artillery and were often cased on-site. Cannon foundries were established throughout the Balkans to furnish the needed ordnance. The Ottomans originally cast them from iron and then later used a single-piece bronze construction, which permitted greater durability and firepower. The bombard was used in addition to traditional sapping activities to undermine solid walls.[i]

The Ottomans also used psychological warfare to undermine the morale of the defenders. Drumming was a viable tool, and the deafening noise from other instruments created auditory confusion. The Ottomans were not averse to displaying the severed heads of enemies within sight of a besieged city's walls. We may think that is dreadful, but Christian armies used the same tactic.

<u>Habsburg Defenses</u>

The Habsburgs were hammered by the Ottomans in the early 16th century but learned how to respond more effectively to their Muslim adversary. A border defense system was created that had a string of fortresses built along the border from the Adriatic Sea to Transylvania. There were significant forts whose garrisons were as large as 1,500 troops, castles with garrisons of 400 to 600 men, and smaller stone and hard-fence castles with 100 to 300 soldiers. These could slow down most Ottoman advances and give the Habsburgs time to raise additional forces.[ii]

The Habsburgs also used a series of sophisticated fortifications to frustrate the attempts of their enemies. Their defensive walls were ordinarily thick stone masonry that could withstand ordinary artillery fire. The fortifications were not always basic curtain walls, though. Bastions were angular protrusions in the wall that could cover more ground with rifle fire and offered better angles of defense.

Ravelins came into use as the years progressed. These were triangular fortifications positioned in front of the main walls and were additional barriers that often included cannons. Redoubts were small, heavily fortified strong points within much more extensive fortifications and were

---

[i] Mediakron.bc.edu. (2023, October 25). Turkish Bombard. Retrieved from Mediakron.bc.edu: https://mediakron.bc.edu/ottomans/turkish-bombard/siege-of-vienna.

[ii] Palffy, G. (2002). The Border Defense System in Hungary in the Sixteenth and Seventeenth Centuries. Retrieved from Academia.edu: https://www.academia.edu/539595/The_Border_Defense_System_in_Hungary_in_the_Sixteenth_and_Seventeenth_Centuries_In_A_Millennium_of_Hungarian_Military_History_Ed_L%C3%A1s zl%C3%B3_Veszpr%C3%A9my_B%C3%A9la_K_Kir%C3%A1ly_New_York_Social_Science_M onographs_Bro.

---

placed to provide heightened defense at critical junctures. Habsburg defenses also included artillery platforms.

Naval Technology

The Battle of Lepanto showcased advances in technology and strategy that worked to the advantage of the Habsburgs. The galleass was the battle wagon that broke the back of the Ottoman fleet. These were massive ships whose crews numbered in the hundreds. They were armed with as many as fifty artillery pieces, with heavy guns mounted in the stern and in the bow of the vessel. The galleass was a floating artillery battery that presaged the enormous man-of-war ships that were common in the 18th century.[i]

Infantry Comparisons

The Ottomans and the Habsburgs relied on professional armies whose soldiers were not farmers called up for thirty days of service. Instead, the Ottomans used the Janissaries as their shock troops, and the Habsburg relied on the Landsknechts. Both the Janissaries and the Landsknechts were professional soldiers.

Ottoman tactics relied on the use of firepower, and the Habsburgs used tight formations that were defensive as opposed to offensive. Both sides relied on sophisticated battlefield tactics. The days of the mass rush were coming to a close. These two rivals made use of the best technology and superior weapons, and both could overwhelm poorly organized enemies.

Diplomacy

Treaties were signed between the Ottomans and the Habsburgs. We can think of these as intermezzos that separated major periods of conflict. The treaties allowed both sides to recover from intense combat and repair damage. However, peace between the two sides was a fleeting moment in time. From the 16th to the 19th centuries, the Habsburgs and the Ottomans battled it out for supremacy in central and southeastern Europe. Some of the diplomatic pacts were more significant than others.

The Treaty of Constantinople, signed in 1533, marked the end of the initial phase of hostilities between the Habsburgs and the Ottomans. What is interesting about this document is the subtle slaps administered

---

[i] Serlin, D. (2014, May 1). Turning the Tide: Venetian Contributions to the Battle of Lepanto. Retrieved from Vtuhr.org: https://vtuhr.org/articles/10.21061/vtuhr.v3i0.21.

by the Ottomans to their enemy. Archduke Ferdinand of Austria was required to recognize Sulieman as his suzerain and needed to pay tribute to the sultan every year. Ferdinand was compelled to renounce claims to all of Hungary except for a western portion. The treaty referred to Charles V as the king of Spain, and Charles was not permitted to call anyone, including himself, "emperor" except Sulieman. For all the pomp and circumstances surrounding the treaty, Sulieman declared the treaty invalid a few years later, and the peace officially ended in 1537 with the Battle of Gorjani.

Modern readers must remember that these treaties are not comparable to the Treaty of Versailles. They were not really documents between a victor and the vanquished. The Habsburgs were making concessions that were considered necessary at that moment. The family was still in control of the Holy Roman Empire, and the monarch of the Spanish Empire was still a Habsburg. What was lost in one treaty could be quickly regained several years later as a result of a successful military campaign.

The Spanish and the Austrian Habsburgs were in almost constant war during the 16th century. The Ottomans happened to be their primary rival, but there were internal revolts and disputes with the Protestants that kept these monarchs incredibly busy. It is to the credit of the Habsburgs that they could withstand enormous pressure and remain the principal ruling family in Europe.

The conflict would not end until the 18th century. Both sides suffered decline due to the lengthy war, which allowed other powers like Britain and France to gain power and challenge the Habsburgs on the world stage. However, the war did end somewhat favorably for the Habsburgs, as they were able to add Hungary and Transylvania to their empire.

Chapter 6: Arts, Sciences, and Habsburg Patronage

The Habsburgs dominated central Europe culturally and politically. The Habsburgs were more than aristocrats who built monasteries so that monks could pray for their blue-blooded souls. Habsburg princes, kings, and emperors were full-blooded patrons of the arts. Their support shaped two significant cultural movements: the Renaissance and the Baroque period.

The Council of Trent played a dominant role in developing the arts. This council created guidelines that told the artists how they could paint religious art. The Council of Trent provided instructions for other areas as well, such as architecture. The Habsburgs were devout Catholics and paid attention to the new guidelines.

There are some differences between what the Spanish and the Austrian Habsburgs did to affect culture. We are going to look at each one and explain how each branch of the family influenced the arts.

<u>Spanish Habsburgs</u>

<u>Art</u>

The Spanish Habsburgs significantly influenced the culture of the Late Renaissance and Baroque period. Their governance was a combination of political power, religious zeal, and artistic patronage. They were staunch defenders of Catholicism, and Charles V's successor, Philip II, followed a rigorous policy of promoting the Catholic faith and fighting what he considered to be Protestant heresy.

A commitment to realism and naturalism characterized Spanish painting under the Habsburgs. The artists employed by the Habsburgs worked to depict the world with accuracy, detail, and precision. Portraiture became a prominent genre, and the Spanish Habsburgs used paintings to project their power and prestige.

Mysticism is evident in the Spanish works of this time. El Greco's art was influenced by his Greek heritage. A viewer can see elements of Byzantine art and a sense of spiritual transcendence in his work.

- El Greco

El Greco was the most prominent Spanish painter. His work showed a dramatic and expressive style that many people at the time could not understand. El Greco studied under Titian and moved to Spain so he could contribute to the building of the monastery of San Lorenzo.

El Greco's work shows brilliant color and manipulation of contrast. His work is noteworthy for body elongation, particularly in works such as *Saint Sebastian*. His masterpiece, the *Burial of the Count of Orgaz*, showcases El Greco's Mannerist method of composition.[i]

The Burial of the Count of Orgaz by El Greco. [85]

[i] Wethey, H. E. (2023, September 23). El Greco. Retrieved from Britannica.com: https://www.britannica.com/biography/El-Greco.

Themes of religious devotion continued into the Baroque period. Philip's successors, notably Philip IV, were major patrons, and the Spanish court was filled with some of Europe's most prominent art patrons. Court portraits were particularly noticeable. The premier painter at the Spanish court was Diego Velázquez.

- Diego Velázquez

Diego Velázquez was a court painter during the reign of Philip IV. His works are a potpourri of commissioned portraits and scenes of everyday life and ordinary people. Velázquez used chiaroscuro, a treatment of light and shadow, in his work. Instead of staying within traditional boundaries, he used naturalism and authenticity in compositions dominated by diagonal structures, complex focal points, and other ways to manipulate the eye. *Las Meninas* is his masterpiece.[i]

Las Meninas by Diego Velázquez. [86]

[i] The Art Story. (2023, October 25). Diego Velazquez. Retrieved from Theartstory.org: https://www.theartstory.org/artist/velazquez-diego/.

There were many other artists who contributed to what can be considered the most significant period of achievement in Spanish art. Bartolomé Esteban Murillo is well known for religious paintings that convey a sense of compassion, tenderness, and piety. His compositions that depicted the Virgin Mary and the Christ child stand out. Francisco de Zurbarán specialized in still-life paintings and displayed a dramatic use of light and shadow with great attention to detail.

Architecture

Imperial Spain was an exporter of artistic innovation, and Spanish colonial architecture in the Philippines and the New World incorporated elements of Spanish Baroque design. While much work was devoted to religious buildings or royal palaces, attention was given to urban planning. Enormous public squares, including the Plaza Mayor, are centers of splendor.

Mudéjar, a blending of Christian and Islamic design elements, was still used by the Spanish Habsburgs. This is interesting because it would not be expected that a family fiercely devoted to the Roman Catholic Church would tolerate any form of Muslim architecture.

An example of architectural coexistence under the Spanish Habsburgs was the Mosque-Cathedral of Córdoba. This Christian cathedral was built in the middle of an enormous Islamic mosque. While Charles V was not impressed by the building, which he saw as a clash of cultures, it must be remembered that another ruler might have ordered the mosque's destruction and built the cathedral on its ruins.

El Escorial

Before the Palace of Versailles was built, there was El Escorial. This complex served as a royal palace, monastery, and burial place for the Spanish monarchs. El Escorial's architectural style is Herrerian, named after the style's principal architect, Juan de Herrera. The scope of El Escorial is massive. There are over 1,200 rooms, and the complex covers 33,000 square meters.

It began to be built in 1563 and was originally intended to be a funerary monument to Charles V, but Philip II decided to expand on the original plans. El Escorial would be both a palace and monastery; a library was later added. It was laid out in a grid plan to emphasize order, balance, clarity, and unity.

Juan de Herrera took over construction management when the first architect died. He believed in severe classicism and drew heavily on the work of Giulio Romano for inspiration. He did not believe in excessive ornamentation. The facade of El Escorial has minimal decoration and focuses on Doric columns to provide a sense of rhythm and structure. The facade is also perfectly symmetrical and uses repetitive elements to enhance a sense of equilibrium.

Precise geometric design is a prominent feature of Herrerian architecture. The complex employs perfect rectangles and squares to create a sense of order. The primary building stone is granite, not marble. It gives a sense of permanence to the structure and a sense of power. That is something the Habsburgs undoubtedly appreciated.[i]

The west façade of El Escorial. [87]

<u>Literature</u>

The Spanish Golden Age also included literary works. The Habsburgs provided financial support and protection to writers, allowing them to devote most of their time to writing. Numerous plays, especially *comedia* (a three-act play with comedic and dramatic elements), sprang from the quills of playwrights like Pedro Calderón de la Barca, Tirso de Molina, and Lope de Vega. The novella took shape during the Habsburg period and would blossom after the Habsburgs left the throne.

---

[i] Kilroy-Ewbank, D. L. (2023, October 25). El Escorial, Spain. Retrieved from Khan Academy: https://www.khanacademy.org/humanities/renaissance-reformation/xa6688040:spain-portugal-15th-16th-century/xa6688040:16th-century-spain/a/el-escorial-spain.

Not all the literature written during this period was fiction. Some major works included the writings of Saint Teresa de Jesus, also known as Teresa of Avila, who wrote in the language of mysticism. Her thoughts are still influential in the modern era.

There was one author who stood out from all the writers during the Habsburgs' time on the throne. He delivered what is considered an enduring classic of Western civilization.

A Survivor

We are familiar with those who commanded the fleets during the Battle of Lepanto and some of the lieutenants. The regular soldiers are often faceless in the annals of history. They lived ordinary lives and died forgotten deaths, for the most part, but there was one exception. This man was the son of a surgeon and was wounded on the deck of a Christian warship. His name was Miguel de Cervantes. He is the most famous Spanish author of all time and wrote the classic *Don Quixote*.

There are books and college classes on this remarkable novel, and its interpretations require more space than this book allows. However, we want to bring up one intriguing analysis of Cervantes's work.

The book is a satire that lampoons chivalry and the feudal age. The writing came at a time of significant change in the Iberian Peninsula. The Reconquista had given way to the Age of Discovery, and Spain was at the forefront. Old traditions and customs were falling away, but some people tried to hang on to the traditions. The global economy was being shaped, and men like Hernán Cortés, who would have been nothing more than a freebooter in earlier times, became fabulously wealthy. *Don Quixote* comes at the birth of modern capitalism and implies that the old notions were losing their grip. Greed replaced virtue, and Spain became incredibly rich. The nation had to find new ways to deal with a strange reality.[i]

The Spanish Golden Age would continue for a while longer. The days of glory would eventually fade away, but the cultural contributions of Spain and the Habsburgs continue to enrich our lives to this day.

---

[i] Woods, A. (2005, July 19). The 400th Anniversary of Don Quixote: Spain in the Age of Cervantes. Retrieved from Marxist.com: https://www.marxist.com/don-quixote-cervantes150705.htm.

<u>Austrian Habsburgs: Northern Renaissance</u>

The Renaissance was much more than Italian paintings and sculpture. Artists were impressed by Italian techniques and incorporated them into their own works. That does not mean that artists from Germany or Flanders only copied the styles of Michelangelo or Titian, though. There was a vibrant Northern Renaissance movement with masters like Hans Holbein and Albrecht Dürer. Their artistic expressions were valuable contributions to the period. The Austrian Habsburgs were significant patrons.

<u>Painting</u>

Art was an essential way of communicating a person's social standing. The aristocracy was just as keen as the royalty was when it came to commissioning and collecting works of art.

Artists were not freelancers in Germany and Austria. They were considered craftsmen and were organized in guilds that had guidelines that needed to be followed. The cities were places where buyers of art could be approached. Albrecht Dürer had no problem selling his prints at local fairs.

The Austrian Habsburgs commissioned artists to paint works for the court. A court appointment was a desired position because it exempted the artist from regulations imposed by a guild. The court artist was expected to paint, stage festivities, and decorate chapels.[i]

Vienna became a cultural center during the Renaissance, and the imperial court attracted numerous artists. Habsburg commissions kept many artists gainfully employed; the rulers wanted artwork for their courts and residences.

Lucas Cranach the Elder worked for the Habsburgs and created portraits such as *Portrait of Emperor Charles V with a Dog*. Giuseppe Arcimboldo worked at the Habsburg court and composed imaginative works that used fruits and vegetables to make faces. *Vertumnus* is an example of his whimsical work. Albrecht Dürer's *Portrait of Maximilian I* is a masterpiece of portraiture.

---

[i] Friehs, J. T. (2023, October 25). Working at Court I: Pro and Contra. Retrieved from The World of the Habsburgs: https://www.habsburger.net/en/chapter/working-court-i-pro-and-contra.

Vertumnus by Arcimboldo depicting Holy Roman Emperor Rudolf II as Vertumnus, the Roman god of seasons. [88]

An artistic giant of the 17th century associated with the Habsburgs was Peter Paul Rubens. This artist was employed by the sovereigns of the Low Countries, Albert VII, Archduke of Austria, and the Infanta Isabella Clara Eugenia of Spain, as their court painter. *The Consequences of War* is one of the paintings Rubens painted for the Habsburgs.

The Consequences of War, also known as The Horrors of War, by Peter Paul Rubens. [89]

Rubens went further than creating portraits. The Spanish Habsburgs used the artist for diplomatic missions and to collect needed information at the royal courts where he worked. Rubens would be both a painter and a diplomat on trips to Spain, England, and the Dutch United Provinces.

The Habsburgs were collectors of art, and their collections displayed incredible pieces. A recent exhibition, "Habsburg Splendor: Masterpieces from Vienna's Imperial Collections," displayed some of the Habsburg artistic possessions. Artists such as Rubens, Tintoretto, Caravaggio, Hans Holbein the Younger, and Velázquez testified to the exquisite taste shown by Habsburg collectors.[i]

<u>Architecture and the Austrian Habsburgs</u>

We typically focus on Michelangelo and Bernini when we think of Renaissance and Baroque architecture. They were great Italian masters, and their styles were extensively copied, but it does not mean that architectural design concepts were only developed in the Italian Peninsula. The Habsburgs played a pivotal role in developing the architecture used in central Europe, and their palaces and imperial residencies show an impressive artistic flair.

The Hofburg was the imperial residence of the Habsburgs and was renovated by Maximilian I, Ferdinand I, and Rudolf II. The religious architecture of the Habsburgs is best exemplified by the restoration of St. Stephen's Cathedral in Vienna.

The Schönbrunn Palace became Habsburg property in 1569 and was originally not much more than a game park. That changed in 1686 when Emperor Leopold II took ownership. Johann Bernhard Fischer von Erlach was assigned the responsibility of designing a palace. Von Erlach's designs planned to make a residence that would rival Versailles and included extensive inclined approaches, elaborate waterworks, and colonnades arranged around a central axis.[ii]

---

[i] The Museum of Fine Arts, Houston. (2023, October 25). "Habsburg Splendor: Masterpieces from Vienna's Imperial Collections". Retrieved from MFAH.org:
https://www.mfah.org/press/major-traveling-exhibition-masterpieces-austrian-habsburg-dynasty-brings.

[ii] Schloss Schonbrunn. (2023, October 25). Architectural History: 17th and 18th Century. Retrieved from Schoenbrunn.at: https://www.schoenbrunn.at/en/about-schoenbrunn/the-palace/history/architectural-history-17th-and-early-18th-century.

The Habsburgs were also interested in creating impressive public buildings. The Spanish Riding School and the Vienna Arsenal are examples of their commitment to architecture. They were willing to draw on the expertise of Italian architects, and the work of Andrea Palladio can be seen in projects commissioned by the imperial family.

Music

France is known for its wine and food, while Italy has a reputation for art. However, Germany and Austria have bragging rights to music, and any musical historian will attest to that. The courts of the Habsburgs hosted composers such as Wolfgang Amadeus Mozart. The Vienna Boys Choir, founded in 1498 by Holy Roman Emperor Maximilian I, is still a world-renowned choral ensemble. Under the Habsburgs, Vienna became a musical hub that welcomed musicians, composers, and other musically inclined professionals.

Maximilian I began the Habsburg family's long association with music when he reorganized his court music in 1498. Vienna became a workshop for musical instruments, notably keyboards and lutes. The Habsburg court chapel became famous for the music it produced. Religious music was very important at the time, and composers employed by the Habsburgs produced motets and masses.[i]

The religious composers produced volumes of sacred music. Cornelius Canis introduced the polyphony style of the Franco-Flemish School to the Habsburg imperial court. His contributions and those of others show sophisticated contrapuntal methods and underscore the Habsburgs' commitment to melody and sound.[ii]

The imperial chapels were testing grounds for sacred and secular music in the Baroque period. They were well known for innovation. The Habsburgs encouraged musical education and created music schools and other institutions that served as spawning grounds for talented performers and composers.

---

[i] OAW. (2023, October 25). Music at the Courts of the House of Habsburg. Retrieved from OAW: https://www.oeaw.ac.at/acdh/projects/music-at-the-courts-of-the-house-of-habsburg.

[ii] Radioswissclassic. (2023, October 25). Cornelius Canis. Retrieved from Radioswissclassic: https://www.radioswissclassic.ch/en/music-database/musician/54261523c37de6c3eba58ffec69f05ab13193d/biography?app=true.

Music was used for diplomatic purposes, and the Habsburgs fostered cultural exchanges with other European courts. It is accurate to say that the Habsburgs founded the laboratories in which the classical music we know and love today was generated.

<u>Science</u>

The Renaissance and the Reformation caused a break with old traditions, and science was where the most significant impact occurred. The Aristotelian and Ptolemaic theories of the heavens came under attack. Copernicus's *De revolutionibus* challenged the old notions of an Earth-centered universe. He believed that the sun, not the Earth, was the focal point of the heavens and that planets revolved around the sun. It was a radical and dangerous notion.

The Roman Catholic Church was committed to the Ptolemaic theory, and it was not alone. The scientific community of the time also embraced Ptolemy. Reputations and careers were built on the false premise of planets revolving around the Earth.

The wrong opinion could have serious consequences for the holder. Galileo Galilei, the leading astronomer of the early 17th century, was forced to recant his belief in the Copernican system. It would take a brave man to challenge the old system. A progressive patron would also be necessary.

Holy Roman Emperor Rudolf II was eccentric. He believed in astrology and was always looking for the philosopher's stone, which could turn base metal into gold. Nevertheless, Rudolf played a dominant role in the scientific inquiry of the 17th century. He had a deep interest in the sciences, and his patronage of prominent scientists and scholars helped advance knowledge. He made his capital, Prague, a center of scientific and intellectual activity, and his support of the sciences made a permanent impression on the development of astronomy, mathematics, and other scientific fields. Rudolph might have seemed a little odd at times, but his support of science was remarkable in an age that still hung on to old beliefs.

Tycho Brahe was an aristocratic astronomer who had a silver nose to replace the one he lost in a duel. He was a Danish citizen and enjoyed the patronage of the king of Denmark, Frederick II (he was not from the House of Habsburg). The observatory he built on Ven Island was famous for its heavenly observations and accuracy of data. Unfortunately,

Frederick died in 1588, and his successor, Christian IV, was not very interested in science. The astronomer needed a new patron.[i]

Brahe's international reputation appealed to Rudolf. The Holy Roman emperor officially became Brahe's sponsor in 1599, and the Dane became the imperial court astronomer. Brahe invited a young mathematician named Johannes Kepler in December 1599 to pay a visit. The world of astronomy would never be the same again.

Kepler's visit turned into a permanent relocation to Prague, where he worked for Brahe and was eventually appointed the imperial mathematician. The two had distinct personality differences. Tycho Brahe was a proud and often abrasive aristocrat. Johannes Kepler was a humble person who once aspired to be a Lutheran minister. Despite these differences, both men brought tremendous talents to the table.

Tycho Brahe was famous for his ability to make highly precise and comprehensive astronomical observations. He meticulously recorded the positions of celestial objects, including planets and stars, for many years. Brahe's records were the foundation points for some incredible astronomical conclusions. He also designed astronomical instruments that produced highly accurate data on heavenly positions.

Johannes Kepler was a gifted mathematician who could analyze and synthesize complex astronomical data. His mathematical insights would be instrumental in unraveling the mysteries of planetary motion.

Tycho Brahe proposed a cosmological theory. He believed that the sun and the moon revolved around the Earth and that the other planets went around the sun. It appears he was trying to create a compromise in which the Earth would be recognized as the center of the universe with only two heavenly bodies rotating around it. It made sense politically, but it was questionable scientifically. Brahe's data, which he accumulated over the years, would ultimately prove his theory was wrong.[ii]

---

[i] Britannica.com. (2023, October 26). Mature Career of Tycho Brahe. Retrieved from Britannica.com: https://www.britannica.com/biography/Tycho-Brahe-Danish-astronomer/Mature-career.

[ii] Redazione. (2018, August 21). Tycho Brahe, Astronomer and Alchemist at the Court of Rudolf II. Retrieved from Progretto: http://www.progetto.cz/tycho-brahe-astronomo-e-alchimista-alla-corte-di-rodolfo-ii/?lang=en.

Brahe died on October 24th, 1601, and Kepler was given the task of completing Brahe's work. Since he had access to the old Dane's statistics, he went to work immediately.

<u>Profound Discoveries</u>

It is essential to remember that the success Kepler achieved was based on a mountain of data. An opponent would have to argue against the facts. It was accepted wisdom that planetary rotations were circular. Kepler proved that Mars does not make its path around the sun in a perfect circle. He was able to show Mars moved in an elliptical route. Moreover, Mars was at times closer to the sun than at other times, and the planet moved faster when it was farther away.[i]

Armed with the figures of his old mentor, Johannes Kepler's calculations produced three laws of planetary motion:

8. The law of elliptical orbits describes planets moving in elliptical paths with the sun at one of the two foci.

9. The law of equal areas states that a line segment connecting a planet to the sun sweeps out equal areas in equal time intervals.

10. The law of harmonics established a mathematical relationship between a planet's orbital period and its distance from the sun.

The third law demonstrates the beauty of mathematics when it is applied to science. Kepler's work with figures replaced complex and convoluted epicycles with a mathematical harmony that elegantly explained the observed data. One did not have to go into long discourses about how the planets moved and why—just do the math!

The partnership between Tycho Brahe and Johannes Kepler exemplified the power of collaboration in advancing scientific knowledge. Brahe's meticulous observations and innovative instruments provided the empirical foundation, while Kepler's mathematical genius and three laws of planetary motion simplified and explained the complexities of planetary orbits. Together, they ushered in a new era of understanding celestial mechanics, leaving an enduring legacy that transformed the field of astronomy.

---

[i] Famous Scientists. (2023, October 26). Johannes Kepler. Retrieved from Famousscientists.org: https://www.famousscientists.org/johannes-kepler/.

The patronage of Rudolf II was instrumental in their success. Brahe and Kepler had the protection of the Holy Roman emperor. The Inquisition would not harass them the way the inquisitors had persecuted Galileo. The two astronomers could pursue truth, and what they discovered was astounding.

Brahe and Kepler did more than challenge the old order: they proved it was wrong. The two did not do this with philosophical arguments but with meticulous observation and complex mathematics. Critics could not attack their character. Instead, the other side would have to prove the data was flawed. Even so, it would take a while for the old ways to die. Isaac Newton would be the one to drive the last nail in the coffin.

There is an irony in all of this. The Habsburgs were devout Catholics and champions of the church. Brahe and Kepler were Lutherans and would have been in serious trouble under ordinary circumstances. However, Habsburg princes were willing to step outside the box and help astronomers seek the truth. Religious opinions were secondary to scientific achievements.

Rudolf was a great patron of science, but he was a poor politician. He was forced to give up the crown of Bohemia to his brother, Matthias, in 1611. Rudolf died in 1612, and it was fortunate for him. Events were darkening the clouds over central Europe. Germany would soon be tossed into a maelstrom in which nearly a third of the population died.

Chapter 7: Religious Tensions and the Thirty Years' War

The Thirty Years' War devastated Europe from 1618 to 1648 and was rooted deeply in political rivalries, religious tensions, and territorial ambitions. There was a real battle between Protestantism and Catholicism, with the Habsburg dynasty, led by the Holy Roman emperors, positioned as staunch defenders of the Catholic faith. The dynamics of this cataclysm started years before the first shots were fired. The beginning of the end was in the waning days of the 16th century.

<u>The Habsburg Crisis</u>

Spain was the dominant European power in the 16th century. However, cracks were starting to show in the facade. The country was involved in an on-again, off-again war with the Dutch Republic as the Dutch fought for their independence. That was a significant drain on the Spanish treasury. The gold from the New World seemed to be cursed. The bullion was used to finance military campaigns instead of economic growth, and Spain suffered as a result. The reign of Philip III (r. 1598–1621) was a disaster. The Spanish Crown kept accumulating debt until, in 1607, the government was forced to declare a moratorium on its debts.[i]

---

[i] Cavendish, R. (2007, November). Spanish Bankruptcy. Retrieved from History Today: https://www.historytoday.com/archive/spanish-bankruptcy.

The Austrian Habsburgs were not faring much better. The Peace of Augsburg granted some breathing room within the Holy Roman Empire, but it did not mean that hostilities had permanently ended. Calvinism was growing within Germany.

The Calvinists had been an insignificant group when the Peace of Augsburg was initially signed. They were a significant minority in central Europe at the dawn of the 17th century. Prominent rulers in Germany, including the elector of Brandenburg, had declared themselves to be Calvinists. Calvinist activism was disrupting an uneasy peace.

Additionally, there were ecclesiastical principalities within the Holy Roman Empire whose bishops became Protestants. Their refusal to return their lands to the authority of the Roman Catholic Church led to sectarian violence, such as the Cologne War (1583–1588).[i]

<u>Religious Debate</u>

Religion in the late 16th century was highly political. The Protestant Reformation, initiated by Martin Luther in 1517, led to the fragmentation of the Catholic Church's hegemony. Lutheranism and English Anglicanism joined Calvinism as substitutes for Roman Catholicism. This religious diversity ignited tensions between adherents of these reformist faiths and the traditional Catholic establishment.

The Counter-Reformation, spearheaded by the Catholic Church and the Habsburgs, sought to counter the spread of Protestantism. The Council of Trent (1545–1563) implemented reforms within the Catholic Church, emphasizing the importance of doctrine and addressing some of the criticisms raised by the reformers.

Sectarian violence became the standard means of settling disputes. France was wracked by holy wars and atrocities, including the Saint Bartholomew's Day massacre in 1572. The Edict of Nantes ended the violence but granted the Huguenot Protestant minority considerable autonomy. In England, the excommunication of Elizabeth I in 1570 encouraged English Catholics to conspire against her. These secret

---

[i] DailyHistory.org. (2023, October 28). How Did the Peace of Augsburg (1555) Lead to the Thirty Years' War (1618-1648). Retrieved from DailyHistory.org:
https://dailyhistory.org/How_did_the_Peace_of_Augsburg_(1555)_lead_to_the_Thirty_Years_War_(1618-1648).

attempts to overthrow the English monarchy culminated in the Gunpowder Plot of 1605 during the reign of King James I.

Both Spanish and Austrian Habsburgs made the suppression of Protestants in their respective domains government policy. The Habsburg commitment to Catholicism went beyond the defense of their own territories. They saw themselves as the protectors of the broader Catholic faith and sought to uphold the authority of the pope in Rome.

The Spark That Caused the Fire

The Thirty Years' War started two years before the actual fighting began. Ferdinand Habsburg was crowned Ferdinand II, King of Bohemia, in 1617. Ferdinand was a pious Catholic determined to return Bohemia to the Roman Catholic faith despite many Bohemian nobles being professed Protestants. His efforts to reinstate Catholicism as the official religion of Bohemia and his attempts to curtail the religious freedoms of Protestants in Bohemia and beyond escalated tensions.

Rudolf II signed the Letter of Majesty in July 1609 during his final years as Holy Roman emperor. This letter was a document of religious toleration permitting the various Bohemian Christian denominations to practice their faith peacefully. Rudolf was making good on a promise his father, Holy Roman Emperor Maximilian II, made to the Bohemian estates in 1575. Ferdinand revoked the Letter of Majesty in 1619, enraging the Protestant nobility.[i]

The Defenestration of Prague

The angry nobles refused to allow Ferdinand's act to go unchallenged. The Defenestration of Prague, which occurred on May 23rd, 1618, was the immediate catalyst for the Thirty Years' War. It took place at Prague Castle. Two Catholic officials, Jaroslav Borrzita of Martinice and Count Vilém Slavata, were confronted by Protestant nobles led by Count Jindřich Matyáš Thurn. The Protestants accused the Catholics of violating the religious liberties granted to them by the Letter of Majesty.

The nobles went one step too far. They forcibly ejected Borrzita and Slavata from a window of Prague Castle. Astonishingly, the two men survived the fall, but the event had far-reaching consequences. The

---

[i] The Bohemian Religious Peace (July 1609). (2023, October 28). Retrieved from GHDI: https://ghdi.ghi-dc.org/sub_document.cfm?document_id=4501.

Defenestration of Prague became a symbol of Bohemian resistance against Habsburg rule and Catholic influence.[i]

Yet, there was another even more inflammatory event that led to armed conflict. The Protestants followed up on their demonstration of disapproval by deposing Ferdinand and raising an army of sixteen thousand men. The crown of Bohemia was then offered to Frederick V, Elector of Palatine (his wife was the daughter of James I of England). The rebels had "crossed the Rubicon," and the Thirty Years' War began.

The Defenestration of Prague and Ferdinand II's role in starting the Thirty Years' War exemplify the complex interplay of religious tensions, political ambitions, and dynastic rivalries that defined this conflict. Ferdinand II's unyielding stance on Catholicism and his actions in response to the defenestration set in motion a war that would devastate Europe for three decades. This period of upheaval would ultimately reshape the political and religious landscape of the continent and leave a lasting legacy in European history.

Historians divide this European conflict into four periods: the Bohemian (1618-1625), the Danish (1625-1629), the Swedish (1630-1635), and the French (1635-1648) phases. We will follow these historical classifications.

<u>The Bohemian Phase (1618-1625)</u>

Ferdinand II was not going to accept his deposal graciously. He intended to fight. He was elected Holy Roman emperor on August 28th, 1619, which permitted him to put the military might of the empire on his side in regaining the Bohemian crown. After his election, he immediately started looking for allies. A logical choice for recruiting supporters was the Catholic League.

It was officially called the Catholic League of German States. The Catholic League was a confederation of Catholic princes and states in the Holy Roman Empire. The league was created in response to the Protestant Reformation and the creation of Protestant alliances within Germany. The Catholic League played a significant role in supporting the Habsburgs throughout the war.

---

[i] Wilson, D. (2020, May 23). The 1618 Defenestration of Prague Explained. Retrieved from History Extra: https://www.historyextra.com/period/stuart/1618-defenestration-prague-facts-history-explained-what-happened-why-castle-protestant-catholic/.

The Catholic League gave Ferdinand an army that, by July 1620, had approximately thirty thousand men. Those numbers gave them military superiority over their Protestant enemies, who could only muster ten thousand soldiers. Something Ferdinand and his allies had in addition to troop superiority was the military leadership of Johann Tserclaes, Count of Tilly.[i]

Count Johann Tserclaes of Tilly, commonly known as Count Tilly, was a prominent military commander. He played a crucial role in the Bohemian phase of the conflict, particularly in the year 1620. The count began his military career in the Spanish Army and earned his reputation in the wars the Spanish fought against the Dutch. Ferdinand appointed Count Tilly as the commander of the Catholic forces, and he played a primary role in Bohemian campaigns.

Count Tilly's army was different than the usual military forces of the time. It was a standing army whose soldiers did not rely on plunder for pay and provision; the government paid and fed the men. Tilly's advantages against Frederick of Bohemia were more than numbers. Tilly was an experienced commander, and Frederick was not a military man. His inexperience would prove costly.[ii]

<u>Battle of White Mountain (November 8th, 1620)</u>

Tilly aggressively took the war to his Protestant enemies. Catholic and Protestant troops met at White Mountain on November 8th, 1620. Tilly's twenty-seven thousand soldiers were disciplined, well trained, and organized into tercios, a highly effective tactical formation used by the Spanish Army. The enemy numbered only fifteen thousand and were mercenaries.

Tilly's forces successfully defeated the less-organized Protestant troops. The battle was a decisive victory for the Catholic Habsburgs, effectively ending Frederick's reign as king of Bohemia.

The Habsburgs held the upper hand after White Mountain, and Ferdinand pressed his advantage with campaigns in Upper Austria and

---

[i] New Advent. (2023, October 23). Johannes Tserclaes, County of Tilly. Retrieved from New Advent: https://www.newadvent.org/cathen/14724c.htm.

[ii] New Advent. (2023, October 23). Johannes Tserclaes, County of Tilly. Retrieved from New Advent: https://www.newadvent.org/cathen/14724c.htm.

Lower Saxony. Ferdinand consolidated his positions in Germany and moved to restore Catholicism.

Attempting to restore the Catholic Church in Protestant territories might have been a tactical error. Ferdinand could have used his winnings to gain concessions from the Protestant German states, but he failed to appreciate such an opportunity. Meanwhile, Protestants in Germany were alarmed at the success of the Habsburgs and looked for a way to counter this menacing threat. They found a new champion in the land of the Vikings.

<u>The Danish Phase (1625–1629)</u>

The Danish phase was a critical stage of the war. The defeat of Protestant forces in the Bohemian phase and the subsequent Catholic consolidation of power led to concerns among Protestant leaders throughout the Holy Roman Empire. They saw the need to counter the growing influence of the Catholic Habsburgs.

Scandinavia became Protestant in the early days of the Reformation, and the countries were solidly Lutheran. King Christian IV of Denmark played a central role. Christian sought to lead the Protestant coalition against the Catholic Habsburgs and gain control of critical territories in northern Germany. He entered the conflict not because of any religious conviction but to exploit opportunities that would permit him to enlarge his German territories. He received generous financial support from the Dutch United Provinces and England. The English also sent troops.[i]

<u>Albrecht von Wallenstein</u>

The Habsburgs continued to have the edge when it came to military leadership. The primary Catholic commander during the Danish phase was Albrecht von Wallenstein. He had a reputation for being a brilliant military leader, and he was also able to raise large numbers of men. Ferdinand made him supreme commander of the Catholic forces in the Holy Roman Empire, and von Wallenstein was dispatched to confront the Protestants.

His strategy was different from Tilly's. Wallenstein put his faith in massive mercenary armies. He raised troops anywhere he could find

---

[i] Infoplease. (2023, October 28). Thirty Years' War: The Danish Period. Retrieved from Infoplease.com: https://www.infoplease.com/encyclopedia/history/modern-europe/wars-battles/thirty-years-war/the-danish-period.

them. He did not care what their religious persuasion was. Many men responded to his recruiting efforts in large numbers because Wallenstein promised the possibility of getting rich from plunder. He was able to recruit and maintain a large army and launch campaigns.

Wallenstein was successful against the Danes. The Danish king used his naval power and was successful in the Baltic Sea, but the land campaigns did not go as well. Wallenstein gained a victory at the Battle of Dessau Bridge (April 25th, 1626) and effectively campaigned against the Protestant leaders Ernst von Mansfeld and Gabriel Bethlen.

It was a bit disturbing that von Wallenstein was more pragmatic than devout. He purchased significant areas of confiscated lands and bought the Duchy of Sagan from Ferdinand. His troops gained a sinister reputation for pillage and plunder. They were guilty of ransacking civilian homes, churches, and business establishments. Brutality and rape were trademarks of his men. Nevertheless, no one could argue with his success. Von Wallenstein's campaigns were fruitful, and his effective leadership achieved the victories that Ferdinand was hoping to achieve.

The Danish phase of the Thirty Years' War ended in 1629 with the Treaty of Lübeck. Christian was permitted to keep all of his pre-war possessions. Still, he had to surrender any claims to Lower Saxon bishoprics, discontinue alliances with North German states, and not interfere with the affairs of the Holy Roman Empire. Denmark received reasonably generous terms, and German Protestants faced rather harsh consequences.

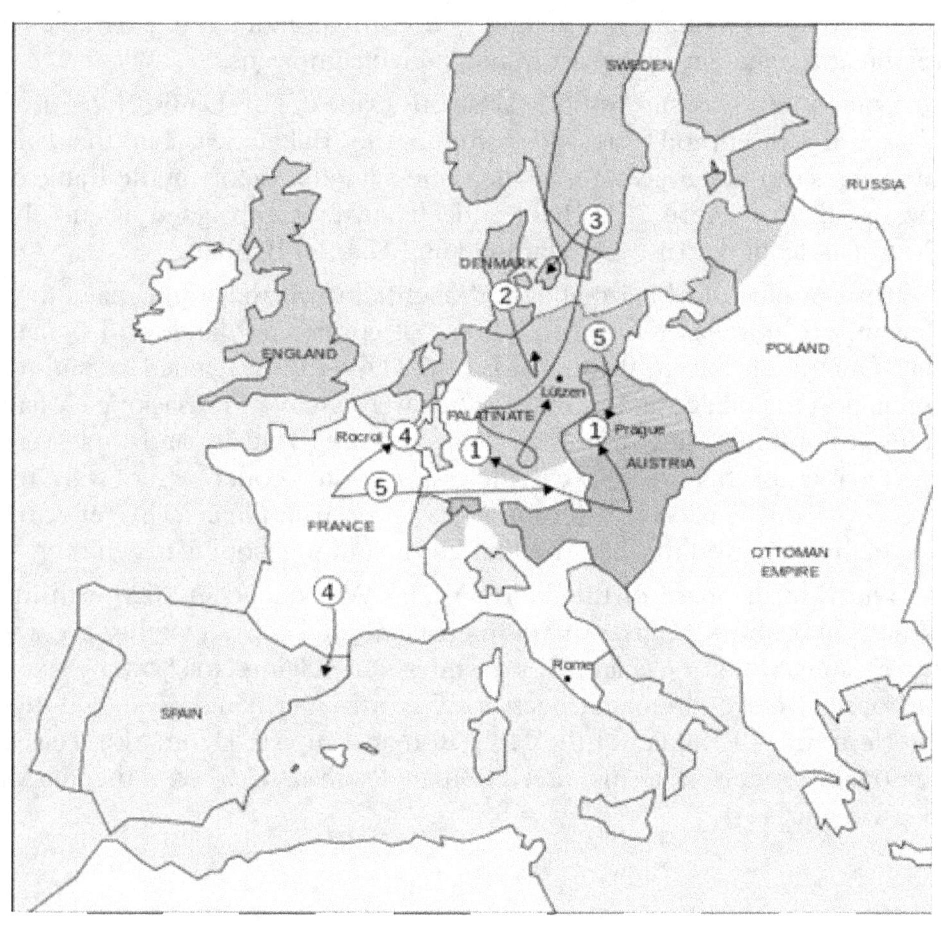

Map of the Thirty Years' War. [40]

<u>Edict of Restitution</u>

The Danish phase further solidified the power and influence of the Catholic Habsburgs under Emperor Ferdinand II. Their control over the empire was more secure, and Protestant resistance had weakened. Ferdinand issued the Edict of Restitution during the peace negotiations. The terms were tough to swallow.

The Edict of Restitution was a controversial decree. It aimed to restore Catholic lands and properties that had been secularized or confiscated by Protestant rulers since the Peace of Augsburg in 1555. The edict was one of the key measures the Catholic Habsburgs took to reestablish Catholicism and Habsburg authority in the empire.

The Roman Catholic Church was to regain various territories, bishoprics, monasteries, and ecclesiastical properties that had been transferred to Protestant hands in the preceding decades, challenging Protestant gains that had been made over the last few decades.

The edict was to be enforced through imperial commissioners whom Ferdinand appointed. These commissioners were tasked with implementing the terms, often against the will of Protestant rulers. The Protestants hotly contested the stipulations, But what could they do? The Habsburg emperor had them in a corner.[i]

The Danish phase ended in a significant Catholic victory, consolidating Habsburg power within the empire and reinforcing the Edict of Restitution. The German Protestants were routed and understandably demoralized. Fortunately for them, hope and salvation would come from the north.

<u>The Swedish Phase (1630–1635)</u>

The Protestants needed a military genius to beat the Habsburgs, and they got one. Gustavus Adolphus, King of Sweden, was a brilliant military commander and an inspiring leader. He was a match for Count Tilly and von Wallenstein.

Unlike King Christian of Denmark, Gustavus Adolphus was a devout Lutheran who viewed the war as an opportunity to defend the Protestant cause and stop the persecution of the faithful. The king had strategic interests as well, as he hoped to secure territory in northern Germany and

---

[i] History Learning. (2023, October 28). The Edict of Restitution. Retrieved from History Learning: https://historylearning.com/the-thirty-years-war0/edict-of-restitution/.

spread Swedish influence in the Baltic region. He was the savior the Protestants desperately needed. Adolphus stepped on the scene at the right time.

Military Reformer

The military genius of the Swedish king is best demonstrated by the reforms he instituted. Sweden was surrounded by powerful enemies with larger populations, and Adolphus recognized that accepted military practices were not feasible for Sweden.

A significant reform he introduced was universal conscription. Military training was tough, and Adolphus was more inclined to use small mobile units over traditional battlefield formations. The king recognized the importance of firepower and developed effective volley-firing tactics. In addition, he shortened pikes to make them easier to use and had light artillery as opposed to the heavy cannons of the day. Adolphus could use cavalry, artillery, and infantry effectively. These were some reasons why Napoleon Bonaparte considered him one of the most outstanding military leaders in history.[i]

A Lightning Bolt

The Catholic forces were used to winning, and their commanders were probably complacent as the Swedish phase began in 1630. It was a mistake, and the Battle of Breitenfeld (September 17th, 1631) proved that Adolphus could face Count Tilly's troops on the battlefield. The Swedes decisively defeated Tilly. The superiority of the Swedish military system shined that day. Breitenfeld was the first major defeat for the Catholics in the war. It was not going to be the last.

Adolphus moved quickly. He took Nuremberg and captured Munich. He then set his sights on Vienna. Ferdinand brought von Wallenstein back into service, and the mercenary general raised a large force and marched into Saxony. The two armies collided at Lutzen on November 6th, 1632, where Wallenstein was defeated. However, it was a Pyrrhic victory for the Protestants. Adolphus was killed, and the Protestant cause's great hero was gone.

---

[i] Smith, S. S. (2015, August 18). Gustavus Adolphus Revolutionized European Warfare. Retrieved from Investors.com: https://www.investors.com/news/management/leaders-and-success/gustavus-adolphus-father-of-modern-warfare/.

Death of von Wallenstein

Albrecht von Wallenstein was a great general who got too involved in politics. He tried to do some independent peace negotiations and raised suspicions and questions about his loyalty. Ferdinand was not going to take any chances; he secretly ordered the general killed. What happened on February 25th, 1634, was recorded by Michael Heubel, a tax collector and judge in the 17th century.

"On February 25, by imperial order, Wallenstein, Generalissimus and Duke of Friedland, was murdered together with the counts Terzky und Kinski by a number of officers in Eger, on account of the discovery of high treason on his part, as desired by the king in Hungary Ferdinand III. I saw the room in Eger with two side doors bearing the ineradicable stain of Wallenstein's blood, and also the staircase down which his corpse was dragged feet first, he who only an hour before had been a great duke and is now become the least and most unworthy of all men – so swiftly can the Lord put down the mighty from their seat."[i]

Two of the best military commanders of the Thirty Years' War were now dead.

The Catholics won at Nördlingen in 1634, but a decisive blow was not made. Both sides still had men on the field as the final phase of the Thirty Years' War began.

The French Phase (1635–1648)

The religious sentiments of 1618 were gone by the time the French phase began. This was a period of realpolitik where Catholic France sought to rein in the Catholic Habsburgs.

There was severe competition between France and the Habsburgs for control over Europe. The Bourbons wanted to reduce the power of the Habsburg family. Furthermore, France wanted to gain territorial rights and strategically important territories that would enhance French influence and provide a buffer against Habsburg holdings.

France entered into a series of alliances and agreements with Habsburg enemies. These included Sweden, the Dutch United Provinces, and various German Protestant states. We may think of it as an irony that a Catholic country would unite with Protestants against

---

[i] Gruber, S. (2023, October 28). Wallenstein: Death by Murder. Retrieved from The World of the Habsburgs: https://www.habsburger.net/en/chapter/wallenstein-death-murder.

another Catholic nation. But this is where geopolitics played a more critical role than religion. France wanted to be recognized as a major power, even if it came at the cost of the Catholic Habsburgs.

Cardinal Richelieu of France played a significant role. He was the chief minister to King Louis XIII and masterminded France's involvement in the war. The French phase introduced the rest of Europe to the French professional army that had been created. France's military leaders, such as the Vicomte de Turenne, played major roles.

The Battle of Rocroi on May 19th, 1643, was a major battle. It was fought between the Spanish and the French, and it established France as the predominant military power in Europe. The rest of the French phase was primarily a game of chess where diplomatic relations and political intrigue were the main activities.

Peace of Westphalia

Ferdinand II died in 1637. Although this major player in the military drama was now off stage, the fighting still continued. Central Europe was exhausted; there had to be a way out.

The Peace of Westphalia was not one document. Instead, it was a series of peace treaties that were signed between May and October 1648 in the Westphalian cities of Osnabrück and Münster. Besides ending the Thirty Years' War, the treaties also ended the Eighty Years' War that Spain had fought with the Dutch Republic.[i]

Principal Terms of the Peace

- "Cuius regio eius religio" was reestablished.

- Spain officially recognized the sovereignty of the Dutch Republic.

- Sweden and France gained significant territories and emerged as political powers in Europe.

- Various states within the Holy Roman Empire were recognized as being sovereign.

- The Thirty Years' War was officially over.

---

[i] Lumen Learning. (2023, October 28). The Peace of Westphalia and Sovereignty. Retrieved from Lumenlearning.com: https://courses.lumenlearning.com/atd-herkimer-westerncivilization/chapter/the-peace-of-westphalia-and-sovereignty/.

After decades of confusion and conflict, stability returned to central Europe. The peace and quiet would allow the healing process to begin.

<u>The War's Consequences for Germany</u>

The Thirty Years' War traumatized Germany. Central Europe would not see such devastation until the two world wars of the 20th century. Cities, towns, and the countryside experienced widespread destruction as marauding armies pillaged and destroyed the land. It is a safe estimate that as many as one-third of the population of Germany and central Europe died during this time.

Trade routes were disrupted, agriculture suffered, and many industries were burned to the ground. High levels of taxation increased the people's suffering. There was a legacy of trauma and grief that worked its way into the culture, and the war remained on the minds of people long after the guns were silent.

What was the final result? Neither side actually won. The Protestants and the Catholics gained little, and the old "cuius regio eius religio" returned. The idea of sovereign states grew out of the ashes of the conflict. However, the consequences of the war would remain for years, and Europe had a difficult time recovering.

The Thirty Years' War did not deal a death blow to the Habsburgs, but it did leave them reeling. The Holy Roman Empire was a shell of what it used to be. It was not a significant force anymore. The Spanish and Austrian Habsburgs faced a time of grave troubles. The 18th century would dawn with one branch collapsing while the other fought desperately for its existence.

Chapter 8: The Spanish Succession

The marriage strategy served the Habsburgs well for generations. The family gained thousands of acres of land without spilling blood or drawing a sword. No one suspected the plan would turn sour. However, on November 6th, 1661, things went horribly wrong.

Philip IV of Spain and Mariana of Austria were husband and wife, but they were also uncle and niece. The couple produced a child whom they named Charles. Any geneticist would immediately note that a child from an incestuous marriage would create severe issues. Habsburgs had intermarried before without any trouble, but now the family custom produced a bona fide nightmare. The consequences of successive inbreeding were apparent in Charles.

The boy had a range of both physical and mental deformities. He had a pronounced underbite, a large jaw, and an elongated face—a condition known as the Habsburg jaw or mandibular prognathism. His health issues extended to his mental faculties; he was described as mentally challenged and suffered from developmental delays. His childhood health was precarious, and he suffered from measles, chickenpox, rubella, and smallpox.

Any one of those maladies would have killed an ordinary child, but Charles survived. These infirmities would not have mattered politically if there were other male children in the family, but Charles was the only surviving son of Philip IV. Philip died in 1665 when Charles was only four years old. A child with extreme physical and mental deformities was now the king of Spain.

There were other instances where children were monarchs. Louis XIV is a great example. The problems of the king's incapacities would not have mattered if capable ministers had surrounded Charles II and the succession was clearly defined. There was one challenge, however, that made things worse. Charles married twice during his life and could not produce an heir. In fact, it is possible the king was impotent. It placed the whole matter of succession in turmoil. A lot was riding on who would succeed this invalid.

Portrait of Charles II, c. 1685. [41]

The Encircling Game

Spain was not the mega-power it had been one hundred years before, but it was still the largest empire in the world. It held large amounts of territory in the Low Countries and in Italy. A capable successor could govern the empire and be an influential European political figure.

Two major players in European politics had a vested interest in who would succeed Charles. The Austrian Habsburgs had a monopoly on the Holy Roman Empire, but the position of Holy Roman emperor was still elected. The Habsburgs were eager to continue having a hereditary monarchy in Spain to ensure the stability of their power in Europe. By having an Austrian Habsburg holding the Spanish crown, they hoped to further strengthen their position in the Holy Roman Empire. Furthermore, having a Habsburg who had close ties with Vienna and control over the Spanish territories could provide the Austrian Habsburgs with access to vast resources, including gold and silver from the American colonies and strategic territories in Italy, the Low Countries, and other regions. These resources could be used to bolster their military and economic strength. They also needed to checkmate an old rival: France.

France was the premier state in Europe and was ruled by Louis XIV, an ambitious monarch who wanted to enhance the power of his family, the Bourbons. The Austrians saw the Bourbons as a growing threat to the balance of power in Europe. Securing the Spanish crown would allow the Austrian Habsburgs to counterbalance Bourbon power and prevent the emergence of a dominant Bourbon superpower.

Ruling Spain would also prevent the Austrian Habsburgs from becoming encircled. If the Bourbons controlled both France and Spain, the Austrian Habsburgs would be geographically surrounded by Bourbon territories, which could potentially isolate and weaken their position in Europe.

Interestingly, the Habsburgs' worries were also the Bourbons' concerns. The Bourbons were motivated by a desire to prevent the Austrian Habsburgs from gaining control of the Spanish crown. Allowing the Habsburgs to hold both Spain and the Holy Roman Empire could create a formidable Habsburg superpower that might threaten the interests of the Bourbon dynasty and its allies. Conversely, the Bourbons understood that securing the Spanish throne would allow them to exert influence over critical regions, such as Italy and the Low Countries, and potentially shift the balance of power in Europe in their favor.

<u>Two Claimants</u>

Contested European successions often resulted in a mad dash to the genealogical tables to discover who had the best claim to an open throne by means of bloodline. The French claimant, Philip of Anjou, claimed his right from his connection to Anne of Austria, Philip IV's older sister, and Maria Theresa, Philip's eldest daughter. The Austrian claimant, Charles, Archduke of Austria, argued that the right of succession was based on his grandmother, Maria Anna, who was the youngest daughter of Philip IV. Philip of Anjou was the grandson of Louis XIV, and Charles was the son of Holy Roman Emperor Leopold I.

The Bourbon claim to the throne was stronger, and Louis XIV schemed to make a Bourbon succession a reality. He signed two separate treaties with William III of England to divide the Spanish Empire in 1698 and 1700 but forgot to ask Charles II what he thought about the arrangements. Charles might have been less than brilliant, but the Spanish king was adamant about keeping the empire intact.[i]

<u>Emerging Alliances</u>

Charles II of Spain was growing physically weaker, and he died on November 1st, 1700. He left behind a will that named Philip of Anjou as his successor. That should have been the end of the story, but it was not.[ii]

England and the Dutch Republic were concerned that a Bourbon king on the throne of Spain would create a Bourbon superpower. They wanted to prevent the Bourbons from upsetting the balance of power in the continent. The Grand Alliance was formed in 1701 and included the Holy Roman Empire, England, and the Dutch Republic.

France was also looking for allies to back the Bourbon candidate. The French renewed their alliance with Spain and added Bavaria as an ally to protect the nation's southern front from war.

Other alliances would be formed in the following years. All of these illustrate the intricate diplomatic maneuverings that took place. Both sides were willing to fight, and all that remained were formal declarations of

---

[i] Lumen Learning. (2023, October 28). War of Spanish Succession. Retrieved from Lumenlearning.com: https://courses.lumenlearning.com/suny-fmcc-boundless-worldhistory/chapter/war-of-spanish-succession/.

[ii] Britannica.com. (2023, October 28). War of the Spanish Succession. Retrieved from Britannica.com: https://www.britannica.com/event/War-of-the-Spanish-Succession.

war. Hostilities began in March 1701 when the French seized Spanish fortresses in the Spanish Netherlands.

The Greatest Habsburg General

Some historians believe that the War of the Spanish Succession was the first world war of the modern era. The Grand Alliance was determined to thwart the French. The Grand Alliance was fortunate to have two of the best military commanders of the 18th century: John Churchill, Duke of Marlborough, and Prince Eugene of Savoy. We know much about the Duke of Marlborough thanks to the writings of his descendant, Winston Churchill. Prince Eugene sometimes gets pushed into the background. That is unfortunate because the short military commander was one of the best generals in Austrian history.

It is ironic that he fought against the French because Prince Eugene was the son of French aristocrats. He was supposed to follow a career in the church, but as a young man, he balked at the idea. He wanted to join the French military, but King Louis XIV blocked his career path. That did not stop the young man. He went to Vienna, where he received a commission in the Austrian army and helped raise the siege of Vienna in 1688.

Prince Eugene was highly successful as a military officer and rose rapidly through the ranks. He played a primary role in driving the Ottomans out of Hungary and was a field marshal when the War of Spanish Succession broke out.[i]

Most military officers at the time gained their positions because of their family connections. Prince Eugene, on the other hand, did it through sheer talent. He had a keen understanding of warfare and had the ability to adapt to different battlefield conditions. Eugene displayed remarkable versatility by excelling in both offensive and defensive operations. He had a wide range of military skills and was equally adept at commanding cavalry charges and infantry engagements. One talent he had that is sometimes overlooked was his ability to work effectively with other military commanders. His relationship with the Duke of Marlborough was a stellar example of his flexibility.

---

[i] Visiting Vienna. (2023, June 7). Prince Eugene: What You Need to Know. Retrieved from Visitingvienna.com: https://www.visitingvienna.com/culture/prince-eugene-savoy/.

Prince Eugene of Savoy. [48]

A Splendid Partnership

The partnership between the Duke of Marlborough (John Churchill) and Prince Eugene of Savoy during the War of the Spanish Succession is often regarded as one of the most successful and effective military collaborations in European history. Their alliance played a pivotal role in achieving significant victories for the Grand Alliance against the forces of France and Bavaria. It was an amazing alignment of two martial stars that delivered substantial victories. There were some key ingredients to their success.

Marlborough and Eugene possessed complementary military strengths. Marlborough was known for his strategic acumen, ability to formulate grand plans, and strong leadership qualities. Eugene, on the other hand, excelled at tactical warfare, displaying remarkable skills in maneuvering troops on the battlefield and making crucial decisions in the heat of battle. Together, they formed a balanced and effective leadership team.

Both men were united by a common purpose: to defeat the forces of France and Bavaria. Their shared commitment to this overarching goal allowed for cooperation and strategic alignment. Marlborough and Eugene developed comprehensive strategic plans that emphasized joint operations. They carefully planned their campaigns and ensured that their forces moved in harmony, preventing the enemy from dividing and conquering them.

They made vital decisions jointly, consulting with each other and seeking consensus. Their partnership was not characterized by rivalry or ego-driven decision-making but rather by a commitment to making choices that would best serve the interests of the Grand Alliance.

The two were flexible. They were open to adapting their plans and strategies based on changing battlefield conditions and enemy movements. This adaptability allowed them to respond effectively to unexpected challenges.

The pair also had mutual respect for each other. They recognized each other's strengths and were willing to defer to the expertise of the other when necessary. This mutual respect formed the basis of their strong working relationship.

They knew how to communicate as well. Despite lingual differences (Marlborough spoke English, while Eugene spoke primarily French and German), they maintained clear lines of communication and exchanged regular correspondence to coordinate their military actions.

All of these qualities would pay off handsomely in the single most crucial battle of the war: the Battle of Blenheim.

<u>The Battle of Blenheim</u>

Military historians count Blenheim as one of the fifteen decisive battles in world history. A French army of sixty thousand men was put against the Grand Alliance army's approximately fifty-six thousand men.

The early days of the war were fought primarily in the Low Countries, but the French, in 1704, decided to take the offensive against Austria with the intention of destroying the Austrian Habsburgs. The Duke of Marlborough was the commander in chief of the Grand Alliance forces, and he marched his army to counter the French in southern Germany.[i]

ⁱ BritishBattles.com. (2023, October 28). Battle of Blenheim. Retrieved from Britishbattles.com:

Marlborough coordinated his movements with Prince Eugene, and Marlborough led his troops on a crossing of the Danube near Donauwörth on July 31ˢᵗ, 1704. This enabled him to join up with Eugene and position their army against the French soldiers under Marshal Tallard and the Bavarian forces commanded by Maximilian of Bavaria.

The French did not expect Marlborough and Eugene to attack. They should have. The forces of the Grand Alliance moved forward on August 13ᵗʰ, 1704, and concentrated on the French center. The battle saw intense fighting, including artillery bombardments and infantry clashes. Tallard's forces initially held their ground, but as the battle progressed, their position weakened.

A decisive moment occurred when Marlborough launched an aggressive cavalry attack on the French center, leading to the collapse of the enemy lines. Marshal Tallard was captured, and Maximilian fled the battlefield. The Battle of Blenheim resulted in a resounding victory for the Grand Alliance.

The myth of French superiority was crushed. The Battle of Blenheim marked a turning point in the War of the Spanish Succession. It halted French expansion into the heart of the Holy Roman Empire and bolstered the morale of the Grand Alliance. It furthermore demonstrated the brilliance of Marlborough and Eugene working together as a team.

<u>A String of Magnificent Victories</u>

After the resounding victory at the Battle of Blenheim in 1704, the partnership between the Duke of Marlborough and Prince Eugene of Savoy continued to yield significant achievements for the Grand Alliance. Their combined military leadership and strategic coordination led to a series of triumphs that further weakened the Bourbon position in the war.

- Battle of Ramillies (May 23ʳᵈ, 1706)

The Grand Alliance achieved a decisive victory over the French and Bavarian forces under Marshal Villeroy. The battle resulted in the capture of a significant portion of the French Army and allowed the alliance to regain control of the Spanish Netherlands.

---

https://www.britishbattles.com/war-of-the-spanish-succession/battle-of-blenheim/.

- Capture of Brussels (June 6th, 1706)

Marlborough and Eugene advanced into the Spanish Netherlands and captured the city of Brussels, a key strategic stronghold. This success further solidified their control over the region.

- Siege of Lille (August 12th–December 10th, 1708)

Marlborough and Eugene jointly conducted the siege of Lille, which was a prominent French stronghold. The siege resulted in the surrender of the city to the Grand Alliance forces and the capture of a substantial French garrison. The fall of Lille was a significant blow to French military capabilities.

- Battle of Oudenaarde (July 11th, 1708)

Marlborough and Eugene defeated the French and Bavarian forces commanded by Marshal Vendôme. The victory prevented a French attempt to relieve the besieged city of Lille and further secured the Grand Alliance's control over the Spanish Netherlands.

- Battle of Malplaquet (September 11th, 1709)

The Battle of Malplaquet was one of the bloodiest engagements of the war, with heavy casualties on both sides. Although the French and Bavarians under Marshal Villars put up a strong defense, Marlborough and Eugene eventually achieved victory. Malplaquet reinforced the Grand Alliance's position and contributed to their continued control over the Spanish Netherlands.

These victories, achieved through the joint leadership of Marlborough and Eugene, significantly weakened the French-Bavarian alliance and expanded the territory controlled by the Grand Alliance. The military successes of Marlborough and Eugene played a crucial role in advancing the interests of the Habsburg monarchy and the broader Grand Alliance during the War of the Spanish Succession.

<u>Politics Intervene</u>

The French were losing on the battlefield, but it did not mean they would lose the war. Politics played a dominating role in the final years of the war.

In 1711, Holy Roman Emperor Joseph I died. He was succeeded by Archduke Charles, which created a conundrum for the Grand Alliance. Charles would not only be the Holy Roman emperor but also the king of Spain, creating a powerful position for the Habsburgs that had not been seen since the 16th century. It would be a severe shift in the balance of power.[i]

Both sides began to maneuver and secretly negotiate for peace terms. The English and French signed the Preliminary Articles of London on October 8th, 1711. France agreed that the Spanish and French crowns would remain separate, and Great Britain was given a thirty-year monopoly on the right to import enslaved people into Spanish American colonies. Other peace negotiations occurred that involved multiple parties, but everyone wanted an end to the conflict.

Finally, two peace agreements were hammered out.

<u>Treaty of Utrecht and Treaty of Rastatt</u>

The principal peace agreement was the Treaty of Utrecht. Its main provisions were the following:

- Recognition of Philip V: The treaty recognized Philip V, the Bourbon claimant, as the legitimate king of Spain with the condition that the French and Spanish crowns would remain separate.

- Territorial changes: Significant territorial adjustments were made in Europe and overseas. Spain ceded several territories to other European powers, including the Spanish Netherlands, Naples, Sardinia, and parts of Milan to the Austrian Habsburgs and Sicily to the Duchy of Savoy. Gibraltar and Minorca were ceded to Great Britain. France ceded Newfoundland, Nova Scotia, and Rupert's Land to Great Britain.

The Treaty of Utrecht was signed on April 11th, 1713, between the major European powers.

The Treaty of Rastatt was a complementary agreement to the Treaty of Utrecht. It confirmed many of the territorial changes outlined in the Treaty of Utrecht, and it addressed issues related to the Holy Roman Empire, including the transfer of certain territories from Spain to the Holy Roman Empire. The Treaty of Rastatt was signed on March 7th, 1714, between the Holy Roman Empire and France.

---

[i] The Royal Hampshire Regiment. (2023, October 28). The War of the Spanish Succession. Retrieved from Royalhampshirereiment.org: https://www.royalhampshireregiment.org/about-the-museum/timeline/war-spanish-succession/.

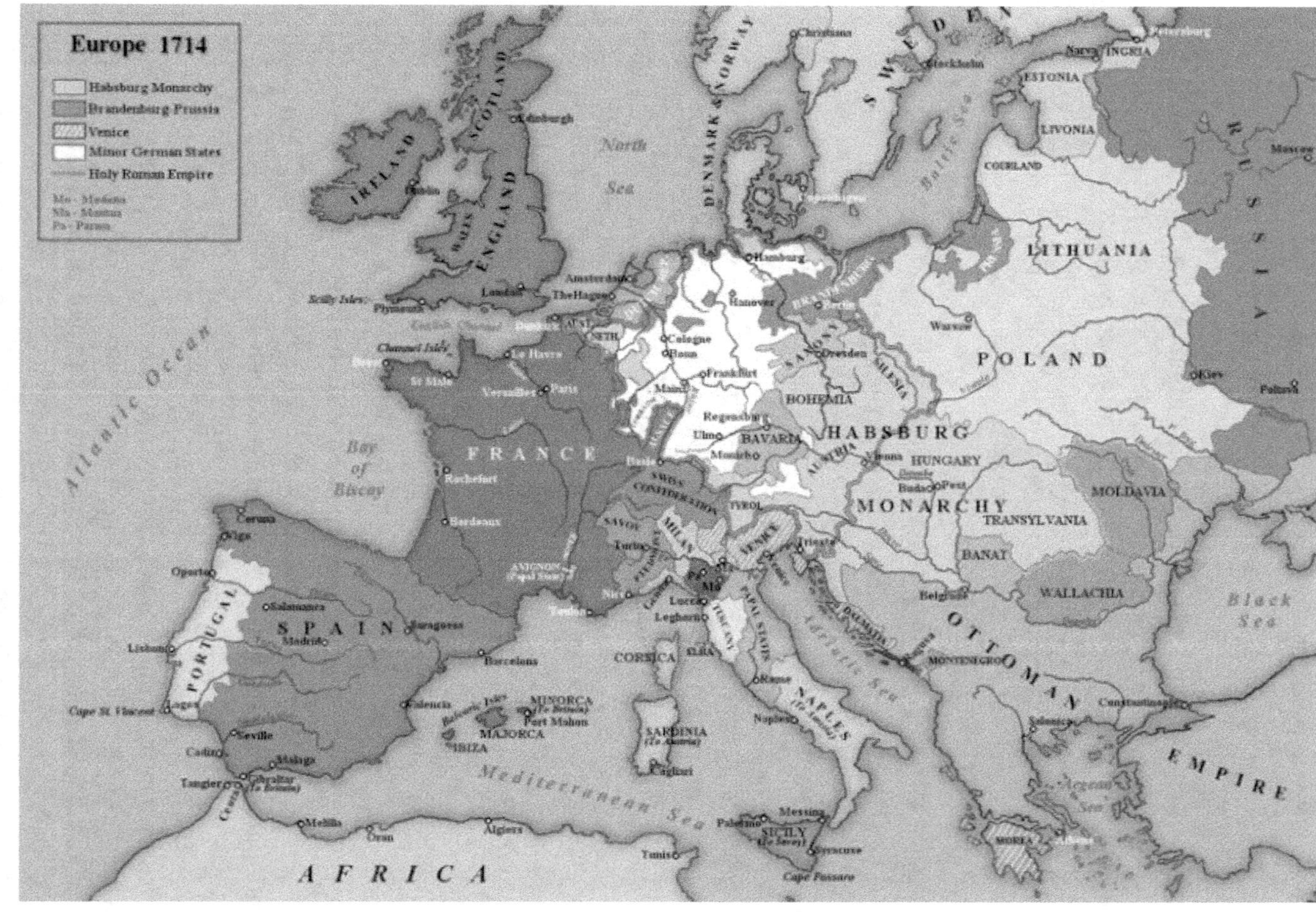

Europe after the treaties. [48]

<u>Pragmatic Sanction of 1713</u>

Concurrently with the peace negotiations, Emperor Charles VI of the Holy Roman Empire sought to secure the Pragmatic Sanction of 1713, which ensured the inheritance of the Habsburg lands by a daughter instead of only a son. The European powers agreed to this arrangement as part of the broader settlement.

These treaties helped establish a more stable and peaceful order in Europe, although they also left lingering tensions and rivalries that would influence later conflicts. The Habsburgs did not get all they wanted, but the acquisition of the Spanish Netherlands gave Austria increased tax revenues. While the Spanish Habsburg line was no more, the Austrian Habsburgs were as powerful as they ever had been.

Chapter 9: The Reign of Maria Theresa

The end of the War of the Spanish Succession saw the Habsburgs lose one crown and risk losing another. Holy Roman Emperor Charles VI did not have a male heir, and it was quite possible that someone outside of the family would become the ruler of the Holy Roman Empire. It was another succession crisis, and the Habsburgs had to win this one or lose all its imperial power.

The Pragmatic Sanction of 1713 outlined the succession after his death. A critical clause in the document was that the eldest daughter of Charles, Maria Theresa, was in the direct line of succession to the throne. Charles spent the last years of his life getting the major European powers to recognize the Pragmatic Sanction. He succeeded in his lifetime, but his succession plan was immediately contested after he died. Albert of Bavaria and Frederick the Great of Prussia both contested the succession. Neither counted on the charisma and courage of a young woman determined to obey her father's wishes.

Queen Elizabeth I of England rallied her troops at Tilbury by saying, "I know I have but the body of a weak and feeble woman, but I have the heart and stomach of a king, and of a king of England too."[i] That

---

[i] Royal Museums Greenwich. (2023, November 8). Queen Elizabeth I's Speech to the Troops at Tilbury. Retrieved from Rmg.co.uk: https://www.rmg.co.uk/stories/topics/queen-elizabeth-speech-

description fits Maria Theresa. She was not inclined to go quietly into the dark shadows of history. Maria Theresa was willing to put up a fight even if her chances appeared slim.

The State of War

Maria Theresa ascended the throne on October 20th, 1740. She was barely settled into her new title when Frederick the Great sent the Prussian army into Silesia on December 16th, 1740. He was not alone in his attack on Habsburg territory. France and Bavaria also took advantage of the situation and launched invasions of Austrian territory. Eventually, Maria Theresa faced an alliance of France, Bavaria, Spain, Sweden, and Saxony, even though several of the members of this alliance had agreed to the Pragmatic Sanction. They saw an opportunity to expand their territory at the expense of the new monarch.[i]

Maria Theresa desperately needed the help of the Hungarian aristocracy if she wanted to protect her crown successfully. She decided to convene a meeting of the Hungarian Diet in Bratislava to make a personal appeal.

The empress traveled to Bratislava to beg for help. There is a legend regarding what she did that convinced the Hungarians to rally for her cause. She faced opposition because she was a woman. To overcome any question of her abilities, Maria Theresa reputedly rode a horse up the steep steps of St. Martin's Cathedral in Bratislava to display her determination and commitment to the Hungarian cause. This act was intended to win the Hungarian nobles' admiration and support. She went further by pleading with the assembled nobles dressed in Hungarian-style clothing and with her infant son in her arms. It is said that the Hungarian nobles were so moved that a general cry of "We will die for our queen, Maria Theresa!" rose up as the Hungarian nobles swore to give their assistance to the embattled monarch.[ii]

Whether the legend is true is a topic for debate. Regardless, Maria Theresa made a formal promise to uphold the rights and privileges of the Hungarian nobility, including their traditional liberties and the autonomy

---

troops-tilbury.

[i] Biography.com. (2021, October 21). Maria Theresa. Retrieved from Biography.com: https://www.biography.com/royalty/maria-theresa.

[ii] History's Women. (2023, November 8). Maria Theresa. Retrieved from History's Women: https://historyswomen.com/women-who-ruled/maria-theresa/.

---

of the Kingdom of Hungary within the Habsburg Empire. This promise was known as her "Hungarian Pragmatic Sanction."

Maria Theresa's willingness to engage directly with the Hungarian nobility and make concessions to preserve their traditional rights earned her their loyalty and admiration. The aristocracy saw her as a ruler who respected their privileges and traditions. Her bold initiative resulted in her coronation as queen of Hungary in St. Martin's Cathedral on June 25th, 1741.

The War of the Austrian Succession plodded on for years. Maria Theresa refused the offer made by Frederick the Great to end the war in return for recognition of Prussian control of Silesia and continued the fight. She had the support of Great Britain but was forced to concede Silesia to Prussia in the Treaty of Dresden, which was signed in December 1745.

The war finally grounded to a halt and was ended by the Treaty of Aix-la-Chapelle, signed on October 18th, 1748. Austria formally gave up Silesia and surrendered the duchies of Parma, Piacenza, and Guastalla in Italy to Spain. Nevertheless, the treaty formalized the succession of Maria Theresa to the Habsburg holdings in Austria. Her throne was secure.

It did not end Austria's involvement in future European wars. Maria Theresa later led her empire into the Seven Years' War and the War of Bavarian Succession.

A portrait of Maria Theresa. "

The Habsburg Reformer

Because Maria Theresa was now Austria's recognized ruler, she could concentrate on a series of reforms to modernize her country. She was a conservative ruler but was open to changes that would improve the administration of her domains and the living conditions of her subjects.

Maria Theresa compiled an impressive record of reforms. These changes touched upon various aspects of governance, administration, education, the military, and the economy.

Administrative Reforms

Maria Theresa centralized the administration of her extensive domains, which included the Holy Roman Empire and other territories. Her administrative reforms aimed to streamline the bureaucracy, make it more efficient, and promote uniform governance across her realms. Critical aspects of her administrative reforms included the following:

- Creation of provincial councils: Maria Theresa established provincial councils in different regions to improve local administration. These councils were responsible for various administrative functions and helped in the collection of taxes and the maintenance of law and order.

- Codification of laws: She undertook efforts to codify and standardize laws in her territories. The Codex Theresianus, a comprehensive legal code, was promulgated in 1766, simplifying legal procedures and providing greater legal clarity.

Educational and Cultural Reforms

Maria Theresa was a staunch supporter of education and culture. Her reforms aimed to promote knowledge and intellectual development. Some of her notable initiatives included:

- Founding Theresianum: In 1746, Maria Theresa founded Theresianum, a prestigious educational institution in Vienna. It served as a model school and academy and trained students for careers in public service.

- Expansion of schools and universities: Maria Theresa promoted the establishment of schools and universities in her realms, These institutions contributed to the spread of education and knowledge. Maria Theresa introduced compulsory schooling for children in all Habsburg hereditary lands in 1774. This was the beginning of mandatory education for large segments of the population.

Military Reforms

Austria's armed forces were out-generaled and out-maneuvered by Prussia in the War of the Austrian Succession. Maria Theresa knew changes were going to be needed.

- Professionalization of the army: She professionalized the Habsburg army by introducing standardized training, uniforms, and discipline. This modernization improved the efficiency and effectiveness of the military.

<u>Economic Reforms</u>

Economic stability and growth were high priorities for Maria Theresa. Her economic reforms aimed to promote trade, support agriculture, and stimulate industry. The following sums up her economic reforms:

- Mercantilist policies: She implemented mercantilist policies to boost domestic production and trade. These policies included tariffs, subsidies, and regulations designed to protect and nurture domestic industries.

- Agricultural reforms: Maria Theresa encouraged improvements in agriculture through land reforms and incentives for landowners to adopt more productive farming techniques, which contributed to increased agricultural output.

- Infrastructure development: She invested in infrastructure development, including the construction of roads and canals, to facilitate trade and transportation within her realms.[i]

Maria Theresa's reforms significantly modernized her realms and promoted their development. While not all of her reforms were universally successful, her reign left a lasting impact on the Habsburg monarchy and the broader European landscape, contributing to its stability and progress during the 18th century.

<u>Diplomatic Revolution of 1756</u>

The Diplomatic Revolution of 1756 was a significant realignment of European alliances that took place in the mid-18th century. It marked a dramatic shift in the balance of power and geopolitical relationships among major European states. The key feature of this diplomatic transformation was the reversal of longstanding alliances and the formation of new partnerships. The Diplomatic Revolution was a response to changing European political, territorial, and strategic considerations.

---

[i] Gruber, S. (2023, November 8). *Maria Theresa: The "Great Reformer."* Retrieved from The World of the Habsburgs: https://www.habsburger.net/en/chapter/maria-theresa-great-reformer.

Maria Theresa of Austria played a pivotal role in the Diplomatic Revolution of 1756. Her diplomatic efforts during this period were aimed at countering the growing power of Prussia and safeguarding the interests of the Habsburg monarchy.

Maria Theresa was a skilled diplomat, and several notable diplomatic accomplishments marked her reign. Among her most significant achievements was the appointment of Wenzel Anton, commonly known as Count Kaunitz, as her chief diplomat and chancellor.

Kaunitz was one of the most influential diplomats and statesmen during Maria Theresa's reign. He played a pivotal role in shaping Maria Theresa's foreign policy and contributing to her diplomatic successes. Kaunitz played a central role in the Diplomatic Revolution of 1756. His most notable diplomatic achievement was the role he played in creating an alliance with France.

A portrait of Kaunitz. "

It was an audacious move. France and Austria had been enemies for centuries, and the friendship agreement that Kaunitz was able to create showed how realpolitik was shaping European diplomacy. France was upset with an alliance Prussia entered into with Great Britain, and the

French needed something to counterbalance that relationship. Kaunitz and Maria Theresa saw an opportunity to make a move against Prussia, and the two decided to ignore the age-old differences between France and Austria.

Negotiations led to the Treaty of Versailles on May 1ˢᵗ, 1756, and then another Treaty of Versailles, signed on May 1ˢᵗ, 1757. France and Austria became allies against Prussia, agreeing to fight against Frederick the Great until Austria regained control of Silesia and Glantz.[i]

While the Diplomatic Revolution did not result in an immediate resolution to European conflicts such as the Seven Years' War, it laid the foundation for the broader realignment of alliances in Europe and contributed to a more complex and multipolar system of power in the continent.

Maria Theresa's decision to ally with France was a diplomatic masterstroke. It signaled her commitment to curbing Prussian expansionism and allowed her to secure critical French support in the event of future conflicts. A treaty signed with Russia at approximately the same time solidified Austria's position in central Europe.

Maria Theresa's diplomatic skills and willingness to form alliances with former adversaries demonstrated her ability to adapt to changing circumstances and prioritize the interests of the Habsburg monarchy.

The Partition of Poland

Austria was involved in the Seven Years' War because it hoped to regain Silesia. The Treaty of Hubertusburg in 1763 ended Austria's involvement in the Seven Years' War. Austria gained some diplomatic successes and regained lost territories, but Silesia was permanently lost. However, Austria later gained some significant regions in Europe at the expense of a neighboring state.

The partition of Poland, one of the most significant events in European history during the late 18th century, involved the division and eventual dismemberment of the Polish-Lithuanian Commonwealth, a once-powerful state in central and eastern Europe. This partition occurred in three stages, with the participation of several European powers, including Austria.

---

[i] New Advent. (2023, November 8). *Wenzel Anton Kaunitz.* Retrieved from NewAdvent.org: https://www.newadvent.org/cathen/08611b.htm.

Poland's government was inherently weak and was torn apart in the late 1760s by a civil war. Poland lacked the political will to resist the pressures exerted on it by Russia and had no support from other European powers. Russia, Prussia, and Austria signed a treaty that partitioned Poland on August 5th, 1772.

As audacious as this blatant land grab was, the Polish Sejm, the country's governing body, ratified the partition on September 30th, 1773. Poland lost nearly half its population and roughly one-third of its landmass. Austria acquired Galicia and Lodomeria (a region in present-day Ukraine and Poland) as its share of the partition.[i]

Austria participated in the partition of Poland to expand its territory and influence in eastern Europe. Maria Theresa acquired Polish territories that were rich in resources and had strategic significance. Moreover, Austria was concerned about the growing dominance of Russia and Prussia in the region. The partition permitted Austria to counterbalance the influence of those two states and prevent either from gaining more power in eastern Europe.

Maria Theresa and the Age of Enlightenment

The Age of Enlightenment was a period marked by intellectual, cultural, and political transformations. Maria Theresa's role during the Enlightenment was complex and multifaceted.

While Maria Theresa implemented some Enlightenment-inspired reforms, she was not immune to criticism from Enlightenment thinkers who called for more radical changes. Some of her policies were conservative, and she maintained a strong central authority.

A combination of reformist policies, cultural patronage, and a degree of openness to Enlightenment ideas marked Maria Theresa's contributions to the Age of Enlightenment. Her reign reflected a balance between the desire for centralized authority and the recognition of the need for modernization and improvement in governance. She abolished torture, limited the judicial authority of landlords over serfs, and removed universities from the control of the Roman Catholic Church. Her agrarian reforms were founded on fiscal and humanitarian reasons. She did not go

---

[i] Britannica.com. (2023, October 17). *Partitions of Poland.* Retrieved from Britannica.com: https://www.britannica.com/event/Partitions-of-Poland.

as far as some reformers hoped, but the changes Maria Theresa instituted had lasting positive effects.[i]

<u>A Patron of the Arts</u>

Maria Theresa made significant cultural contributions during her rule. Her patronage of the arts played a pivotal role in shaping the cultural landscape of the Habsburg monarchy during the 18th century. She was particularly fond of music and opera. Maria Theresa supported the Viennese court's musical life and was known to attend performances regularly. She helped court composers like Joseph Haydn, who served in her court. Haydn's music and compositions contributed significantly to the Classical period of music. Maria Theresa also patronized renowned artists, including painters like Martin van Meytens.[ii]

Culture was incorporated into Maria Theresa's diplomatic efforts as well. She exchanged gifts and artistic treasures with other European courts. These exchanges fostered cultural ties and promoted the Habsburg monarchy's prestige.

Maria Theresa's patronage and support of the arts made Vienna a major European cultural center. She left a lasting legacy that enriched the cultural heritage of the Habsburg realm and contributed to the broader cultural developments of the 18th century.

Maria Theresa died on November 29th, 1780. Her reign was marked by significant accomplishments in various fields, including governance, administration, culture, and diplomacy. Her ability to navigate the challenges of her time and leave a lasting legacy makes her one of the most notable rulers in European history. Historians consider her one of the most important Habsburg rulers.

---

[i] Keithly, D. M. (2008, April 3). *Maria Theresa.* Retrieved from Enlightenment-revolution.org: https://enlightenment-revolution.org/index.php?title=Maria_Theresa.

[ii] History's Women. (2023, November 8). Maria Theresa. Retrieved from History's Women: https://historyswomen.com/women-who-ruled/maria-theresa/.

Chapter 10: The Napoleonic Era and the Age of Metternich

Maria Theresa was succeeded by her son Joseph II, who also instituted reforms to improve government and society. His younger brother, Leopold II, followed him; his reign lasted only two years.

Austria was involved in a war against the Turks during the reign of both monarchs. That conflict, which was part of a treaty obligation to assist the Russians, was the last Austro-Turkish war. It was finally concluded by the signing of the Treaty of Sistova in 1791.

Unfortunately, Leopold permitted the cancellation of many of his older brother's reforms and increased the power of the secret police. Perhaps what influenced the end of those progressive reforms could have been a response to what was happening in France.

The French Revolution broke out in 1789 and severely attacked the old order. Francis II (later Francis I of Austria), who succeeded Leopold II, opposed the French Revolution and the treatment of France's king, Louis XVI. Relations between the two allies grew strained to the point where the French declared war on Austria in April 1792, beginning a series of conflicts that would wrack Europe for the next twenty-three years.[i]

---

[i] Britannica.com. (2023, November 8). Conflicts with Revolutionary France, 1790-1805. Retrieved from Britannica.com: https://www.britannica.com/place/Austria/Conflicts-with-revolutionary-

<u>Sheer Military Incompetence</u>

Austria fought five wars with France during this troubled period and lost four of them. Austria was a key player in the War of the First Coalition (1792–1797), forming alliances with other European monarchies to counteract the revolutionary French forces. The empire had initial successes but quickly stumbled against the French and began to lose consistently.

Fighting the French in Italy was a total disaster. Austria had the misfortune of dealing with a military genius named Napoleon Bonaparte. Napoleon led a highly skilled, disciplined army. The French troops were well trained and experienced; they clearly understood Napoleon's innovative tactics. The Battle of Marengo in 1800 is a prime example of this. The Austrian army's inability to adapt to the rapidly changing battlefield conditions contributed to its defeat. Austria faced resource limitations, including difficulties maintaining and supplying its troops in Italy. The financial and logistical strain of sustaining a campaign in Italy placed additional burdens on the Habsburg monarchy.

The Austrian army was large but suffered from rigidity, worn-out strategies, and obsolete battle tactics. There were highly competent commanders, such as Archduke Charles (son of Emperor Leopold II), but there were also instances of less capable leadership. Austria's officers were often appointed based on social status rather than merit, and many were inexperienced or incompetent.

Austria's army relied on linear formations and slow maneuvers. The French, on the other hand, were using modern innovations, such as moving troops in column formations and the corps system. Poor leadership at Rivoli in 1797 was the reason for the Austrian defeat.

Napoleon consistently out-maneuvered and out-fought the Austrians in Italy. The consequence of the poor Austrian performance was the Treaty of Campo Formio in 1797. Austria was forced to cede Lombardy to France.

Lombardy's loss was a significant blow to Austria's influence in Italy. This territory became part of the Cisalpine Republic, a French client state. Austria was required to recognize the Cisalpine Republic and the Ligurian Republic. Austria also gave up the Austrian Netherlands and recognized the French annexation of the left bank of the Rhine.

Some consequences harmed Austria years after the guns fell silent. The French occupation of Italian territory exposed the local population to the revolutionary ideals of liberty, equality, and nationalism. Those ideas had a lasting impact on the Italian Peninsula, contributing to the emergence of nationalist sentiments and movements that would shape the course of Italian unification in the 19th century.

Map of central Europe after the Treaty of Campo Formio."

<u>Third Coalition Disaster</u>

The Third Coalition was a military alliance formed in 1805 to respond to the expanding ambitions of Napoleon Bonaparte and the French Republic during the Napoleonic Wars. The expanding ambitions of Napoleon Bonaparte prompted this alliance. Its member nations were Austria, Great Britain, Russia, Naples, Sweden, and Sicily. Archduke Charles was a principal commander of the Third Coalition forces.

Austria attacked Bavaria, France's ally, on September 10th, 1805. Napoleon responded by marching into central Europe. The Third Coalition was confident of victory since the Russians and Austrians who confronted the French outnumbered the French two to one.

Napoleon moved rapidly and surprised Austrian General Karl Mack von Leiberich at Ulm on October 19th. The Austrians suffered a horrific defeat, losing almost all of Mack's army. The road was now opened for the French to march on Vienna. As Francis fled his capital, Napoleon entered Vienna on November 14th, 1805. The Third Coalition still had an army in the field, and Napoleon moved against it.[i]

The French emperor understood the intentions of the coalition forces and initiated a series of rapid and daring maneuvers. He feigned weakness, enticing the coalition to pursue him while he concentrated on his forces. He chose a battlefield at Austerlitz that offered significant advantages. The terrain included a gently sloping plateau known as the Pratzen Heights advantage.

The Battle of Austerlitz commenced on December 2nd, 1805. The coalition forces launched attacks on the French center, which Napoleon had deliberately weakened. The French right and left wings executed a well-coordinated counterattack, driving a wedge between the Russo-Austrian forces and isolating their left wing on the Pratzen Heights. Napoleon, using brilliant strategy and execution, destroyed the coalition army and gave the French a magnificent victory.[ii]

The Habsburgs were humiliated. The Treaty of Pressburg, signed on December 26th, 1805, shortly after the Battle of Austerlitz, formalized

---

[i] PBS.org. (2023, February 10). The Ulm-Austerlitz Campaign, 1805. Retrieved from PBS.org: https://www.pbs.org/empires/napoleon/n_war/campaign/page_6.html.

[ii] Mark, H. W. (2023, July 13). Battle of Austerlitz. Retrieved from World History Encyclopedia: https://www.worldhistory.org/article/2253/battle-of-austerlitz/.

both the terms of the armistice between Austria and France and Austria's shame. Austria ceded significant territories to France and its allies. This included the loss of Venetia (Venice and its territories), Tyrol, and other regions in northern Italy. Other Austrian lands were distributed among the French allies. The Holy Roman Empire, which the Habsburgs had governed for hundreds of years, was formally dissolved on August 6th, 1806, when Francis abdicated the throne.

Because of the defeat at Austerlitz, Austria underwent a period of military reorganization and reform. This period of reform aimed to address some of the shortcomings exposed at Austerlitz and prepare Austria for future conflicts. In the meantime, Austria was a defeated nation, and its military was discredited.

<u>Diplomatic Maneuvers</u>

Frustrated on the battlefield, the Habsburg rulers of Austria considered diplomacy to checkmate Napoleon. It would be challenging to find another skilled diplomat like Kaunitz, but Austria was fortunate to find an equally adept man at handling international negotiations.

Klemens von Metternich was skilled in diplomacy and rose through the ranks until he was made foreign minister of the Austrian Empire in 1809. He understood it would take more than cannons and bullets to defeat Napoleon. Subtle and effective diplomacy, combined with some luck, might achieve the goal.

Metternich faced many significant challenges from 1809 to 1814, the later stages of the Napoleonic Wars. These challenges tested his diplomatic skills and statesmanship as he navigated the complex and ever-shifting European political landscape. Maintaining a delicate balance in Austria's relations with Napoleon Bonaparte was a constant test. Metternich had to engage in diplomacy with the French emperor while safeguarding Austrian interests.

As Metternich decided what to do on the diplomatic front, events were unfolding that had terrible results for the Austrian Empire. The Fifth Coalition against Napoleon was formed. The War of the Fifth Coalition pitted Austria and its allies against the French. (There was a Fourth Coalition (1806–1807), but Austria did not participate.) Napoleon's victories at Aspern-Essling and Wagram forced the Austrians to sue for peace and endure another humiliation.

The Treaty of Schönbrunn, signed on October 14th, 1809, forced Austria to give up even more land, including access to the Adriatic Sea.

Austria was required to become part of Napoleon's Continental System and reduce its army to 150,000 men. A contemporary British magazine best summarized the impact of the treaty on Austria:

"This Treaty is certainly one of the most singular documents in the annals of diplomacy. We see a Christian King, calling himself the father of his people, disposing of 400,000 of his subjects, like swine in a market. We see a great and powerful Prince condescending to treat with his adversary for the brushwood of his own forests. We see the hereditary claimant of the Imperial Sceptre of Germany not only condescending to the past innovations on his own dominions, but assenting to any future alterations which the caprice or tyranny of his enemy may dictate with respect to his allies in Spain and Portugal, or to his neighbours in Italy. We see through the whole of this instrument the humiliation of the weak and unfortunate Francis, who has preferred the resignation of his fairest territories to restoring to his vassals their liberties, and giving them that interest in the public cause which their valour would have known how to protect."[i]

The Habsburgs had failed miserably on the battlefield. They next decided to use a strategy they had successfully used in the past: marriage.

<u>Marie Louise and Napoleon</u>

Napoleon divorced his wife Josephine on December 15th, 1809, for failing to produce a male heir. This dissolution created an irresistible opportunity that Metternich wanted to exploit. There was competition from Russia, though, as Napoleon had expressed a wish to marry Tsar Alexander I's sister. Despite that, Metternich used his diplomatic skills and flattery to convince Napoleon that the Austrian candidate, Archduchess Marie Louise, the daughter of Emperor Francis, was the best choice. The French emperor finally agreed, and the two were formally married on April 1st, 1810.

---

[i] Robertson, Angus. *The Crossroads of Civilization: A History of Vienna.* 2022.

Marriage of Napoleon I and Marie Louise. [47]

Metternich scored a major coup with the marriage. Firstly, it established a familial connection between the Austrian and French imperial houses, potentially providing a degree of influence and leverage in future negotiations with Napoleon. The marriage alliance also brought a temporary respite to the ongoing conflict between Austria and France. It allowed Austria to secure a period of relative stability and avoid further military confrontations with Napoleon. Austria desperately needed time to regroup, and Metternich was able to guarantee that.

Napoleon's Mistakes

The French were the dominant military power in Europe, and defeating Napoleon on the battlefield was nearly impossible. It appeared only the French emperor could defeat himself. And that is precisely what happened.

Napoleon made two major blunders that would destabilize his control over Europe. The first was his invasion of Spain in 1808. Napoleon overthrew the Bourbon monarchy, putting his brother Joseph on the Spanish throne. A guerilla war on the Iberian Peninsula broke out that tied up thousands of French soldiers who were needed elsewhere. The second error in judgment was the invasion of Russia in 1812.

Napoleon's Grande Armée was destroyed in the winter snow of Russia; only a tiny fraction of the soldiers made it back alive. The Russian debacle made Napoleon vulnerable. The Sixth Coalition was thus formed.

The War of the Sixth Coalition

The primary members of the Sixth Coalition were Austria, Prussia, Russia, Great Britain, Spain, Sweden, Portugal, and Sardinia. Its goal was to overthrow Napoleon. Metternich initially tried to mediate peace, but his proposal included dismantling the Confederation of the Rhine, which Napoleon refused to do. Formal declarations of war from the coalition members followed, and Austria declared war on France in August 1813.

The most significant battle of the War of the Sixth Coalition was the Battle of Leipzig, also known as the Battle of the Nations, fought from October 16th to October 19th, 1813. It was a massive confrontation involving hundreds of thousands of troops from both sides. It was a decisive coalition victory over Napoleon's forces and marked the war's turning point, as the defeat forced Napoleon to retreat from Germany.

Metternich tried one last time to broker a peace. The Frankfurt proposals were presented to Napoleon in November. The terms called for France to return to its borders as they existed before Napoleon's expansions, permitting France to keep Belgium, Savoy, and the Rhineland. Napoleon would have to withdraw French forces from various conquered territories in Europe.

Napoleon initially showed some interest in the Frankfurt proposals, as he recognized that his position had weakened considerably after the defeat at Leipzig. However, he sought to negotiate from a place of strength and attempted to buy time for his military efforts. Ultimately, the negotiations did not lead to a peace agreement.[i]

---

[i] Mark, H. W. (2023, September 4). War of the Sixth Coalition. Retrieved from World History Encyclopedia: https://www.worldhistory.org/War_of_the_Sixth_Coalition/.

The coalition finally invaded France and forced Napoleon to fall back to Paris. Napoleon was forced to abdicate, which he did on April 11th, 1814. The French threat was now gone, and the European powers would meet to redraw the continent's borders. The meeting, known as the Congress of Vienna, would be Metternich's finest hour.

<u>The New Europe</u>

The Congress of Vienna took place in Vienna, Austria, from September 1814 to June 1815. It aimed to reorganize Europe and establish a new balance of power in the continent. Representatives from Austria, Prussia, Russia, Spain, Great Britain, Portugal, Sweden, and France were in attendance.

A vital goal of the Congress of Vienna was to restore legitimate monarchs to their thrones. This would include the restoration of the Bourbon monarchy in France with Louis XVIII as king.

The Congress of Vienna intended to create a framework for stability and peaceful diplomacy in Europe. Its members understood a need for pragmatic solutions to prevent future conflicts.

The Congress of Vienna established the Concert of Europe, a series of international congresses and diplomatic meetings to resolve conflicts and maintain the balance of power in Europe. This system played a role in European diplomacy for several decades.

Significant territorial adjustments were made in Europe. Borders were redrawn, and some states gained or lost territories. Notable examples include the expansion of Prussia and the formation of the Kingdom of the Netherlands, which included the former Austrian Netherlands (Belgium).

Metternich's primary objective was to safeguard Austrian interests and restore the Habsburg monarchy to a position of prominence in Europe. He sought to regain territories lost during the Napoleonic Wars, particularly in Italy and central Europe. He advocated for establishing a balance of power in Europe to prevent any single state from becoming too dominant. This approach was instrumental in shaping the post-Napoleonic order.

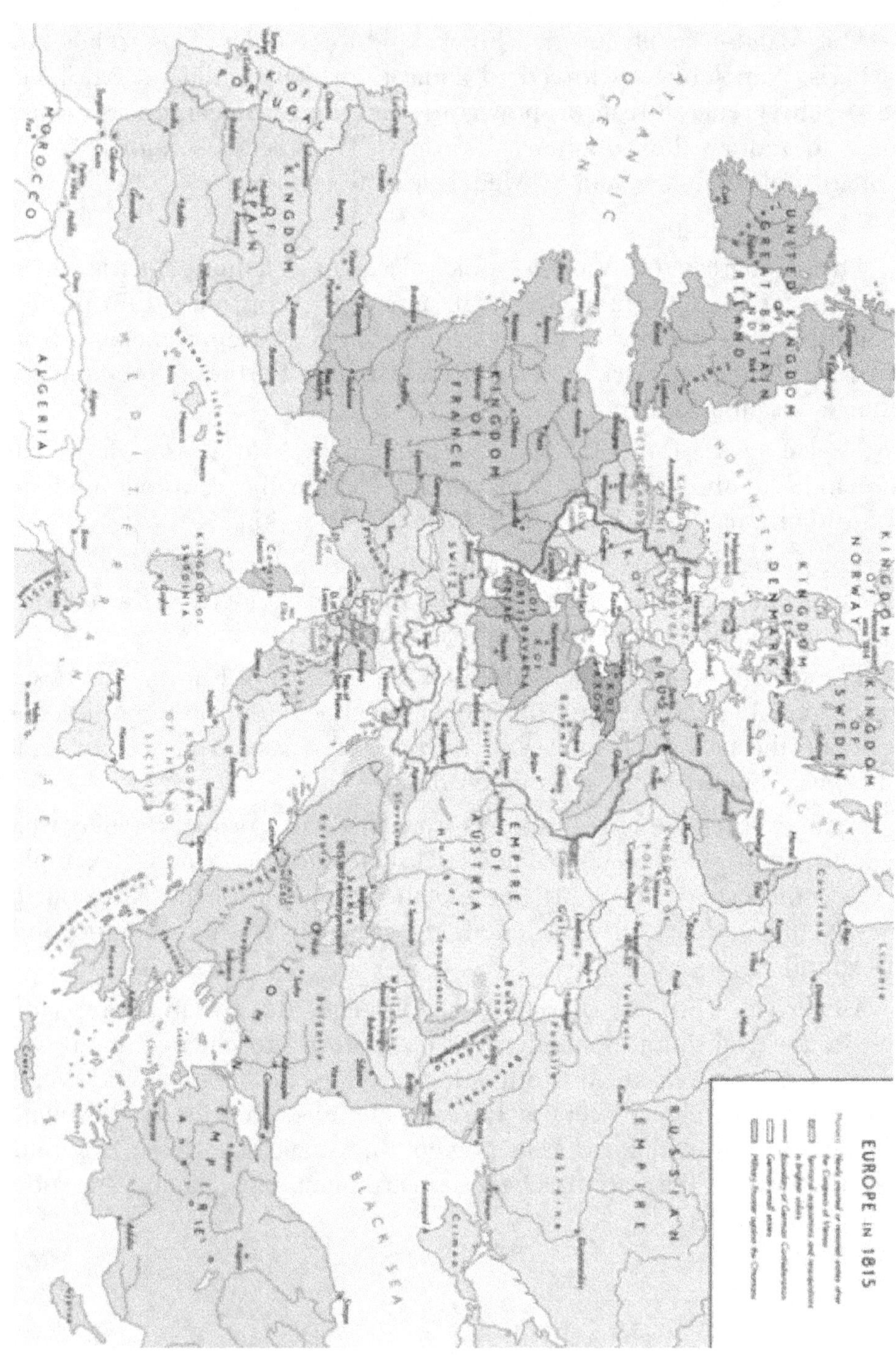

Europe after the Congress of Vienna. [48]

His negotiating skills enabled him to mediate disputes and engineer compromises successfully. Metternich would be a dominant figure in European politics for decades to come.[i]

Age of Metternich

The Age of Metternich represents a significant phase in European history that unfolded during the early to mid-19th century. It was a time of political upheaval and social change, marked by the aftermath of the Napoleonic Wars and the rise of nationalist and revolutionary movements.

Metternich's influence on European diplomacy and the balance of power was profound. His primary goals during this era were centered around maintaining conservative monarchies, containing revolutionary forces, and preserving the equilibrium of power among European nations.

Following the upheaval of the French Revolution and the Napoleonic Wars, many European monarchies had been threatened or overthrown. Metternich, representing the interests of the Austrian Empire and other conservative states, sought to restore and maintain these traditional monarchies. He believed that solid and legitimate monarchies were essential for stability and the preservation of the social hierarchy. Consequently, many exiled monarchs were restored to their thrones, and the influence of revolutionary movements was curtailed in many parts of Europe.

An essential means of maintaining stability during this period was the Concert of Europe. Major European powers cooperated diplomatically to address common issues and contributed to preserving the balance of power. This framework facilitated discussions and negotiations, reducing the likelihood of significant conflicts. One negative result was that the more conservative members used the Concert of Europe to restrict liberal movements.

While it cannot be denied that this era suppressed liberal and nationalist aspirations, it also brought relative stability to a continent that had been in turmoil for years. Klemens von Metternich's diplomatic efforts and policies left a lasting mark on European politics and paved the way for a more peaceful, albeit complex, era in European history.

---

[i] History Guild. (2023, November 11). The Congress of Vienna. Retrieved from Historyguid.org: https://historyguild.org/the-congress-of-vienna/.

Under Metternich's influence, the Austrian Empire became a bastion of European conservatism. Austria was a key player in the Holy Alliance, which sought to maintain the conservative order in Europe. The Holy Alliance was a coalition of European monarchies formed after the Napoleonic Wars to promote conservative principles, suppress revolutionary movements, and maintain peace. While it did help to maintain the status quo, the day finally came when the Holy Alliance could no longer hold back the tide of liberalism. Habsburg Austria was caught up in the current.

Chapter 11: The Dual Monarchy

The Dual Monarchy, known as Kiegyezés in Hungarian, was a pivotal moment in the history of the Habsburg Empire. The Austro-Hungarian Compromise of 1867 created a dual monarchy, transforming the Austrian Empire into the Austro-Hungarian Empire. The compromise was a response to growing nationalist sentiments within the Austrian Empire and sought to balance the aspirations of the Austrian and Hungarian populations while maintaining Habsburg rule.

<u>Revolution in the Air</u>

To understand the Austro-Hungarian Compromise of 1867, one must first grasp the turbulent history of the Habsburg Empire in the 19th century. The empire was a vast, multi-ethnic state that included numerous nationalities, languages, and cultures. The Habsburg rulers faced the challenge of governing these diverse territories while preserving the power and unity of the empire.

Klemens von Metternich wanted to create stability in a Europe that had been devastated by the Napoleonic Wars. His model of governance had a reactionary design because he believed that the status quo ensured peace and quiet. The Austrian statesman hoped to create a lasting era of peace, but he would be disappointed.

The French Revolution and the Napoleonic era unleashed a yearning for greater personal freedom and the end of authoritative monarchies. Despite the Congress of Vienna and the harsh repression of European monarchies, the desire for liberty, equality, and fraternity was in the air. The French Revolution had let the genie out of the bottle, and it refused to go back in.

<u>The Status of the Austrian Empire</u>

The Austrian Empire, which was under the rule of the Habsburg dynasty in the early 19th century, was a multi-ethnic conglomerate consisting of various nationalities, including Germans, Hungarians, Czechs, Poles, Italians, and many others. This diversity created a complex political and social landscape, with different ethnic groups often asserting their distinct identities and demands.

Emperor Francis I and his successor presided over an absolutist monarchy characterized by centralized control and limited political representation. Dissatisfaction with the conservative and autocratic regime simmered among various segments of the population, setting the stage for revolutionary movements.

The Habsburgs did enact some reforms in the 1830s. However, these reforms were insufficient to address the deep-seated issues of national identity and political representation. The Habsburg monarchy remained the absolute power, and discontent continued to simmer beneath the surface.

Yet, the Austrian Empire also experienced economic growth and prosperity. The population of the empire increased, and the significant budget deficits caused by the Napoleonic Wars were nearly erased.

<u>1848, Annus Revolutionis</u>

A local uprising in January 1848 in Sicily spread like a forest fire to France, Germany, Italy, and Austria. These revolts sought to challenge established monarchies. Uprisings occurred throughout the Austrian Empire. Groups wanted to achieve either independence or greater autonomy. On March 13th, 1848, Metternich was forced to resign. A series of liberal governments followed, but the political situation continued to get out of control.

Austria's forces had to confront a volatile situation in northern Italy, and there was also unrest in Bohemia. The insurgents in northern Italy were defeated by Field Marshal Joseph Radetzky in 1849, and a period of repression in Lombardy-Venetia sponsored by the Austrians was severe. The trouble in Prague was put down, but Austria faced a more significant problem that, if unresolved, would tear the empire to pieces.

<u>The Hungarian Question</u>

Hungary was a diverse and multi-ethnic region within the Austrian Empire, encompassing not only ethnic Hungarians but also various minority groups, including Slovaks, Croats, Serbs, and Romanians. This ethnic diversity added complexity to Hungary's quest for autonomy and self-determination. The Hungarian Diet wielded significant power within the kingdom, and Hungary enjoyed a degree of independence in domestic affairs.

There had been some economic hardships in Hungary, which sparked discontent. A larger instigator of unrest was the spread of liberal ideas in a land where aristocrats ruled. On March 15th, 1848, Hungarian intellectuals, including Lajos Kossuth, met in Pest and drafted a revolutionary document called the Twelve Points.

The brainchild of Sándor Petőfi, the Twelve Points were a call for individual liberties and a practical blueprint for a nation. Petőfi insisted on freedom of the press and no more censorship. He also demanded the end of separate laws for the nobility and equality under the law. Religious liberty should be granted; the days of state-sponsored religion would be over. The final vestiges of the feudal system, particularly serfdom, were to be done away with.

The ideas for a nation-state were dramatic. The Twelve Points insisted that Hungary be a nation and not a part of the Austrian Empire. A national bank and a separate currency would be instituted along with an independent government with a national assembly of members whom the people elected, not the aristocracy.

The demands were presented to a weakened Austrian government, which initially accepted the demands on April 11th, 1848. Lajos Kossuth emerged as a charismatic leader of the Hungarian Revolution. His impassioned speeches and emotional commitment to Hungarian independence galvanized support for the cause. Ultimately, Kossuth declared an independent Kingdom of Hungary.[i]

---

[i] Sellers, W. (2023, March 13). Opinion: The Forgotten Hungarian Revolution. Retrieved from Alabama Political Reporter: https://www.alreporter.com/2023/03/13/opinion-the-forgotten-hungarian-revolution/.

Kossuth inspiring followers in a speech he gave in 1848. [49]

A significant problem with all of this was the way the Hungarians treated ethnic minorities. There were many ethnic groups in Hungary, but most of their needs were largely ignored. Croats, Slovaks, Serbs, and other groups within Hungary preferred the protection of the central government in Vienna. War broke out in the autumn of 1848 as Hungarians fought the Austrians and Croats.

Austria finally appealed to Russia for help. Russian troops assisted in ending the armed conflict in Hungary. The Hungarian attempt at liberty was officially over, but there were still issues that desperately needed to be addressed. The Austrian Empire could not exist in its current form, and its many minorities would continue to insist on some degree of independence. Vienna knew there had to be a resolution to the problems that surfaced in 1848.[i]

---

[i] Heritage History. (2023, October 30). Hungarian Revolution. Retrieved from Heritage-History.com: https://www.heritage-history.com/index.php?c=resources&s=war-dir&f=wars_hungarian.

<u>Franz Joseph, The Last Best Hope of the Habsburgs</u>

Russian regiments restored calm in the Austrian Empire, but they could not restore the status quo. The past imperial authority had been violently compromised. Hungary was another war waiting to happen, and other ethnic minorities were demanding concessions. The Habsburgs had to come up with a workable answer to the problems the 1848 unrest brought out of the shadows.

In the past, the Habsburgs were able to produce a monarch at critical times to meet impossible challenges. This happened in 1848 when Franz Joseph became the Austrian emperor. He was eighteen years old, but he quickly showed he had the maturity of someone twenty years older. Franz Joseph understood the gravity of the situation and the potential threat posed by the revolutionary movements.

He initially sought to maintain the traditional absolute monarchy and resist the demands for constitutional reforms and national self-determination. He was proclaimed emperor on December 2nd, 1848, after the former emperor, Ferdinand, abdicated. That abdication was the final act in a year in which the old order had been purged. Metternich had resigned, and Emperor Ferdinand approved a Hungarian constitution, which kept the emperor as monarch; that constitution was suspended in 1849. The arrival of Russian troops ended the crisis in Hungary. Unfortunately, Franz Joseph had a new set of problems to the south in Italy.

Franz Joseph in 1892. [50]

<u>Creation of the Italian State</u>

The 1848 revolutionary wave that swept across Europe reached the Italian states, and many Italians sought to overthrow their rulers and establish independent, unified nation-states. The Lombardy-Venetia region was a particular hotspot for revolutionary activity.

The First Italian War of Independence started in 1848 with rebellions in Milan and Venice. On March 23rd, 1848, the Kingdom of Sardinia-Piedmont, led by King Charles Albert, declared war on Austria, intending to liberate northern Italy from Habsburg rule. Franz Joseph was able to win this contest, but one of the Italian leaders, Giuseppe Garibaldi, would give the Austrians headaches in the future.

Italy was caught up in a revolutionary spirit known as irredentism, which called for the liberation of Italians living under foreign rule and their incorporation into a unified Italian state. This meant the Habsburg possessions in Italy would be targeted.

Austria also faced France in the Second War of Italian Independence. Fighting against the French was a hopeless situation, and the Battle of Solferino on June 24th, 1859, saw Austria give Lombardy to France, which, in turn, transferred the territory to Sardinia.

Meanwhile, the situation in Hungary was still simmering in the background.

<u>An Untenable Situation</u>

Austria had Hungary under tight military control after the Hungarian Revolution of 1848, but the people in Hungary had not calmed down. The status quo was no longer something that could be maintained. Either some agreement had to be reached, or Austria would be continually fighting to keep control over Hungary. The latter was an expensive option, and Austria could not afford the cost.[i]

The threat of non-stop warfare was not the only motivation behind a permanent solution. Emperor Franz Joseph wanted to maintain the unity and stability of the Austrian Empire. He recognized that the empire faced significant challenges, including the rise of Hungarian nationalism. By agreeing to a compromise, he aimed to secure Hungary's loyalty and cooperation, which would contribute to the empire's stability.

---

[i] DBpedia.org. (2023, October 30). Austro-Hungarian Compromise of 1867. Retrieved from DBpedia.org: https://dbpedia.org/page/Austro-Hungarian_Compromise_of_1867.

Economic considerations also played a role. Hungary, with its fertile lands and agricultural resources, sought control over economic policies that would benefit its own economy. This was particularly important given Hungary's rustic nature.

<u>The Negotiators</u>

Emperor Franz Joseph relied on Friedrich Ferdinand von Beust to navigate the complexities of the negotiations. Von Beust was motivated by the emperor's objectives, seeking a compromise that would satisfy Hungarian demands while preserving the Habsburg monarchy's influence in foreign affairs and defense.

The principal Hungarian negotiators were Ferenc Deák and Count Gyula Andrássy. Deák is often referred to as the "Sage of the Country" and was a prominent Hungarian statesman. His primary motive was to secure greater political and economic autonomy for Hungary. He was a moderate nationalist who believed that cooperation with the Habsburg monarchy was more beneficial than outright separatism.

Andrássy advocated for a compromise that would grant Hungary substantial autonomy. His motives were aligned with Deák's in seeking a peaceful resolution to the Hungarian question. He believed securing Hungary's rights and privileges through negotiation was preferable to risking armed conflict.

What is significant about the negotiations is that there were no strong adversaries at the table. Both sides wanted to avoid war, and everyone was looking for an agreeable way in which Austria and Hungary could still maintain a relationship while giving the latter greater autonomy than before.

<u>The Ausgleich</u>

The year 1866 was a terrible one for Austria. It was involved in the Third Italian War of Independence and fought against the Kingdom of Italy, which was supported by Prussia. Furthermore, Austria was fighting Prussia in the Austro-Prussian War. By the time the shooting stopped, Austria had ceded Venetia to France, which then handed it over to Italy. This marked another significant loss of Italian territories under Franz Joseph's rule. The next year, 1867, would be much better for Austria and the Habsburgs.

The Austro-Hungarian Compromise of 1867, also known as the Ausgleich, was a pivotal event in the history of the Habsburg monarchy. This compromise established the dual monarchy of Austria-Hungary, transforming the political structure of the Austrian Empire. The Austria-Hungary Compromise of 1867 consisted of several key points.

- Establishment of the Dual Monarchy: The Austro-Hungarian Compromise recognized Austria and Hungary as two separate yet equal states within a shared monarchy. Emperor Franz Joseph I remained the common head of state, serving as the emperor of Austria and the king of Hungary.

- Hungarian autonomy: Hungary was granted considerable autonomy in domestic affairs. It had its own parliament (the Diet), government, and legal system, allowing Hungarians to legislate and administer their internal affairs independently.

- Shared institutions: While domestic affairs were largely the purview of each state, certain areas were managed jointly, like foreign policy, defense, and finance. Shared ministerial councils, known as common ministry councils, were established to oversee these shared matters.

- Language rights: The Austro-Hungarian Compromise recognized the Hungarian language alongside German as an official language of the empire, signifying the linguistic diversity within Austria-Hungary.

A compromise only happens when both sides concede points to arrive at a consensus. Austria acknowledged Hungary's autonomy in domestic affairs, allowing the Hungarian Diet to legislate and govern independently. Austria also recognized the restoration of Hungary's historic constitution and the Hungarian legal system. Hungary recognized the Habsburg monarchy and Emperor Franz Joseph I as the common ruler. Hungarian leaders agreed to participate in the common ministries responsible for foreign affairs, defense, and finance, in which they had a say but did not hold absolute control.[i]

[i] Study.com. (2023, October 30). The Dual Monarchy of Austria-Hungary. Retrieved from Study.com: https://study.com/learn/lesson/hungarian-austrian-dual-monarchy-ausgleich.html#:~:text=The%20Ausgleich%2C%20or%20the%20formal,Ferenc%20Deak%2C%20and%20other%20delegates.

The Austro-Hungarian Compromise of 1867 had significant long-term consequences:

- Stability: In the short term, the compromise provided a degree of peace to the Habsburg monarchy by addressing the Hungarian question and providing a framework for governance.

- Nationalism and ethnic tensions: While the compromise successfully quelled immediate nationalist demands, it did not fully address the underlying ethnic and national tensions within the empire. The multinational character of Austria-Hungary continued to be a source of conflict and discontent.

Unfortunately, the compromise created an asymmetrical structure, with Hungary having more autonomy and influence in domestic affairs than Austria. This imbalance fueled resentment and tensions within the empire.

The Austro-Hungarian Compromise's legacy is marked by the precarious coexistence of diverse ethnic groups and the eventual dissolution of Austria-Hungary in the aftermath of World War I, which marked the end of the Habsburg monarchy.

Chapter 12: The End of the Habsburg Dynasty

The Austro-Prussian War was short, and it heralded the end of an era in central European history. Austria was no longer the premier German state; the new Kingdom of Germany had replaced it. The Habsburg Empire was now Austria-Hungary. It was still an enormous state in Europe, but Great Britain, France, and Germany now contested for pride of place. The Habsburgs' power was eclipsed, but that did not mean their empire was a backwater. Austria-Hungary would play a significant role in the cultural and intellectual life of Europe in the late 19th century.

<u>The Cultural Mecca of Europe</u>

Vienna, the capital of the Habsburg Empire, emerged as a vibrant cultural hub during the late 19th and early 20th centuries. It is often referred to as the "City of Dreams." Vienna experienced a remarkable cultural renaissance in the late 19th and early 20th centuries. This period, known as the "Viennese fin de siècle ("end of the century"), was characterized by a flourishing of artistic, intellectual, and social movements that propelled the city onto the global stage. A convergence of factors, such as political stability, imperial patronage, and a rich cultural tradition, gave rise to Vienna's prominence as a cultural hub.

At the end of the 19th century, Vienna was the destination for many of the empire's subjects. Italians, Slovaks, Poles, Slovenians, Moravians, Germans, and Slovaks immigrated to the capital city, attracted by its many opportunities. In 1910, Vienna had a population of two million and was a liberal and cosmopolitan center. The Viennese melting pot welcomed universal forms of communication and artistic expression.[i]

<u>The Arts</u>

The Vienna Secession was a groundbreaking art movement that emerged in 1897 as a reaction against academic conservatism. It was the formal beginning of modern art in a country with a conservative tradition. Led by a group of avant-garde artists, including Gustav Klimt, Koloman Moser, and Josef Hoffmann, the Secessionists sought to break free from traditional artistic norms. Their motto, "To each age its art, and to art its freedom," encapsulated their desire for creative autonomy. The work of this art group is the Austrian version of the Art Nouveau style of painting.

The Vienna Secession was known for intricate symbolism, sensuality, and decorative patterns. The Secessionists built the first permanent exhibition space dedicated to displaying contemporary art, which still exists.[ii]

The Kiss by Gustav Klimt. [51]

[i] The Economist. (2016, December 24). How Vienna Produced Ideas That Shaped the West. Retrieved from Economist.com: https://www.economist.com/christmas-specials/2016/12/24/how-vienna-produced-ideas-that-shaped-the-west.

[ii] The Art Story. (20232, October 31). Summary of the Vienna Secession. Retrieved from Theartsotry.org: https://www.theartstory.org/movement/vienna-secession/.

Die Musik

Vienna's significance in music has been undeniable throughout history, particularly during the late 19th and early 20th centuries. This period witnessed a dynamic interplay of traditionalism and innovation, exemplified by the composers who either adhered to or challenged established norms. From late Romanticism to the pioneering works of the Second Viennese School, Vienna stood at the forefront of musical exploration. It earned its title as "The City of Music."

The late 19th century in Vienna was marked by the presence of Johannes Brahms, a composer known for his mastery of classical forms and profound emotional depth. Brahms, with his four symphonies, numerous chamber works, and songs, played a pivotal role in preserving and advancing the Romantic tradition. Brahams was both a traditionalist and an innovator. He followed the basic structures of the Classical tradition but used the intense expression of the Romantic movement when creating his works.[i]

Johann Strauss II was a composer of light music that is still immensely popular. Referred to as the "Waltz King," Strauss is one of the most iconic figures in the history of Viennese music. His music and compositions are closely associated with Vienna, and he played a pivotal role in shaping the city's musical and cultural identity during the 19th century.

His melodies were known for their charm, elegance, and infectious rhythms, making them immensely popular at social events and balls. Strauss also composed operettas, light operas known for their humor and catchy tunes. His most famous operetta, *Die Fledermaus* (*The Bat*), premiered in 1874 and remains a staple of the operetta repertoire. "The Blue Danube" is known by most people today. His waltzes continue to have public appeal.

Johann Strauss II's music became synonymous with the elegance, grace, and joie de vivre of Viennese society during the 19th century. His compositions captured the spirit of the city and reflected the optimism and charm of the Habsburg era. The music he wrote was a central part of Vienna's vibrant ball culture. His compositions were featured at countless

---

[i] Classicfm.com. (2023, October 31). Johannes Brahms. Retrieved from Classicfm.com: https://www.classicfm.com/composers/brahms/.

balls, including the famous Vienna Opera Ball.[i]

There were significant venues where the music of Vienna was performed. The Vienna Philharmonic, founded in 1842, was a vital institution. It became renowned for its annual New Year's Concert, which celebrated the Strauss family's waltzes and other Viennese classics. The Vienna State Opera was a premier venue for operatic performances. During this period, it showcased works by composers of the day, including Richard Strauss and Gustav Mahler.

Intellectual Discourse

Vienna's cultural renaissance extended beyond the visual arts to encompass literature, philosophy, and music. The city was home to some of the most influential intellectual circles in Europe. The city's coffeehouses, such as Café Central and Café Griensteidl, served as meeting places for artists, musicians, and intellectuals. These establishments facilitated the exchange of ideas and contributed to the city's vibrant cultural scene.

The Vienna Circle originated in 1907 and began to formulate philosophical concepts of a positivist view of science. The psychoanalytic movement, which started in Vienna, produced substantial insights into psychology and the study of human behavior.

Sigmund Freud is considered the father of psychoanalysis. He developed a groundbreaking approach to understanding the human mind, which he initially called the "talking cure." Freud's theory emphasized the role of the unconscious mind and the impact of repressed thoughts, memories, and desires on an individual's behavior. His work challenged prevailing psychological and psychiatric paradigms. The concept of the "talking cure" involved free association and open dialog to explore a patient's unconscious thoughts and emotions. This approach aimed to uncover repressed traumas and conflicts, thereby providing insight and relief to individuals suffering from mental disorders.[ii]

---

[i] Classicfm.com. (2023, October 31). Johann Strauss II: A Life. Retrieved from Classicfm.com: https://www.classicfm.com/composers/strauss-ii/guides/johann-strauss-ii-life/.

[ii] Christopher Marx, C. B. (2017, September 17). Talking Cure Models: A Framework of Analysis. Retrieved from National Library of Medicine:
https://www.ncbi.nlm.nih.gov/pmc/articles/PMC5601393/#:~:text=The%20%E2%80%9Ctalking%20cure%2C%E2%80%9D%20then,the%20patient%20from%20hysteric%20symptoms.

Freud's colleagues and students, including Carl Jung, Alfred Adler, and Otto Rank, played significant roles in developing psychoanalysis as a field of study and clinical practice. The psychoanalytic movement of the late 19th century was a revolutionary development in psychology and the understanding of the human mind. This movement laid the foundation for modern psychoanalysis and profoundly influenced the fields of psychology, psychiatry, and psychotherapy. It was part of the exciting time of expression and innovative thoughts that made Vienna and Habsburg Austria-Hungary shine.

<u>The Creeping Shadows</u>

Cabaret is a popular musical that depicts café society with all its delights and sophistication. It is juxtaposed against the fall of the Weimar Republic and the militancy of national socialism. This is nearly the same setting for late Habsburg society. Vienna's cultural vitality in the late 19th and early 20th centuries was a testament to the city's ability to foster artistic, intellectual, and musical innovation. The energy and vitality distracted people's attention from what was happening outside of the cultural circles.

Europe had not seen a major conflict since the Franco-Prussian War. There were localized wars in the Balkans, but nothing compared to the Napoleonic Wars. The happy scenes were soon to come to an end as the twilight years of the Habsburgs began.

<u>Prelude to a War</u>

The period from 1900 to 1914 was marked by a complex interplay of political, diplomatic, economic, and military factors in Europe that contributed to the outbreak of World War I. Austria-Hungary, under the rule of Emperor Franz Joseph, was a central player in the events that led to the war. While Franz Joseph might not have been personally seeking war, his actions and policies did not prevent the escalation of tensions.

The major European powers, including Austria-Hungary, were engaged in imperial rivalries and competition for colonial territories. This animosity created tensions between these powers, especially Germany, France, and Great Britain.

The complex system of alliances, such as the Triple Entente (France, Russia, and Great Britain) and the Triple Alliance (Germany, Austria-Hungary, and Italy), created a situation where a regional conflict could quickly escalate into a larger war. Austria-Hungary had the support of Germany, while Serbia had the backing of Russia.

The Balkans

Balkan nationalists saw an opportunity with the decay of the Ottoman Empire to end hundreds of years of Turkish control. Several wars, beginning in 1912, saw various regions in the Balkans struggle for independence or border expansion. It was not just the Ottomans versus the Christians; Bulgaria, Serbia, and Romania were also locked in intense struggles with each other.[i]

The region was not stable, and there was an opportunity for Austria-Hungary to make territorial gains. This was risky because fervent nationalism was driving emotions to agitated states. Despite the potential hazards, Austria-Hungary annexed Bosnia and Herzegovina in 1908, which angered Serbia.

The major alliances had interests in the Balkans. Russia had a historical and cultural connection to the Slavic peoples of the Balkans, particularly in Serbia. France had historical alliances with Russia, and Great Britain was concerned about maintaining the balance of power in Europe.

The Major Alliances Drift toward War

Barbara Tuchman's book *The Guns of August* provides a detailed analysis of the relationships between the Triple Entente and the Triple Alliance in the years leading up to the outbreak of World War I. The leaders within both alliances made assumptions about their adversaries' intentions, which played a role in the escalation of tensions.

A naval arms race already existed between Germany and Great Britain. Germany's expansion of its High Seas Fleet and Great Britain's response with the construction of new battleships added to the overall sense of insecurity. Detailed war plans, such as the Schlieffen Plan in Germany, were created with the assumption of an impending conflict. These plans involved complex timetables and troop movements that required meticulous execution.

Military posturing was rapidly replacing pragmatic diplomacy in resolving differences. A fundamental assumption was that alliances were a deterrent to war. The possibility of a chain reaction, including mobilizations and counter-mobilizations, was viewed as making the

---

[i] Hall, R. C. (2018, April 4). War in the Balkans. Retrieved from International Encyclopedia of the First World War: https://encyclopedia.1914-1918-online.net/article/war_in_the_balkans.

outbreak of a major war unlikely. Only a madman would start the martial ball rolling. Perhaps all it would take was a passionate nationalist.

The Shot Heard 'Round the World

Gavrilo Princip was a teenage member of the Young Bosnia movement. Learning that the heir to the throne of Austria-Hungary, Archduke Ferdinand, and his wife were paying a visit to Sarajevo, Bosnia, Princip and his comrades hatched a plan to assassinate the archduke. The conspirators made their way to Sarajevo. On June 28th, 1914, after multiple attempts by the assassins, Princip fired his pistol at point-blank range and killed the couple.

Austria-Hungary blamed Serbia for the assassination and issued an ultimatum on July 23rd, 1914 (the July Ultimatum) that, if not met, would result in war. Russia made it clear that it would support Serbia. Austria-Hungary sought assurances from Germany of support, which were granted. One month after the death of Archduke Ferdinand, on July 28th, Austria-Hungary declared war on Serbia. Germany, France, Russia, and Great Britain then issued declarations of war. World War I began.[i]

Emperor Franz Joseph of Austria-Hungary was not the principal instigator of the conflict, but his leadership and decisions as the monarch of Austria-Hungary were instrumental in the chain of events that led to the outbreak of war. Rather than actively pursue diplomatic solutions to the crisis, Franz Joseph and his government opted for a path of military action against Serbia.

Austria-Hungary in World War I

Austria-Hungary played a significant role in World War I as one of the Central Powers (Germany, Austria-Hungary, Bulgaria, and the Ottoman Empire). The empire faced numerous challenges on various fronts. Austria-Hungary was heavily involved in the Eastern Front of the war, where it faced off against Russia. The eastern theater of the war saw significant fighting, and Austria-Hungary struggled with the vast expanse of the front and the pressure exerted by the Russian army.

Austria-Hungary also dealt with the Italians. Italy, which was initially a member of the Triple Alliance but later switched sides to join the Triple Entente, declared war on Austria-Hungary on May 23rd, 1915. The two

---

[i] History. (2021, June 25). Austria's Archduke Ferdinand Assassinated. Retrieved from History.com: https://www.history.com/this-day-in-history/archduke-ferdinand-assassinated.

countries confronted each other in an Alpine war that mirrored the Western Front in its stalemates.

Austria-Hungary faced significant military challenges during the war. Its forces struggled on multiple fronts, and the empire's military and logistical capabilities were stretched thin. The Dual Monarchy often relied on German support, particularly from 1917 onward.

The war imposed a heavy economic and social burden on Austria-Hungary. The empire faced shortages of food and supplies, which led to discontent and unrest among the civilian population.

Emperor Franz Joseph, who had ruled for over six decades, died on November 21st, 1916. He was succeeded by his grandnephew, Charles I, who attempted to seek a separate peace with the Triple Entente. However, these efforts were unsuccessful, and Austria-Hungary remained committed to its alliance with Germany.

By 1918, Austria-Hungary was in a state of disarray. Its armies were on the retreat on multiple fronts, and the internal cohesion of the empire was eroding due to ethnic tensions and nationalist movements. It was increasingly clear that Austria-Hungary was going to lose the war. Strikes and street demonstrations served to drive the final nail into the coffin. On October 17th, 1918, the Hungarian Parliament declared Hungary's independence, effectively dissolving the Austro-Hungarian Empire.

The Final Dissolution

With the dissolution of the empire and the signing of the Armistice of Villa Giusti with Italy on November 3rd, 1918, Austria-Hungary effectively withdrew from World War I. Charles I went into exile, and the empire disintegrated into several successor states.

The end of the empire became official with the Treaty of Saint-Germain-en-Laye on September 10th, 1919, and the Treaty of Trianon on June 4th, 1920. Austria lost 60 percent of its old territory, and Hungary lost 72 percent of its former territory. The land was divided among several existing nations, and new states were created. Austria passed the Habsburg Law on April 3rd, 1919, which dethroned the Habsburgs and banished them from all Austrian territory.

Austria's association with the Habsburg dynasty, which had existed for hundreds of years, was over. All that was left of the Habsburgs were the magnificent palaces, the stunning art collections, and the beautiful music. All their political power was gone.

The dissolution of Austria-Hungary after WWI. [53]

Conclusion

The Habsburg dynasty lasted longer than many ruling families. Hundreds of years of Habsburg rule in central Europe created countries and instituted policies that impacted the modern era. The influence the Habsburgs had on the culture and the politics of Europe and beyond is significant.

Although the Habsburgs did engage in war, their greatest success came with diplomacy. They used marriages and treaties to gain more with less bloodshed. It reminds us that negotiations can be more effective than guns and bullets.

The cultural gifts that the Habsburgs left were tremendous. We can still view the artwork and the architecture the Habsburgs commissioned. It is thanks in part to the Habsburgs that astronomy progressed beyond the opinion of Aristotle and is based more on science and mathematics than Christianity. We are the beneficiaries of the patronage that the Habsburgs generously provided.

Unfortunately for the Habsburgs, diplomacy finally failed them in the early years of the 20th century. The Habsburgs fell victim to nationalism and extreme policies that made war the only way to resolve issues.

The Habsburgs were a unique ruling family in Europe's history. They added more to Western civilization than they ever took from it. Anyone who has seen the Schönbrunn Palace in Vienna or El Escorial in Spain will know that. The family legacy provided new standards for culture and the arts, and they were an amazing line of monarchs. They were prominent contributors to Western civilization.

Part 3: History of Prussia

An Enthralling Overview of Major Events and Figures in Prussian History

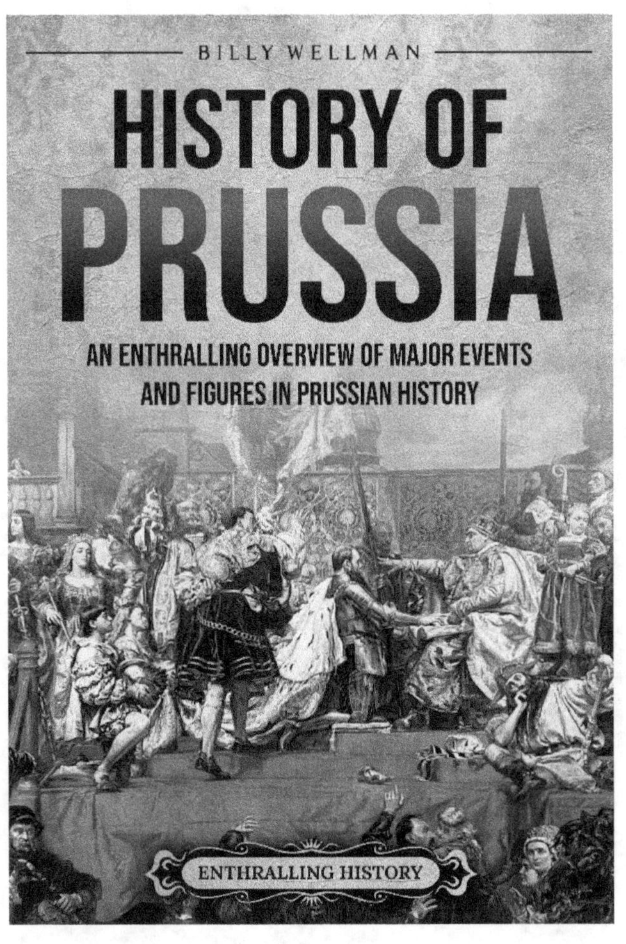

Introduction

Prussia no longer exists, but it is not an ancient nation. The memory of Prussia actually still lives vividly in the minds of many Germans, Poles, and Russians, and that memory is met with equal parts heartache, headache, and indifference. This book will explore the history of the land that would become Prussia, the people who inhabited it, and the dramatic collapse of this nation that was once among the most powerful in Europe.

Prussia's erasure from the map was so thorough that even its heartland has been absorbed into a different country entirely. The core of what was once Prussia is now the Kaliningrad Oblast, a Russian province separated from the rest of Russia by hundreds of miles and wedged between Lithuania, Poland, and the Baltic Sea. The city that was once Königsberg—Prussia's intellectual and cultural capital—is now Kaliningrad, and its streets are filled with Russian speakers rather than German ones. Germans maintain the strongest cultural memory of this land, but with Kaliningrad's overwhelmingly Russian population, any return to its former identity seems a distant dream. Prussia exists now only in history, in memory, and in the long shadow it casts across European politics.

Chapter 1: Origins and Foundations of Prussia

Baltic Tribes 1200 CE. [58]

The people who occupied the region that bore their name for the longest period were a group known as the "Old Prussians." These people spoke a common Baltic language, also known as Old Prussian, and were made up of several tribes, including the Sambians, Bartians, Nadruvians, and Pomesanians, among others. Their occupation of the land called Prussia and Brandenburg has been documented from the Iron Age (the 5th century BCE) until the Middle Ages. They worshiped pagan deities, which would eventually be used by others as the justification for conquering their land and converting them to Christianity.

The Romans knew of the Baltic tribes, whom they called the Aesti, meaning easterners, which was what their German neighbors called them. The Balts collected amber on the seashore, which was generally worthless to them but was worth more than gold to the Romans, who traded for it through German intermediaries. In exchange for amber, the Old Prussians received iron, weapons, Roman coins, and jewelry. Still, due to the long distance from the Baltic tribal lands to Rome, there is little Roman documentation about the details of how the Old Prussians lived. It is generally accepted that the Old Prussians were native to the area, but this, too, remains unknown for certain.

In the Early Middle Ages, more detailed descriptions of these people emerged. Legend says that the Old Prussians were brought together by a pair of brothers, Widewuto and Bruteno, who came from overseas. Widewuto was elected the *kriwe-kriwajto*, the highest leader among the Old Prussians and the intermediary between gods and men. He was obeyed by all the Baltic tribes; he would be similar to the pope of the Catholic Church. The other brother, Bruteno, instructed the people to worship the gods Patrimpas (god of spring and fertility), Perkūnas (god of thunder and justice), and Patulas (god of death). Images of these gods were placed in the trunk of an evergreen oak that grew in the holy place of Romuva, where the kriwe-kriwajto lived. The Old Prussian nobles would meet in this holy grove to make decisions on war and rule.

The Latvians were neighbors of the Old Prussians, and in Latvia, there is a place named Romuva, or the place of peace. It is believed that this was a common name for holy locations. In Romuva, no trees were cut down, no animals were hunted, and people could make sacrifices to the three high gods and possibly to the creator of everything, Deivs, who created the lesser gods and started the engine of the world.

The Old Prussians also worshiped a host of lesser gods, including a god of corn, a god of health, and *berzduki* and *markopoli*, which were house gnomes and spirits, respectively. Priests and priestesses were unmarried or widowed men and women who carried out religious rituals, including the sacrificing of animals, spoils of war, and, during hard periods, captives. They also blessed the land and dwellings and acted as teachers, soothsayers, and seers. Many of the priests lived with the kriwe-kriwajto in Romuva.

Legend says that when Bruteno and Widewuto reached a hundred years of age, they divided the land among Widewuto's sons. They told their people to remain peaceful and honor their gods, and then they climbed onto a funeral pyre in Romuva and sacrificed themselves for their people. The people elected a new kriwe-kriwajto from among their ranks.

According to Old Prussian beliefs, the brothers ascended to the world of the gods through fire. This was why the Old Prussians burned their dead, along with their weapons and tools, and why they sacrificed humans to appease the gods.

Bruteno and Widewuto were then worshiped as gods of farming, especially livestock. Stone images of the brothers were placed to mark the borders of various tribal lands. The Old Prussians remained true to their promise to the brothers, and the tribes remained peaceful with each other. When they were threatened, they banded together to fight off their common enemy.

The early history of the Old Prussians before the 10th century remains shrouded in mystery. We know they traded amber with the Romans through Germanic intermediaries and that this valuable trade brought them into contact—and likely conflict—with neighboring peoples. Later medieval chronicles and legends speak of ancient battles with Slavic tribes and invasions from all directions, but separating historical fact from folklore is nearly impossible with the limited sources available. What is clear is that by the time written records became more reliable in the late 10th century, the Old Prussians had established themselves as a fierce and independent people who would resist outside control for centuries to come.

The question of outside influences on Old Prussian culture remains debated among historians. From across the Baltic Sea came Scandinavian Vikings. The extent and nature of their presence in Prussia are not completely understood. Some historians, citing archaeological evidence from the Midgard Historical Center in Norway and the State Archaeological Museum in Warsaw, have argued that the Yotvingians (also called Sudovians), a people living in or near Old Prussian territory, were descended from Viking settlers who came from Scandinavia onto the Baltic coast in the 9th century. They point to burial practices that differed from those of the Old Prussians. The Yotvingians buried their dead near dwellings rather than cremating them. Swords with runic inscriptions have also been found in the Masurian Lake District. However, most modern scholars classify the Yotvingians as a separate Baltic tribe related to the Old Prussians rather than as descendants of Norse settlers. Whatever their origins, if Vikings did settle in significant numbers among the Baltic peoples, they never came to dominate the region. Viking raids in the Baltic were generally focused on plunder rather than conquest, and most raiders returned to Scandinavia or continued eastward to places like Kyiv (Kiev).

The first well-documented attempt to bring the Old Prussians under outside control came from the newly Christianized Kingdom of Poland. Mieszko I, the first Christian ruler of Poland, had unified various Slavic tribes under his rule in the late 10th century. His son, Bolesław I the Brave, became the first king of Poland. Along with expanding his kingdom, Bolesław also sought to convert the pagan Prussians by sending the missionary Adalbert, Bishop of Prague, in 997.

The details of Adalbert's mission come primarily from hagiographies (accounts of saints' lives written by Christians years after the events), so they must be treated with some caution. According to these accounts, Adalbert entered Prussian territory with only a small group of companions, including his half-brother Radim, a Pole named Benedict-Bogusza, and an interpreter. The Old Prussians, an oral society that relied heavily on face-to-face interactions, distrusted this stranger who read from books. In the first village where Adalbert preached, the bishop was reportedly struck on the head with an oar by a chieftain, and he and his companions were forced to flee. After being chased out of two more settlements, Adalbert and his group were set upon by an angry mob, possibly led by a local priest. The mob killed Adalbert and cut off his head. King Bolesław later bought Adalbert's remains from the Prussians for their weight in gold. Adalbert was subsequently made a saint in the Catholic Church, and tales about his martyrdom made Prussia more widely known in Christian Europe.

The failure of Adalbert's mission did not end the conflict between the Old Prussians and their Christian neighbors. The historical record for the next two centuries is fragmentary, but chronicles mention various clashes. In 1166, Henry, Duke of Sandomierz and a veteran of the Second Crusade, was killed in battle against the Prussians. Beyond such scattered references, we know little about the details of Polish-Prussian relations during this period. What is clear is that the Old Prussians maintained their independence and their pagan religion into the 13th century, despite the growing pressure from Christianized neighbors.

By the early 13th century, Polish rulers were making more concentrated efforts to subdue Prussia. The Kingdom of Poland had fractured into competing dukedoms, and one of these rulers, Konrad I, Duke of Masovia, sought to expand his territory northward into Prussian lands. His campaigns met with fierce resistance and Prussian counter-raids. Facing continued difficulty in conquering the region, Konrad made a fateful decision around 1226. He invited the Order of Brothers of the German House of Saint Mary, better known as the Teutonic Knights, to help defeat the Prussians. This invitation would change the course of Prussian history. The Teutonic Knights, a military-religious order that had fought in the Crusades in the Holy Land, brought their organizational skills, their military expertise, and the backing of the pope. Their arrival marked the beginning of a sustained and ultimately successful campaign to conquer and Christianize Prussia.

Chapter 2: The Teutonic Knights: Prussia's Medieval Crusaders

The story of the Teutonic Knights might not have captured the public imagination like other orders, such as the Templars, but its story is certainly cinematic in scope. The Teutonic Knights were late arrivals among the medieval military orders. By the time they were founded in 1190, the Knights Templar and the Knights Hospitaller had already established themselves as powerful forces in the Crusader States. The Teutonic Order originated during the siege of Acre, when German merchants from the towns of Bremen and Lübeck established a field hospital for their sick and wounded countrymen. The German crusaders were attempting to recapture the city of Acre, an incredibly important port on the coast of the Levant. King Guy of Jerusalem granted the German merchants a plot of land and a street in Acre once the city was taken. The Germans prevailed, and the hospital was established in the newly conquered city.

The hospital was recognized as a religious fraternity by Pope Celestine III in 1196, and in 1198, it was formally transformed into a military order. It was officially called the Brothers of the Hospital of St. Mary of the German Nation. The name "Teutonic" comes from the Latin phrase "of the Germans," *Theutonicorum,* which itself derives from the Teutones, an ancient Germanic tribe. Unlike the older military orders whose leadership had long been established, the Teutonic Order's first grand master was Heinrich Walpot von Bassenheim, a Rhenish knight from a noble family. He led the order from 1198 until his death around 1200.

From its inception as a military order, the Teutonic Knights required their knight-brothers to be of noble or knightly origin, following the model of the Templars and Hospitallers. The knights were first and foremost dedicated to Jesus Christ and were exempt from secular justice. They were abstinent and renounced their personal property and free will once they joined. Living arrangements were simple, and meals were shared. Like the Templars, they wore a white mantle, but theirs bore a large black cross instead of a red one. They were to live by strict rules of behavior that produced chaste, humble, obedient, and charitable men. They were, in essence, warrior monks. They were led by a grand master, who was elected by a council of thirteen, who were in turn elected by officials within the organization.

The order was not just knights and monks. It also consisted of laymen who were employed as workers, warriors, and knights' retainers. They wore only a white mantle with no cross. The members of the order came from various backgrounds. While most were German, some were Polish and Slavic.

The Teutonic Order existed mostly on the periphery of the Crusader States until the reign of Frederick II, who was crowned Holy Roman emperor in 1220. One of Frederick's chief advisors was Hermann von Salza, the fourth grand master of the Teutonic Knights. Under Salza's leadership and through his political connections, the Teutonic Order received recognition equal to the Knights Hospitaller and the Knights Templar. Pope Honorius III and his admiration for Salza helped the order rise in prominence.

Salza's origins are unclear, but it seems he was descended from a family of ministeriales (unfree nobles who made up much of the German knighthood in the High Middle Ages). The ministeriales formed a unique place in German society, as they were of high birth but not considered freemen, a requirement for many organizations. Salza had possibly been part of the Fifth Crusade, and either there or during the Sixth Crusade, he formed his bond with Frederick. He most likely helped to arrange for the emperor's marriage to Isabella, the princess of Jerusalem, and the eventual sidelining of Isabella's father, the king of Jerusalem. Frederick then took the title of king of Jerusalem, though this was disputed at the time for several reasons, not least of which was the fact that he had been twice excommunicated and could not, therefore, legally be on a crusade.

Upon returning to Europe, Frederick and Hermann von Salza took part in the War of the Keys, which was the first military action taken by a pope against one of Europe's royal houses. It is not clear if Salza or the Teutonic Knights fought in the war. However, peace negotiations were resolved through the intervention of the grand master and several German princes. Frederick's excommunication was finally lifted in 1230.

Before this, the order had already embarked on its first major military venture outside the Holy Land. In 1211, King Andrew II of Hungary invited the Teutonic Knights to the region of Burzenland in southeastern Transylvania to defend against incursions by the nomadic Cumans. The order built five castles in the region and settled German colonists there. However, as the knights grew more powerful and autonomous, Hungarian nobles became alarmed. When the Teutonic Knights attempted to place themselves directly under papal authority rather than that of the Hungarian crown in 1224, King Andrew responded by expelling them from Transylvania in 1225, though he allowed the German settlers to remain.

After this setback, Duke Konrad I of Masovia contacted Hermann von Salza and asked for support from the Teutonic Knights in conquering and converting the Old Prussians in what would be known as the "Prussian Crusade." Konrad's offer was even more enticing than King Andrew's had been because the duke of Masovia promised the order that for their efforts in converting the pagan Prussians, they would be rewarded with territories along the Vistula River. Salza realized the opportunity that this presented. Emperor Frederick approved the plan, so Salza approached the pope, resulting in the Golden Bull of Rimini of 1226. This established that the territories granted to the order would be sovereign, and it made the grand master a prince of the Holy Roman Empire. The order would also be free from all imperial "taxes, burdens, and services."

The other missionary force in Prussia, the Cistercian monks, became allies to the Teutonic Knights, and the two orders became pillars of this new crusade. While the Old Prussians had held off previous attempts at conquest, by the 1230s, their territory was already being threatened by the slow encroachment of Christian German settlers from the south and west. German settlements were springing up all along the Baltic coast. The Teutonic Knights were once again late to the scene. While their numbers were few to begin with, they had something the Old Prussians lacked and something the German settlers needed: order, organization, and coordination. Salza recognized the significance of this new crusade. As the age of chivalric warfare was beginning to evolve, the Teutonic Knights were securing for themselves a clear legacy in the form of a new state.

By 1230, the order had established itself around Kulm and Lübau, and Duke Konrad had handed these lands over to them. To avoid becoming a pawn between the empire and the papacy, Salza had the pope declare the land the property of Saint Peter. However, it was not long before the Polish nobility, including the duke, began to consider the order an unwelcome intruder. The order's position was not initially strong militarily or financially. They were assisted by land grants on the island of Sicily by Frederick, who had taken them from the Templars and the Order of St. John. Additionally, their numbers began to increase as the crusade attracted German warriors and knights seeking spiritual merit. Most of the actual fighting was done by German crusaders who were not members of the order itself. Since this was a crusade sanctioned by Rome, participants could have their sins forgiven.

The order pushed east across the Vistula, building castles as they went. The local Prussian tribes seemed hindered by internal conflicts and unable to mount a unified resistance initially. In 1239, Hermann von Salza died, never having set foot in the nation he was creating. In 1255, Otakar, King of Bohemia, joined the crusade. In Samland, they built a new fortress named Königsberg, which bore on its coat of arms a knight with a crowned helm.

Unlike the crusades in the Holy Land, the campaign in Prussia was focused on creating a permanent Christian state through military conquest and colonization. The Teutonic Order's official mission was to convert the pagan Prussians to Christianity; this was their papal mandate and crusading justification. In practice, however, the campaign relied heavily on military force rather than peaceful conversion. The Teutonic Order conducted mass forced baptisms under armed supervision, destroyed pagan shrines, and suppressed traditional Prussian religious practices.

Tensions emerged between the Teutonic Order's stated religious mission and the political reality. While the Treaty of Christburg in 1249 promised civil liberties to Prussian converts, these rights were often not honored, particularly after the major uprisings that started in 1260. As a minority ruling over a conquered population, the German knights maintained control through military superiority and a feudal system that kept most Prussians subordinate regardless of their religious status. The conquest was marked by brutal suppression. Prussians who resisted conversion were killed, enslaved, or driven into exile, while those who converted found themselves under the tight control of a foreign military order.

Obviously, the conquest was far from smooth. The Old Prussians mounted fierce resistance, and the campaign was marked by numerous setbacks and revolts. Major uprisings erupted around 1260 and continued for over a decade. The Prussians proved to be formidable opponents, and it took the order decades of sustained military effort to subdue them. When the Teutonic Order finally suppressed the last major resistance in the early 1280s, they demanded complete subjugation. Prussian nobles were placed under feudal obligations that stripped away any remaining independence.

At the same time, successive waves of German immigrants led to the gradual Germanization of Prussia. The German language became increasingly dominant. Christianity spread, and by the 14th century, there was little left of the Old Prussians as a distinct people. Prussia had, in many ways, become a German territory under the rule of the Teutonic Order.

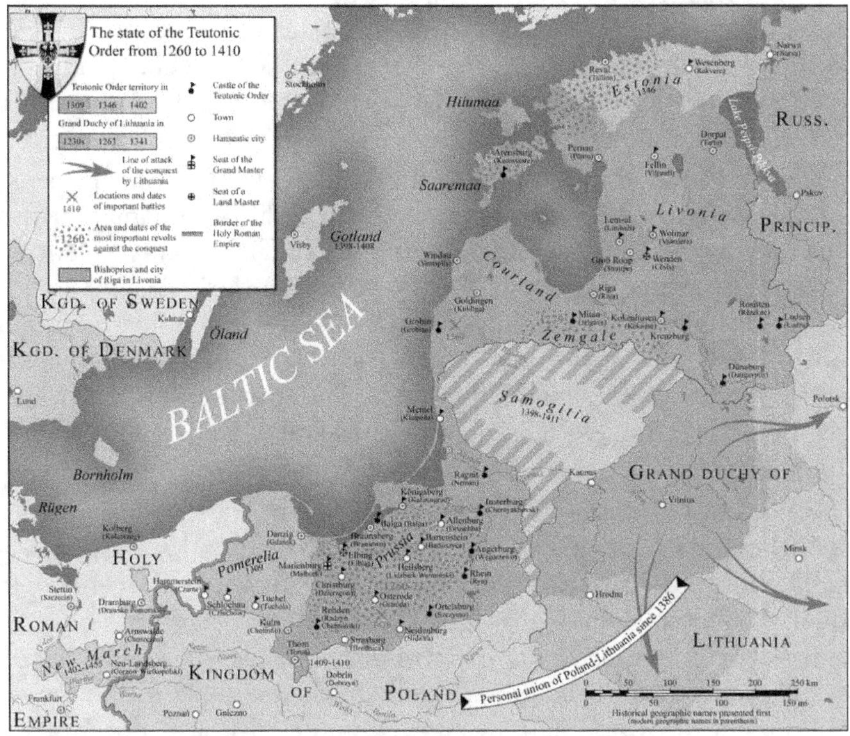

The spread of the Teutonic Order from 1230 to 1410.[54]

After the conquest and subjugation of Prussia, the order turned its sights to the lands to the west of the Vistula: Polish-owned Pomerelia (a sub-region of Pomerania). Standing in their way were the margraves of Brandenburg, who considered themselves the heirs of Pomerelia. They swooped in to occupy the city of Danzig. King Vladislav of Poland called on the Teutonic Knights to expel the Brandenburgers, which the order completed in 1308. The order then demanded a payment that the king could not afford, but it declared that it would be content to keep Danzig and the rest of Pomerelia. At the same time, they paid off the Brandenburgers to renounce their claim to the land. The order now controlled the Vistula estuary and would eventually connect their territory to the rest of the empire.

Yet, their expansion was curbed by a new alliance between the Poles and the "heathen" Lithuanians whose rule extended from the Baltic to Kiev. Through marriage and the forced conversion of the Lithuanians, the union between them and the Poles was not just a barrier to Teutonic expansion but a threat to the continued survival of Prussia as a Germanic state. To push back against their neighbors' aggression, Grand Master Ulrich von Jungingen assembled a large army for a decisive confrontation. Contemporary sources provide varying estimates of the forces involved at the Battle of Grunwald in 1410, with the Teutonic army likely numbering between twenty thousand and twenty-seven thousand men, including knights, mercenaries, and auxiliaries.

Jungingen gambled everything on this battle. The Teutonic forces were soundly defeated, not just by the size of the Polish-Lithuanian army but also by superior tactics. Grand Master von Jungingen was killed in the fighting, along with most of the Teutonic Order's leadership. The Teutonic Order survived, though, by successfully defending its capital at Malbork Castle during the subsequent siege. After several weeks, the Polish-Lithuanian forces lifted the siege, and the Peace of Toruń was signed in 1411, though it required substantial reparations from the Teutonic Order.

The new grand master, Heinrich von Plauen, was more content with consolidation than expansion, but eventually, his hand was forced. The landed nobility of Prussia, composed mainly of those descended from German immigrants, had grown to dislike the Teutonic Order. The Peace of Toruń required large payments to Poland, which the order could only raise through heavy taxation. Internal conflict within the order got out of control. King Vladislav allowed bands of Poles and Lithuanians to raid the Prussian borderlands.

Grand Master von Plauen failed to receive help from Hungary, so he attempted to take the fight to the Poles. However, he was met with failure, largely due to the divisions within the order. In 1440, the Prussian nobility founded the Prussian League, which formed an alternative government that eventually opposed the order. They looked for protection from their strongest neighbor, Poland.

The result was the Second Peace of Toruń of 1466, which declared that the western territories of the Teutonic Order's state, including Pomerelia and the city of Gdańsk, would be ceded to Poland as Royal Prussia. The Teutonic Order retained control of eastern Prussia, but it was now a fief of the Polish crown, so the grand master had to swear fealty to the king of Poland.

As a show of defiance, the order elected grand masters with strong German backgrounds. In 1511, the grand master was Margrave Albert of Brandenburg-Ansbach. Under him, the order became a secular institution, and Prussia became a secular state. The black cross disappeared from the mantle and shield. The Teutonic Order was essentially over.

The order undoubtedly played a major role in the formation of the Prussian state. While the Teutonic Knights brought administrative structures modeled on the Holy Roman Empire and established an economic system based on large-scale agriculture, their rule came at a tremendous cost to the native Old Prussians. The conquest involved decades of brutal warfare, forced conversions, and the systematic suppression of Prussian culture and religion. Many Old Prussians were killed, exiled, or reduced to serfdom, particularly after the major uprisings of the 1260s–1280s. Those who remained were gradually assimilated through Germanization, a process the Teutonic Order accelerated but did not start.

By the 14th century, the distinct Old Prussian language and culture were fading, replaced by the German language, law, and customs. While some Prussian nobles who submitted to the Teutonic Order retained certain privileges, and some Prussians served as auxiliaries or converts within the new society, the relationship was fundamentally one of conquest and domination rather than partnership. The Teutonic Order's legacy in Prussia is a complex one. They established systems of governance and agriculture that would shape the region's future, but this development was built upon the subjugation and cultural erasure of the indigenous population.

Chapter 3: The Margraviate of Brandenburg and the Hohenzollern Dynasty

A margrave is a German nobleman who ranks above a count. Margraves in the 14th and 15th centuries were princes of the Holy Roman Empire. The Margraviate of Brandenburg began in the Northern March (Nordmark). This area is equivalent to the modern German state of Brandenburg, located in the northeast of the country.

The first margrave in that region is believed to have been Gero I in 937, though he was not the margrave of Brandenburg. Gero expanded his originally modest holdings into the vast territory called Marca Geronis or March of Gero, which was considered a super-march. The Slavic rebellion of 983 disrupted the power dynamics of the region for some time, and the area was largely under the control of the Slavic Lutici alliance, which fell in the middle of the 11th century. The rule was somewhat restored by Prince Pribislav-Henry, a Slavic-Christian prince and the last ruler of the Hevelli tribe (a Slavic tribe) in the Nordmark. Pribislav, upon his death in 1150, left the territory to the House of Ascania, an Old Saxon noble family.

Albert the Bear of Ascania declared himself the margrave of Brandenburg, thus firmly establishing his march, which he expanded through crusades against the nearby Slavic Wend tribes. The Margraviate of Brandenburg, controlled by the House of Ascania, was officially established in 1157. Albert accompanied Emperor Frederick Barbossa in his campaign in Italy, distinguishing himself in the taking of Milan. When Albert died in 1164, he divided his territory between his six sons.

The Margraviate of Brandenburg passed to his eldest son, Otto, whose godfather had been none other than Prince Pribislav. Otto married Judith, a member of the House of Piast, the ruling family of Poland. She was the sister of Boleslaw IV and Mieszko III, both dukes of Poland. Otto did not expand his territory and instead focused on stabilizing the region. The Margraviate of Brandenburg, at that time, did not correspond to the current state of Brandenburg; it was the eastern land of the River Havel and the Zauche Plateau to the south. In Zauche, Otto founded the Lehnin Abbey, which remains a part of Brandenburg to this day.

When Otto I died in 1184, his eldest son, Otto II, took over the margraviate. From 1198 to 1199, Otto II devastated the Danish in Pomerania and consolidated his power to the east. He supported Philip of Swabia as king of Germany until Otto's death in 1205. He did not leave an heir from his marriage to Ada of Holland, his father's widow and his stepmother. The margraviate then passed to his younger brother and stepson, Albert II, the youngest son of Otto I and Ada of Holland.

Albert had joined the German Crusade of 1197 and was present in the Holy Land for the founding of the Teutonic Order. After Albert took over as margrave of Brandenburg, Philip of Swabia was assassinated in 1208. He had supported Philip, but after his death, he supported Philip's adversary, Holy Roman Emperor Otto IV. Albert secured areas like Teltow, Prignitz, and parts of the Uckermark, but lost Pomerania to the House of Griffin. When Albert died in 1220, his sons, John I and Otto III, ruled jointly as margraves. The brothers expanded the margraviate and died a year apart in 1266 and 1267.

The margraves of Brandenburg's relationship with Prussia and the ruling Teutonic Order at the time was complicated, to say the least. Many members of the House of Ascania joined the order and fought to secure Prussia, but there was also conflict between the rulers of Brandenburg and Prussia. The territory of Pomerelia remained an area of conflict for many years. It had been Christianized, and in 1217, the ruler of Gdańsk, Swietopelk II, declared himself the duke of Pomerelia. A civil war erupted between him and his brothers, with one side siding with the Teutonic Knights and Swietopelk allying with the Old Prussians, who revolted against the Teutonic Order in 1242. When Swietopelk died in 1266, his dukedom passed to his sons, who began another civil war. One son, Mestwin II, allied himself with the margraves of Brandenburg, the co-rulers John II, Otto IV, and Conrad I, who were all sons of John I. The longest-lived and most well-known of these was Otto IV, known as "with the arrow" because he lived for about a year with an arrow sticking out of his head.

The Brandenburgers were allowed, per the provisions of a treaty signed between them and Mestwin II, to keep troops within Pomerelia for a certain amount of time while Mestwin battled his brother and uncle for supremacy. Once the time was up and Mestwin had established himself as the sole ruler of Pomerelia, the Brandenburgers refused to remove their troops. This led to a conflict between the previous allies, which resulted in Mestwin calling for help from Poland.

Pomerelia became a fief of Poland, but after Mestwin's death and an attempted Polish takeover, the Ascanians made their move to take Pomerelia. In the struggle, the Teutonic Order took control of Danzig in 1308. The exact circumstances of this takeover, including the degree of violence, negotiations, and the ultimate treaty arrangements through which Brandenburg relinquished its claims, remain debated among historians, though it is clear that the Teutonic Order eventually secured the city through a combination of force and diplomacy.

In this same year, Waldemar the Great of the House of Ascania came into power in Brandenburg. Waldemar secured the rest of Pomerelia for Brandenburg, but he relinquished his claim to all lands east of the River Leba in 1309 to the Teutonic Order. Waldemar died childless, and the margraviate fell to the young Henry II, his cousin, who was the last margrave of Brandenburg from the House of Ascania.

Henry II only lived for about a year after becoming the margrave. Brandenburg passed to the House of Wittelsbach, and the new margrave was Louis V, called "the Brandenburger." He ruled as the margrave of Brandenburg from 1323 to 1351 and the duke of Bavaria from 1347 to 1361. Louis was the son of Louis IV, the Holy Roman emperor.

Louis V was not of age to rule when he became margrave. His regent was Berthold VII, Count of Henneberg. One distantly related member of the Ascanian family, Rudolf I, Duke of Saxe-Wittenberg, had to be bought off to renounce his claim to the margraviate. When Louis came of age, he married Princess Margaret, daughter of King Christopher II of Denmark, to strengthen the standing of the Wittelsbach dynasty.

However, Louis was never very popular in Brandenburg. Civil unrest eventually created another Brandenburg-Pomeranian war, part of a series of conflicts that lasted from the 13th century until 1637, when the House of Griffin (also known as the House of Pomerania) died out. The Pomeranians were forced to abandon the Uckermark after suffering defeats, but they were able to avoid Brandenburg's dominance by becoming a papal fief in 1330.

In 1336, Louis joined the Teutonic Knights in the Lithuanian Crusade. The Lithuanians, led by Duke Margiris, are remembered for their valiant last stand at the hill fort of Pilėnai, the location of which remains unknown to scholars. According to later accounts, some of which historians have identified as embellished, some four thousand people sheltering at the fort committed mass suicide in a tragic and dramatic act of defiance that continues to inspire Lithuanians to this day. In 1338, Louis concluded a peace with the Lithuanians in which he gave up any ownership of the land but retained rights of succession.

Louis naturally sided with his father in a political standoff with Pope Benedict XII. He backed his brother-in-law, Valdemar IV, as king of Denmark, which strengthened relations with the Danish court even after Louis's wife died in 1340. From that point onward, he spent most of his time in Bavaria and Tyrol. In 1342, he married the Tyrolean countess, Margaret, even though she was not technically divorced from her previous husband, a Luxembourg prince named John Henry.

Louis, through his paternal grandmother's line, was of the House of Habsburg as well as the House of Wittelsbach. The Habsburgs and Luxembourg were often rivals in the dynastic struggles of Europe. However, Louis's father, Louis IV, was considered the safest choice for Holy Roman emperor over Fredrick the Fair of the House of Habsburg. When Countess Margaret expelled her husband, John Henry, from Tyrol, Emperor Louis supported her claim that their marriage had not been consummated and pushed his newly widowed son, Louis V, to marry Margaret to add her lands to the expanding lands of the House of Wittelsbach. The newest pope, Pope Clement VI, however, excommunicated the couple even though the emperor had employed two well-regarded scholars to support his cause. Regardless, Louis's marriage went through.

In 1347, Holy Roman Emperor Louis IV died. Louis V succeeded him as duke of Bavaria. However, he was not selected to be the next emperor; this role went to Charles IV of Bohemia and the House of Luxembourg. Charles also happened to be the elder brother of Louis's wife's ex-husband, John Henry.

The House of Wittelsbach elected Günther von Schwarzburg as the anti-king of Germany. Though this attempted overthrow failed, it led to several years of strife between Charles and Louis, which erupted into war. After losing much of Brandenburg and repelling an attack on Tyrol, Louis V was faced with civil unrest after the appearance of a "false Waldemar," who claimed to be the dead Waldemar, Margrave of Brandenburg from the House of Ascania. This was likely a ploy by Charles to undermine Louis's power, but it did not work. Peace was finally reached between the two sides in 1350, when the Wittelsbachs regained Brandenburg and retained all their other possessions. The margraviate of Brandenburg was then given to two of Louis's brothers, Louis VI the Roman and Otto V the Bavarian.

When Louis the Roman first took over Brandenburg, the "False Waldemar" was still causing trouble within the margraviate. However, with the peace with the emperor, this was quickly stamped out. Louis the Roman was married to Princess Cunigunde, daughter of Casimir III, King of Poland. Through this marriage, he hoped to gain the Polish crown when the king died, but his wife died first. Louis then married Ingeborg of Mecklenburg, daughter of the duke of Mecklenburg.

The Golden Bull of 1356 made Brandenburg an electorate, meaning that the margrave would be a member of the electoral college that selected the next Holy Roman emperor. About a decade later, in 1365, Louis the Roman died without an heir in Berlin. The Electorate of Brandenburg then passed to his brother, Otto V.

In 1366, Otto married Catherine of Bohemia, daughter of Holy Roman Emperor Charles IV, a member of the House of Luxembourg. Twenty-four-year-old Catherine was already a widow. She had been married to Rudolf of Austria for nine years. Otto promised his father-in-law the power of succession in Brandenburg upon his death.

After becoming sole elector in 1365, Otto spent extended periods at the court of his father-in-law in Bohemia rather than governing his own territory. He even handed Brandenburg's administration to Charles IV for six years, essentially allowing the emperor to run the margraviate while Otto remained the nominal ruler.

Financially, Otto's rule was disastrous. He sold Lower Lusatia, which he had already pledged to the Wettin dynasty, to Charles IV in 1367, trading away Brandenburg territory for quick cash. He renewed old border disputes with Poland and turned a brief friendship with Pomeranian dukes into renewed hostility.

By 1371, Otto's financial situation had become so bad that he could not mount an effective defense of Brandenburg. Charles IV had successfully isolated him by winning over potential allies. When Charles invaded in 1371, Otto had neither the money, the army, nor the political support to resist. Otto resigned from the electorate in exchange for a large monetary compensation and retired to Bavaria. Otto V was the end of the Wittelsbach dynasty in Brandenburg.

The House of Luxembourg now controlled the electorate. The emperor placed his son, Wenceslaus, in the seat of power. The prince was twelve years old and had already been the king of Bohemia for ten years. Historically, the young boy is known as Wenceslaus IV of Bohemia. Born in 1361, Wenceslaus was the son of Emperor Charles IV and his third wife, Anna von Schweidnitz, a member of the Polish Piast royal family. Though Charles IV had a higher regard for his heritage along his mother's line, through his father, he was a scion of the House of Luxembourg, which included Holy Roman Emperor Henry VII.

When Charles died in 1378, Wenceslaus was just seventeen years old. He became his father's heir to both the Kingdom of Germany and the Holy Roman Empire. However, his hold on those governments was often tenuous, and he faced many challenges to his rule.

Upon Charles's death, Brandenburg went to Wenceslaus's younger half-brother, Sigismund, who was just ten years old. Sigismund eventually became more focused on his role as the king of Hungary, so he gave the Electorate of Brandenburg to his cousin, Jobst of Moravia. Six years later, Jobst joined a rebellion of nobles against Wenceslaus, who had been unable to secure the imperial crown and was barely hanging on to the German one. In 1400, Wenceslaus was removed from the throne, and Rupert of the House of Wittelsbach became the new king of Germany (a role also known as the "King of the Romans").

When Rupert died in 1410, there was a period of tension, with Jobst, Sigismund, and Wenceslaus all vying for the throne. However, Jobst died in 1411, and Wenceslaus agreed to give up the German throne in exchange for remaining king of Bohemia. Sigismund became not only king of Hungary and Germany, but he also became the Holy Roman emperor in 1433. In exchange for supporting Sigismund in his bid for the throne, Frederick VI of the House of Hohenzollern became the new elector of Brandenburg.

The Hohenzollern family originated in the Swabia region of southern Germany. Their center was originally Hohenzollern Castle on Mount Hohenzollern in the Swabian Alps. The family is mentioned in historical documents that date back to the 11th century. Frederick III, Count of Zollern, became Frederick I, Burgrave of Nuremberg, in 1192. The burgraviate remained in the Zollern family for over two centuries, passing through several generations until Frederick VI, Burgrave of Nuremberg, became Frederick I, Elector of Brandenburg, in 1415.

Frederick was born in Nuremberg in 1371 and fought alongside Sigismund against Ottoman forces in 1395. When Frederick's father died, he co-ruled Nuremberg with his brother, John, and also inherited the Principality of Ansbach. After supporting Sigismund and receiving Brandenburg, Frederick fought against the unruly nobles of Brandenburg to secure his authority. Frederick moved the capital of Brandenburg to Berlin.

Eventually, Frederick tired of his duties and passed on the role of margrave to his son, John, in 1426, though he kept the electorate title for himself. John, called "the Alchemist," was not particularly interested in governance, and his rule was largely ineffectual. He spent most of his time trying to turn ordinary materials into gold, hence his nickname. In 1427, Frederick persuaded John to take the mineral-rich lands of Bayreuth. Eventually, he handed over the administration of Brandenburg to John's younger brother, Frederick II, nicknamed "the Iron."

Frederick II focused his attention on pacifying the restless nobles of Brandenburg and avoided imperial politics. In 1440, Frederick I died, and Frederick II became elector in his own right while John the Alchemist retired to pursue his passion. In that same year, tensions rose when Frederick II announced his plans to build a residence on the Cölln island in the Spree River next to Berlin. This meant that parts of the city would be forcibly obtained by the electorate at the loss of the city.

In 1448, this spilled over into open revolt when citizens poured into the excavated land of what would become the Stadtschloss or the Berlin Palace. This palace would be the seat of the electors of Brandenburg, kings of Prussia, and German emperors in future centuries. In the mid-15th century, Frederick called in his troops. The rebellion was stopped, and construction continued. In 1454 and 1455, Frederick concluded the Treaties of Cölln and Mewe, in which he secured the Neumark (New March), which had previously been lost to the Teutonic Order, for the Electorate of Brandenburg. In 1470, Frederick abdicated in favor of his younger brother, Albrecht Achilles, and retired to the principality of Bayreuth, where he died a year later.

Albrecht III Achilles was the third son of Frederick I and the fourth margrave of Brandenburg from the House of Hohenzollern. The imperial crown was now securely in the hands of the Habsburgs. Albrecht had fought alongside Holy Roman Emperor Albert II in his war against the Hussites, an early Protestant group formed by Jan Hus. Albrecht was a member of the Order of the Swan, a knightly order formed by Frederick II and based on the medieval tale of the Swan Knight. As a knight, Albrecht was known for being virtuous and skilled. He gained the nickname "Achilles" after the great Greek warrior of legend.

After Frederick I's death in 1440, Albrecht was given the Principality of Ansbach. He attempted to expand his territory by various means but was largely unsuccessful. After the abdication of his brother Frederick II, he gained control of all the Hohenzollern lands, the most important being the Electorate of Brandenburg. After a war with Pomerania, he secured the Duchy of Pomerania as part of Brandenburg. In 1486, he handed control over Brandenburg to his eldest son, John Cicero.

John established the Berlin Palace as the permanent residence of the elector of Brandenburg, thus making Berlin the capital. When he died in 1499, he was the first member of the House of Hohenzollern to be buried in Brandenburg. His son, Joachim I Nestor, became elector after his death. Joachim proved to be a firm but sensible ruler. He established order through stern measures, improved the administration of justice, encouraged commerce, and listened to the needs of the growing towns in his domain. In 1519, after the death of Holy Roman Emperor Maximilian I, Joachim's electoral vote was highly sought after by the two rivals for the throne of the Holy Roman Empire, Francis I of France and Charles of Burgundy (King of Spain). Joachim backed the winning Charles, who became Emperor Charles V, though relations between the elector of Brandenburg and the emperor were fairly cool.

Joachim was able to secure the Electorate of Mainz for his brother Albert, which gave the House of Hohenzollern two of the seven electoral votes to approve the Holy Roman emperor. The bribery needed to obtain this position was significant. To pay off his debts, Albert was given papal authority to sell indulgences to his parishioners. As a result, Albert became the focus of Martin Luther's sermons in nearby Saxony. Joachim was a great supporter of the Roman Catholic Church, and the Hohenzollerns were, at that point, opposed to the Reformation movements within the church. Yet he could not stop the tide of the Protestant movement. His wife, Elizabeth of Denmark, converted to Lutheranism and fled to Saxony.

While Joachim struggled with the Reformation in Brandenburg, his cousin faced an even more dramatic transformation far to the east. Albert of Brandenburg-Ansbach, from a cadet branch of the Hohenzollern family, had been elected grand master of the Teutonic Knights in 1511. The military order that had once been the scourge of the pagans now found itself in dire straits. Decades of warfare with Poland had drained its coffers and reduced its territory. The Second Peace of Thorn in 1466 had left the Teutonic Order's remaining lands (the region around Königsberg in East Prussia) as a fief of the Polish crown. The Teutonic Order owed fealty to the very kingdom it had once sought to conquer.

By the 1520s, the Teutonic Order was sinking under a mountain of debt estimated at over 200,000 gulden. Its very purpose—crusading against pagans—had become obsolete. The Reformation offered Albert an escape from this dying institution. In 1522 and 1523, he traveled to Wittenberg and Nuremberg to consult with Martin Luther and other Protestant reformers. Luther's advice was radical: dissolve the Teutonic Order, convert to Lutheranism, and transform the monastic state into a hereditary secular duchy.

Albert took Luther's counsel to heart. After securing the support of the Prussian estates and local knights who were weary of the Teutonic Order's papal ties and mounting debts, Albert made his move. On February 10th, 1525, he resigned his position as grand master, formally converted to Lutheranism, and proclaimed the dissolution of the Teutonic Order in Prussia. The transformation required legitimacy, which only the Polish king could provide. Negotiations with King Sigismund I of Poland culminated in the Treaty of Kraków, which was signed on April 8th, 1525. Two days later, on April 10th, Albert knelt before the Polish king in Kraków's market square and paid homage, becoming Albert, Duke of Prussia. He was the first duke of a new secular state.

The Duchy of Prussia had been born, and it was unlike anything Europe had seen before. It was the first Protestant state, and it had been created through the abandonment of monastic vows and the secularization of church lands. Albert could now marry, establish a dynasty, and rule as a secular prince. The transformation did not bring radical social change. The former commanders of the Teutonic Order simply converted to Lutheranism and retained their positions in the social hierarchy. However, it fundamentally altered the political landscape of northeastern Europe. Prussia was no longer a crusading order answerable to the pope but a hereditary duchy answerable to Poland.

The new duchy remained a Polish fief, requiring Albert and his successors to pay homage to the Polish crown and provide military support when called upon. This vassalage would endure for over a century, something that rankled future Hohenzollern rulers who dreamed of sovereignty.

Joachim died in 1535, still a stalwart Catholic. He never reconciled with his Protestant wife and seemed unaware of just how momentous his cousin's actions in faraway Prussia would prove for the future of their house.

His eldest son, Joachim II Hector, became the elector of Brandenburg. Joachim II had been forced by his father to sign a document promising to remain a Roman Catholic so he could remain heir to Brandenburg. However, after his father's death, Joachim II began to turn toward Protestantism. He did not openly convert until Charles V abdicated his throne and his brother, Ferdinand I, became the new Holy Roman emperor.

Previously, a pogrom in Brandenburg had forced Jewish citizens to flee the region. Under Joachim II, they were allowed to return after the Jewish advocate Josel of Rosheim pleaded their case directly to him. Joachim II spent lavishly, indulging in various passions to the point that he racked up a debt of 600,000 thalers by 1540. He tried to pay off his debt by confiscating church property and raising taxes.

In 1541, Joachim II joined Holy Roman Emperor Ferdinand in battling the Turks as they pressed into eastern Europe. He participated in the Siege of Buda, the capital of the Kingdom of Hungary. However, he was defeated and then defeated again in the Siege of Pest in the following year. Joachim II died in 1571. By that time, the Duchy of Prussia had already passed to Albert Frederick, who was a member of the Ansbach branch of the Hohenzollern family.

John George, Joachim II's eldest son, inherited the Electorate of Brandenburg, as well as a large amount of debt. He raised the grain tax, which heavily burdened the common people while the nobles— particularly the landed Junkers of Brandenburg's rural estates—were largely exempt. These Junker families, the estate-owning nobility east of the Elbe, controlled vast grain-producing lands worked by peasant labor and jealously guarded their tax exemptions and other feudal privileges.

John George once again banished the Jews from Brandenburg. A staunch Lutheran, he did allow Calvinist refugees from the Netherlands to enter his domain. In 1577, possibly because Duke Albert Frederick was exhibiting signs of mental illness, John George became co-regent of Prussia. He died in 1598, leaving Brandenburg to his son, Joachim Frederick, who reigned for ten years. The electorate then passed to Joachim Frederick's son, John Sigismund, in 1608.

When Duke Albert Frederick of Prussia died in 1618, John Sigismund was declared the new duke of Prussia by the Polish king. Brandenburg and Prussia were now combined. They had separate administrations, but both were ruled by John Sigismund of the House of Hohenzollern. John Sigismund was born Lutheran, but he converted to Calvinism. Because most of his subjects were Lutheran or Roman Catholic, he had initially drawn up plans of mass conversions within both regions, but he faced protests, particularly from his wife, who was a devout Lutheran. John Sigismund suffered a stroke and died in 1619.

His successor and son was George William. He was born in Cölln in 1595 to the elector of Brandenburg and his wife, Anna of Prussia. George William's mother was the daughter of Duke Albert Frederick, so he was truly the direct male heir to both Brandenburg and Prussia. George William married Elizabeth Charlotte of the Palatinate (a region in today's southern Germany). They had one son and two daughters.

George William proved to be an ineffective leader. This was not helped by the eruption of the Thirty Years' War in 1618, which broke out just before he became elector and duke. He tried to remain neutral in the fight between Holy Roman Emperor Ferdinand II and his Lutheran opponents, but the war entered his territory anyway, leading to widespread looting by Catholic forces. When George's brother-in-law, Gustavus Adolphus of Sweden, intervened in the war, George reluctantly aligned with him. However, despite their ties, Swedish-Protestant troops still plundered parts of Brandenburg. After Gustavus was killed, George William withdrew from the war, leaving the government in the hands of a subordinate. He died in 1640 and was succeeded by his son, Frederick William.

Chapter 4: The Great Elector, Frederick William

Frederick William was twenty years old when he succeeded to the throne. He had hardly any experience in government or administration. He had grown up with a deep admiration of Gustavus Adolphus. Frederick William was educated in Küstrin instead of Berlin due to the Thirty Years' War, which had caused a lot of devastation to Brandenburg and Prussia. In 1634, he traveled to the Netherlands and studied mathematics, Latin, history, and warfare in Leyden. He spoke German, French, Dutch, and Polish. Frederick William grew to sympathize with the Dutch and the House of Orange's struggle against the Catholics, the Spanish, and the House of Habsburg.

Frederick William, the Great Elector of Brandenburg and Duke of Prussia.[55]

When his father decided Brandenburg should fight the Swedes and join the Habsburgs' side of the war, Frederick found himself in opposition to his father and his father's powerful advisor, Adam, Count of Schwarzenberg. Frederick was effectively banished from his father's court and political life in general. When Elector George William died, Brandenburg and the House of Hohenzollern were at an all-time low. The most important holdings, economically speaking, were in Prussia, where the duke of Prussia, thanks to the Teutonic Order's consolidations, still held vast domains and a large number of subjects. While Brandenburg's population had decreased by half during the Thirty Years' War, Prussia was not hit as hard. Still, the situation Frederick William found himself in was not an enviable one.

At first, Frederick William relied on the guidance of his mother. She sought to clarify and quantify the problems facing the Hohenzollerns. It was determined that the continued war against the Swedes was too costly, but upsetting the alliance with the Habsburgs was equally impossible. No solutions were forthcoming.

However, Frederick William immediately realized the need for an effective, possibly permanent army. He did not dismiss Schwarzenberg but instead gradually diminished his powers to the point of insignificance. Frederick also tried to appease the nobles, whom he was supposed to consult on important matters, but he found them more concerned with their own gains than the needs of the nation. Their main complaint was against the army running amok.

Frederick agreed to reduce the army in Brandenburg, which was seemingly in contradiction to his desire for a standing army. Yet it was not a true contradiction. The army in Brandenburg was a motley crew of ill-trained troops who were a worse menace to the people than previous invading armies. Their combat value was dubious at best. For Frederick to build the army he wanted, he had to dissolve the current one.

In 1641, Schwarzenberg died unexpectedly. A few months later, an armistice with Sweden was concluded. Frederick William had to walk a fine line. While he could not continue the war with the Swedes, the ceasefire greatly concerned King Vladislav IV of Poland. Frederick William, as duke of Prussia, was a vassal to the Polish crown, so he kept Vladislav largely in the dark about his dealings with the Swedes.

In the same year as the peace deal with Sweden, Frederick William was able to reassert his power over Prussia and was granted the ability to impose an excise tax, which would become one of the most important sources of funds for Brandenburg-Prussia. The nobility of Prussia also benefited from this tax, so it helped to keep them satisfied and unlikely to cause trouble for the elector.

The social dynamics of Brandenburg-Prussia were particularly complicated since medieval serfdom was still practiced in areas like Pomerania and parts of the Uckermark. In both Prussia and Brandenburg, there were high and low nobility. In Prussia, east of the River Elbe, rural society was stratified. At the top were peasants who owned large farms and fulfilled their obligations by providing horses and laborers to their lord. Below them came cottagers with smaller plots of land (less than thirty hectares) who owed manual service. Then there were the cottagers who worked as full-time laborers during harvest season. At the bottom were servants who lived in or near the lord's premises and served him directly. These peasants could not leave the estate, get married, or learn a trade without their lord's permission. Serfs could be bought and sold like livestock.

To the west of the Elbe, the situation was not nearly as strict. In dealing with the nobility, Frederick William had to remember each noble's standing and culture. He also had to deal with different religious beliefs. While Frederick William was a Calvinist, most of his subjects were Lutheran. So, he adopted a stance of general religious tolerance.

In 1644, Frederick began to build his army, cautiously at first. He entrusted recruitment to his close confidant, Johann von Norprath. Norprath conducted the recruitment in the Lower Rhine region to avoid the suspicions of the Swedes. Garrisons in Brandenburg and Prussia were also increased. Frederick's goal was a well-trained standing army, and by 1646, he had about three thousand recruits in Cleves. The money to pay the soldiers came mostly from Prussia, but the payments were kept secret from both the Swedes and the nobles. The various sources of funds were kept so secret that many remain unknown to this day. Frederick William did raise some taxes without the consent of the nobles, which met with strong opposition.

Then, in 1648, what must have seemed like an endless war was finally concluded when the Holy Roman Empire signed a peace treaty with Sweden and then another with France. These treaties became known as the Peace of Westphalia and marked the end of the Thirty Years' War. It had been a war primarily centered around Holy Roman Emperor Ferdinand II's desire to see Roman Catholicism as the only religion in the

Holy Roman Empire, but it had spread into a war that engulfed much of Europe and decimated Germany's population. It was one of the longest and most destructive wars in European history. Elector Frederick William had never experienced European peace until the treaties of Westphalia were signed.

Brandenburg-Prussia did not profit much from the Peace of Westphalia, except for the end, if temporary, of foreign armies marching across its borders. Frederick's nation remained relatively insignificant and was vulnerable partly because the east and west were separated, with the Swedes gaining the Pomeranian region after the war. Frederick's role as elector in the Holy Roman Empire did not afford him as much leverage, and his role as a vassal to the king of Poland was a burden. This was especially true in 1655 when war broke out between Poland and Sweden. Due to Poland's internal weaknesses, Frederick William abandoned his liege lord. The Swedes were victorious. They, in turn, imposed overlordship on Prussia.

The king of Poland, John Casimir, had been forced out of his kingdom but soon returned with greater support. Frederick William put his new army to the test in the three-day Battle of Warsaw. The army proved more than effective. When Austria and Russia threw their support behind Poland, Frederick William took the opportunity to demand that Sweden withdraw the bonds of vassalage and recognize Frederick as the sovereign duke of Prussia in his own right in exchange for his support of Sweden in the war. The Swedes agreed to those terms in the Treaty of Labiau in 1656.

The next year, Holy Roman Emperor Ferdinand III died. The imperial election would not occur until July 1658, when Ferdinand III's son, Leopold, came of age. Frederick William's electoral vote would be valuable in that election, but he had already secured his greatest prize months earlier. During the Second Northern War, Frederick William had switched sides from Sweden to Poland. Poland desperately needed his military support. In September 1657, in the Treaty of Wehlau, King John II Casimir of Poland agreed to end Prussia's vassalage. After more than a century as a Polish fief, Prussia was finally sovereign.

Sweden felt betrayed by Frederick William's actions and renewed hostilities with Brandenburg-Prussia. Frederick responded by securing an alliance with Austria and Poland. Frederick took a force of thirty thousand men composed of Brandenburg, imperial, and Polish troops.

They attacked the Swedes and drove them out of Schleswig and Holstein, just south of Denmark.

The victory was short-lived, as both the Holy Roman Empire and Poland gave up their support. In 1660, a peace was settled between Brandenburg-Prussia and Sweden in the Treaty of Oliva. All occupied territories were restored to their pre-war owners. Frederick had conquered most of Swedish Pomerania, but he was forced to give it back to the Swedes. His dream of uniting all of Pomerania under Brandenburg rule would have to wait.

After twenty years of rule, Frederick William's only successes appeared to be the formation of a standing army and the sovereignty of Prussia. These were certainly great successes, but Frederick William was an ambitious ruler who desired more. He mainly wanted to turn his nation into a formidable European power at all costs. The sovereignty of Prussia at least removed an avenue of power for the nobles, who often conspired with the Poles to undermine the rule of the elector. Frederick decided to pursue a policy of absolute authority, which the nobles quickly opposed.

The heart of the opposition was in Königsberg under the chairman of the city council, Hieronymus Roth. Frederick William left Danzig and landed with two thousand men. They marched into the city center. Faced with overwhelming force, the citizens gave Roth up. He was found guilty of treason and imprisoned for the rest of his life in the fortress of Peitz. A worse fate was met by Colonel Christian Ludwig von Kalckstein, who openly opposed the elector and managed to flee to Poland, only to be captured by Frederick William's men. He was beheaded in 1672. The message was clear. The nobles could no longer rely on Polish protection.

Frederick William soon instituted taxes and stationed troops in Königsberg without the approval of the nobles. He was met with no opposition. He faced even less opposition in establishing absolute authority in Brandenburg.

His next goal was a centralized and uniform government for all the lands he controlled. To do this, Frederick William introduced a uniform system of taxation. Despite the benefits, it was still not enough to pay for a peacetime army of seven thousand and a wartime army of almost thirty thousand troops. So, he relied on subsidies from larger allies like France, Spain, the Netherlands, Denmark, and Austria. These allies came and went with great frequency. And it was not just his allies that he could not fully trust. He also could not depend on the officers in his army. Frederick William tended to rely on foreign-born generals, the most well known being Field Marshal von Derfflinger, who was an Austrian of humble origins.

In the late 1660s and into the 1670s, Brandenburg-Prussia was caught in the machinations of the absolute monarch of France, Louis XIV. France was sometimes an ally and sometimes an enemy. Louis ran political circles around the likes of Frederick William. In December 1674, the elector received the alarming news that a Swedish army, allied with France, had invaded Brandenburg. Frederick William's army had already arrived at the winter quarters on the other side of central Germany. The challenge of getting the army to Brandenburg fell to Derfflinger, who divided his forces into smaller sections to increase mobility while keeping communication open.

In just two weeks, the army was back in Brandenburg. The Swedes, surprised by the sudden arrival and unaware of the Prussians' true numbers, quickly fell back. Derfflinger caught up to them. Though he had fewer troops and less artillery, the Swedes suffered a demoralizing defeat at the Battle of Fehrbellin. This feat helped to bolster the reputation of not just the Brandenburg-Prussian army but also of Frederick William himself, who was soon being hailed as the "Great Elector."

Derfflinger followed this success with a broader campaign in Swedish Pomerania. Frederick William realized he might finally be able to evict the Swedes if he continued the push. He allied himself with Denmark, whose fleet pressured Swedish positions in the Baltic. The campaign became protracted and lasted into 1677. Frederick William's goal was to capture the city of Stettin to secure control of the Oder River. After a siege and bombardment by land and sea, the city paid homage to him in January of 1678.

However, Frederick William's hopes for Brandenburg-Prussia to be respected by the great powers of the day were short-lived. France encouraged Sweden to undertake another campaign against Brandenburg in the winter of 1678/79. As his allies dwindled, Frederick concluded the Peace of Saint-Germain-en-Laye in June of 1679, which returned Pomerania to Sweden.

Perhaps recognizing the futility of opposing France, Frederick William instead decided to join Louis XIV. Secret negotiations began. Frederick hoped to turn the alliance against the hated Swedes, while Louis hoped for Prussian assistance in the annexation of German territories, which Louis chose to call "reunions."

In 1681, when Louis's army besieged and captured the imperial city of Strasbourg, Frederick William's alliance with the French made him a traitor in the eyes of many. However, Frederick kept his alliance with Louis, and in 1683, it seemed to bear fruit when the French agreed to drive Sweden out of Germany. Yet, these treaties were never ratified, and Frederick William's dreams of obtaining Pomerania would never be realized.

In that same year, France found the Holy Roman Empire completely distracted by the presence of an Ottoman army outside the city of Vienna. The Battle of Vienna, which was waged between the Holy Roman Empire and the Polish-Lithuanian Commonwealth and the Ottoman Empire and its vassals, was a decisive victory for the Holy Roman Empire and Poland. It was the turning point in the expansion of the Ottomans into Europe. They would gain no more territory after the battle, and many of the lands they had conquered in Hungary would be returned to Emperor Leopold I. Brandenburg-Prussia was not involved in the fight at all, and its absence was duly noted.

France abandoned Frederick William as an ally, so Frederick tried to ally himself with the Habsburgs and the Holy Roman Empire, but he was rebuffed. He was told that as an elector, he had a duty to support the empire. Peace was finally settled between France and the Holy Roman Empire, which was much to the benefit of France. There was no profit for Frederick or even the Germans.

As Frederick William approached the end of his life, his legacy seemed uncertain at best. In 1682, he gave a charter to the Brandenburg Africa Company in the hopes of getting in on the profitable slave trade. This company founded two colonies, Gross-Friedrichsburg and Fort Dorothea. Neither colony was profitable during Frederick's lifetime.

While Brandenburg-Prussia had become a formidable power, it was not the great power that Frederick had hoped for. It was often a pawn in political affairs and subject to the whims of France, the Holy Roman Empire, and Sweden. It was not a great commercial power either. Yet Frederick William is still remembered as the "Great Elector," not because he raised Prussia to the heights of a great European power, but because he laid the foundation upon which later leaders built Prussia's power.

After a reign of forty-eight years, Frederick William died at the age of sixty-eight. He left behind a military and government organization that had been much improved since he had taken over at twenty years old. It was a system that would greatly benefit the leaders who followed him.

Chapter 5: Prussia's Age of Enlightenment

King Frederick II's Roundtable at Sanssouci by Adolph von Menzel features Frederick II, King of Prussia, as well as Enlightenment thinkers Voltaire, d'Argens, La Mettrie, and Algarotti, among others.[56]

The Great Elector left behind an army of thirty thousand troops when he died. The question of how to pay for this army led his successors to continue attracting immigrants to Prussia. The revocation of the Edict of Nantes in 1685 had brought some twenty thousand French and Walloon Huguenots into his domain. These emigrants possessed highly developed commercial and industrial skills and were often better educated than the native population.

Besides the army and these industrious new citizens, Frederick William's greatest legacy was the sovereignty of Prussia, which he had secured in 1657. The Great Elector's successor, his son Frederick III, had a singular goal. While he left the administration of his nation to a series of prime ministers, Frederick sought to raise his title of duke of Prussia to the title of king. His situation as the elector of Brandenburg made him technically a vassal of the Holy Roman Empire, which meant that he could not be a king there. However, as the sovereign ruler of Prussia, he felt he had a right to a royal title.

Yet, while Holy Roman Emperor Leopold I did not need to confer the crown on Frederick, the emperor did need to give his approval and recognition. This meant that Brandenburg-Prussia would need to maintain its alliance with the Holy Roman Empire at all costs. Negotiations began just two years after Frederick William's death. Leopold agreed to the deal in the Crown Treaty of November 1700 after a war with France erupted. Leopold needed Prussian troops. In January 1701, Frederick crowned himself King Frederick I, King in Prussia. He chose "in Prussia" instead of "of Prussia" because West Prussia was still part of Poland, and he wanted to avoid objections from the Polish monarchy, which viewed the coronation as illegal.

King Frederick I's reign was also noted for the founding of the Prussian Academy of Arts in 1696 and the Academy of Sciences in 1700. He died in 1713 and was followed by his son, King Frederick William I, known as the "Soldier King."

Pragmatic and harsh, Frederick William cut many of his father's expenditures, including shutting down the Academy of Sciences as an economic measure. He concerned himself with every detail of the ruling of his country and is considered an absolutist monarch. Unwilling to spend the money needed to maintain them, Frederick William sold off the West African colony his father established and disbanded the Prussian Navy. He made considerable changes to military training and equipment. He died at the age of fifty-one in 1740, leaving the country to his son, King Frederick II, also known as "the Great."

What followed was a flowering of arts and sciences that made Prussia a center for the European Enlightenment. Frederick II reopened the Academy of Sciences in 1740, inviting thinkers of all kinds to come to Prussia to study and teach.

Let's now take a look at some of the leading Enlightenment luminaries with ties to the Prussian state.

Christian Wolff.[57]

Christian Wolff (1679–1754)

Christian Wolff was born on January 24th, 1679, in Breslau in Silesia (part of modern-day Poland) to parents of modest means. He was able to attend school and eventually went to the University of Jena to study theology, physics, and mathematics. He then moved to the University of Leipzig in 1702, where his work caught the attention of many academics, including the German philosopher Gottfried Wilhelm Leibniz. The two struck up a correspondence that lasted until Leibniz died in 1716. Wolff took up a position as a professor of mathematics at the University of Halle in Prussia. There, he lectured in math and natural science, eventually tackling traditional philosophy as well.

He published a series of textbooks on logic, metaphysics, ethics, politics, and physics from 1713 to 1723. These textbooks became popular partly because the first editions were written in the German vernacular; Latin versions were printed later. This allowed greater access to Wolff's concepts among his countrymen.

He enjoyed a stellar reputation among other intellectuals but ran afoul of the theology department at Halle (a group of Pietist Lutherans) when he espoused the doctrine of predeterminism. The escalating conflict with the Pietists, including controversy over his lectures on Chinese philosophy and their implications for the autonomy of moral reasoning, led to the involvement of King Frederick William I. He banished the philosopher from Prussia in 1723, only giving him forty-eight hours to leave or face execution.

Wolff's expulsion only enhanced his reputation and brought him to the attention of other Enlightenment luminaries like Voltaire. He accepted a position at the University of Marburg. In 1733, attempts were made to entice Wolff back to Prussia (in 1734, Prussia rescinded the 1723 arrest warrant and offered him various positions), but Wolff declined these overtures. However, with the ascension of King Frederick II in 1740, the enlightened monarch made Wolff an offer he could not refuse. Wolff accepted the king's invitation to return to Halle, initially as vice-chancellor and later as chancellor of the university in 1743. Christian Wolff died in Halle in 1754.

Wolff is often seen as the intellectual bridge between Leibniz and Immanuel Kant and is often described as a follower of Leibniz. This characterization is misleading for several reasons. While Leibniz was older than Wolff, the majority of Leibniz's most important philosophical works, including *The Principles of Nature and Grace, Monadology*, and *New Essays on Human Understanding*, were published posthumously, after Wolff had already developed and published his own philosophical system. The correspondence between the two thinkers primarily was over mathematics, which was Wolff's focus at the time. Leibniz himself even commented that Wolff knew very little of his philosophical ideas, writing, "Mr. Wolff has adopted some of my opinions, but since he is very busy with teaching, especially in mathematics, and we have not had much correspondence together on philosophy, he can know very little about my opinions beyond those which I have published." Because of this, it is important to see Wolff as a great independent thinker of the Enlightenment, especially for his work in bringing new philosophical thought to Prussia.

Pierre Louis Maupertuis.[58]

Pierre Louis Maupertuis (1698–1759)

Born in Saint-Malo, France, in 1698 to a moderately wealthy family of merchants, Maupertuis was privately tutored in mathematics. He eventually moved to Paris to establish himself as a mathematician. In 1723, he was admitted into the Académie des Sciences. He developed and extended the work of Isaac Newton, whose theories were less widely accepted on the Continent outside England. In 1736, he led the French Geodesic Mission sent by King Louis XV to Lapland. This expedition helped prove a theory held by Newtonians that the Earth was oblate and not prolate by measuring the length of a degree of arc of the meridian. This garnered Maupertuis a good deal of respect and acclaim within European scientific circles.

Four years after the expedition, he was invited to Berlin by King Frederick II. After being taken prisoner at the Battle of Mollwitz in 1741 and released, he returned to Paris, where he was elected director of the Académie des Sciences in 1742. He returned to Brandenburg-Prussia in 1745, and Frederick chose him to be the president of the Royal Prussian Academy of Sciences in 1746. This organization was founded by Frederick I in 1700 upon the advice of German philosopher Gottfried Wilhelm Leibniz. It was a French-language institution because, at the time, French was the language of science and culture.

Maupertuis served as president of the Royal Academy until 1753, when the controversy with Voltaire and his deteriorating health caused him to leave Berlin, effectively ending his presidency. Though he briefly returned in 1754, he left again for France and spent his final years traveling for his health, dying in Basel in 1759. He was often at odds with fellow philosophers and had well-known controversies with Johann Samuel König and Voltaire.

Voltaire.[59]

Voltaire (1694–1778)

Frederick the Great and Voltaire began a correspondence in 1736 when Frederick was still the crown prince. Frederick was raised in Prussia but became deeply influenced by French Enlightenment culture. They shared a firm conviction in the importance of religious tolerance backed by skepticism in traditional religions. Frederick saw in Voltaire another luminary to add to his growing collection in Berlin. Voltaire saw in Frederick a great philosopher king, an enlightened monarch who would finally create a free, just, and peaceful nation. They would both be disappointed.

In 1750, Voltaire came to Brandenburg-Prussia after numerous invitations from King Frederick II. He was welcomed by the other French expatriates there, including Maupertuis. He was given the position of chamberlain, which had very few duties, and was given an annual salary of twenty thousand French livres. He had rooms at the Sanssouci and Charlottenburg palaces.

After approximately two and a half years, Voltaire angered Frederick, first by his involvement in a financial scandal and then after the publication of his satirical book *Docteur Akakia*, in which he criticized Maupertuis's theories and questioned the mathematician's ethics. Frederick ordered official copies of *Docteur Akakia* to be confiscated and publicly burned. Voltaire offered to resign his position. Frederick initially refused but then accepted.

However, as Voltaire was heading back to France, he was detained in Frankfurt by Frederick's agents for over three weeks. This detention was over manuscripts of poetry Frederick had loaned to Voltaire and wanted back. It was a prime example to Voltaire that Frederick was not the enlightened monarch he had hoped for. He was just another despot ruling according to his whim. Voltaire would satirize Frederick in many works. In his posthumous publication, *Mémoires pour Servir à la Vie de M. de Voltaire*, he explicitly mentioned Frederick's homosexuality, describing how the king regularly invited pages, young cadets, and lieutenants from his regiment to have coffee with him and then withdrew with the favorite, framing this in a manner intended to degrade the king.

Their eventual clash seems, in hindsight, inevitable. While Frederick was a philosopher and king, he also tended toward authoritarian rule. Voltaire, ever the skeptic and challenger of the status quo, the epitome of the Enlightenment rebel, could never have survived long under

Frederick's thumb. Despite their falling out, they continued to correspond. After the Seven Years' War, they largely reconciled, though they would never again meet in person.

Carl Philipp Emanuel Bach.[60]

Carl Philipp Emanuel Bach (1714–1788)

C. P. E. Bach was the fifth child and second surviving son of Johann Sebastian Bach and his first wife, Maria Barbara. The younger Bach attended university at Leipzig and then at Frankfurt-on-the-Oder in 1735. He studied law but was trained in music by his father. In 1738, he obtained an appointment in Berlin, serving Crown Prince Frederick of Prussia. When the prince ascended the throne as King Frederick II (the Great) in 1740, Bach joined the royal orchestra. He was renowned for playing the clavier, a keyboard instrument, and composed over one hundred sonatas and concert pieces for the harpsichord and clavichord.

Bach spent much of his time in Berlin, which, under the direction of Frederick the Great, had become a center for arts and culture. Bach became friends with other musicians and literary figures like Gotthold Ephraim Lessing. In 1746, he rose to the post of chamber musician and wrote several well-regarded pieces, including symphonies, cantatas, and other sacred vocal works. In 1753, he published his influential treatise on the playing of keyboard instruments, which was highly valued by Haydn and Beethoven.

In 1768, Bach was allowed to leave his post in Brandenburg-Prussia to become the director of music in Hamburg. There, he focused on choral work, which gained widespread appreciation. He died in Hamburg in 1788.

Jean-Baptiste de Boyer.[61]

Jean-Baptiste de Boyer, Marquis d'Argens (1704–1771)

Born into a devout Catholic family, Jean-Baptiste de Boyer, Marquis d'Argens, was a rationalist author and critic of the Catholic Church. He was disinherited by his family and began a career as a writer, publishing a book in 1735 and the six-volume *Lettres juives* between 1736 and 1740. In 1742, he accepted an invitation from Frederick the Great to be the royal chamberlain in Berlin. He remained there for most of his career.

He met and befriended Voltaire, but unlike Voltaire, d'Argens was not just opposed to absolute monarchy. He was also highly critical of religious authority and traditional institutions. Interestingly, he does not appear to have quarreled with Frederick the Great like his more famous friend. D'Argens finally returned to France in 1769.

Julien Offray de la Mettrie.[62]

Julien Offray de la Mettrie (1709–1751)

Mettrie, like his fellow countryman Maupertuis, was born in Saint-Malo to a prosperous merchant family. He attended the Collège du Plessis in Paris and was initially interested in becoming a clergyman, although he later turned away from the church. Mettrie attended the Collège d'Harcourt, where he studied natural philosophy before graduating in 1728. He then studied under the renowned Dutch physician Hermann Boerhaave.

Mettrie returned to his home region of Saint-Malo to begin practicing as a physician. He went on to be appointed surgeon in the French Guards during the War of the Austrian Succession. It was around this time that he made the acquaintance of Maupertuis.

While in Paris, Mettrie suffered from a fever, which led him to believe that mental faculties like emotion were accounted for by organic changes in the brain and nervous system. The publication of his *Histoire naturelle de l'âme* caused an outcry, and he was forced to take refuge in Holland. There, he wrote his most famous work, *L'Homme machine* (*Man a Machine*), which espoused materialistic and partly atheistic concepts.

In 1748, Mettrie was forced to leave Holland for Berlin due to hostility against his works. In Berlin, he joined Maupertuis. Frederick the Great named him the court reader and allowed him to practice as a physician. Mettrie wrote *Discours sur le bonheur*, which appalled many Enlightenment thinkers with its purely hedonistic and sensualistic rhetoric. For this, Mettrie was largely written out of the history of the Enlightenment for about one hundred years.

He died in Berlin at a feast at which he was said to have devoured a large amount of food and died of a gastronomic illness as a result. Frederick the Great delivered his eulogy, in which he described Mettrie as a good devil and fine physician but a terrible writer.

Francesco Algarotti.[68]

Francesco Algarotti (1712–1764)

It is believed that Francesco Algarotti, a Venetian polymath, became Frederick the Great's close companion when the Italian was touring northern Europe with Lord Baltimore in 1739. Frederick came to the throne the next year and began to correspond with Algarotti, who had not only an encyclopedic mind and a handsome face but was also known to have had amorous relationships with both men and women. Frederick referred to Algarotti as his "dear swan of Padua."

It was through Algarotti that Frederick obtained some of his most prized works of art. One statue, reportedly of a nude Roman boy, was said to have been placed just in front of the king's bedroom window at Sanssouci, the king's new summer palace. Frederick made Algarotti a count, as well as Algarotti's brother. Together, they toured Prussia and met with Voltaire. However, it must be noted that Algarotti—and perhaps Frederick as well—were not interested in a monogamous relationship. Algarotti is thought to have carried on various romantic liaisons across Europe.

Algarotti's greatest contribution to the Enlightenment was perhaps his desire to spread the teachings of Isaac Newton throughout the Continent. He was a noted art collector and acquired several important works of the 18th century. He died of tuberculosis while living in Pisa.

Immanuel Kant.[44]

Immanuel Kant (1724–1804)

Immanuel Kant, perhaps the last great Enlightenment thinker, was born in Königsberg, the capital of East Prussia. Unlike the many French, German, and Italian philosophers, artists, and musicians who were drawn to Prussia by the magnetism of Frederick the Great, Kant was truly a native son.

Kant's father was a harness maker of modest means. Like the theologians of the University of Halle, Kant's parents were Pietists, an evangelical branch of Lutheranism. Kant went to a Pietist school as a child, where the focus was on classical learning, religious instruction, and moral discipline. It could be said that Kant's forced focus on emotion and dependence on divine grace helped form his later interest in autonomy and rationality. While Kant might have hated his schooling, he loved his parents, who taught him hard work, honesty, and independence.

He attended the University of Königsberg, then known as the Albertina. He quickly found a passion for philosophy, which incorporated mathematics, physics, logic, ethics, metaphysics, and natural law. There, he was introduced to the work of Christian Wolff and Leibniz. Still, there were many in the faculty of the school who opposed Wolff's views. Kant's favorite professor, Martin Knutzen, was a Pietist influenced by the English philosopher John Locke. Through Knutzen, Kant was introduced to the works of Isaac Newton.

After university, Kant acted as a private tutor to children in East Prussia. In 1755, after both of his parents had died and his finances remained insecure, he returned to the Albertina as a lecturer. He would teach philosophy there for the next forty years.

In 1755, Kant published several works, one of which was *Universal Natural History and Theory of the Heavens*, in which he developed what would become known as the nebular hypothesis on the formation of the solar system. However, the book was published anonymously and initially had little impact. In the years after this seeming failure, Kant gained a reputation as an excellent lecturer and an intellectual. His finances were bolstered by the large number of students who attended his classes; they paid him directly.

Kant unleashed another round of publications in the early 1760s. These works of philosophy helped give him a wider audience, but they were not seen as particularly groundbreaking. They drew on British philosophers like David Hume, Francis Hutcheson, Newton, and the

Swiss thinker Rousseau. In 1770, Kant gained the position he had longed for: the chair of philosophy and logic at the Albertina. With this, he became more financially secure and expanded his lecture repertoire.

Kant published a new work known as the *Inaugural Dissertation*, which marked a significant departure from both German rationalism and British sentimentalism. Kant introduced concepts that he would keep for the rest of his life. For instance, he believed understanding consists of both sensibility and reason, that time and space are forms relative to human sensibility, and that moral judgments are based purely on reason. Kant worked for a decade refining his ideas and then, in 1781, released another burst of publications, including *Critique of Pure Reason* (second edition in 1787), *Metaphysical Foundations of Natural Science* (1786), and *Critique of Practical Reason* (1788).

With these and many other publications, Kant came to dominate German philosophy. He gained widespread acclaim and international fame. Kant continued to publish into the 1790s and was once even censured by the new king of Prussia, Frederick William II, nephew of Frederick the Great. Many German philosophers began to move away from Kantian ideas in order to distinguish themselves in the competitive academic environment of German universities.

Kant retired from teaching in 1796. He died in 1804 at the age of seventy-nine, leaving behind a library's worth of work for future generations to ponder.

Chapter 6: Frederick the Great

Europe in 1740 when Frederick the Great came to the throne. Notice Brandeburg and Prussia.[65]

Europe at the time of Frederick's death.[66]

The crown prince of Prussia's relationship with his father was problematic. King Frederick William thought young Fritz, as he was then called, was too enamored with French culture, which he saw as effeminate and overindulgent. The king hated everything French and flew into a rage at the mere mention of the great European power. Fritz grew to hate his father's strict rule.

A crucial moment in the prince's life was when he planned with some compatriots to leave Prussia for England but was caught before he could make his escape. The king brought Fritz up on charges of desertion and had him court-martialed. The prince was saved when the court rejected the charge, but his companion and possible lover, Lieutenant von Katte, was sentenced to death and beheaded in front of Fritz. The king toyed with taking Fritz out of the succession but was eventually convinced against it. How much the episode affected Fritz remains unclear, but afterward, he appeared to mature and began earnestly preparing himself for the throne.

Crown Prince Frederick, known as "Fritz."[67]

Fritz drifted away from his Calvinist upbringing. Unlike his father, he came to believe that royal power came from the state, not from God. Frederick, as a religious skeptic, created a devotion to duty and the state. By then, he was twenty-eight years old and prepared for what would come.

In May of 1740, King Frederick William, the "Soldier King," died in Potsdam. His son, King Frederick II, took the crown. With it came a large and disciplined standing army. Prussia was a highly militarized state. The Prussian infantry was arguably unrivaled in discipline and firepower. His title, like his grandfather and father before him, was still "King in Prussia." Frederick II recognized that Brandenburg-Prussia would always be at a disadvantage as long as its territory remained fragmented. One of his goals was to acquire territory to connect and round off his kingdom.

Frederick's loyalty to the state did not falter once he acquired the crown. Many times, he gave instructions that if he were ever captured, then his counselors should do nothing to save him. "I am king only when I am free," he told them. "I shall sacrifice myself for the state ... no ransom must be offered."

The monarch subordinated himself to the state, but this must not be confused with the people, for they, too, served the state and had to be willing to sacrifice themselves for the needs of the kingdom. Frederick would be every bit the absolutist monarch as his father and the king he most admired, Louis XIV. Still, he held to his Enlightenment ideals. He limited the use of torture, reorganized the Academy of Sciences with Maupertuis at its head, and began construction of the Berlin State Opera. He also remained focused on his goal of turning Prussia into a great power. He did not have to wait long to make his move.

In October 1740, Holy Roman Emperor Charles VI died unexpectedly, leaving the Habsburg lands to his daughter Maria Theresa of Austria. Russia was preoccupied with the death of the tsarina, who died just three days before. Frederick felt confident in challenging Maria Theresa's right to the lands and asserted his own right to the richest of the Austrian provinces, Silesia.

His claims were ambiguous. He claimed it through some old treaties with the House of Hohenzollern, but it was still enough of a pretense for Frederick to prepare for war. He approached his ministers and generals to determine the best way to capture Silesia. One minister suggested diplomacy. Frederick instead decided to march into Silesia. What followed would be known as the First Silesian War.

Frederick was hedging his bets on quick and decisive action. The occupation of Silesia was relatively easy until Frederick was surprised by the arrival of an Austrian army in the Battle of Mollwitz. While the Prussian cavalry fell into disarray and Frederick actually took flight for fear of being captured, the Prussian infantry persevered and won the day. Frederick took the opportunity to fine-tune the cavalry. The French and the Electorate of Bavaria joined the War of the Austrian Succession against the Austrians, with Great Britain and Russia joining the Austrian side. Charles of Bavaria was soon elected Holy Roman Emperor Charles VII.

In the Battle of Chotusitz, Frederick's new cavalry performed much better, but it was the infantry again that won the field. It was a major victory for Frederick and resulted in the Treaty of Breslau in 1742, in which Prussia gained all of Silesia and Glatz County. The Austrians only retained a small area called Austrian (or Czech) Silesia.

However, the peace did not last long. After Maria Theresa's Austrian forces expelled the French beyond the Rhine, Frederick drove his army toward Austria, beginning the Second Silesian War in 1744.

At first, Frederick's advance into Austrian territory was unsuccessful. He had no support from his ally, France, while Austria received troops from Saxony and had the assistance of the British. He lost almost seventeen thousand men to desertion in a few months' time. In January of 1745, Holy Roman Emperor Charles VII died, and Bavaria made peace with Austria. Frederick decided, against the military theory of the time, to withdraw to Silesia and wait for his enemy to come to him.

An Austrian and Saxon army of seventy thousand soon crossed the Sudeten Mountains to Hohenfriedberg. Contrary to Austrian expectations, Frederick attacked their left flank, pushing through the Saxons and then the Austrians. Their total casualties numbered around ten thousand. It was a dramatic Prussian victory and restored Frederick's reputation. Still, the Austrians did not surrender.

Maria Theresa's husband was crowned Holy Roman Emperor Francis I, despite Frederick's vote against him. In the fall of 1745, Frederick was preparing to winter in Silesia when he received word that the Austrians planned to attack. He had just twenty-two thousand troops; the Austrian commander, Prince Charles of Lorraine, led an army of thirty-nine thousand. Frederick decided to strike first.

This time, it was the Prussian cavalry that distinguished itself. Frederick gained another impressive victory. His reputation soared, and the prefix "the Great" began to enter the public consciousness. The Prussian Army pushed on and defeated the Saxons in December. Maria Theresa finally ended her campaign to recapture Silesia, and peace was concluded on Christmas Day 1745.

Frederick proceeded to open Silesia's resources to the rest of Prussia. While he still held the formal title "King in Prussia," by this point, many referred to him simply as "King of Prussia." Frederick focused on domestic affairs, furthering judicial reforms and establishing universal policies throughout his nation.

The ten-year period after the Second Silesian War was the time of the informal "Round Table of Sanssouci," where Frederick entertained Enlightenment thinkers at his new summer palace. Frederick composed flute music, which he performed, showcasing a genuine talent for musical composition beyond that of a mere amateur. In the early 1750s, Frederick finally met Voltaire, and a relationship based on admiration and hope quickly turned to one of criticism and disappointment on both sides.

All the while, Frederick continued to build his army and enrich his war chest. At the same time, it seemed his enemies were encircling him. In the early 1750s, Austria and Russia began aligning diplomatically. By 1756, they had a formal alliance aimed mainly at countering Prussian power. In 1755, Great Britain concluded the Convention of Westminster with Frederick, which promised mutual neutrality and protection for Hanover during the imminent Anglo-French war over the North American colonies. Frederick had hoped for an agreement with France as well, but France instead entered into a defensive alliance with Austria as part of the Diplomatic Revolution (the reversal of long-standing alliances in Europe). The Franco-Prussian relationship dissolved in 1756, and the French showed no interest in renewal.

In the ring forming around Prussia, Frederick felt Russia was the greatest military threat, but he believed Russia would only attack if goaded by the Austrians. Frederick was right to fear the Russian military, but he underestimated their own interest in curbing Prussian power. In 1756, Russian leadership began planning a military campaign to counter Prussia's growing influence in central Europe.

Throughout 1756, Russian and Austrian troop movements heightened Frederick's concern of an impending attack. Deciding on a preemptive strike, in August, he occupied Saxony. After a prolonged siege, the Saxon army capitulated in October and was forcibly incorporated into the Prussian Army. This would prove to be a mistake because entire units of Saxons soon deserted en masse. This began Prussia's involvement in the global war of the European great powers: the Seven Years' War (1756–1763).

France was suffering at the hands of the British and so turned its defensive alliance with Austria into an offensive one in 1757. Sweden also joined the anti-Prussian alliance, as did the Holy Roman Empire. Frederick moved his armies in the spring of 1757, which led to the Battle of Prague, in which the war hero Field Marshal Kurt von Schwerin was killed. Still, the Austrians suffered heavy losses, with casualties numbering around fifteen thousand, making it one of the bloodiest battles of the war.

This did not annihilate the Austrian army, which withdrew to the fortress of Prague. Frederick began to lay siege to the city. Another Austrian force was on the way to bring relief to those inside Prague. When Frederick faced this larger force at the Battle of Kolín, he was defeated. Soon after, the French and their allies advanced into Saxony. On November 5th, 1757, Frederick led an army of about twenty-two thousand men against a combined French and Imperial force of over forty thousand. The Prussians were able to surprise the enemy and completely rout their foe. Napoleon Bonaparte would later call Frederick's tactics in this battle, the Battle of Rossbach, the work of a genius. The French would no longer play a major role in the Seven Years' War in central Europe.

Idealized Frederick the Great as a standard bearer.[68]

Frederick had no time to celebrate. He soon learned that the Russians were attacking East Prussia and that the Austrians had invaded Silesia. He decided to attack the Austrians first, though they occupied the high ground and were entrenched. Frederick concentrated his forces at the Austrian center but at the last minute reformed and hit the unsuspecting left wing. The Battle of Leuthen was a resounding defeat for the Austrians, who fled to Bohemia.

The Russians, upon rumors of the death of Tsarina Elizabeth, withdrew from East Prussia in late 1757. The rumors turned out to be false. In 1758, the Russians returned and occupied Königsberg. Frederick responded, and the Prussians and Russians faced each other for the first time in open battle.

The Battle of Zorndorf lasted all day, with both sides displaying extreme tenacity and bravery. Only the coming of night ended the hostilities. At dawn, the Prussians were surprised to see the Russians had withdrawn from the field. The Russians suffered around sixteen thousand to seventeen thousand casualties, while Frederick lost about twelve thousand. It was not the resounding victory that Frederick had hoped for. Yet, the Prussians had stopped the Russians from driving further into Prussia and from linking up with Austrian forces.

Lack of material and men forced Frederick to fight a defensive war to secure his possessions, including Saxony. When a force of Russians and Austrians, about sixty thousand strong, pushed into his territory, Frederick met them at Kunersdorf in 1759. The Prussians were soundly defeated, and the king came close to being captured. The Russians and Austrians did not follow up on their success but went their separate ways to pursue their separate aims.

Frederick temporarily lost Dresden and had to abandon Saxony. The Austrians, with a force of around fifty thousand, planned to annihilate Frederick's army of roughly equal size. However, Frederick outmaneuvered his foe and won the Battle of Torgau in November of 1760. Still, he could not complete his objective of recapturing Dresden due to a continued lack of supplies and manpower. He raised troops from pressed foreigners and cadets as young as fourteen. He eventually gathered almost 100,000 troops, but their offensive capacity was doubtful.

Prussia's future looked grim, and it might have been if not for the timely death of Tsarina Elizabeth. She was succeeded to the throne by Peter III, who was a great admirer of Frederick's. He reversed Russia's policy on Prussia and recommended peace. Peace was signed between Russia and Prussia in May 1762. Frederick had hopes of an alliance with Peter against the Austrians, but his dream ended with the overthrow and death of Peter III in July 1762.

However, France and Great Britain had agreed on peace, and soon, Maria Theresa finally agreed to end the conflict with Prussia. Frederick was forced to give up what he claimed in Saxony, but he retained Silesia. Frederick agreed to the treaty because he had, like much of Europe, tired of war for the time being. The Seven Years' War had been a huge drain on men and money. Nations had found themselves simply incapable of going on.

A period of reconstruction began. Frederick wanted to use the peace to build up his army. He had learned from his predecessors and from his own experience that a standing army was crucial to Prussia's survival and growth. Petty criminals and vagabonds were pressed into service. By 1776, the Prussian Army would number over 187,000 soldiers.

In 1764, a general crisis in trade and commerce struck Berlin, as well as Amsterdam and Hamburg. Frederick envisioned a novel approach to addressing such issues. He came up with a plan in which capital and money were concentrated in the hands of the state as well as manufacturing and trade. To this end, he proposed creating a central bank, the Preußische Giro- und Lehnbank. But the idea got no further because of pushback from merchants and the overwhelming issues of administration.

Frederick purchased a porcelain factory in Berlin, which became the Königliche Porzellan-Manufaktur, which still exists today as KPM Berlin. Under Frederick, the KPM became a model employer with regular working hours, no child labor, and health insurance coverage. Frederick was also the company's first great customer, ordering 200,000 Reichsthalers' worth of ceramics from the company's founding until his death.

Frederick forced the expansion of potato planting and large-scale dairy farming. The number of cattle in Prussian territory doubled by the end of the 18th century. He increased the excise tax on brandy, beer, and meat but abolished it on flour. The result was a significant increase in revenue—possibly up to 23.5 million thalers from 1766 to 1786. Much was spent on welfare purposes, but plenty was put back into the state treasury. The king attracted outside settlers. In the years after the Seven Years' War, the population increased by about 1.25 percent per year.

In 1764, Frederick the Great secured a formal alliance with Russia, strengthening ties between the two powers. Following the death of King Augustus III of Poland, a contested royal succession unfolded within the Polish-Lithuanian Commonwealth. With support from both Prussia and Russia, Stanisław August Poniatowski, a pro-Russian candidate, was elected king. The Russo-Prussian alliance allowed both states to exert influence over Polish affairs. In the years that followed, as Russia became embroiled in war with the Ottoman Empire (beginning in 1768) and internal unrest deepened in Poland, Frederick skillfully maneuvered politics. These developments culminated in the First Partition of Poland in 1772, in which Prussia, Russia, and Austria each annexed portions of Polish territory. The result was Prussian control of West Prussia, finally linking Prussia with Brandenburg.

In 1780, Frederick's great antagonist, Maria Theresa, died. Her son, Joseph II, succeeded her. Joseph tried to expand territorially, but Frederick checked him at every move. France, Britain, and Russia were too concerned with their own affairs to get involved in a central European squabble. Then, on August 17th, 1786, Frederick the Great died at the age of seventy-four. No other Prussian monarch had accomplished as much as he had.

Frederick's reign had not just brought Prussia onto the global stage, but he had also inspired future generations of Germans. As Goethe wrote of Frederick, "What mattered Prussia to us? It was the personality of the Great King which affected the emotions of us all." People, especially writers looking to define what it was to be German, looked to Frederick as the leader, regardless of whether they were Prussians and despite the fact that Frederick was typically critical of German writing, preferring the French in almost all art forms.

Frederick the Great's legacy is ambiguous to the modern reader. His idolization as the ultimate German "hero" and a paragon of duty and militarism has been stained by his later incorporation into Nazi propaganda. Adolf Hitler was a great fan of Frederick's and carried a portrait of the Prussian monarch with him, even in his bunker during the final days of World War II. After World War II, Frederick's role in history was downplayed, but renewed interest in him has emerged at the end of the 20th and into the 21st centuries.

Frederick's patronage of the arts is seen as a positive. His sense of duty to his country marks him as a clear example of Enlightenment absolutism, though his military efforts often contradict certain Enlightenment ideologies. Military historians regard him as a great leader and strategist, and his battles are still studied around the world. Napoleon was an admirer of the king. Frederick is still considered a model of "servant leadership," a concept in which the role of the leader is to serve the greater good.

Frederick also wrote several works in his lifetime. As crown prince, he received some notoriety for penning *Anti-Machiavel*, which attempted to argue against Machiavelli's principles in his Renaissance work *The Prince*. Several volumes by Frederick were published after his death, including a two-volume history of the Seven Years' War. Also published posthumously were two memoirs, *The History of My Own Times*, and an instruction book originally written to his generals. He is also remembered for his flute compositions.

Before Frederick became king, he was married to Elisabeth Christine of Brunswick-Wolfenbüttel-Bevern, who would be queen through his entire reign and would outlive him by eleven years. It is fairly certain that Frederick was gay and that this remained his primary orientation for most of his life. However, the exact nature of his relationships remains speculative. Frederick and Elisabeth's marriage remained childless, and Frederick would be succeeded by his nephew, Frederick William II. Certain letters survive that indicate quite clearly that Frederick had same-sex affairs with men, such as his secretary, Claude Darget. Voltaire commented openly about Frederick's homosexuality. Frederick's younger brother, Prince Henry, is also believed to have been gay.

Chapter 7: Prussia and the Napoleonic Wars

Frederick the Great's younger brother, Prince Augustus William, and his wife, Princess Luise Amalie of Brunswick-Wolfenbüttel, welcomed their son, Frederick William, into the world in 1744. He came to the throne in 1786 at the age of forty-one and was immediately cast in the shadow of his predecessor. Frederick William II moved away from the strict regime of his uncle, which was welcomed by many. Yet, the administration of the kingdom was steered into carelessness and neglect. It is almost certain that whoever followed Frederick the Great on the throne would be compared to him and fall short. However, Frederick William was noted for his love of theater, art, gossip, and his mistresses, as well as his disinterest in listening to his ministers or taking an active part in governing Prussia.

At the end of the 18th century, Prussia's societal dynamics were beginning to shift. The population was still largely peasants with a small number of nobles, but the gradual development of trade and early industrial activity contributed to the emergence of a modest middle class. Frederick the Great had promoted a centralized, bureaucratic state and did not actively support middle-class political influence. Frederick William proved to be a weaker monarch. He was unable to provide consistent leadership in response to these changes. His government moved away from enlightened absolutism, reverting to a more bureaucratic authoritarianism with a focus on maintaining control and stability.

Frederick William had been forced into a marriage with Princess Elisabeth Christine of Brunswick-Wolfenbüttel (not the same Elisabeth Christine who was married to Frederick the Great), which resulted in one daughter. His second marriage to Princess Frederica Louisa of Hesse-Darmstadt produced seven children, including the future Frederick William III. His first mistress, Wilhelmine Enke, was a commoner and the daughter of a horn player in the royal orchestra. He had five children with her. He ended his physical relationship with Wilhelmine several years before taking the throne, but she remained a close companion and confidant. In 1794, he raised her from commoner status to the countess of Lichtenau. He continued several other affairs, including two with the queen's ladies-in-waiting, Julie von Voss and Countess Sophie Dönhoff.

Wilhelmine introduced Frederick William to architect Carl Gotthard Langhans, who would go on to design the famous Brandenburg Gate. Berlin breathed new life with the ascendancy of a new monarch. Germans took the place of Frenchmen in the Academy of the Sciences. Immanuel Kant, a native Prussian, continued publishing, as did Johann Georg Hamann and Johann Gottfried Herder. Literary and scientific clubs grew, not just in the capital but also throughout the kingdom.

The Brandenburg Gate.[69]

Frederick William left foreign policy largely in the hands of Count Hertzberg, who had served faithfully under his uncle. Hertzberg worked under the traditional view that Austria and the Habsburgs were the great enemies of Prussia. However, after a series of diplomatic maneuvers, the death of Emperor Joseph II, and the outbreak of revolution in France in 1789, Hertzberg's power waned. When Frederick William became more involved, the two were often at odds.

The need for a common front against revolutionary France led to the unlikely alliance of Austria and Prussia, which was concluded in 1791. They agreed to war against France, in which Prussia promised to provide twenty thousand men, although it initially sent many more. Russia took this opportunity to invade Poland in the hopes of territorial gain. Prussia and Russia had reached an understanding (of which Austria was unaware at the time), and Prussia also invaded Poland in 1793, capturing Danzig, among other prizes. The Poles mounted a brave defense but were ultimately crushed in 1795.

Meanwhile, the war with France made little headway. Despite popular assumptions, the people of France did not view Prussian, Austrian, or Imperial forces as liberators. The French continually pushed the allies back, and the Prussian coffers that Frederick the Great had left full began to empty. Frederick William's health declined rapidly while he was cared for by his first love, Wilhelmine Enke. He died at the age of fifty-three on November 16th, 1797. His son, Frederick William III, ascended to the throne. He was twenty-seven years old.

Educated under the guidance of his father's court and the values of his great-uncle Frederick the Great, Frederick William III was a more prudent ruler than his father. Despite his great-uncle's religious skepticism, he was instructed by religiously minded teachers. He would remain devout his whole life. In 1793, he met Princess Louise of Mecklenburg-Strelitz. This was one of the few love matches of the Hohenzollern dynasty. While Frederick William III was reserved, she was outgoing. They complemented each other perfectly. They had nine children together.

Frederick William immediately cut royal expenditures upon gaining the throne. He dismissed his father's ministers. But while he certainly had determination, he lacked the trust in his advisors to delegate responsibilities. This severely undermined the effectiveness of his administration.

It was not long into his reign that the rise of Napoleon led to the Napoleonic Wars, which started in 1803. Frederick William and his advisors wished to remain neutral in the conflict. However, the queen believed Prussia must join the other European forces to stop Napoleon, who had crowned himself emperor, from gaining any more power. Prussia was drawn into the conflict in 1806 and joined in the twin battles of Jena and Auerstedt in October of that year. The French decimated the Prussian Army. The Prussians had superior numbers, but their casualties were almost four times those of the French. They were unable to react to the speed and decisiveness of Napoleon's armies. The French then defeated the reserve army and marched into Berlin.

When Napoleon entered Berlin, one of his first stops was to the tomb of Frederick the Great in Potsdam. "Gentlemen," he told the generals gathered around him, "if this man were still alive, I would not be here." In peace negotiations, Napoleon demanded that Prussia give up all its territory west of the River Elbe. Frederick William was willing to agree to these terms, but then Napoleon changed his mind and demanded that Prussia allow French troops to use Prussian lands as a staging ground for an invasion of Russia. In a rare moment of decisiveness, Frederick William rejected the offer.

The royal household was now in Königsberg with the French Army at their heels. Napoleon began to rally support for his invasion of Russia. He offered Austria the region of Silesia back, but the Habsburgs kept their neutrality. Saxony, however, went to the French side, and the elector was made king under Emperor Napoleon.

In 1807, East Prussia became a theater of war. There, the French had large numbers of troops who lived off the land, damaging the common people's farms and crops. Napoleon was able to push the Russians back to Lithuania. Then, at Preussisch-Eylau, Napoleon fought a bloody and indecisive battle against the Russians, who had support from Prussian forces. Although Napoleon was not defeated outright, it was one of his first serious setbacks. However, the Russians did not press their advantage, and Napoleon was able to slip away and regroup.

The Prussian king, now advised by ministers like Karl August von Hardenberg (his chancellor and chief reformer who had modernized Prussia after the 1806 defeat), refused the offer. Napoleon pressed on, gaining control over much of Silesia and Pomerania. Prussia secured alliances with Sweden, Russia, and Great Britain. The terms of the Russian agreement stated the aim was to push the French back across the

Rhine and to establish a German confederacy to replace the Holy Roman Empire, with Austria and Prussia as equal powers.

However, to Frederick William's dismay, Russia concluded a ceasefire with Napoleon. Prussia paid the heaviest price in the resulting Treaty of Tilsit, losing significant territory, including lands west of the Elbe, much of its Polish provinces, and its influence in Saxony. Some of the western provinces were incorporated into the newly created Kingdom of Westphalia, with Napoleon's youngest brother, Jérôme Bonaparte, placed on the throne.

The result of this defeat and humiliation was a renewed desire for reform, which had already been on the minds of many officials. The disaster proved to be the opportunity many had hoped for. It would be known as the Prussian Reform Movement. It was not a revolution but rather a reconstruction from within the existing institutions of the Prussian state.

The reforms were widespread. Royal subjects became citizens, echoing the French Revolution. The state was to be the focal point of the community, and feudal restrictions separating subjects by estate would be abolished. Four main reformers gave progress direction, though many others worked at all levels of government: Baron Heinrich Friedrich Karl vom und zum Stein (chief minister who abolished serfdom), Prince Karl August von Hardenberg (chancellor who continued economic reforms), General Gerhard von Scharnhorst (military reformer who opened the officer corps to merit), and Wilhelm von Humboldt (education minister who founded the University of Berlin).

The foreign-born Baron Stein had served under Frederick the Great. Stein recognized a lack of communication between the various departments in the Prussian government and saw that skilled ministers were reduced to messengers while inexperienced members of the royal cabinet made most of the decisions. He envisioned a centralization of power and the establishment of a council of ministers. Stein was a great follower of Adam Smith and wanted to make guilds accessible to all trades, crafts, and professions.

Stein hit a significant barrier when he proposed to eliminate the royal cabinet. His unwillingness to yield on this issue led to a forced resignation and his departure from Prussia. However, he was invited back, thanks to the work of Hardenberg, returning in 1807. Stein and Hardenberg, who had once been adversaries, joined forces and set their sights on the liberation of serfs in all of Prussia.

The serfs would no longer be tied to a lord and his estate, giving them more opportunities, but they also lost many of their legal protections. The nobility was eager to comply with the change because, under the old system, they were obligated to provide for peasants on their land even if their profits suffered. The new system would allow the landholders to evict tenant farmers without notice and consolidate their holdings to maximize their returns.

Stein worked to allow cities to become more self-governed and made it so that more citizens could become burghers, city residents who held the exclusive right to own property and conduct business. However, many groups remained excluded, including most Jewish people, due in part to prevailing prejudices of the time.

Stein also helped to establish the idea that the various lands under Frederick William III's control would officially be known as "Prussia." This completed the unification of Prussia, which had begun in the days of the Great Elector. Stein made drastic cuts to streamline the government. Fifty percent of all public servants lost their jobs. One of Stein's last acts before leaving office under pressure from Napoleon was to suggest to Frederick William that he should place Wilhelm von Humboldt at the head of the administration of culture and education.

Humboldt had developed a concept of national education whose goal was to produce free men capable of fully developing themselves for the benefit of the state. At the heart of this was the concept of the Volk (the people), which did not originate from Humboldt. The Volk were united not within the borders of a nation but by the German language.

Humboldt's reforms widened the number of people who received an education. He also reorganized the education system to ensure efficiency. He helped found the Frederick Wilhelm University of Berlin. Humboldt accomplished all of this in a little over a year and then left his post due to personal issues with Hardenberg in 1810.

Karl August von Hardenberg was, like Stein, not native to Prussia. In 1810, at the age of sixty, he became the chancellor of the state and was entrusted to conduct Prussia's affairs. Hardenberg was hard on subordinates who dared to disagree with him, which was what led to Humboldt's resignation.

Prussia faced French demands for contributions, so Hardenberg confiscated many church lands and sold them cheaply to pay the French. He abolished most tax exemptions and allowed broader participation in trade with some exceptions, which undermined the authority of the guilds.

The nobility greatly opposed Hardenberg. This opposition was often expressed with blatant antisemitism. Adding to these conservative fears was the Edict Concerning the Rights of the Jews. The result of Hardenberg's edict was that approximately seventy thousand Jews officially became Prussian citizens. In 1812, Hardenberg declared that the Jewish people should have the same rights and duties as any other citizen.

At the same time, the military situation was changing in Prussia. A Hanoverian-born officer in service to Prussia, General Gerhard von Scharnhorst recognized the need for reforms in the army. As director of the Prussian Military Academy, he sought to modernize the army, abolish the recruitment of foreigners, end corporal punishment, and limit advancement based on seniority in favor of a system based on merit.

Scharnhorst believed in opening the commissioned ranks to members of the middle class and advocated a shift toward a citizen army rather than an aristocratic professional force. In the aftermath of Prussia's defeat and the imposition of a forty-two-thousand-man cap on its standing army, he introduced the Krümpersystem, under which recruits were rapidly trained, cycled out, and replaced, creating a large reservoir of trained manpower beyond the treaty limit. He also supported the creation of a militia (later the Landwehr), laying the foundation for a broader national defense based on compulsory, universal-style service, though full universal conscription was legally formalized only later.

Scharnhorst purged the senior officers. Of the 143 generals who were active in 1806, only a few remained after he had finished. Corporal punishment was abolished. Training became more focused on the field and the rifle range instead of the parade grounds.

Frederick William III did not turn a blind eye to these reforms. He let men like Hardenberg, Stein, Humboldt, and Scharnhorst do as they wished but only to a point. He recognized the need for reforms, but like his predecessors, he was cautious of political upheaval. His fear was unfounded. If the reforms did anything, it was to instill in the middle class a sense of patriotism and duty to the state, which curbed any influence of revolutionaries. The king remained in power, while the middle class was able to expand its own power and gain more control of the government.

Prussia remained a buffer state between France and Russia, its independence severely limited. Frederick William was required to pay a substantial indemnity, which resulted in the creation of the general income tax. To the surprise of the French, Spain rose in a unified revolt against Napoleon's power. Many hoped that a similar spirit would be raised in Germany. Austria made attempts to ally with Prussia to oppose the usurper. Frederick William would not agree to an alliance unless Russia was involved, and at the moment, Russia was not interested in a war with France.

Due to the revolt in Spain, Napoleon was forced to withdraw several troops from Prussia. In 1809, Austria declared war on France. In Prussia, Stein had been forced to resign under pressure from Napoleon, who saw him as an agitator. Scharnhorst counseled Frederick to declare war on France, as did Queen Louise. Major Ferdinand von Schill from the Prussian Army took it upon himself to wage a campaign against Napoleon, but he was found and killed in May of 1809. Not long after this, Austria signed a peace treaty with France.

It was clear that attitudes were changing, and it soon became apparent that Russia and France were on the brink of war. The French-imposed Continental System had strained Russia's economy, cutting off vital trade with Britain. Though initially aligned with Napoleon, Tsar Alexander grew increasingly uneasy, especially as French influence crept eastward through the reconstitution of a Polish state under French protection. Russia viewed the Duchy of Warsaw as a direct threat to its borders. At the same time, mutual distrust deepened. Napoleon suspected the Russians would abandon the alliance, while Alexander resented France's overreach. As Russia began to loosen its enforcement of the trade blockade, relations further deteriorated. War seemed inevitable, and both sides quietly began to prepare. Frederick William offered an agreement to the French but sent Scharnhorst on a mission to St. Petersburg to conclude a secret alliance there.

Napoleon amassed an army of over 600,000 men for his invasion of Russia in 1812. A significant portion of these forces were Germans. Napoleon advanced, but the Russians pulled back. His army was swallowed by the vastness of Russia. The Russians burned crops as they went, leaving nothing for Napoleon's forces to eat. The French were finally forced to retreat after a few costly victories. This was when the Russians began to truly attack Napoleon's retreating forces.

Prussian soldiers captured by the Russians sometimes joined anti-French units, including the so-called German Legion, which was supported by ex-minister Stein. The Prussian forces in East Prussia were under the command of General Yorck. He continually offered to coordinate with the Russians. He even sent messages to Frederick William to direct him, but the monarchy was, as ever, vacillating. Yorck took it upon himself to sign the Convention of Tauroggen in December 1812, allying with the Russians and beginning the War of Liberation.

It was now 1813. The beloved Queen Louise had been dead for three years. Though Frederick William viewed Yorck's actions as insubordinate, he did not charge the general, and he went along with the Russian alliance. In fact, he seemed invigorated by the new war. He created the Order of the Iron Cross, issued his famous "An Mein Volk" ("To My People") proclamation, and universal conscription was put into place. All of Prussia became unified in their desire to defeat Napoleon and reclaim their country. One of the volunteer units made a point of being German and not purely Prussian. Their uniform of black, red piping, and gold buttons later came to be associated with the German national colors—black, red, and gold.

In August of 1813, Austria joined the Allies. Three Coalition armies converged on Leipzig: the Austrian Army of Bohemia under Field Marshal Karl Philipp Schwarzenberg, the Swedish Army of the North under Crown Prince Charles John, and the Prussian Army of Silesia under Field Marshal Gebhard Leberecht von Blücher.

Blücher was seventy-one years old and had returned to active service when Prussia rejoined the war against Napoleon. A career soldier who had risen through the ranks on merit rather than noble birth, he embodied the spirit of Prussia's military reforms. Known for his aggressive tactics and unrelenting energy, Blücher had earned the nickname "Marshal Forward" for his tendency to push relentlessly toward the enemy. Where other generals hesitated or waited for perfect conditions, Blücher attacked. This mentality, combined with the tactical brilliance of his chief of staff August von Gneisenau, made him a formidable commander.

The resulting Battle of Leipzig (also called the Battle of the Nations) was waged over four days, from October 16th to 19th. On the first day, Blücher's army engaged French forces in the northern sector at Möckern, where his troops fought Marshal Marmont's corps in brutal close combat. Though the Prussians took heavy casualties, Blücher's persistence wore down the French defenses. His victory at Möckern prevented Napoleon from concentrating his forces and paved the way for the decisive defeat that followed.

By the final day of battle, Napoleon's position had become untenable. The Coalition armies closed in from all sides, and on October 19th, Blücher's forces stormed Leipzig itself. The battle involved approximately 560,000 soldiers and led to 133,000 casualties, making it the largest battle in European history before World War I. Napoleon was forced to retreat westward, and French dominance over Germany collapsed.

For his role at Leipzig, Blücher was promoted to field marshal and given the title prince of Wahlstatt. He became a hero of Prussia's War of Liberation, a symbol of the nation's resurgence after the humiliations of 1806.

At the Congress of Vienna, which concluded the Napoleonic Wars, Prussia regained its place as a great power. Hardenberg and Humboldt attended the congress. Frederick William was also in Vienna, working behind the scenes. Prussia acquired significant territory, including much of Saxony, parts of the Duchy of Warsaw (Poland), Danzig, and the Grand Duchy of the Lower Rhine, along with other lands lost during the Napoleonic Wars.

Chapter 8: Prussia's Economic and Social Revolution

While the Congress of Vienna restored and expanded Prussia's borders, the country and its people had been rocked by years of war. A complete restoration was needed to pull the country out of the trauma of the turn of the 19th century, and it would not be found in more war or political maneuvers but in economic growth and development. After the Napoleonic Wars, Prussia remained largely agrarian and less industrialized than Britain, which had already entered the Industrial Revolution. Prussia found itself behind the times, but it still benefited from the reforms established years before. It also had one of the most progressive education systems in Europe. This created generations of thinkers, engineers, and entrepreneurs who would utilize everything Prussia had to offer to bring about its own industrial development.

After Napoleon's abdication and exile to Elba, he famously returned and gathered an army, only to be finally defeated at Waterloo in 1815. The two great leaders who faced Napoleon were Lord Wellington of Britain and the aged hero of Leipzig, Prussian Field Marshal Blücher. Napoleon was once again exiled, this time to St. Helena, where he died. With Napoleon defeated, Prussia was able to focus on securing what it had and expanding where it could.

Economic measures were already enacted that promoted trade and cooperation among German states. Though Austria held German provinces, Prussia was increasingly seen as the rightful leader of any

German organization. There was pressure on Frederick William to acknowledge a constitutional monarchy instead of the patchwork absolutism he enjoyed. The king and his allies did everything they could to avoid this.

In 1818, Prussia secured a large loan from the banking house of Rothschild, allowing the government not only to function but also to pursue economic interests and support industrial development. This was especially noticeable in Westphalia. There, the well-traveled provincial president Ludwig von Vincke, an admirer of British self-governance, promoted economic modernization. The newly developed coalfields in the Ruhr became the backbone of Prussia's economic strength.

A road-building program began in the early 19th century and expanded steadily over the next decades. By the late 1840s, Prussia had built a large and growing network of state-owned roads. The railway was also a revolution in the country's transportation system. The first line opened in 1838 between Berlin and Potsdam.

Frederick William III was not impressed. He complained that his peace and quiet were suffering just to be "a few hours earlier to Berlin." However, most of the country welcomed the new speed. By 1844, Prussia had several hundred kilometers of track. Four years later, the total had nearly tripled. In 1840, Prussians began building their own locomotives instead of importing them.

Prussia was outpacing many smaller German states economically. For example, while pig-iron and steel production in regions like Saxony remained modest in the 1830s, Prussia, aided by its mineral resources, was quickly scaling up output across multiple smelters. One significant case was the firm now known as Krupp. Alfred Krupp dropped out of school to manage his family's failing steelworks at the age of fourteen, inheriting the secret of producing high-quality cast steel. Over the following decades, as demand for steel for railways and industrial machinery surged, Krupp's business turned a profit. The quality of his cast steel proved so high that by the 1850s and 1860s, he began producing artillery. He eventually supplied weapons to many countries and earned the nickname "The Cannon King." From humble beginnings, he built a massive industrial fortune and established a foundation for Prussia's—and later Germany's—steel armaments dominance.

August Borsig (1804–1854), the son of a carpenter from Silesia, started his industrial career with limited capital. Borsig initially built equipment for sugar refineries but soon transitioned to the manufacture of locomotive parts. In 1840, he built his first complete locomotive, which performed as well as the English-made engines being imported into the country at the time. He eventually opened additional works to supply the increased demand for trains. At the time of his death in 1854, he had built several hundred locomotives. By 1872, his company had become one of the largest producers of locomotives in Europe.

Steam engines had first been introduced to Prussia in the 18th century, but it was in the 19th century that they saw widespread use. By the 1830s, steam power had begun to transform factories, mines, and workshops across the kingdom. In the west, Prussia's newly acquired territories along the Rhine (gained at the Congress of Vienna in 1815) proved economically vital. Prussia's coal-rich regions became the center of this early industrial shift. The Saar region, which had once been under Napoleon's control but was now part of the Prussian Rhineland, saw sharp increases in coal output through the 1820s and 1830s. The Ruhr Valley, also part of these western acquisitions, saw production expand rapidly after 1815, helped by improved mining techniques and rising demand for fuel. These regions would soon become the heart of Prussia's heavy industry. Steam power and coal were laying the foundations of a new industrial economy.

Industrialization required not just laborers but also skilled engineers and technicians. To answer this need, the Royal Technical Institute (a predecessor of the Technical University of Berlin) was established in 1821. To demonstrate Prussia's advancements to an international audience, exhibitions were organized in 1822, 1827, and 1844.

As is so often the case, those who suffered the most from industrialization were those at the bottom of the social hierarchy. The Stein-Hardenberg reforms had done much to help the middle class, but they had led to many peasants losing their small landholdings, as the nobility was able to evict tenant farmers more freely. Peasants who managed to retain their small holdings could not compete with the large-scale farmers around them and had to sell their land and move to cities to become factory workers.

Conditions at Prussia's factories were notably bad. Workdays were long and dangerous, with little time off. Child labor was rampant. The government's solution of setting a minimum age of nine for workers did little to help the issue. It would take several more decades before workers were given a voice.

Interestingly, the arts prospered at this time. Gottfried von Schadow, the famous sculptor of the chariot and four horses atop the Brandenburg Gate, had a pupil named Christian Daniel Rauch (1777–1857). Rauch completed several noteworthy works in the early 19th century, including a statue of sleeping Queen Louise, which was placed in her mausoleum. It is a defining piece of neoclassical sculpture in Prussia. Rauch also sculpted monuments to Blücher and Scharnhorst, as well as a colossal equestrian statue of Frederick the Great, which is today considered a masterpiece of the Berlin school of sculpture and marks a transition to realism in the capital.

Queen Louise of Prussia by Christian Daniel Rauch.[70]

Gottfried Schadow's son, Friedrich Wilhelm Schadow (1789–1862), and Alfred Rethel (1816–1859) were both well-known German painters. Schadow is perhaps better known as a teacher and Rethel for his historical paintings, drawings, and eccentric character. Felix Mendelssohn (1809–1847) moved with his family as a young child to Berlin and eventually studied under German composers Ludwig Berger and Carl Friedrich Zelter. A prolific composer from an early age, Felix composed thirteen string symphonies between the ages of twelve and fourteen. Mendelssohn was favorably compared to Mozart. In 1833, he was made musical director at Düsseldorf. He then moved to Leipzig and eventually Britain.

Great thinkers like Georg Wilhelm Friedrich Hegel (1770–1831) also lived at this time. Hegel held the chair of philosophy at the University of Berlin from 1818 until his death. There were well-known female thinkers as well. Bettina von Arnim was a German Romantic author and composer. Her most famous books were reworkings of correspondence with real people.

Rahel Varnhagen (1771–1833), the daughter of a Jewish merchant, was born in Berlin and went on to host one of the most prominent salons in the late 18th and early 19th centuries. She is remembered for her vast amount of correspondence and the famous intellectuals who came to her salon, including the Humboldt brothers, Wilhelm and Alexander.

Wilhelm von Humboldt was, of course, a minister and diplomat, but he was also a philosopher. His studies of languages, particularly Basque, remain influential to this day. Wilhelm's younger brother, Alexander (1769–1859), is remembered as a leader in botanical and geographic studies. Between 1799 and 1804, he traveled extensively in the Americas and wrote about his journey over the course of several years and twenty-one volumes. Other luminaries include the historian Leopold von Ranke and jurist and historian Friedrich Carl von Savigny. Karl Marx might have joined them if he had not been denied a lectureship at Berlin University.

The political climate of Prussia was charged in the 1830s. Tensions rose between the government and the Catholic Church when a dispute broke out between the church and the Prussian government over the terms under which mixed Catholic-Protestant marriages could be recognized by the Catholic Church. This had been accepted by previous bishops under pressure, but the new archbishop of Cologne refused to comply with the state's terms. At the same time, constitutionalists were agitating for a constitutional monarchy.

On January 7th, 1840, Frederick William III died. The throne passed to his son, Frederick William IV.

The younger Frederick had been his mother's favorite son. When she died when he was only fourteen years old, the prince saw it as a punishment from God. He had been a child when his family was forced to flee the approaching French soldiers, and like many royalty who lived during the French Revolution, he feared the power of the mob might topple his own power. As crown prince, he did not care for the reforms of Stein and Hardenberg. He fought in the Wars of Liberation that drove the French out of Germany. He became a Romanticist with a nostalgic view of the Middle Ages.

Frederick William IV's accession to the throne was cheered by the population at large. Many liberals who had gone into exile were welcomed back, including the famous Brothers Grimm. (The Grimms had been among the "Göttingen Seven," professors who had been dismissed and exiled from Hanover in 1837 for protesting the king's abolition of the constitution.) Alexander von Humboldt was appointed state councilor. However, the king also appointed his close friends to high positions, men who were conservatives with the religious fervor of Pietist revivalism. Many wondered if Frederick William would be a liberal or a Pietist monarch, but in truth, the king wanted to be both.

He delivered public speeches, something his father had never done. However, his words bordered on religious sermons with little political value. Many liberals came to believe he was not a man of action as they had hoped. The king's concept of monarchy was fundamentally different from that of many of his ancestors. He did not see himself as the first servant of the state but instead believed he held his crown by the grace of God. He deeply trusted in the power of divine will, and this led to inaction at important moments.

Frederick William IV supported the "German" cause to return Germany to its medieval splendor, but he appeared not to realize that this would mean losing his kingdom to a German emperor. He eased the troubles between the state and the Roman Catholic Church. He believed this was the first step toward reconciliation between Catholics and Protestants. He also restarted the building of the Cologne Cathedral.

In 1843 and 1844, the cotton market was depressed, and the weavers of Silesia were hit particularly hard. The Silesian weavers' protest of 1844 reflected growing hardship and discontent in the industrial working class.

In 1847, after years of economic woes and bad harvests, several revolts broke out in Prussia. King Frederick William IV had tried to avoid constitutionalism, but the crises of his country forced his hand. On February 3rd, 1847, he published a decree that created the United Diet, a legislative assembly. This assembly would meet when summoned by the king for matters such as approving new taxes or loans. However, the decree seemed too little, too late.

In 1848, the Second French Republic was proclaimed, and a tide of revolution swept through Europe. It began in Cologne on March 3rd, 1848, with a mass demonstration of workers, which spread through the Rhineland. Frederick William tried again to appeal to the people's liberal demands, but his proclamations fell short of expectations. The German intelligentsia met in Heidelberg in March of 1848 and resolved to press for a German, not a Prussian, national assembly. They wanted a German constitution and for a preliminary parliament, the Vorparlament, to be convened that month in Frankfurt am Main. They resolved to maintain the freedom of the press and adopted the national colors of black, red, and gold.

On March 18th, thousands gathered outside the royal palace in Berlin. The crowd demanded reforms: a constitution, freedom of the press, civil liberties, and Prussia's leadership in creating a unified German nation. The king addressed the crowd and appeared to promise reforms, but tensions remained high.

As troops attempted to clear the palace square, two shots rang out. Whether they were fired accidentally or deliberately remains disputed. In the chaos that followed, soldiers opened fire on the crowd. The violence continued through the afternoon and into the evening, with hundreds of civilians killed or wounded. Bodies were carried through the streets, and fury at the military spread throughout Berlin.

Open revolt broke out. The revolutionaries, made up of the working class, students, artisans, and burghers, erected over a thousand barricades throughout the city. Street fighting continued through the night of March 18th. Military leaders advised the king to both flee the city and crush the rebellion with overwhelming force. Frederick William instead issued another proclamation, asking the Berliners to return peacefully to their homes. When this proved ineffective, he made a fateful decision. He ordered troops to withdraw from the inner city. Amid the confusion, the revolutionaries celebrated what appeared to be a victory.

The king's brother, Prince William of Prussia, whom many held responsible for ordering the troops to fire on March 18th, fled the country in disguise, eventually reaching England. The revolutionaries formed a citizen militia to maintain order and prevent looting. In response to continued demands for reform, Frederick William appeared before crowds wearing a black, red, and gold sash—the colors of German liberalism and unification. He famously declared, "Prussia henceforth merges with Germany." Still, the Prussian government was in disarray, and the statement remained largely rhetorical.

The primary issue of a unified German state was the question of who would be at its head. The major German powers were Prussia and Austria. The men at the Frankfurt convention wanted a broad German Empire headed by a hereditary royal family but governed by a constitution. The Habsburgs of Austria refused to participate because they rejected constitutionalism and ruled over many non-German provinces.

A "lesser Germany," excluding Austrian lands and placing Frederick William IV as German emperor, was proposed. However, Frederick would not accept the convention's terms. He had no interest in their constitution and remained opposed to democratization in his kingdom. New revolts broke out, and this time, Frederick responded with force. The revolutions were violently suppressed. The Revolution of 1848 had failed.

The Frankfurt Parliament had grand ambitions, but it was too divided and lacked real power. Western Europe viewed the revolution warily. A unified Germany, potentially stretching from the North Sea to the Black Sea, was seen as a major threat to the balance of power. France was prepared to ally with Russia to suppress it. Britain, while sympathetic to liberal ideas, opposed a strong German central power.

Things returned, for the most part, to the status quo, but the whole of Germany—and especially Prussia—had been greatly shaken. Many Germans turned away from revolutionary politics. What did not subside was the steady progress of industrialization. Prussia saw a substantial increase in the use of steam engines during the mid-19th century, although exact figures vary. Germany's railway network expanded rapidly, covering thousands of kilometers by the 1860s.

Mechanization gradually replaced artisans, and factories grew larger. Textile manufacturing became increasingly mechanized during this period. The textile sector underwent consolidation, resulting in a decrease in the number of companies. Industry continued to expand, with shareholding companies growing rapidly, particularly in railways, mining, steel, iron, banks, and insurance. Prussia, and to a greater extent Germany, was on the verge of great change.

Chapter 9: German Unification

In 1847, a thirty-two-year-old Junker nobleman from an estate near Schönhausen married Johanna von Puttkamer and gained social and financial stability that supported his entry into public life. That same year, he became a representative in the newly created Prussian United Diet. He made a name for himself as an ultra-conservative royalist, but it also became clear that he was a capable politician who quickly learned to maneuver through the evolving legislative system of his country. Initially, when he entered Prussian politics, he opposed German unification, believing it would compromise Prussia's independence.

His strong support for the monarchy did not go unnoticed. In 1851, King Frederick William IV appointed him as Prussia's representative to the German Confederate Diet in Frankfurt. This envoy's name was Otto von Bismarck, and he would come to be considered the architect of the German Empire.

Born in 1815, Bismarck was the son of a landowning Junker and former Prussian military officer. His mother was the daughter of a senior government official. He spent much of his youth between the family estates in Schönhausen and Kniephof (in Farther Pomerania, now part of Poland). He was well educated and had knowledge of several languages, including English, French, and Russian. He studied law at the University of Göttingen in Lower Saxony and then at the University of Berlin from 1833 to 1835.

Bismarck later undertook a period of agricultural study while managing the family estate and serving in the Landwehr (the Prussian reserve army). He had hoped for a diplomatic career, but his early civil service posts were short-lived. Though regarded as eccentric in his youth, he displayed considerable charm and intelligence, traits that later served him well in politics.

After his mother's death in the early 1840s, Bismarck returned home to manage the family estate. He later became engaged to Johanna, whom he knew through her cousin, who was married to one of his close friends. Johanna was known to be quiet and modest but also sharp-witted. With their marriage, Bismarck's political career began in earnest with his 1847 election to the United Diet. The following year, a revolution broke out in Prussia.

While King Frederick William IV was making concessions to the revolutionaries, Bismarck, in his role as a loyal monarchist, reportedly tried to persuade the king's sister-in-law, Augusta, to support replacing the king with her son, Prince Frederick William. She refused. The liberal revolutionaries were eventually divided by internal conflicts, and conservatives regained power, promising reforms but ultimately preserving much of the existing political structure.

In 1849, Bismarck was elected to the Prussian Landtag (the lower house of Parliament). He remained generally opposed to the liberal nationalist vision of German unification, though he accepted an appointment as a Prussian delegate to the Erfurt Union Parliament in 1850—a short-lived attempt by Prussia and several smaller German states to unify Germany without Austria. Bismarck attended in order to safeguard Prussian interests, not to promote unification, and the effort soon collapsed.

In 1851, Bismarck was appointed Prussian envoy to the Diet of the German Confederation in Frankfurt. There, he frequently clashed with the Austrian representative, Friedrich von Thun und Hohenstein, and insisted on equal treatment, such as the right to smoke or remove his jacket during sessions. One notable incident resulted in a duel with fellow Prussian deputy Georg von Vincke; neither party was injured.

Bismarck spent eight years in Frankfurt, during which his political views evolved. Distanced from the Prussian court, he began to adopt a more pragmatic approach. He came to believe that Prussia needed to form alliances with other German states in order to challenge Austrian dominance, and his thinking on unification began to shift. He increasingly felt that both conservatives and moderate liberals could support a

German unification that preserved the traditional social order under Prussian leadership.

Bismarck disapproved of Prussia's neutral stance during the Crimean War and believed the kingdom should maintain a close alliance with Russia while keeping ties with Napoleon III's France. In 1857, King Frederick William IV suffered a debilitating stroke, and his brother Wilhelm became regent. Wilhelm, seen as a moderate conservative, started the so-called "New Era," implementing changes in leadership and policy direction. Bismarck was removed from his post in Frankfurt and reassigned as ambassador to Russia. Though this was technically a promotion, Bismarck felt sidelined from developments in Germany.

Nevertheless, during his four-year posting in St. Petersburg, Bismarck remained informed about Prussian affairs, thanks in part to his close relationship with Albrecht von Roon, the minister of war. Roon, along with General Helmuth von Moltke, shared Bismarck's conservative yet pragmatic outlook. The three men would become the central figures in the drive for German unification under Prussian leadership.

In 1861, King Frederick William IV died, and his brother ascended the throne as King Wilhelm (or William) I. Frederick William IV had said in his will that he hoped Wilhelm would repeal the constitution, but Wilhelm ignored his dead brother's wishes. He inherited a government strained from the tension between the Landtag and the monarchy.

In 1862, a crisis arose in which the legislature refused to approve a military spending increase to reorganize the Prussian Army. King Wilhelm threatened to abdicate in favor of his son, who was believed to be more liberal. However, Albrecht von Roon was able to convince the king that the only person capable of handling the crisis was Otto von Bismarck. Bismarck was recalled, and Wilhelm appointed him minister president and foreign minister.

Despite the king's misgivings about Bismarck, Otto soon had a powerful hold on the monarchy. He desired to maintain the power of the monarchy above all else, and he looked for a way around the current crisis. The constitution stated that a budget must be approved by the legislature and the monarchy, but it did not specify what to do in the case of a deadlock. Bismarck argued that the previous year's budget could be used to keep the government functioning by the continuation of tax collection, thus avoiding catastrophe.

Bismarck focused on German unification, envisioning Prussia as the leading entity in a German nation. In 1862, he delivered an often-quoted speech in which he said that unification would not be won with speeches and majority decisions but with iron and blood. However, his censorship of the press made him generally unpopular, and the liberal legislature demanded that the king dismiss him. The crown prince opposed Bismarck, and the queen continued to dislike him after how he had acted during the 1848 revolution. However, this did nothing to dissuade the king from believing that Prussia would only prevail with the aid of Bismarck.

Prussia's circumstances changed with the death of King Frederick VII of Denmark in 1863. The Danish king died without a direct heir, triggering a succession crisis over the duchies of Schleswig and Holstein. These territories occupied a complicated position. Holstein was predominantly German-speaking and a member of the German Confederation, while Schleswig had mixed Danish and German populations. Both were ruled by the Danish king, but they were not incorporated into Denmark itself.

The succession question had been temporarily settled by the London Protocol of 1852, which designated Prince Christian of Glücksburg as heir to both the Danish throne and the duchies, but it required the duchies to remain separate from Denmark proper. However, when Christian ascended as King Christian IX in November 1863, he immediately signed the November Constitution, which integrated Schleswig directly into the Danish kingdom. This was a clear violation of the 1852 agreement.

Bismarck saw an opportunity. He convinced Austria to join Prussia in demanding that Denmark reverse the constitution. When Denmark refused, Bismarck had his justification for war. In February 1864, Prussian and Austrian forces invaded, beginning what became known as the Second Schleswig War.

Austrian and Prussian troops entered Schleswig in February 1864. The Danish troops were outnumbered and poorly led, facing grueling retreats amid harsh winter conditions. Danish attempts to block invasion routes proved unsuccessful.

The Prussians continued to push through Schleswig, and military operations extended into Jutland. This had not been part of the original plan, but Bismarck improvised and convinced the Austrians of the need for force to settle the question of the provinces and the German Confederation for good. The war continued into the summer. Attempts were made to come to a ceasefire, but the negotiations often fell apart. By July, most of Jutland had been occupied by the German forces. Only the Danish islands remained.

In October 1864, after agreeing to abandon claims to the duchies, Denmark signed the Treaty of Vienna. Denmark handed over Schleswig, Holstein, and the Duchy of Lauenburg to the Prussians and Austrians. By giving away these provinces, the Danes lost roughly 40 percent of their land area and about one million citizens.

Prussia came out of the conflict as the superior force. The reorganization of their army proved more than effective, and this led the other nations of the German Confederation to see Prussia as the only country able to protect a unified Germany from outside aggression. Prussia and Austria agreed to administer Schleswig and Holstein jointly, but Bismarck was clearly already envisioning the duchies as part of the German nation without the Austrians' involvement.

The joint Austro-Prussian victory immediately created a new problem: what to do with the conquered territories. Both powers claimed rights to the duchies, but neither could agree on their future status. Should they become independent German states? Be annexed directly? Given to a German prince? The two victors spent months in tense negotiations.

Finally, in August 1865, they reached a compromise in the Convention of Gastein. Austria would administer Holstein, Prussia would govern Schleswig, Lauenburg would be sold to Prussia (for 2.5 million Danish rigsdaler), and both powers would jointly control the strategic port city of Kiel. This arrangement satisfied no one. It merely postponed the inevitable confrontation between the two German powers. The joint administration was awkward and unworkable from the start, with each power suspicious of the other's intentions in their respective zones.

In January 1866, a crisis erupted between the two powers that governed Schleswig-Holstein. The Austrian governor of Holstein had permitted the estates to call up a general assembly. Prussia protested this decision, saying that it undermined its authority. Austria countered that this was not true, but not wanting to take any chances, they reinforced their troops along their border with Prussia.

In April, Bismarck secured a crucial alliance with Italy. The newly unified Italian kingdom still lacked Veneto, the wealthy northeastern province that remained under Austrian control. Bismarck promised that if Italy joined Prussia in a war against Austria, Veneto would be theirs. Italy agreed, and Austria immediately mobilized its southern army along the Italian border. By May, all three powers had mobilized, making war inevitable.

Austria attempted to use its traditional leadership position in German affairs to isolate Prussia. In June, Austria brought formal charges against Prussia before both the Frankfurt Diet of the German Confederation and the Holstein Diet, accusing Prussia of violating the Convention of Gastein and threatening German unity. Prussia's response was dramatic. Bismarck declared the joint administration of Schleswig-Holstein null and void, and Prussian troops marched into Holstein, expelling the Austrian garrison.

The German Confederation immediately called for mobilization against Prussia, voting to place federal troops under Austrian command. Most of the German states, including Saxony, Hanover, Bavaria, Württemberg, Baden, and Hesse-Kassel, sided with Austria, viewing Prussian aggression as a threat to the traditional German order. Only a handful of smaller northern states joined Prussia.

Bismarck declared the German Confederation, an institution that had existed since 1815, dissolved, and Prussian armies immediately invaded Saxony, Hanover, and Hesse-Kassel before they could fully mobilize. The Austro-Prussian War, which would determine the future shape of Germany, had begun.

Years later, Bismarck would claim he had orchestrated the entire crisis with a calculated view toward German unification under Prussian leadership and even with an eye toward an eventual confrontation with France that would complete that unification.

Some suggest that Bismarck was embellishing his intentions for his later aggrandizement. Some historians argue that Bismarck was a Prussian expansionist and only nominally committed to the idea of German unification. His alliance with Austria had been to gain control of Schleswig-Holstein, and his later turn against the Austrians was to secure the duchies for Prussia alone. Of course, it is impossible to know with complete certainty. What is certain is that Bismarck's actions led directly to the declaration of war between Austria, Prussia, some of the German states, and Italy.

The war that would determine Germany's future lasted just seven weeks, earning it the nickname the "Seven Weeks' War." Prussian forces quickly overwhelmed their opponents. In the north, Hanoverian forces resisted stubbornly but were defeated at Langensalza on June 27th and forced to surrender two days later. Prussian columns swept through Saxony, Hesse-Kassel, and other states that had sided with Austria, facing little organized resistance.

The decisive campaign unfolded in Bohemia. Austrian forces under Ludwig von Benedek assembled a massive army—over 200,000 men—supported by Saxon contingents. The Prussian armies, divided into three separate columns under the overall command of Field Marshal Helmuth von Moltke, converged on the Austrian position near the fortress town of Königgrätz (modern-day Hradec Králové in the Czech Republic).

On July 3rd, the two armies clashed in one of the largest recorded battles in Europe. Nearly half a million soldiers fought across a twelve-mile front. The battle hung in the balance for hours until the Prussian Second Army, commanded by Crown Prince Frederick William, arrived on the Austrian right flank in the afternoon. Caught in a pincer, Austrian forces broke and retreated in disorder, suffering over forty thousand casualties to Prussia's nine thousand. It was a catastrophic defeat that shattered Austrian military power.

Meanwhile, on the Italian front, the war went less smoothly for Prussia's ally. Despite numerical superiority, Italian forces were defeated by the Austrians at Custoza on June 24th and in a naval battle at Lissa in the Adriatic on July 20th. However, these Austrian victories came too late. Königgrätz had already decided the war, and Austria was forced to divide its armies between two fronts, fatally weakening the Bohemian campaign.

Prussia's rapid victory stemmed from several advantages. The Prussian Army was equipped with the Dreyse needle gun, a breech-loading rifle that could fire five times faster than the Austrian muzzle-loaders and could be loaded while prone, giving Prussian infantry devastating firepower. Even more important was Prussia's railway network, which allowed Moltke to mobilize and concentrate armies with unprecedented speed. While Austrian troops were still marching toward concentration points, Prussian forces had already deployed via rail and invaded enemy territory.

By late July, Bismarck faced a delicate situation. Prussia had won decisively, but King Wilhelm I and the Prussian generals wanted to march on Vienna and impose a humiliating peace on Austria. Bismarck vehemently opposed this. He feared that France, which had been watching the war nervously, might intervene if Prussia appeared too threatening. More importantly, Bismarck wanted Austria weakened but not destroyed. He still saw Austria as a potential future ally and wanted to avoid creating lasting enmity. After fierce arguments with the king and military leadership, Bismarck prevailed.

The Peace of Prague, signed on August 23rd, 1866, was surprisingly lenient to Austria. Austria paid no indemnity and ceded no territory to Prussia. Only Veneto went to Italy, which was transferred through French mediation to save Austrian pride. However, the treaty's political consequences were revolutionary. Austria was permanently excluded from German affairs, ending centuries of Habsburg leadership. The German Confederation was formally dissolved. Prussia annexed Schleswig-Holstein, Hanover, Hesse-Kassel, Nassau, and Frankfurt, growing dramatically in size and population. The remaining German states north of the Main River were organized into a new North German Confederation under Prussian dominance, while the southern states (Bavaria, Württemberg, Baden, and Hesse-Darmstadt) remained independent but were forced into secret military alliances with Prussia.

In seven weeks, Bismarck had fundamentally reordered Germany. Austria was expelled, Prussia was the dominant power, and the path toward German unification under Prussian leadership was clear.

The Hanoverians proved especially resistant to annexation. Their king, King George V, protested along with the population. Prince Frederick William of Hesse-Kassel condemned the annexation and the end of the Electorate of Hesse. A strong anti-Prussian undercurrent continued for years afterward, disrupting Prussia's plans. Still, the process continued.

The North German Confederation was initially only a military alliance, but within a year of its creation, it had established a federal constitution with the king of Prussia as its monarch. A new parliament was created, called the Reichstag, based on universal male suffrage. A combined conservative and liberal coalition worked to establish a Northern German system of government.

Bismarck had, seemingly against all odds, accomplished exactly what he set out to do. He was not loved by his countrymen or even well liked. He was often at odds with fellow ministers and even the king, but he had made himself indispensable. And that power had upended the order of power in the German Confederation. Austria was not only no longer the superior power, but it was also excluded from German politics completely.

Bismarck's "soft peace" with Austria allowed the two countries to resume stable relations not long after the war. Austria was too concerned with the Italians and pan-Slavic movements to make a lasting enemy of Prussia. The German states, which had largely sided with Austria in the war or had remained neutral, now found themselves yoked to the Prussian wagon. Bismarck did all this even though he commanded no army, led no political party, and was not a member of the royal family. Yet, Bismarck had little time to gloat because larger enemies were just beyond the horizon.

Tensions with the Second Empire of France and Emperor Napoleon III had begun before the ink had dried on the Peace of Prague. Napoleon had hoped that France would gain land in Belgium and along the Rhine as a reward for not joining the war against Prussia, but the war had ended too quickly for him to take advantage of the situation. Bismarck did not necessarily want to avoid war with France, but he was certainly wary. France might find a ready ally in Austria, or Russia might join the war against Prussia. However, if Prussia could defeat France, it would only help to solidify the various German states.

A pretext for war came in 1870 with the question of Spanish succession. When the Spanish throne became vacant, Prince Leopold of the Hohenzollern-Sigmaringen branch was offered the crown. Napoleon III, alarmed at the prospect of Hohenzollern rulers on both his eastern and southern borders, pressured Leopold to withdraw. Leopold complied, but Napoleon III demanded more. He wanted a binding guarantee that no Hohenzollern would ever accept the Spanish throne. Since King Wilhelm of Prussia was the head of the entire House of Hohenzollern, Napoleon sent his ambassador, Count Vincent Benedetti, to meet Wilhelm at the spa town of Ems in July 1870 to extract this humiliating promise.

Wilhelm politely but firmly refused to give such a guarantee and sent Bismarck a telegram describing the meeting. Bismarck saw his opportunity. He edited the telegram to make it appear that Wilhelm had brusquely dismissed the French ambassador and that the ambassador had been insulting to the king. He then released this doctored version (called the Ems Dispatch) to the press on July 13th, 1870. The edited text enraged both nations. The French felt humiliated, and the Germans felt their king had been insulted. Bismarck later admitted he had made the telegram sound "like a red rag to the Gallic bull." France declared war on Prussia on July 19th, 1870.

In the German states, France was seen as the aggressor. German patriotism swelled to face the common foe. Bismarck's concerns about Austrian or Russian involvement proved unfounded, and his belief that war would unify Germans against France was realized. The southern German states—Bavaria, Württemberg, Baden, and Hesse-Darmstadt—honored their secret military alliances with Prussia and sent their armies to join the fight.

The war was a catastrophe for France. Prussian and allied German forces, again benefiting from superior organization, railway mobilization, and the needle gun, won decisive victories at Wissembourg, Spicheren, and Wörth in early August. By September 1ˢᵗ, the main French Army under Marshal MacMahon was trapped at Sedan near the Belgian border. After a day of fierce fighting, with 17,000 French dead and wounded and 104,000 captured, including Napoleon III himself, the French Army surrendered. The emperor was taken prisoner and eventually went into exile in England, where he died in 1873.

However, the war was not over. The French declared a Third Republic and continued fighting under a government of national defense. The French forces under Marshal Bazaine surrendered at Metz in October with 173,000 men. Paris endured a brutal four-month siege through the winter of 1870/71, with civilians reduced to eating rats, cats, and zoo animals as food supplies dwindled. The city finally capitulated in January 1871. The Franco-Prussian War formally ended with the Treaty of Frankfurt in May 1871, which imposed harsh terms. France had to pay a massive indemnity of five billion francs and ceded Alsace and most of Lorraine to Germany. These territories had significant German-speaking populations but also many French speakers. This humiliation would poison Franco-German relations for decades and help sow the seeds of World War I.

Bismarck used the momentum of this military victory to bring about German unification. During the siege of Paris, he negotiated with the southern German states, offering them significant concessions to join the North German Confederation. These included control over their own railways, postal services, and independent military commands in peacetime, as well as special voting arrangements in the Bundesrat, the upper legislative house representing the states, which sat above the popularly elected Reichstag. Bavaria, in particular, received substantial autonomy in return for joining.

On January 18th, 1871, in the Hall of Mirrors at the Palace of Versailles (which was deliberately chosen to humiliate France on its own soil in the very palace built by Louis XIV as a symbol of French grandeur), King Wilhelm of Prussia was proclaimed the first German emperor (Kaiser Wilhelm I). Bismarck became the first chancellor of the German Empire. The ceremony was attended by German princes, military commanders, and officials. The French notably did not attend. They watched helplessly as their historic palace became the birthplace of a unified German state.

The new empire was a federation of twenty-five different states—four kingdoms (Prussia, Bavaria, Württemberg, and Saxony), six grand duchies, five duchies, seven principalities, and three free cities (Hamburg, Bremen, and Lübeck). The emperor was "first among equals" and presided over the Bundesrat. For the first time since the Holy Roman Empire had dissolved in 1806, Germany was united under one government, and that government was led by Prussia.

Chapter 10: End of an Era: Prussia's Dissolution and Legacy

When Wilhelm gained the title of emperor, Otto von Bismarck became the chancellor of the German Empire. He was also raised to the rank of prince. He retained all of his previous offices and gained so many new ones that he was now virtually in control of much of the domestic and foreign policy. Europe entered a period of relative stability among the great powers after 1871, and Bismarck became a leading European figure.

After the Franco-Prussian War, Bismarck supported the annexation of Alsace-Lorraine from France. Many in Germany approved of this. The Prussian Army argued that the territory offered a better defensive frontier. The annexation embittered France, and relations between Germany and Russia also became occasionally strained, although Bismarck worked to maintain a balance of alliances. Germany secured close ties with Austria-Hungary and later Italy.

Bismarck had been largely opposed to German colonization, viewing overseas territories as expensive distractions that could entangle Germany in conflicts with Britain and France. But in 1883, he reversed his stance, and Germany began to acquire overseas colonies in Africa and the South Pacific. Germany joined the Scramble for Africa and acquired territories, including Togoland, Cameroon, German South West Africa (later Namibia), and German East Africa (parts of present-day Tanzania, Rwanda, and Burundi). Bismarck's motives for expanding the German Empire have been debated by historians. Some say he yielded to pressure to keep pace with other European powers, while others claim it was part of his domestic realpolitik.

Throughout his chancellorship, he maintained that he was doing all he could to avoid another European war. His domestic goals moved toward the creation of a welfare state that promoted loyalty to the state and the crown, but he made sure to create welfare programs that would be acceptable to conservatives. He pushed through a bill that provided sickness insurance for German workers; this, along with other state benefits, slowed the tide of Germans emigrating to the United States.

However, Bismarck's total control was shaken with the death of German Emperor Wilhelm I in 1888 after a short illness. He was ninety years old. Wilhelm was succeeded by his son, Frederick, who was already suffering from throat cancer. Frederick III reigned for only ninety-nine days before dying on June 15th, 1888, dashing liberal hopes that he would reform the empire along more constitutional lines. He was succeeded by his son, Wilhelm, who was crowned Emperor Wilhelm II the same day, making 1888 the "Year of the Three Emperors."

Wilhelm II was born on January 27th, 1859. His mother was Victoria, Princess Royal, the eldest daughter of Queen Victoria of Britain. His birth was traumatic, and as a result, he was born with a withered left arm. Some have speculated, though never proven, that he might have also suffered a minor neurological injury. He was the eldest grandson of Queen Victoria, and his parents hoped to give him a liberal British education. However, he was heavily influenced by Prussian culture, which centered around the military and masculinity.

Wilhelm II attended the University of Bonn, where he studied law and politics. On his eighteenth birthday, his grandmother gave him the Order of the Garter. He showed a strong intellect, but this was often overshadowed by his tempestuous demeanor. While he originally worshiped his father, a hero of the wars of unification, he grew to become ambivalent toward both his parents as he came to adulthood. He did idolize his grandfather, whom he referred to as "Emperor Wilhelm the Great."

At twenty-one, he was allowed to join the First Regiment of Foot Guards and begin his military career. For the rest of his life, he would rarely be seen out of uniform. In 1881, he married Princess Augusta Victoria of Schleswig-Holstein, known as "Dona," with whom he would have seven children. The marriage was happy, and Augusta Victoria would prove a devoted, conservative influence throughout his reign.

As crown prince, Wilhelm undertook various diplomatic missions with mixed results, often demonstrating the impulsiveness and tactlessness that would characterize his reign. In 1886, he traveled to Russia to attend the wedding of his cousin, Grand Duke Paul. His meeting with Tsarevich Nicholas (the future Tsar Nicholas II) went poorly. Wilhelm lectured the younger Nicholas on military matters and reportedly behaved in an overbearing manner that offended the Russian court. The incident foreshadowed the personal tensions that would complicate Russo-German relations in the coming decades.

Wilhelm spent much of the 1880s frustrated by his lack of real power and grew increasingly at odds with his liberal parents, particularly over their Anglophile sympathies. He gravitated toward conservative military circles and became known in Berlin for his brash opinions and desire to see Germany assert itself more forcefully in European affairs. In 1888, after the death of his grandfather and then his father, he became the German emperor and king of Prussia at the age of twenty-nine.

Wilhelm II.[71]

Wilhelm II had admired Bismarck for a time, but as emperor, he opposed Bismarck's careful foreign policy and desired for Germany to grow in power and influence. Wilhelm did not like Bismarck's control over the government, as he felt his job as monarch was not just to reign but also to rule his empire.

The break between Wilhelm and the "Iron Chancellor" came after repeated disagreements concerning a series of anti-socialist laws that Bismarck had supported. Bismarck had pushed these laws through in the 1870s to suppress the growing Social Democratic Party, banning socialist organizations and publications. Wilhelm, however, wanted to let the laws expire, believing a softer approach toward workers would better serve the empire. The emperor also showed sympathy toward workers' associations, which the chancellor opposed. Bismarck's Kartell, a political coalition between the German Conservative Party and the National Liberal Party, lost its majority in Parliament. Bismarck, who had spent much of the 1870s waging the Kulturkampf—a bitter political campaign to reduce the Catholic Church's influence over education and civil affairs—had seen that struggle end in failure. His anti-Catholic laws had only unified and strengthened the Catholic Center Party rather than weakening it. By the mid-1880s, Bismarck had quietly rolled back most of the Kulturkampf legislation. Now, he needed votes in the Reichstag, so he attempted negotiations with the very Catholic Center Party he had once tried to destroy. This reversal angered the emperor.

After a heated argument at Bismarck's estate, the chancellor wrote a letter of resignation and left the German government. Bismarck had been, for better or worse, steering the course of Germany since unification, and now, the Kaiser (the emperor) took control. Bismarck apologists argue that Wilhelm's "New Course" was the beginning of the end for the stability of the German Empire. They say that Bismarck's forced resignation set the stage for the collapse of the empire and Prussia, as well as the carnage of the world wars. It is hard to pinpoint a single moment as the root of such earth-shattering events, but Bismarck's departure certainly changed the direction of Germany's policies.

Others argue that Bismarck's dismissal was long overdue. He had alienated almost every faction within Germany at one time or another in the search for scapegoats. Matters outside Germany also played a large role in shaping what the next century would bring. Bismarck was certainly a great statesman, but he was also an aging representative of a generation that needed to step aside and allow the next generation to take its place. He died in 1898, at eighty-three years of age.

Kaiser Wilhelm initially focused on domestic affairs, primarily the protection of workers' rights. However, by the turn of the 20th century, he was looking into foreign matters more closely. He began to build a German navy that, he hoped, would rival the British navy and set Germany up as a world power.

It was around this time that his personality was most noticeable to observers. He was intelligent and forceful but also restless and lacking in dedication. Bismarck had said that the Kaiser wanted every day to be his birthday. Many found him to have unrealistic ideas and to be ignorant of the real world. He believed in social Darwinist ideas like "survival of the fittest" and was often seen as unstable, romantic, erratic, and highly insecure.

He was a first cousin of George V, King of Britain, and he admired the British even though he also hated them. His other royal relatives included Queen Maud of Norway, Queen Victoria Eugenie of Spain, Queen Marie of Romania, and Tsar Nicholas II of Russia. He desperately wanted the approval and attention of his grandmother, Victoria, but he despised his uncle, Bertie, who became King Edward VII upon the death of his mother. He attended both Victoria's funeral in 1901 and Bertie's funeral in 1910. In 1913, he hosted his daughter's wedding. Both King George V and Tsar Nicholas II were in attendance.

The Kaiser came to see Japan as a serious threat to Europe, especially after the Russo-Japanese War. During the Boxer Rebellion in China, he gave a speech to departing German soldiers that included racist imagery and a call to fight like the Huns, giving no quarter. The term "Hun" would later be used by Allied troops in anti-German propaganda.

Wilhelm visited the Ottoman Empire, where he showed support for Sultan Abdul Hamid II. In 1905, he traveled to Tangier, Morocco, where he delivered a provocative speech declaring German support for Moroccan independence and Sultan Abdelaziz, directly challenging French plans to establish a protectorate in Morocco. His actions sparked the First Moroccan Crisis, bringing Europe to the brink of war. An international conference at Algeciras in 1906 largely sided with France, humiliating Germany and heightening international tensions. The crisis demonstrated the dangers of Wilhelm's impulsive diplomacy.

In 1908, Wilhelm gave an interview to *The Daily Telegraph*, a British publication, that proved disastrous. In the interview, he made a series of tactless remarks, including claiming that the English were "mad" and that most Germans were anti-British while insisting he personally was England's friend. He also claimed credit for helping Britain win the Boer War and made provocative comments about Japan and Russia. The interview caused outrage not just in Britain but across Europe and within Germany itself. The Reichstag criticized the emperor, and even his own government condemned his indiscretion. This event severely damaged his political reputation, and he became increasingly withdrawn from public life.

Then, in June of 1914, Archduke Franz Ferdinand of Austria, heir to the Austro-Hungarian throne, was assassinated in Sarajevo by a Serbian nationalist. The aging emperor of Austria, Franz Joseph I, saw an opportunity to crush Serbia, which Austria blamed for fostering nationalist movements that threatened the empire. Austria-Hungary issued an ultimatum to Serbia on July 23rd, with terms deliberately designed to be unacceptable. Serbia accepted most terms but rejected those that would violate its sovereignty. On July 28th, Austria-Hungary declared war on Serbia.

The European alliance system pulled the great powers into the war. Russia, bound by a treaty to protect fellow Slavs in Serbia, began mobilizing its massive army on July 30th. Germany, Austria-Hungary's ally, faced a strategic dilemma. German war planning, embodied in the Schlieffen Plan, assumed Germany would have to fight both Russia and France simultaneously. The plan called for a rapid knockout blow against France through Belgium before Russia could fully mobilize and then shift the forces east to face the Russians. Once Russia began mobilizing, Germany felt compelled to act. Germany declared war on Russia on August 1st, 1914, and on France two days later, on August 3rd.

The German invasion of neutral Belgium on August 4th brought Britain into the war. Britain had guaranteed Belgian neutrality by treaty, and the German violation of that neutrality, which was dismissed by German Chancellor Bethmann Hollweg as a "scrap of paper," gave Britain both a legal obligation and a strategic imperative to intervene. What began as a regional Balkan crisis had exploded into a continental war. It would soon become a world war.

Wilhelm became less and less involved in the government and the actual events of the war. He was increasingly relegated to ceremonial duties and public morale-boosting appearances. The real head of the government was Theobald von Bethmann Hollweg, who served as chancellor from 1909 to 1917. The war that many had predicted would be "over by Christmas" dragged on for years, bogging down into brutal trench warfare on the Western Front. German morale suffered greatly as casualties mounted, and the Allied naval blockade created severe food and material shortages at home.

By 1916, Germany had effectively come under military rule. Field Marshal Paul von Hindenburg, the hero of the Eastern Front, was appointed chief of the General Staff, with General Erich Ludendorff as his deputy. Together, Hindenburg and Ludendorff established what became known as the "Silent Dictatorship," sidelining civilian leadership and making all major strategic decisions. Bethmann Hollweg was eventually forced out in 1917 due to conflicts with the military leadership over war aims and his more moderate policies. Hindenburg and Ludendorff pushed for unrestricted submarine warfare. They wanted to sink ships without warning, including neutral vessels, which outraged the United States.

In January 1917, British intelligence intercepted and decoded a telegram from German Foreign Secretary Arthur Zimmermann to the German ambassador in Mexico. The telegram proposed a military alliance. If the United States entered the war, Germany would support Mexico in reconquering Texas, New Mexico, and Arizona. These territories had been lost to the United States in the 19th century. Britain shared the decoded telegram with the American government, and when it was published in American newspapers in March 1917, public fury erupted. The combination of unrestricted submarine warfare and the Zimmermann Telegram's brazen attempt to incite war on American soil made US entry into the war inevitable. The United States declared war on Germany in April 1917.

With Russia's exit from the war due to the Bolshevik Revolution of 1917, Germany transferred hundreds of thousands of troops from the Eastern Front and launched massive offensives in the spring of 1918. Some hoped these final gambles would bring victory, but the offensives soon stalled. By September of that year, both sides were almost completely exhausted. The arrival of fresh American troops on the Allied side—ten thousand per day by the summer of 1918—sealed Germany's fate. The German Army began to collapse, and Ludendorff demanded that the government seek an armistice.

Germany was thrown into chaos during the revolution of 1918–1919, also known as the "November Revolution." In late October 1918, with defeat imminent, German sailors at Kiel mutinied when ordered to make a final suicidal sortie against the British fleet. The mutiny spread rapidly to other ports and cities. Workers' and soldiers' councils formed across Germany, echoing the Russian Revolution. By early November, the revolution had reached Munich, where a republic was declared, and then Berlin itself.

On November 9th, 1918, mass demonstrations erupted in the capital. The German Empire was dissolving, and Kaiser Wilhelm recognized he would have to give up the imperial crown. He hoped to retain the Kingdom of Prussia, but the German constitution had tied the empire and Prussia together. This meant that if he abdicated one, he was abdicating the other.

His abdication was announced by the last chancellor of the German Empire, Prince Maximilian of Baden, without the Kaiser's knowledge, but there was little Wilhelm could do. The Socialist Workers' Party, which had taken control, declared Germany a republic. In the end, the military and even diehard royalists like Paul von Hindenburg abandoned the cause of restoring the throne. Wilhelm belatedly released his formal abdication of both thrones on November 28th, officially ending the five-hundred-year reign of the House of Hohenzollern in Prussia.

Wilhelm fled to the Netherlands on November 10th, 1918, just one day before the armistice ended the fighting. The Dutch government granted him asylum despite Allied demands for his extradition to face trial as a war criminal for his role in starting the war. He purchased Huis Doorn, a manor house near Utrecht, where he lived in exile for the remaining twenty-three years of his life. He spent his time chopping wood, studying archaeology, hosting visitors, and writing his memoirs in which he blamed everyone but himself for Germany's defeat. He maintained that he had been betrayed by socialists, Jews, and disloyal generals. This "stab-in-the-back" myth would poison Weimar politics.

Wilhelm lived long enough to see Adolf Hitler come to power. He initially expressed some support for the Nazi restoration of German military strength but grew disillusioned with Hitler's radicalism and vulgarity. When the Netherlands was invaded and occupied by Nazi Germany in 1940, Wilhelm refused Hitler's offer of protection and remained at Huis Doorn. He died there on June 4th, 1941, during the Nazi occupation, having lived to see a second and even more catastrophic world war engulf Germany and Europe. Hitler allowed him a small military funeral, but he forbade Nazi officials from attending. Wilhelm was buried in a mausoleum at Huis Doorn, where he remains to this day.

The new republic, later called the Weimar Republic, was home to the large Free State of Prussia. This was the successor of the Kingdom of Prussia. The leading figure and minister president from 1920 to 1932, excluding two brief interruptions, was Otto Braun. Braun was able to keep Prussia fairly stable, which was not true for the rest of Germany. Prussia remained largely industrial, and unemployment was fairly low. Otto Braun was successful in settling with the House of Hohenzollern over the former royal family's possessions. The Hohenzollerns received large landholdings and financial compensation (reportedly about fifteen million Reichsmarks), while the state kept the royal palaces, parts of the estates, the coronation regalia, works of art, the royal library, and the royal theater. Still, Prussia was not immune to the escalating radicalization on both the left and the right. Conflicts broke out between Communists, Social Democrats, National Socialists, and the police, specifically in Berlin.

Prussia had a particularly strong police force. While the commanders were from varied backgrounds, the officers were mostly ex-soldiers who saw the enemy primarily as Communists and the left. When the Berlin police banned traditional May Day demonstrations in 1929, Communists defied the order and took to the streets. Police opened fire on demonstrators in working-class neighborhoods like Wedding and Neukölln. "Bloody May" ended with 33 dead (mostly civilians), around 200 injured, and more than 1,200 arrested. The Communist Party (KPD) believed the problem was with the Social Democratic Party (SPD), which they saw as the main enemy. The KPD was accused of planning to overthrow the government, which could not be proved. The National Socialists or Nazi Party (NSDAP) saw the other parties as the problem. Joseph Goebbels, the Nazi Party's chief propagandist and leader in Berlin, declared that getting control of Prussia was the key to controlling Germany.

The Prussian government, specifically Otto Braun and his followers, actively opposed Adolf Hitler and the rise of the Nazis. The Prussian authorities monitored Nazi activities closely and gathered evidence of unconstitutional behavior, which they presented to the national government, but it was too little, too late. The NSDAP became the largest party in the Prussian Parliament in the April 1932 election, though it did not have a majority.

On July 20th, 1932, the national government under Chancellor Franz von Papen used Article 48, the emergency powers provision of the Weimar Constitution, to depose the elected Prussian government in what became known as the Preußenschlag ("Prussian Coup"). Papen claimed Prussia could no longer maintain order after clashes between Nazis and Communists, though this was largely a pretext. He appointed himself Reich Commissioner for Prussia, removing Braun and the SPD-led government from power. Otto Braun and the SPD leadership considered armed resistance using the Prussian police, but they ultimately decided against it, fearing such action would trigger a civil war and provide an excuse for even harsher repression. This bloodless coup removed the last major democratic bulwark against Nazi power. With Prussia, which made up nearly two-thirds of Germany's territory and population, now under authoritarian national control, the Weimar Republic's days were numbered.

When Hitler became chancellor in January 1933, Hermann Göring was appointed Reich Commissioner of the Interior for Prussia in February. Göring immediately purged the Prussian civil service and police. Political undesirables, particularly supporters of Braun and the SPD, were systematically removed and replaced with Nazi Party members. The Prussian police became a major instrument in enforcing Nazi rule. The Gestapo, the Nazi secret police force, grew out of the Prussian police under Göring's direction.

The formal end of Prussian autonomy came quickly. Without the votes to secure a majority, the NSDAP used political manipulation to remove and, in many cases, arrest opposing politicians and then secure an absolute majority in the newly formed Nazi-controlled parliament. The Prussian Parliament essentially dissolved in October 1933. In January 1934, the Law on the Reconstruction of the Reich abolished Prussia's administrative autonomy entirely. From that point forward, Prussia existed only as a geographic designation with no real governmental power. The Prussian administration was stripped down, leaving Göring with most of the authority. Hitler himself exercised ultimate control over Prussia through the centralization of power. This structure remained for over a decade until the end of World War II and Nazi Germany's defeat at the hands of the Allied Powers.

Germany was divided into occupation zones, and almost everything east of the Oder-Neisse Line—roughly one-quarter of pre-war German territory—became part of Poland. Most of this lost territory had been Prussia's historic heartland: Pomerania, Silesia, Brandenburg east of the Oder, and most of East and West Prussia. The northern third of East Prussia became Soviet territory. The ancient city of Königsberg was renamed Kaliningrad, and the region became the Kaliningrad Oblast, a Russian enclave between Lithuania and Poland. This area remains part of Russia to this day.

Between 1945 and 1950, an estimated twelve to fourteen million Germans fled or were forcibly expelled from former Prussian and other eastern German territories now under Polish and Soviet control. Hundreds of thousands died during the expulsions from exposure, starvation, and violence. Russians, Poles, and Ukrainians were resettled in these emptied territories, completely transforming the region's demographics.

The Control Council Law No. 46, signed February 25th, 1947, officially dissolved Prussia as a legal and political entity. The Allied Control Council declared that Prussia, "which from early days has been a bearer of militarism and reaction in Germany," had ceased to exist. The remaining Prussian territories in western Germany were divided into smaller states, which are today part of the unified Germany. Of the current sixteen states of Germany, none carries the name Prussia. After the war, Berlin was divided between East and West and featured the famous wall bearing its name. Berlin, which was once the capital of the Prussian state, is now the capital of the nation of Germany.

Conclusion

While Prussia has largely faded from most of the world's memory, it is still certainly remembered in Germany and the areas that were once a part of this remarkable nation. Prussia's legacy is complex and hard to place in the modern world, but it is there regardless. Many today might only recognize the name as it relates to the famous "Prussian Blue" or "Berlin Blue," a synthetic pigment of a deep blue color that was most likely first created in the early 18th century by paint maker Johann Jacob Diesbach in Berlin. Others may think of Prussians as a military-centered culture known for battling Napoleon, Austria, Russia, and many other European powers. What is perhaps lost is that the Prussians were artists, businessmen, and philosophers as well.

Great, dynamic, and controversial characters have played major roles in Prussian history, from outsiders like Voltaire, who influenced Frederick the Great's intellectual life, to native Prussians like Immanuel Kant and Frederick the Great. From the early medieval beginnings of the Old Prussians and then the Teutonic Knights to the German unification orchestrated by the Iron Chancellor, Prussia has played a key role in European and global history. The history of Prussia is so closely intertwined with that of Germany that the two are inseparable. One cannot talk about modern Germany without mentioning how the national colors of black, red, and gold were associated with German volunteers during the wars against Napoleon, many of whom served under Prussian command, or how Otto von Bismarck came to define Germany and how Kaiser Wilhelm of the House of Hohenzollern played a role in the outbreak of World War I.

To define modern Germany or even modern Europe, one must look to the history of Prussia to see how the evolution of German identity was formed. It is certainly a story worth telling. At one point, Prussia was a backwater and, by the accident of hereditary titles, came to be connected to the elector of Brandenburg. With that little bit of power, great Prussian leaders leveraged their way from subservience to the Holy Roman emperor to sovereign kings. From there, they spread to control huge swaths of land along the Baltic Sea and down into the German hinterlands. Eventually, the Prussians, descended from a mixture of German, Polish, Lithuanian, and Scandinavian peoples, came to rule a great central European empire that had colonies in Africa and the South Pacific.

The German emperors, all descended from the House of Hohenzollern, which came from Brandenburg and then Prussia, were among the most powerful of Europe's leaders. Where once Prussia had been fearful of Austria, Russia, and France, they began to dominate them in negotiations and political maneuvering. Yet, it was perhaps that great ambition of the Prussian people that led to their eventual downfall in the First World War. Still, the state of Prussia carried on, although it could not stop the rise of the Nazi Party and the eventual destruction of the state after the end of the Second World War.

Prussia no longer exists. It cannot be picked out on a map. The pieces that once made the whole are spread between different nations, and none carry the once powerful name of Prussia as a state, though the name survives in cultural and historical institutions. Yet, the legacy and the lessons that Prussia has to give remain as strong as ever. The cities of Prussia remain, many as great as ever. The palaces of its kings still stand. However, these are not the things that carry on Prussia's legacy. Rather, it is the story of the rise and fall of one of the most extraordinary powers of the world that will keep Prussia alive in the centuries to come.

Part 4: History of Germany

An Enthralling Overview of Major Events and Figures

Introduction: Germany Before It Was Germany

It sounds like a terrible oxymoron to say it, but it needs to be said anyway. Germany is both ancient and relatively new. The history of this unique part of the world can be traced back to the ancient past, but the actual modern-day state of Germany dates back only to 1871. This nation-state is quite young in comparison to many other modern-day nation-states. Even that upstart newcomer, the United States of America, is older than Germany since the US was established in 1776!

However, when we speak of German history, we are considering more than the establishment of the modern-day state of Germany. Before the current boundaries of Germany were established, there were many other incarnations of Germanic statehood.

This historic land rests at an important crossroads, where Western Europe meets Central Europe. Other nations, such as France, Spain, and Great Britain, are clearly defined by geographic boundaries. Many of these boundaries date back for centuries. The boundaries of Germany are not as clearly defined, though, and they are not created so much due to rivers, mountains, and oceans as they are to abstract thinking.

It is a region where countless people groups have moved back and forth during the course of history and have established various coalitions among each other. This regional evolution can actually be traced as far back as the Neanderthals, who were named after Germany's "Neander Valley," where their skeletal remains were found. The Neanderthals, which are considered to be the hominid cousins of modern humans, made their way into Central Europe after the end of the last Ice Age.

The Neanderthals thrived for quite some time before facing a massive extinction event. No one is sure what exactly happened to the Neanderthals, but it is believed they were deeply affected by the arrival of the *Homo sapiens* (modern humans). Either these early humans killed them or interbred with them; perhaps it was a combination of both. At any rate, the people who followed in their footsteps began to settle down and farm the land. With their food source secure, they began to perfect their language and culture. Since these people groups existed before any historical records, they are categorized by the artifacts that they left behind. The Funnelbeaker culture, for example, named after the prevalent pottery they crafted, is believed to have thrived in the region by 3900 BCE and remained a prevalent presence all the way until 600 BCE.

Prehistoric peoples, such as the Funnelbeakers, would soon be supplanted by a much more sophisticated tribal group known as the Celts. The Celts would come to dominate much of Central and Western Europe, spreading from the mainland all the way to Great Britain. The Celts would eventually butt heads with the growing Mediterranean power of the Romans.

In 390 BCE, Celtic tribes actually raided Rome, which was the capital of what was then the Roman Republic. These Germanic peoples first entered into the historical record due to their encounters with the Romans. As time passed, the growing powerhouse of Rome had to come to grips with the wild Germanic tribes on its frontiers. All oxymorons aside, this confederation of roving warriors was Germany before it was Germany.

Chapter 1: Ancient Germanic Tribes

The notion of a nation-state named Germany taking up space somewhere in Central Europe is so ingrained in the modern consciousness that it can be a bit jarring to realize that Germany, as we know it today, did not exist for much of recorded history. It is true that there have been Germanic peoples, languages, customs, principalities, and even various pseudo-empires for thousands of years. However, the modern-day nation-state of Germany did not actually come about until the 19th century.

As mentioned, Germany's history goes much deeper than that. The first designation of a Germanic region came about because of Julius Caesar. Yes, this would-be dictator of the Roman Republic led his armies into the wilderness of Central Europe, where he encountered fierce Germanic tribes. He ended up calling the region Germania.

After Julius Caesar died and the Roman Republic had transformed itself into the Roman Empire, Roman Emperor Augustus became determined to bring the Germanic tribes north of the empire to heel. He sent troops over the borders of Roman Gaul (France), past the Rhine River, and into Germania itself.

The Romans were initially able to subdue the Germans, but in 9 CE, something unexpected happened. A revolt broke out, and a massive German force surrounded the Roman positions. The Battle of Teutoburg Forest saw an entire legion of Rome's best troops pulverized. The Romans retreated, and the outposts in Germania were lost. Augustus was so shocked by this outburst that he did not even try to retake this lost ground. It was not until he was succeeded by Emperor Tiberius in 14 CE that further expeditions were sent to try and tame the Germans.

Tiberius was not all that successful, and after several failed attempts, he decided to maintain the Roman borderlands at the Rhine and leave it at that. Just west of the Rhine, the Romans established the provinces of Germania Superior and Germania Inferior.

Perhaps the best-known historical reference about Germania from that time is the work of Roman historian Tacitus, whose work *Germania* sought to describe the region and its people as the Romans understood them at the time. This work, said to have been crafted around 98 CE, described the Germanic tribes as being wild and untamed.

As an indication of their perceived warlike nature, he famously described the Germanic rite of passage for Germanic youths as being the gifting of arms, whereas for Romans, it was the donning of a toga.[i] Both represent articles of importance for both civilizations, with the Roman toga representing intellectual refinement and responsibility and the German sword representing unbridled power.

A Roman bronze figure depicting a Germanic man.[73]

---

[i] Ozment, Steven. *A Mighty Fortress*. 2004. Pg. 22.

Even though Tacitus described the Germans as barbarians, he expressed admiration for their tenacity. He especially admired the fact that the Germans seemed to choose tribal leaders based on their exploits in battle. Leadership was based more on merit than heredity.

Another interesting observation that Tacitus had about these Germanic tribes was what he contended to be their rather transparent nature. Rather than behaving in the cunning Machiavellian mannerisms that the Romans were used to, he described the Germans as holding nothing back as it pertained to their feelings. As Tacitus put it, they "blurted out their innermost thoughts—every soul [laying itself] bare."[i]

One could argue that this trait of candid openness has been passed down, as it is something we can see in German culture today. Many who visit Germany have been struck by the forthright nature of German conversation. And if anyone has ever taken a course in German, they might be forewarned not to take an expression such as "Wie geht es Ihnen?" ("How are you?") lightly. In the English-speaking world, we frequently greet one another with this inquiry, expecting nothing more than a simple reply of "Doing good." But if you were to ask a German, "Wie geht es Ihnen?" you might get an unexpected earful. Ask a random stranger on a German street how they are doing, and they might enter into a diatribe about how they woke up with a terrible headache, were late for work, and were reprimanded by their boss!

The people of Roman Gaul and Roman Germania tended to blend together. Germanic tribes raided one another on each side of the Rhine as much as they intermarried each other. Even though today we have a distinct conception of those who are French and those who are German, this was not the case back then.

Germanic peoples fit into a wide category of tribes in both Germania and Gaul, so there is much confusion as to who should be considered Germanic in the first place. Historians still struggle to figure out whether a revered figure such as Charlemagne should be considered French or German. Most, however, contend that Charlemagne and his Frankish brethren were an amalgamation of the two. They were pseudo-French and pseudo-German since neither nationality existed at the time. The ancestors of these regions prolifically intermingled with one another.

---

[i] Ozment, Steven. *A Mighty Fortress*. 2004. Pg. 22.

This intermingling created the powerhouse known as the Kingdom of the Franks. Again, some see the origin of France in the Franks, while others see Germanic roots. Nevertheless, the Frankish kingdom did stem from Germanic tribes that settled in Central and Western Europe.

The Franks were not the only Germanic tribe in the region at the time. They had plenty of competitors, primarily in the form of the Visigoths, the Ostrogoths, the Lombards, and the Vandals. Of these four groups, the Visigoths proved the most problematic for the Romans.

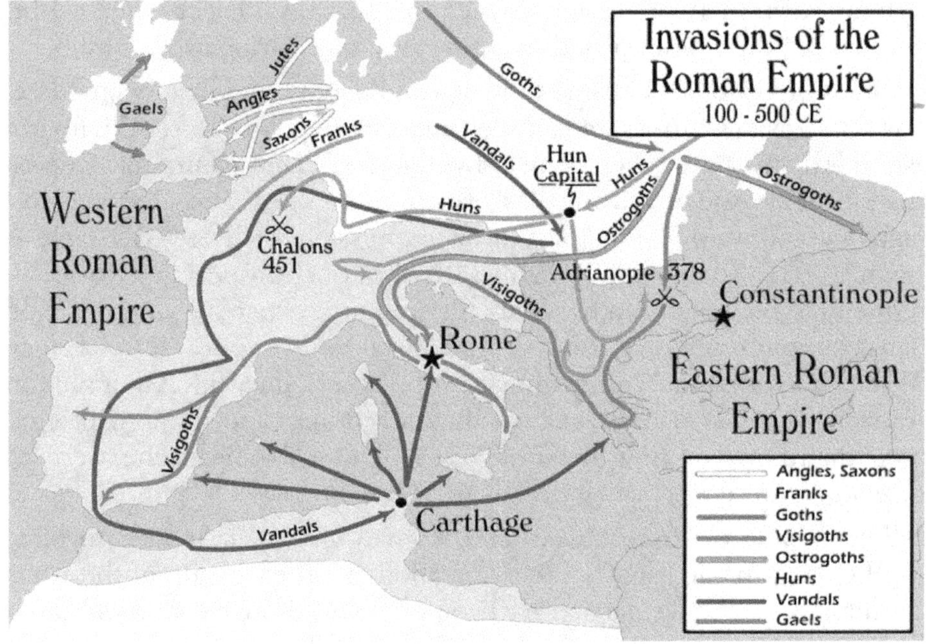

Invasions of the Roman Empire by Germanic tribes.[78]

The Visigoths took part in numerous engagements against the Romans in the late 4th and early 5th centuries CE, culminating in a brazen invasion of Rome itself in 410. This invasion was led by Visigoth chieftain Alaric. Alaric and his warriors sent a tremendous shock through the Roman Empire, as they sacked the city of Rome of all of its valuables, depleting the average Roman of their morale.[i]

However, perhaps even more consequential than the sacking of Rome was the fact that many of the Germanic tribes had become integrated into

---

[i] Benjamin, G. Craig. *The Big History of Civilizations.* 2016. Pg. 184.

the Roman military. Toward the end of the Western Roman Empire, Germanic warriors were increasingly used as auxiliary troops. These Germanic peoples fought alongside the Romans and became quite acquainted with Roman culture.[i]

After the inevitable fall of the Western Roman Empire in the 5th century, a long succession of various Germanic warring tribes led to the rise of the Franks, who were led by their indomitable leader, Clovis. This Germanic warlord was well acquainted with the Romans. He had served with them on various campaigns prior to Rome's collapse. He was influenced by both Roman governance and the Roman Catholic religion.

Clovis is said to have experienced a profound conversion to Christianity, and in what was considered "Germanic custom," his people followed suit. This was how the Franks became Christian. Their descendants would eventually cobble together a Germanic superstate, which included modern-day Germany, France, and northern Italy. This German kingdom, which was breathed into existence in the 9th century, would come to be known as the Holy Roman Empire.

---

[i] Ozment, Steven. *A Mighty Fortress*. 2004. Pg. 25.

Chapter 2: The Rise of the Holy Roman Empire

In 768 CE, Charles the Great, better known as Charlemagne, came into a great inheritance. He was bequeathed an extensive domain that reached from central Germany all the way to the Pyrenees. Charlemagne was a successful ruler and was soon able to expand his domain even farther until his power reached all the way into central Italy.

This brought Charlemagne into close contact with the pope of the Roman Catholic Church, Leo III, who was a virtual head of state over his own dwindling holdings in Rome. Ever since the fall of the Western Roman Empire, the pope had been wheeling and dealing with a multitude of warlords in order to keep his head afloat. There was still an emperor in the Eastern capital of Greek-speaking Constantinople, but the Eastern emperor, who was traditionally held responsible for protecting the pope, could often do very little when push came to shove.

This led the popes to become Machiavellian realists in temperament, siding with whoever was best suited to preserve them and the church. However, Pope Leo III had run afoul of his usual benefactors. He had just succeeded the previous pope, Adrian I, and there were factions that did not approve of his succession. Two of Adrian's nephews, Paschalis and Campulus, in particular, did not approve of the new pope and began to stir up trouble.[1]

---

[1] McCabe, Joseph. *A History of the Popes.* 1939. Pg. 172.

Paschalis and Campulus (just like their uncle Adrian) were from a prominent Roman family and felt entitled to try and influence public discourse as they saw fit. They were dismayed when Leo III was elected as pope, and they wanted to let their discontent be heard. They galvanized others to their cause.

On April 25th, 799, during the religious feast day of St. Mark, some of the most vocal of these dissenters struck.[i] Pope Leo III was leading a religious procession through the streets of Rome. The pope was riding on top of a horse, and the rest of his clergy followed behind. Riding alongside the pope were none other than Paschalis and Campulus.

At first sight, it seemed that the two brothers had temporarily put aside their differences with the pope in order to show solidarity for the religious holiday. But this was not the case. The two had secretly stationed a group of heavily armed men along the procession route, and they were ready to ambush the pope. And sure enough, as soon as the pope approached them, they jumped up from their positions and began their assault.

They knocked the pope right off his horse and then pulled him to the side. They attempted to cut out the pope's tongue and blind him. This was a sign of disgrace back in those days. Someone who had their eyes and tongue removed was typically seen as not only being adequately chastised but also being entirely eliminated as a threat. It would be difficult for leaders (kings, emperors, and even popes) to continue in a leadership role after being blinded. And how could they issue orders without their tongue?

It is not entirely clear what happened next or how extensive Pope Leo III's injuries were in the aftermath. There are legendary stories about this event. They claim that the pope's eyes were indeed cut out but later miraculously reformed in his eye sockets.[ii] Other accounts insist that there were enough papal supporters on hand that day, and they were able to intervene and drive the attackers off before anything too damaging occurred.

At any rate, in the aftermath of this terrible altercation, Pope Leo III turned to the powerful King Charlemagne, who had expanded his reach all the way to his doorstep, for protection. Some of the nobles protested

---

[i] McCabe, Joseph. *A History of the Popes.* 1939. Pg. 173.

[ii] McCabe, Joseph. *A History of the Popes.* 1939. Pg. 173.

this protection and sent an indictment to Charlemagne, which accused the pope of various crimes, including corruption and the general mismanagement of the papacy. Charlemagne sent some of his own nobles to investigate these claims, but they ultimately found no fault with the pope.[i]

Pope Leo III ultimately returned the favor Charlemagne had given him. In acknowledgment of Charlemagne's growing power and the Eastern Roman Empire's shrinking influence, Pope Leo III crowned Charlemagne emperor on Christmas Day, December 25th, 800 CE. Some believe that Pope Leo III did this under duress, but there is no evidence to say one way or the other. It is possible that Pope Leo III did this to strengthen his own position. What would be better for the papacy than to align with the strongest ruler in Europe?

Although it is a complicated narrative to pinpoint exact dates to, some mark this day as the moment that the Holy Roman Empire was born. Other scholars believe the Holy Roman Empire began with Otto I because Charlemagne's empire did not last that long.

This move sent shockwaves throughout the Christian world and would ultimately lead to a schism between the East and the West. The Great Schism would not occur until 1054, but the long process of disentanglement between the Eastern and Western Churches had already begun by 1000 CE. Although the pope really had no choice but to cozy up with the powerful Charlemagne, the Eastern heads of state and church cried heresy, and fractures between the Latin Catholic Church and the Greek Orthodox Church began to emerge.

Interestingly, as much as Charlemagne's crowning was met with disdain by Eastern Christians, he was actually recognized by Eastern Muslims. This footnote in history is overlooked, but it has been said that in this pre-Crusades world, Charlemagne set up embassies in Jerusalem and even Baghdad. He was apparently eager to shore up diplomatic relations with the Islamic powerbrokers of the Middle East.

His efforts were successful to some degree. In October 802 CE, Caliph Harun al-Rashid of the Abbasid dynasty sent Charlemagne a rather extravagant gift to congratulate him on his coronation. Fittingly acknowledging the new "elephant in the room," he sent the new Western

---

[i] McCabe, Joseph. *A History of the Popes.* 1939. Pg. 174.

Roman emperor (a title disputed by the Eastern Roman emperors) an elephant. The caliph also sent extravagant silk robes, exotic spices, expensive perfumes, and even a water clock. However, the elephant, supposedly named Abu al-Abbas, was the most frequently cited gift in the chronicles of the day.

Charlemagne apparently loved his elephant, and he also liked the idea of keeping diplomatic doors open in the Middle East. As much as Christianity and Islam were at odds during this era, Charlemagne was willing to set aside religious differences if he could forge a mutually beneficial alliance. It also cannot be forgotten that both Charlemagne and the caliph had a potential common enemy in the form of the disgruntled Byzantines.

At the time, the Byzantines were ruled by Empress Irene. Considering the disparity between male and female rulers at the time, Empress Irene was not always given the recognition she deserved. The fact that now the pope had turned his back on her in favor of Charlemagne did not help this situation.

The Byzantine empress was not happy with Charlemagne's claim as emperor, but even if she were able to raise a sufficient army to challenge the forces of Charlemagne in battle, she had to worry about the caliph allying with Charlamagne. That would open up a second front right in the Byzantine ruler's backyard.

There was also another, perhaps even more practical, reason for Charlemagne to align himself with Caliph Harun al-Rashid and the Abbasid dynasty. The Abbasids had toppled and supplanted a previous Islamic dynasty, the Umayyads. The Umayyads were driven out of Baghdad but had set up their new base in Córdoba, Spain, which was still under Islamic rule at the time of Charlemagne's coronation.

The Umayyads presented a real threat to Charlemagne's southern borders. By having an alliance with the Abbasids, Charlemagne gave himself considerable breathing room. Neither the Umayyads nor the Byzantines were ready to stoke the wrath of the powerful Abbasids and Franks.

All of this goes to show that Charlemagne the Great was not just a powerful warrior king. He was also a pragmatic political broker. He knew the realpolitik of the day and sought to use it to the best of his advantage.

Charlemagne was a benevolent patron of the pope and the Catholic Church. He left the pope in control of Rome and even gifted him more territory while maintaining control of much of northern Italy, France, and Germany.

Empress Irene was deposed in 802 and was succeeded by Emperor Nikephoros I. The East and the West would then come together briefly when the Byzantine emperor agreed to the Treaty of Aachen, which acknowledged Charlemagne as the emperor of the West as long as Charlemagne promised to stay away from Mediterranean territory that the Byzantines had been desperately attempting to cling to, such as the important port city of Venice.

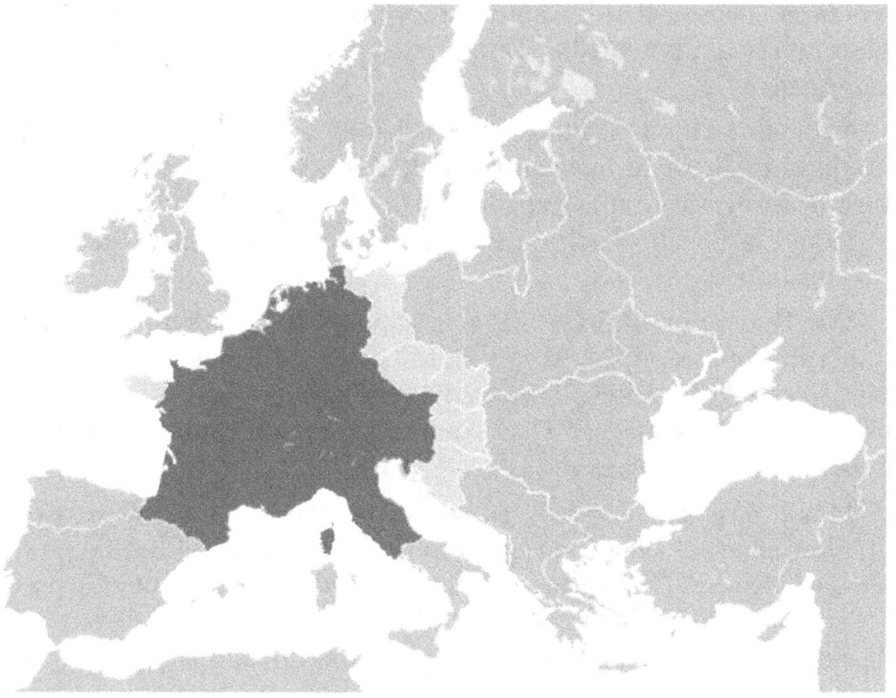

The Carolingian Empire in 814 CE.[74]

Charlemagne ultimately died in 814 CE and ceded his realm to his son, Louis the Pious. Louis found governing the large empire difficult and decided to divide the territory between his three sons: Louis, Lothair, and Charles the Bald.

No sooner than this new system was devised, the three successors began to squabble over it. Arguments over just who would get what led to armed conflict. The matter was finally resolved in 843 CE by way of the Treaty of Verdun.

This treaty handed over the region of West Francia, which basically made up the modern borders of France, to Charles the Bald. The region known as East Francia, which roughly consisted of what we now know as Germany, went to Louis. Lothair got the short end of the stick, as he was given an exceedingly narrow strip of land locked directly between West and East Francia. It was dubbed Lotharingia.

Lotharingia was narrow, but it was long, reaching from northern Italy all the way up to the Netherlands. It was also entirely indefensible. Poor Lothair must have known that he faced armed aggression from both of his brothers on either side of his domain if he angered them.

East Francia roughly constituted the boundaries of modern-day Germany and was made up of the German duchies of Franconia, Saxony, Swabia, and Bavaria. These lands would later be tied together in a confederation under King Henry the Fowler in 919 until the end of his long reign in 936. As one may guess, this king was an avid hunter and was dedicated to the fine art of falconry. The term "Regnum Teutonicorum" came to designate the lands of King Henry. The term can be roughly translated as "Kingdom of the Germans."

Henry managed to incorporate Lorraine back into the German kingdom, seizing this thoroughly French territory in 925 CE. He also took control of Bohemia and pushed into Saxony. He invaded Denmark toward the end of his reign, thereby making the region of Schleswig part of his dominion as well. Henry put several fortifications in place along the frontiers of the kingdom and kept a wary eye on the Magyars, who were saber rattling to the east.

Upon Henry's death in 936, Otto I was made king by the archbishop of Mainz and Cologne at the city of Aachen. He truly had his work cut out for him. One of his greatest accomplishments was securing the Bavarian Eastern March, which had been under threat for some time by the encroaching Hungarian Magyars. Otto defeated the Magyars, and the Bavarian Eastern March would go on to become German-speaking Austria.

Otto also managed to push traditional Germany's eastern border all the way to the Oder River. This is the current eastern boundary of Germany today. Otto then threw his weight around in Italy and managed to gain authority over who could become an abbot or a bishop.

This powerful clout in the Catholic Church came with the supposed responsibility of the German king being the protector of the Roman

Church and the pope. Otto was officially recognized as the Holy Roman emperor of the German nation. It is a confusing term, and it would later inspire the derision of great satirists, such as Voltaire, who once remarked that the Holy Roman Empire was neither holy nor Roman nor even a true empire. However, it was a term that would remain in force for quite a long time.

The Holy Roman Empire between 972 and 1032 CE.[75]

The empire certainly was not without its problems. The emperor being in charge of the appointments of bishops and abbots was a source of major disagreements. The first real crisis between the Catholic church and the German state took place during Henry III's reign. Henry reigned from 1046 to 1056, and during this period, the Catholic Church found itself in a transitional moment. Henry III had to deal with a papal crisis, which left the Roman Catholic Church without an effective leader on the papal throne. At one point, three different popes claimed to be the pontiff—Benedict IX, Sylvester III, and Gregory VI. Henry III settled the matter by deposing all of them before appointing Suidger of Bamberg, otherwise known as Clement II, as the next pope. Although the pope had crowned the first Holy Roman emperor, Charlemagne, in the year 800, Henry III started a new tradition of having the Holy Roman emperor essentially become a papal kingmaker.

During the last couple of years of Henry III's reign, the fractures between the Western and Eastern Churches finally came to a head, resulting in the Great Schism in 1054. The Great Schism happened because of differences in the ritualistic practices of the two churches and the notion of where the ultimate earthly authority should be placed. The pope believed he was the supreme ruler, while the patriarch believed differently. The Eastern Church had long criticized the Western Church's seeming subordinance to Western rulers, such as Henry III, and decided to cut ties for good.

After Henry III's death in 1056, the papacy sought to reform the system so that the Catholic Church would have more say over who would become pope than the state. This discord came to a head in 1078 with the Investiture Controversy, which was launched under Pope Gregory VII. This set Pope Gregory VII at odds with Holy Roman Emperor Henry IV. Henry was just fine with the system of bishopric and abbot appointments and was deeply dismayed that this pope wanted to interfere with the status quo.

Henry even went as far as to try and annul Gregory's status as pope. He began to refer to him as "Hildebrand." This was Pope Gregory VII's original name prior to him becoming pontiff in 1073. Henry was trying to assert that Gregory should have never become pope in the first place and that his current status was invalid.

Gregory's rise to the position of pope was not without its controversy. Henry seized upon the discontent with his election and used it to criticize him. He also convened a group of German bishops who were under his sway and had them sign a letter that officially condemned and castigated the pope. The letter was filled with all kinds of anti-pope propaganda and innuendo, accusing Pope Gregory of a multitude of infractions. At one point, it even insinuated that Gregory was having an improper relationship with one of his parishioners. Copies of the letter were made, and they were circulated all throughout the Holy Roman Empire. It was designed to be as scandalous and incendiary as possible, but Pope Gregory refused to back down. In fact, he took the drastic step of excommunicating Henry.

Henry was seen as a heretic at odds with the Roman Catholic Church. This was not an easy thing for Henry to face at the time, and it meant that many of those who were supposed to be under his charge began to actively question his own authority to reign. In essence, both the pope and the Holy Roman emperor were insisting that neither one of them was legitimate or fit enough to lead.

The two heads of the Western medieval world had become completely at odds with each other. Henry IV, however, underestimated the support that the pope had from German nobles and was ultimately forced to beg the pope for forgiveness. Henry IV is said to have stood barefoot in the snow outside of the Castle of Canossa in the Alps, where the pope had taken refuge. Henry asked the pope to rescind his excommunication.

Pope Gregory realized that it was in his best interest to do so, and he finally relented and did just that. In this round of battles between the Catholic Church and the Holy Roman Empire, the pope was clearly victorious, as were the various German princes who supported the pope instead of Henry IV. From this point forward, the German princes and, later, the German electors would be crucial for the Holy Roman emperor's election and ability to maintain power.

Yes, the Catholic Church had won this round, but this was not the end of the story. As soon as the pope took back his excommunication of Henry IV, a civil war ensued between Henry and a substantial portion of the German princes who did not back him. It seems that even though the pope was willing to grant clemency to Henry IV, not all of the powerful German princes were as willing to do so. These wily opportunists believed once a heretic, always a heretic, and they preferred to ignore the absolution that the pope had rendered. Henry IV, who was scorned by his peers, would ultimately die in 1106. He was unable to regain the footing he once held.

Henry perished with half his realm still up in arms against him, including his own son, Henry V. Ultimately, Henry V's bid to side with the pope and his father's rivals cost him his own power during his reign. Henry V had to deal with the Concordat of Worms, which had him give up almost all of his control of the influential bishoprics in northern Italy.

A considerable amount of power had shifted from the office of the Holy Roman emperor to the pope and the German prince-electors, whose prestige had increased. The Holy Roman Empire had essentially developed into what can only be termed an electoral monarchy. Just like the president of the United States is elected by an electoral college scattered over all fifty states, the Holy Roman emperor would be elected by special electors from all across the Holy Roman Empire. Such a comparison is very general, of course, but the similarities provide a decent example.

The electors developed the notion that the emperor was primus inter pares, or "first among equals." The Holy Roman emperor was not really any greater than the electors; he was simply the one who was chosen to be in charge. This concept would be important, not just during the election of emperors but also during their reign. Powerful electors would hold much clout and would often weigh in on important matters of state.

Martin Luther, for example, famously rocked the Catholic Church with his calls for reformation, yet it was an elector who ended up holding the balance of power. Even though both the pope and the sitting Holy Roman emperor wanted to punish the rebellious monk, he was actively protected by a powerful German elector. This elector managed to thwart any direct action being taken against Luther.

It did not stop Luther from being condemned and excommunicated. It also did not stop the Holy Roman emperor from declaring Luther an outlaw and basically suggesting that if any random citizen of the realm were to dispatch with Luther, they would not be punished. However, it did stop any direct official action from being taken by either the Catholic Church or the Holy Roman Empire.

We will discuss these happenings in greater depth in the next chapter, but for now, it is important to know that this weakening of executive power helped to make such things as Luther's Reformation possible in the first place.

Chapter 3: The Rise of Barbarossa and the Teutonic Knights

After Henry V perished on May 23rd, 1125, he was succeeded by Lothair III, who was elected by a group of imperial prince-electors. He was already in his fifties at the time, so it was generally accepted that his reign would be brief. He reigned until his death in 1137 at the age of sixty-two. Stepping into the void was Conrad III. Conrad was just an interim ruler. His nephew, Frederick Barbarossa, was designated as his heir apparent.

Frederick was a force to be reckoned with. An intellectual and a warrior, he reigned as king of the Germans from 1152 to 1155. In the fateful year of 1155, he was made Holy Roman emperor. Frederick often found himself at odds with many of the German

A golden bust of Frederick Barbarossa.[76]

princes, just as many of his predecessors had. In order to offset these difficulties, Frederick sought to gain greater support in Italy. He cozied up to power brokers in Italy's powerful northern cities. He also became a favorite of Pope Adrian IV by putting down an insurrection in Rome.

Frederick would become the most known for his crusading efforts. Although the Germans were latecomers to the Crusades, Frederick would become an enthusiastic Crusader during a pivotal phase of the conflict. During Frederick's reign, Jerusalem fell to Islamic warlord Saladin in 1188.

The First Crusade, which was called in 1095, had seen the successful capture of Jerusalem by Crusader forces, and just short of a century later, the Crusaders' grip on Jerusalem had slipped. Holy Roman Emperor Frederick was determined to lead the charge to take it back. He hooked up with French King Philip Augustus (Philip II) and the leading light of England, Richard the Lionheart, and set out for what would become known as the King's Crusade, which was, in reality, the third major official Crusade to the Middle East.

Initially, Barbarossa and his countrymen seemed poised to make a real difference in the conflict, but after Barbarossa perished in a freak accident, all hell broke loose. Frederick Barbarossa had tried to cross a river on horseback but had underestimated the force of the water that flowed through it. Stories differ, but most say he drowned in the water due to his heavy armor.

It was clear to most that he had drowned, even though a legend would develop insisting that Frederick did not die but instead somehow entered into a state of suspended animation. The most popular of these myths suggests that he was slumbering under Mount Kyffhäuser in Thuringia. It may seem a bit unusual, but such myths were fairly common. In this tale, one can even see echoes of the British story of King Arthur. In both legends, it is suggested that the slumbering monarchs are simply waiting for the day their countrymen might need them most. At any rate, as of this writing, no one has heard from Frederick or King Arthur.

Frederick's death threw the Holy Roman Empire into chaos. It was indeed a chaotic period, but something very notable in German history occurred. Around this time, an order of German knights was established.

Previously, the Knights Templar and the Knights Hospitaller had been the ones to carry out heroic deeds in the Holy Land. Around the year 1190, the order of German crusaders known as the Teutonic Knights was established. The Teutonic Knights made their base in the coastal city of

Acre in the Levant and took part in the Third Crusade, which sought to recover Jerusalem.

The Teutonic Knights began in a similar fashion as the Hospitallers. The Hospitallers were known for establishing special hospitals to take care of the wounded. The Teutonic Knights began by establishing the Order of the Hospital of St. Mary. In the aftermath of the fall of Jerusalem, which saw refugees flood into Acre, such field hospitals were crucial.

Once the Order of the Hospital of St. Mary began to move beyond just tending the wounded to take part in military operations, they shifted from being just caregivers to being a branch of warriors in their own right. They also found a lucrative side gig by keeping watch on the port city of Acre, collecting tolls from those who passed through.

The situation in Acre would soon become untenable. As Islamic armies began to drive the Christian Crusaders into the sea, the Teutonic Knights would eventually have to move their base of operations out of the Levant. In 1210, under the leadership of Teutonic Grand Master Hermann von Salza, the knights relocated to Transylvania. This was done at the request of the king of Hungary. At that time, Transylvania was on the fringes of Christian Europe, with various factions warring against each other. It was also on the front lines of the ongoing struggle between the forces of Islam and Christianity since Transylvania was in the path of the rising Muslim power, the Ottoman Turks, who were pushing out of Asia Minor (modern-day Turkey) into the Balkans of southeastern Europe.

In return for their efforts in this dangerous region, the king of Hungary pledged to give the Teutonic Knights special perks and privileges, such as tax-exempt land. This allowed the Teutonic Knights to take over large tracts of land in the wild border regions of Hungary and Transylvania. They brought German settlers with them who would not have to bother forking over money to the king.

The situation initially worked well enough, but by 1225, the Hungarians became wary of this growing German enclave and forced the Teutonic Knights and their followers to relocate once again. This change of plans, facilitated by official papal marching orders, led the knights to take part in the Prussian Crusade. The region known as Prussia no longer exists, but during the time of the Teutonic Knights, it was a vast swathe of relatively untamed land along the Baltic coasts of northeastern Europe.

With the backing of the pope and Poland's Duke Konrad I of Masovia, the Teutonic Knights launched their own personal holy war against the pagan residents of the region. The Teutonic Knights would prove to be highly successful in forcibly converting the locals and wresting lands away from them.

It seems the establishment of permanent castles by the Teutonic Knights broke the Prussians' backs. Prior to this, both Polish and German nobles launched attacks on the pagan Prussians. The warfare was usually effective at first, but after initially driving the Prussians back, they would regroup and overwhelm the Polish and German intruders. It was only once formidable forts were established up and down the Vistula River that the Teutonic Knights were able to effectively stand their ground.

Their fortresses were formidable, and the knights were highly skilled at defending them, even from a multitude of Prussians. The Vistula River provided an obvious source of easy transport since waterways such as these were basically the superhighways of the medieval world.

This strategic initiative finally put a dent in the Prussian armor, and the Teutonic Knights and the Germans who settled around their fortresses would continue to expand their reach into the Prussian frontiers.

In the meantime, the Holy Roman Empire had gained a dynamic new ruler in the form of Frederick II. Frederick reigned from 1225 until his death in 1250. He left a lasting impression not just on his realm but also on all of world history. Frederick II ruled through a combination of martial might, diplomacy, and outright bribery. The bribes were mostly needed to hold back rebellious German princes in his own backyard, while martial might and a surprising degree of diplomacy were used during his efforts during the Crusades.

Holy Roman Emperor Frederick II.[77]

Frederick II famously negotiated an agreement with the Muslim powers of the Middle East to allow Christians to temporarily have control of Jerusalem so long as a kind of sharing agreement was arranged with the locals. This level of diplomatic cooperation was relatively unheard of at the time, and the arrangement, as unique as it was, was generally despised by both local Muslims and local Christians.

Frederick II was known as a cultured and skilled statesman. Even so, conflicts in Italy, where Frederick sought to exert his authority, would lead to a falling out with the pope. Due to these difficulties, Frederick II was excommunicated on more than one occasion.

Despite the success of the Teutonic Knights and Frederick II's impressive feats of diplomacy, following Frederick II's demise in 1250, the Holy Roman Empire had lost considerable clout on the international scene. The century that followed would see the power and prestige of the Holy Roman Empire continue to wane until it constituted little more than a very loose confederation of oligarchs under a very weak figurehead.

As noted, Frederick II had been excommunicated on multiple occasions, which had allowed a conglomeration of unruly German princes to reign over their own autonomous regions. The Holy Roman Empire had been weakened and fractured, and the other great powers of Europe were content to keep it that way. It was much better for them to have a weak and divided Holy Roman Empire than to have a powerful nation on their doorsteps.

However, their actions unwittingly provided the perfect breeding ground for the Reformation. Due to the decentralized and autonomous regions of the German realm, Martin Luther was allowed to rail against the pope and find refuge among German prince-electors who were willing to shelter him.

Chapter 4: The Reformation and Martin Luther

"I hoped the pope would protect me, for I had so fortified my theses with proofs from the Bible and papal decretals that I was sure he would condemn Tetzel and bless me. But when I expected a benediction from Rome, there came thunder and lightning instead, and I was treated like the sheep who had roiled the wolf's water. Tetzel went scot-free, and I must submit to be devoured."

-Martin Luther[i]

It can be said that by the time of the 14th century, the Holy Roman Empire, as well as the world, was going through quite a bit of change. As it pertains to the Holy Roman Empire, a major event occurred in 1356. An imperial decree called the Golden Bull was issued by Holy Roman Emperor Charles IV. According to this decree, succession to the throne would be overseen by seven prince-electors. These seven important prince-electors of the German confederation would wield the power as it pertained to who would be elected as the next Holy Roman emperor. This decree would remain in effect without much change until the Thirty Years' War in 1648.

---

[i] McGiffert, Cushman. *Martin Luther: The Man and His Work.* 1911. Pg. 101.

In between all of this, something else eventful happened: the Reformation of the Catholic Church. By this point, the Holy Roman Empire had become a highly decentralized group of cities, regions, and princes. Unlike the rigid conformity held in much of the rest of Europe, differences of opinion were allowed. However, under the right circumstances, they could easily flourish.

Today, we can admire such rugged individualism, but in the past, this state of affairs was often likened to anarchy. In 1495, Holy Roman Emperor Maximilian I was inspired to establish the so-called "Eternal Peace." This decree was made at an official proceeding of the Holy Roman Empire's deliberating body known as the Diet of Worms. The Diet of Worms was basically a council that took place in the city of the same name. This council did not seek unification exactly; rather, it focused on compromise and cooperation between the different factions of the realm that were so often at odds with each other.

This was an act of near desperation on Maximilian's part. He wanted to bring some order to a realm that was slipping out of the emperor's grip. Some important changes to the civil structure were achieved, such as the creation of an imperial tribunal where grievances could be aired. This was certainly an improvement to the ad hoc system of crime, punishment, and deliberation that previously existed. For a brief moment, the decree seemed to promise some sense of unity in the realm.

However, Maxmillian would perish in 1519, and he had barely accomplished this task. In fact, the realm was more turbulent than ever, as the electors of the Holy Roman Empire vigorously debated who they would elect to the position of Holy Roman emperor. The electors ultimately settled upon Maximillian's grandson Charles V. However, they did so with a series of stipulations.

In exchange for the electors' support, they had Charles agree not to utilize any of the empire's resources for dynastic purposes. He also had to pledge not to bring any foreign troops on German soil. Perhaps most important as it pertains to the coming Reformation was the fact that Charles also pledged not to embark upon any important matters of imperial policy without first consulting with appropriate German counsels, also known as diets.

This agreement would see Martin Luther, who was branded a heretic by the Catholic Church, appear before the Diet or Council of Worms to plead his case. If Charles had not made such agreements and was not so dependent upon the support of the seven electors, Martin Luther could have simply been dragged off to Rome and thrown behind bars.

Before we get too far ahead of ourselves, let us first give a basic summary of how the Reformation itself emerged. The Reformation began on the evening of October 31ˢᵗ, 1517. On this day, a little-known German monk by the name of Martin Luther posted a series of complaints, critiques, and philosophical musings to the doors of Wittenberg Church. This series of notes posted to the church doors would become known as the *Ninety-five Theses.*

Contrary to what you may think, Luther did not choose October 31ˢᵗ because it was Halloween. He actually chose October 31ˢᵗ because it was the day before All Saints' Day, sometimes also known as All Hallows' Day, which takes place on November 1ˢᵗ. He knew that celebrations would begin on All Saints' Day, and multitudes of people would be going in and out of the church's doors. Luther wanted his theses to be the first things these people saw. And they definitely saw them.

It was exceedingly rare for anyone to criticize church doctrine, so the arguments nailed to Wittenberg's doors came as a surprise. Luther's thoughts sparked a dialogue that spread like wildfire.

He had many criticisms of the church, but he strongly disagreed with the pope and his subordinates collecting indulgences. These were offerings of money to clergy with the express promise that the clergy would pray for the deceased in order to lessen their time in purgatory.

One can get into a lengthy debate about the existence of purgatory itself. Many Protestants eventually stopped believing in it altogether. If you were to speak with non-Catholic Christians today, they might be of the opinion that the Catholic Church made the whole thing up. This, however, is not the case.

Purgatory (whether you believe in it or not) was a belief derived from scripture. The notion of purgatory comes from a very specific interpretation of the scripture and is no more "made up" than the belief in the rapture. Now one might disagree with the interpretation of the scripture, but the idea of purgatory is not something that some Catholic priest just arbitrarily made up.

The notion that one could take alms for the dead and pray to save their soul was validated through the scripture as well. Catholics point to a verse in the Book of Maccabees. The Book of Maccabees is considered by most Protestant churches today as part of the Apocrypha (a collection of biblical books that are considered not to be part of canon scripture), but it is still important to both Christianity and Judaism. The Book of Maccabees contains the story of Hannukah.

Maccabees was written during a troubling time in Jewish history when outside powers were trying to dominate the land. After soldiers fighting in one of these many struggles perished, prayers for the deceased were called. Judas Maccabeus took alms for the dead and, assuming their souls to be trapped in an in-between state (like purgatory), prayed for their release.

As we are told in 2nd Maccabees 42-45:

"The noble Judas called on the people to keep themselves free from sin, for they had seen with their own eyes what had happened to the fallen because of their sin. He levied a contribution from each man and sent the total of two thousand silver drachmas to Jerusalem for a sin offering—a fit and proper act in which he took due account of the resurrection. For if he had not been expecting the fallen to rise again, it would have been foolish and superfluous to pray for the dead. But since he had in view the wonderful reward reserved for those who die a godly death, his purpose was a holy and pious one. And this was why he offered an atoning sacrifice to free the dead from the sin."[i]

Of course, one could argue that this was a weak interpretation of the scripture. Fair enough. Martin also dared to challenge it. He even criticized the authority of the pope himself.

Catholics believe that the pope has been imbued with power from on high because of Christ's words to Peter, whom Catholics consider to have been the first pope. Jesus told Peter (whose name actually means rock) that he was the rock on which he would build the church and that the gates of hell would not prevail against it.

Jesus further told Peter that he was going to give him the keys to the kingdom. Peter was told that whatever he bound on Earth would be bound in heaven and that whatever he loosed on Earth would be loosed in heaven. Peter went on to establish the first church in Rome before he was executed by the pagan-believing Romans. This is why he was considered the first pope.

---

[i] *The New English Bible with the Apocrypha.* 1970.

All subsequent popes were believed to have inherited Peter's keys to the kingdom and to have been imbued with the same binding and loosing power. It was for this reason that a pope and his subordinates felt they could claim they had the power to bind (by way of excommunication) or loosen (by way of lessening one's time in purgatory).

The basic reaction against Martin Luther by the Catholic Church was, "Who the heck is this guy?" and "Who does he think he is to question the already established interpretation of scripture?" The learned clergy of the church just could not believe that someone like Luther would think he knew more than thousands of years of Catholic theologians and that he would dare to spread his interpretation of the Bible.

Even more importantly, the officials in the Catholic Church wanted to stop Luther before his new-fangled ideas infected the masses. In 1520, a papal bull was issued that declared Luther's views were akin to poison. The church really did not want Luther's views to spread too far. Containing Luther's thoughts was deemed all the more imperative in light of the invention of the printing press.

The printing press had been around before 1440 outside of Europe, but it was vastly improved by a German inventor named Johannes Gutenberg. The printing press now used a mobile, metal type instead of wood blocks. The Gutenberg press allowed for information to spread so much faster than old-fashioned handwritten letters ever could.

However, the pope and the Holy Roman emperor had a problem. Wittenberg was the capital of the Electorate of Saxony. The elector of Saxony was crucial to Holy Roman Emperor Charles V's continued success.

The elector of Saxony, Frederick the Wise, ended up throwing in his lot with Martin Luther. Thanks to the support of Frederick the Wise, Luther could continue his revolt against the church without being burned at the stake for heresy.

Frederick did not entirely subscribe to Luther's views. His primary motivation was to ward off outside intervention against a notable, well-known, and increasingly popular local scholar. Frederick was also a huge benefactor of Wittenberg University, where Martin Luther taught. Frederick had actually founded it, and he was not about to let one of his scholars be yanked around. Since Luther had the protection of the elector of Saxony, he was able to send his words off to the printers, allowing for the wider dissemination of his ideas throughout the realm.

Things came to a head when Luther was excommunicated on January 3rd, 1521. Despite this blow, the Catholic Church wanted to give Luther a chance to recant his beliefs. He was called to give an account for himself and present his ideas to the Diet of Worms in 1521. However, Luther failed to convince his detractors, and the label of heretic would remain firmly in place.

Martin Luther making his case in front of the Diet of Worms.[78]

The Holy Roman emperor, who was in attendance, although did not take direct action, declared that Luther was an outlaw. This declaration basically rescinded all of Luther's rights as a citizen and allowed (practically even encouraged) anyone who felt compelled to apprehend him. This meant that any random citizen could kill Luther and would not be held accountable for their actions.

So, even though Luther was not being dragged away in chains by the Holy Roman emperor's entourage, the world had become very dangerous for this Protestant reformer. And as dangerous as it was for Luther, it was very dangerous for others too. Soon, many parts of Germany would be engaged in open warfare between the factions that supported Luther and those who did not. Luther finally made his way back to Wittenberg in 1522 and attempted to somehow get on top of the events that were spiraling out of control. He found that some of his previous supporters were making matters worse for him by stoking fires of revolt and even spreading views that were not his own. For instance, Andreas Karlstadt began to declare infant baptism as a false belief.

There are many Christians today who may speak of one needing to reach the age of accountability in order to be even considered a sinner. This is the notion that one may be too innocent to even know what sin is. However, Saint Augustine, who lived from 354 to 430 CE, trashed this concept a long time ago. He argued that babies were born sinners.

It sounds almost ridiculous, but Augustine actually made a good point. He argued that since a baby is born crying, it is a clear indication of their self-centered, sinning nature at work. Babies are not crying to help others or be of service; they are crying because they want something. They want food, water, warmth, or attention. According to Augustine, this is clearly the selfish, sinful nature of humanity at work. Martin Luther agreed with Augustine's take and found infant baptism quite necessary.

However, Martin Luther had opened up a Protestant Pandora's box, and zealous reformers such as Karlstadt were taking things much further than Luther had intended to take them. At one point, Karlstadt even declared that Martin Luther was a greater stumbling block to reform than the pope. This was a decidedly bizarre conclusion to reach, considering that Martin Luther was the one who had kicked off the Reformation in the first place.

Feelings of disenchantment with Luther among Protestants were seconded by another early Reformation leader, Thomas Müntzer. Thomas Müntzer felt that Luther did not go far enough and called him out for his relatively cozy relationship with the German nobility.

Martin Luther was indeed quite cozy with members of the elite, most especially the elector of Saxony since his protection was vital to his very existence. Reformers such as Müntzer brought up this fact to ridicule Luther as being too soft. Müntzer even railed against Luther by likening him to a "fattened swine."

Luther was just as disenchanted with the Protestant factions. He castigated overly zealous reformers such as Karlstadt and Müntzer as "rioting murderous spirits."

Luther's fears of riots erupted in earnest in 1525 when radical reformers kicked off what became known as the German Peasants' War. This uprising was largely composed of the poorer classes of German society, who had been goaded and convinced by religious radicals like Müntzer to take up arms against the upper class in an attempt to change the status quo—religious, social, and otherwise.

Martin Luther came out strongly against this disturbance. In fact, Luther wrote a fiery tract entitled *Against the Murderous, Thieving Hordes of Peasants*. The title should be pretty clear about what is talked about in this piece.

Luther stated that the peasants who killed and robbed the rich and landed estates while claiming to be doing so in the name of God were the worst kind of blasphemers. He further insisted that the rich nobles had every right to crush the revolt since they were the true wielders of authority. They were merely putting down an uncouth, sinful insurrection of the ugliest kind.

Luther went on the record to state, "Our peasants, however, want to make the goods of other men common, and keep their own for themselves. Fine Christians they are! I think there is not a devil left in hell; they have all gone into the peasants.."[i]

The German authorities eventually crushed the revolt, and Thomas Müntzer was rounded up and killed. The Protestants were certainly in disarray at this point, and it was for this reason that the monk who started it all—Martin Luther—felt compelled to bring some sort of clarity to the madness. He tried his best in 1530 to once again restore some stability by consolidating the views of his theological doctrine with his Augsburg Confession.

This confession of faith expressed Martin's belief in the nature of God, the nature of original sin, and, most importantly, his notion of justification by faith. Luther used biblical references to support his views, especially justification by faith, as he did not wish to follow edicts from the pope requiring penitential works.

Although supported in some sense through the writings of the Apostle Paul, Luther runs into a seeming contradiction since James, in the Book of James, clearly states, "Faith without works is dead." Martin Luther steadfastly disagreed, so much so that he even suggested taking the Book of James out of the Bible and insisted that it was faith and not works that justified the believer.

Martin Luther died in 1546. The turmoil of the Protestant Reformation still very much affected Central Europe. The very year of Luther's death, Holy Roman Emperor Charles V, with renewed

---

[i] McGiffert, Cushman. *Martin Luther: The Man and His Work*. 1911. Pg. 256.

determination to stamp out the Protestants once and for all, sent troops to take on the Protestant stronghold of Saxony.

No longer living in fear of losing the elector of Saxony, Charles captured and imprisoned the elector of the realm, John Frederick I. He then installed his own handpicked elector, Maurice von Wettin.

However, if Charles V thought he could tamper with the "electoral college" of the Holy Roman Empire and tilt the game in his favor by inserting his own elector, he was mistaken. No sooner than Maurice was made elector of Saxony, he turned against the Holy Roman emperor. He allied himself with the other Protestant princes, as well as with France, leading to the outbreak of what became known as the Princes' Revolt in the year 1552.

The outbreak of the Princes' Revolt proved that force would not solve the problems in his realm. Realizing as much, a few years later, in 1555, he convened the nobility at the Diet of Augsburg and issued the Peace of Augsburg, which stipulated that the princes of the various cities in the German realm could basically choose for themselves whether they wished to remain Catholic or Protestant.

Tired and defeated, Charles V died a short time later. The Peace of Augsburg, with its grand concessions that allowed more free will among the princes, was a bandage at best. Even so, it would remain in place for some sixty years before this wound was torn wide open once again in what would become known as the Thirty Years' War.

Chapter 5: The Thirty Years' War and the Peace of Westphalia

In 1618, a violent conflict erupted. This would signal the start of the Thirty Years' War. The origin of this conflict lay in the Holy Roman Empire's desire to maintain control over the electoral state of Bohemia, which was under the influence of the Habsburg dynasty. The Habsburgs, who ruled Austria from 1282 to 1918, first came to prominence in the year 1273. During that fateful year, German prince-electors elected Rudolf of Habsburg as king of the Romans (sometimes also interchangeably called king of the Germans). Being designated as king of the Romans placed Rudolf just a stepping stone away from being hailed as the next Holy Roman emperor.[i]

---

[i] Murray, V. *The Crusades: An Encyclopedia.* 2006. Pg. 1063.

Map of the Thirty Years' War.[79]

The trouble began with the rise of Ferdinand II, who reigned from 1619 to 1637, to the throne of the Holy Roman Empire. Ferdinand II was not satisfied with the results of the 1555 Peace of Augsburg. Upon rising to prominence, he sought to roll back the clock, take away previous religious freedoms, and enforce Catholic doctrine. Even though the Peace of Augsburg allowed German princes to determine whether their realms would adhere to Catholicism or Protestantism, Ferdinand II was hell-bent on making everyone in the empire once again become obedient to the Catholic faith.

Just about as soon as it was learned that these changes to the status quo were underway, Protestant leaders began to make their displeasure known. In the Bohemian lands that now make up part of Austria and the modern-day Czech Republic, the reaction was immediate and deadly. The noble lords of the realm decided to shoot (or at least toss) the emperor's messengers. They hurled these diplomats from the window of Prague Castle. Amazingly, the dignitaries reportedly survived since they landed on a large pile of dung in the castle's moat.

Holy Roman Emperor Ferdinand II was none too pleased when he heard of what had happened. This incident marked the beginning of an insurrection in Bohemia, which spread to other Protestant strongholds across the realm. The Holy Roman emperor was not going to take this insurrection lightly and marshaled the strength of his sister's nephew, Philip IV of Spain.

The Bohemians had the backing of Norway, Sweden, Denmark, and much of the rest of the northern reaches of the Holy Roman Empire. They also gained the support of the Ottoman Empire, which, although an Islamic state, viewed the Catholics as their traditional enemies and opted to join forces with the Protestants.

The conflict initially went very badly for the Protestants. The first major battle of the war took place at White Mountain just outside of Prague in 1620. The imperial forces easily overran the Protestant forces and managed to gain control of Bohemia. This was a devastating blow to the German princes, who struggled to present a stable enough coalition to ward off the imperial troops.

A major development occurred in 1630 when Lutheran-believing Swedish Protestants took up an invitation from the embattled Protestants. They were not doing this so much out of their own goodwill to help the Protestants but rather to create a reliable buffer zone between them and imperial power.

The Swedes wished to make northern Germany a friendly pit stop and proxy just south of Sweden and the rest of Scandinavia. The Swedes made a direct alliance with Lutheran Saxony and Calvinist Brandenburg. This was a tenuous alliance since the Saxons and the people of Brandenburg did not want the Swedish king, Gustavus Adolphus, to get too powerful. They wanted the Swedes' help in pushing out imperial troops, but they did not want the Swedes to become the unquestioned power player as a result. In other words, they did not want to trade one bully for another.

Holy Roman Emperor Ferdinand II seemed to realize just how desperate the German Protestants were and decided to attempt some last-ditch bargaining with them. It was made known to the electors that the Edict of Restitution might be amended if all parties could somehow come to the table. The Protestants, as desperate as they were, were wary of bargaining with the emperor at this point. In April of 1631, after meeting at a Protestant assembly in Leipzig, they issued the Leipzig Manifesto, which stated their desire to defend their German Protestant liberties in the face of aggression.

The following month, forces of the Holy Roman Empire burned the Saxon city of Magdeburg to the ground. It has been said that some twenty thousand Protestants were killed. This only drove the Protestants and Swedes closer together, and in September of 1631, they scored a major win at the Battle of Breitenfeld. In this exchange, the Holy Roman Empire army suffered two deaths for every three soldiers that had been placed on the battlefield. This was a devastating blow for the Holy Roman Empire, which was having a hard enough time rallying its own troops.

By this point, the Swedes had made their way into Pomerania and Prussia. Even though they were allegedly fighting for the German Protestants, those same Protestants began to grow increasingly resentful of the Swedish presence on their soil. The Swedes would ultimately be pushed out. In September 1634, the Swedes and their Protestant allies were decimated by imperial troops. It is thought that some twelve thousand Protestants were killed in this exchange. This was enough to send the Swedes packing, and by November, they were leaving northern Germany.

Now that the Swedes were gone, the princes of northern Germany had to find a new ally. That new ally came in the unexpected form of Catholic France. This brings us to one of the most pivotal moments of this complicated and confusing decades-long debacle.

In 1635, France joined the conflict. This was done under the hand of France's infamous Cardinal Richelieu. France's actual ruler at this time was nine-year-old Louis XIII. A nine-year-old, of course, is not old enough to call the shots on their own, so France was governed by a core group of royal advisers until Louis XIII came of age.

Cardinal Richelieu was serving as the prime minister of France when the decision was made for French forces to get involved in the brewing conflict in Central Europe. Most would have assumed that the predominantly Catholic French would have sided with the Catholic forces of the Holy Roman Empire, but the French sided with the Protestants! This was pure and simple Machiavellian strategizing on the part of Richelieu, who, despite the fact of being a Catholic priest, could not resist the opportunity to inflict serious damage on one of France's major geopolitical rivals.

Just the mere thought of France weighing in like this was enough to make both sides consider possible negotiations. Shortly after this development, in May 1635, Saxony and Brandenburg's electors signed the Peace of Prague with the Holy Roman emperor. Known as a victory of pragmatism over religion, the Peace of Prague stipulated that the crown and the electors would work together to keep foreign powers, such as France, out of the conflict.

While the terms of this peace were still being hashed out, Holy Roman Emperor Ferdinand II perished in 1637. The interesting thing is that although peace was being made within the Holy Roman Empire, the former ally of northern Germany, Sweden, was beginning to get worried. It was in Sweden's best interest to keep imperial forces out of northern Germany to create a buffer zone. Sweden had to put its nose into these matters and stir up enough trouble to derail the peace process that had been started. France had similar concerns and was soon demanding to have certain stipulations met.

This led to extensive talks in 1641 in Münster and Osnabrück between imperial representatives (who stood in for German Protestants) and Sweden and France. These terms would be discussed over the next few years, and intermittent fighting continued to break out.

From our modern vantage point, it can be difficult to understand why it took so long to bring a complete end to the fighting. All sides wanted to stop the war at this point. Yet, it proved exceedingly hard for them to do so. Perhaps the best example of such a situation in more modern times is the Vietnam War. The war began between the French and the North Vietnamese immediately after the Second World War.

The French desperately fought the North Vietnamese insurgency until the US took over support for South Vietnam in the late 1950s. The US then began putting boots on the ground in the 1960s. The war quickly turned into an unwinnable quagmire, yet rather than de-escalating the conflict, the US sent more and more troops. By the 1970s, it was clear to just about everyone that the US had to end the war and get out of Vietnam.

Even so, the US could not just pull out overnight. Instead, what ensued was a very complicated set of negotiations on how the United States would exit Vietnam. These talks stretched on until the US finally left for good in 1975. The final phase of the Thirty Years' War produced a similar situation.

Just like in Vietnam, vested interests were at stake. Many sides had fought and suffered for several years, and they were so entrenched that no one knew how to pull their troops out easily. There was also the postwar state of Central Europe to consider. All of these things had to be hammered out in what would become the 1648 Peace of Westphalia.

This treaty had to satisfy all of those who had become involved. And for the most part, it did. It gave the Swedes some chunks of Pomerania, including important ports on the Baltic. This seemed to satisfy the Swedish demand for a buffer zone between it and the Holy Roman Empire. The French, for their part, were bought off by giving them some footholds along the Rhine, as well as the coveted regions of Alsace and Lorraine.

As for the German princes, they were given what they wanted in the first place. They were given the right to rule their immediate domain as they saw fit, and their Protestant subjects were free to remain Protestant. Another noteworthy development was the fact that Fredrick William, the great elector of Brandenburg-Prussia, was handed East Pomerania. This would be crucial in the development of a much more powerful state known as Prussia later on.

The Holy Roman emperor had been reduced to little more than a figurehead. The German princes had to recognize him as their overlord, but what exactly did that mean? The only real point that was stipulated to the German princes was not to get involved with foreign affairs that went against the wishes of the emperor.

So, the patchwork of German kingdoms within the Holy Roman Empire became even more autonomous than they had been before. It was a tenuous, fragile existence that was hatched out by the Peace of Westphalia, and it would not be long before the foreign intrigue that the German princes had been forbidden to engage in would threaten to tear the whole empire asunder.

Chapter 6: The Enlightenment and the Rise of Prussia

"The whole garrison of Berlin had turned out. A great show of princes, generals and so forth. I mingled with the crowd and was struck with the interest manifested by the lowest people in things military. Not a trace of the former animosity against the military which used to be noticeable among the lower classes. The commonest working man looked on the troops with the feeling that he belonged or had belonged to them."

-Prince Chlodwig zu Hohenlohe-Schillingsfürst[i]

The region we know today as Germany has been a center of commerce for thousands of years. Commercial goods and ideas have flowed freely throughout Europe and beyond due to Germany. This was the land that gave birth to Wolfgang Amadeus Mozart, Franz Joseph Haydn, Johann Sebastian Bach, Immanuel Kant, and Ludwig van Beethoven.

Intertwined with this increasing sense of culture and identity, the patchwork of states that made up the Holy Roman Empire were becoming more assertive and distinct in their own right. The Peace of Westphalia ensured further regional autonomy, leading to the rise of what chroniclers of German history have dubbed the Kleinstaaterei, or small stateships.

---

[i] Retallack, James. *Imperial Germany: 1871-1918.* 2008. Pg. 19.

The small states were in control of their own destiny and actively shaping their future. This was certainly the case as it pertained to powerful German states such as Bavaria, Saxony, Austria, and Brandenburg-Prussia. These regions were so autonomous that they had their own religious preferences, their own bureaucracy, and even their own armies.

The Holy Roman emperor was ostensibly considered the overlord of all of these principalities, but he was really just a peer among equals. He was barely able to keep it all together. The emperor of the Holy Roman Empire would soon find himself cast in Prussia's prominent shadow. At the dawn of the 1700s, Austria would form the base of the Holy Roman Empire, and the Habsburgs became the hereditary rulers.

At this time, Prussia had a population of just around three million. By the 1750s, Prussia boasted one of the region's strongest military forces and was expanding its borders. The bureaucracy of the Holy Roman Empire was huge and cumbersome. The main arbiter of disputes between the many parts of the empire was the imperial body known as the Reichstag. Although the Reichstag of this period did not have a fixed location, from 1664 to 1806, the Reichstag meetings most commonly convened in the Bavarian city of Regensburg. Individual states had their own bureaucratic machinery, but the larger, overarching Reichstag served the main purpose of vetoing direct decrees from the emperor. A similar analogy would be a US president or British prime minister consistently faced with a Congress or Parliament filled with members from the opposing party. The Holy Roman emperor was perpetually paralyzed unless he could somehow get the Reichstag to agree to go along with his bidding.

The emperor was also not well equipped to protect these principalities from outside threats. A prime example of this was the crisis of the Austrian succession, which morphed into the devastating Seven Years' War. This would prove to be one of the most pivotal wars of the century as it pertained to the fate of Central Europe. The reasons for the war are both simple and complex. The root of the conflict revolved around the succession of one would-be potentate, Maria Theresa, to the Austrian throne. However, the war becomes exceedingly complicated because of all of the motives of the other power players involved and the inevitable agendas that got mixed up in this whole mess.

Maria Theresa was the daughter of Holy Roman Emperor Charles VI, and she had the right to succeed her father as ruler of the House of Habsburg. Holy Roman Emperor Charles VI specifically set out a decree in 1713 known as the Pragmatic Sanction for this very purpose.[i] The decree stipulated that Maria Theresa could succeed her father if he had no male heir to the Austrian throne, which the Habsburgs had dominated for so long.

The Habsburgs were a dynastic family line that stemmed back to the rise of Rudolf I as king of Germany in 1273 CE. Rudolf acquired what was then known as the Dutchy of Austria, which was a principality of the Holy Roman Empire. In 1508, Holy Roman Emperor Maximilian I came to power. Maximilian was of the Habsburg line, and from here on out, the House of Habsburg would rule the Holy Roman Empire. The makeup of the empire changed when Maximilian gained control of the Netherlands by way of his marriage to Mary of Burgundy even though she perished before he officially became emperor.

This set the stage for further consolidation of the realm by Maximilian's grandson, Charles V, who was elected as the new Holy Roman emperor in 1519. Along with the lands he took over from Maximilian, Charles V ended up inheriting the Spanish throne and its colonies from his father, Philip the Handsome, who had married Joanna the Mad of Spain (yes, these are actual titles).

The domain that Charles V ended up controlling was mind-bogglingly large, and as such, he was constantly on the move from one part of the empire to another just to make sure that everything was in order. A weary, sick, and tired Charles V abdicated in 1556, allowing his son, Philip II of Spain, and his brother, Ferdinand I, to effectively split their inheritance. Ferdinand I gained Austria and other imperial holdings, while Philip was left with control of the Netherlands, part of Italy, and the vast Spanish Empire, which at that point controlled much of South America and parts of North America. He also controlled the Philippines, which was named after Philip, of course.

The Habsburgs centered around Austria controlled much of what had traditionally been the Holy Roman Empire, as well as additionally acquired lands in Eastern Europe. Charles VI, the father of Maria Theresa and whose succession caused the crisis, was both the Holy Roman emperor and the head of the vast Habsburg domain. Charles VI died on October 20th, 1740 without a male heir. There were those who

---

[i] Middleton, John. *World Monarchies and Dynasties.* 2005. Pg. 360.

believed that Maria Theresa should be allowed to succeed her father, but there were those who came out in clear opposition. All factions had their reasons behind either supporting or opposing Maria Theresa's succession. Those who supported her succession pointed to the Edict of Pragmatic Sanction, which had been issued by Charles VI and ensured that hereditary possessions could be inherited by a female heir if necessary.

However, this edict did not say that a female heir could become a Holy Roman empress. And since the Habsburgs had such a stranglehold on the office at this point, the succession of Maria Theresa created a quandary. Maria Theresa and her inner circle had a solution. It was proposed that she would not become Holy Roman empress; instead, her husband, Francis Stephen, would be elected as Holy Roman emperor.

Frederick II the Great, the leader of mighty Prussia, disagreed. Although no one to this day can say exactly what was in Frederick's heart, it has long been suggested that his ulterior motive in coming out in opposition to the succession was seizing Austrian Silesia, a wealthy province, for his own and incorporating it into Prussia. Frederick argued against Maria Theresa's succession and then made claims to Silesia.

Frederick II of Prussia.[80]

These developments kicked off the War of the Austrian Succession on December 16th, 1740. It was then up to all of the other great powers of the day to weigh in, depending on their own self-interests. And weigh in they did. Great Britain, the Netherlands, the Kingdom of Sardinia, and the Electorate of Saxony came out on the side of Maria Theresa. However, France supported Prussia.

Initially, it did not look too good for Prussia since Frederick's only reliable ally was the Electorate of Bavaria. However, Frederick's mighty army quickly won a series of stunning victories in the First Silesian War. The Prussians were skilled in warfare strategies and were notoriously good at pummeling the weakest enemy positions before forcing entire defensive lines to scatter. Frederick employed such a tactic during the bloody fighting at Mollwitz in 1741. In 1742, the Prussians scored another major victory.

By this time, Frederick was calling himself the king of Prussia. This was important because his father had gone by the more subservient title of king in Prussia. By stating that he was the king *of* Prussia (including the newly conquered lands in Austria), he was shaking off any notion that he was subordinate to any other overlord.

These hammer blows resulted in the Treaty of Breslau, which ceded Silesia and Glayz County to Prussia. Prussia then invaded Bohemia, kickstarting the Second Silesian War.

Frederick and his Prussian forces scored more wins in the second round of fighting, getting the best of the battles centered around Soor and Hohenfriedberg. These conquests in Silesia led to a virtual doubling in the size of Prussia's territory and boosted its overall revenue significantly as well.

All of these developments led to the 1745 Treaty of Dresden. This, again, forced Austria to recognize the Treaty of Breslau, but Frederick finally acknowledged Maria Theresa's husband as the rightfully elected Holy Roman emperor. However, Frederick's Prussia had unquestionably become a major player in Europe.

And Frederick, the man who had initiated the bloody conflict, was being hailed as "Great." Not since Charlemagne had a figure risen up with such vigor and audacity. Frederick was poised to take on the whole world. However, he was a pragmatic realist instead of a world conqueror. After coming out on the winning side of the Silesian wars, he knew that his hand had been fully played. He had won the wars, but it had come at a high cost in both blood and treasure, the latter of which he sought to replenish by utilizing the rich resources of the newly seized lands, as well as by raising taxes on his older domains.

Frederick was an absolutist. He believed that he should have absolute authority over his realm, but he also believed that he was an "enlightened" absolutist. This means that Frederick was an advocate of many of the ideals of the European Enlightenment, which had taken a firm hold on much of Western Europe at the time.

Although the Enlightenment is mostly considered the plaything of philosophers, it actually dovetails with the Scientific Revolution, which had begun just prior. The discoveries of great scientists, such as Johannes Kepler, Francis Bacon, Isaac Newton, and Galileo Galilei, managed to provoke the minds of many philosophers. Galileo, in particular, provoked them in a couple of ways. He proved that Earth is not the center of the universe.

Prior to Galileo's discovery that the Earth revolved around the sun and not the other way around, most people believed that the Earth was literally center stage. Everything revolved around it. This was a common misconception. When we look up into the skies, not realizing that the Earth is moving underneath our feet, it does appear as if the sun is rising and setting—that the sun is the one doing the moving and the Earth is standing still. Galileo's findings proved that this was not the case, and it was (for lack of a better word) earth-shattering, or at least it was enough to shatter some of humanity's hubris.

Another way a scientist like Galileo provoked the mind of the philosopher was the reaction of authoritarian rulers to their findings. Rather than celebrate Galileo's discovery, the authorities (both religious and secular) sought to suppress what Galileo had discovered. These social gatekeepers seemed to think that Galileo's revelation that Earth was not as unique as people had once thought was dangerous and needed to be kept from the public at all costs. They forced Galileo to recant his writings.

In the years that followed, philosophers began to reflect on these things and began to consider how damaging and stifling authoritarian gatekeepers of society could be to free thought and the advancement of human knowledge. It was in this way that the Scientific Revolution jumpstarted the Age of Enlightenment, which had the philosophically minded reconsider the structure of society and even human nature itself.

Soon, philosophers such as Thomas Hobbes, John Locke, Voltaire, and Rene Descartes explored the depths of the human soul to find answers to some of humanity's deepest questions. Ironically enough, these musings even resonated with later authoritarian rulers such as Prussia's Frederick the Great.

This led to a peculiar creation of leaders known as enlightened despots or enlightened absolutists. Some philosophers agreed with the concept. French philosopher Voltaire (who eventually befriended Frederick) was a well-known supporter of the notion of "philosopher kings."

At any rate, despite the carnage Frederick had unleashed, he truly believed that he—being the enlightened authoritarian despot that he was— had his people's best interests at heart and sought to create a state that would uplift the masses. Even so, by the eruption of the Third Silesian War in 1756, which would become a theater of the Seven Years' War, the notion that Frederick had his people's best interest at heart would become increasingly strained.

This war was a mixed bag for Prussia in the sense that the Prussians lost as many battles as they had won. Prussia saw incredible reversals, and on two different occasions, the mighty city of Berlin was occupied by enemy forces.

The year 1757 saw the worst defeat for the Prussians in the Battle of Kolín, which is said to have taken the lives of over nine thousand Prussian troops. Prussia rallied, and shortly thereafter, Prussian forces, even though facing numerically superior armies, scored two subsequent victories in the Battles of Rossbach and Leuthen, the latter of which left all enemy combatants on the field either dead or taken prisoner.

The Prussians scored another victory after this smashing win at the Battle of Zorndorf, but it was considered a Pyrrhic one. Although sixteen thousand Russians were killed or injured, as many as thirteen thousand Prussians were as well. Since Prussia, under normal circumstances, was not able to field an army as large as the Russians could, this "victory" was indeed a costly one.

The Prussians suffered a string of defeats from 1758 to 1759. The first defeat was the Battle of Hochkirch, which left one-third of Frederick's forces in ruins. The Battle of Kunersdorf was much worse since only a fraction of the Prussians involved were left alive. The army that went into the battle was some forty-eight thousand strong. It is said that some twenty thousand men were killed or injured. Even worse, it has been estimated that half a million civilians perished in all of this endless fighting.

The war ultimately came to a close by means of diplomacy. The war officially ended with the Treaty of Hubertusburg in 1763. The treaty basically returned all belligerents to their pre-war status quo. Even so, Prussia was the clear winner for being able to stand toe to toe with Austria without losing territory. By doing so, the Prussians demonstrated that they were a force to be reckoned with.

Once the fighting was over, Frederick tried his best to rebuild and remake Prussia into not only a military power but also a cultural power.

He made Berlin a major city and enacted democratic reforms such as freedom of the press and fairly progressive social programs for his citizens.

Frederick began the process of codifying Prussian law in 1780. The laws in these legal books were progressive for the era. They reduced the reasons for capital punishment, forbade torture, and sought to stymie arbitrary arrests. Such things are rights that most of us take for granted in the Western world. But yes, before a nation like the United States had even fully fleshed out the Bill of Rights, Frederick was giving his people similar rights under his own legal code.

Chapter 7: The Napoleonic Era and the Confederation of the Rhine

Prussia's Frederick the Great, who had befriended French philosopher Voltaire, liked to style himself as an enlightened despot. However, he was still a despot. This was demonstrated at the end of the Seven Years' War. Upon hearing of the dismal figures of death and destruction, Frederick decided to "shoot the messenger." He was so irked by the findings that he is said to have had the bureaucrat who informed him of the sobering statistics put behind bars.

Even so, he was not nearly as despotic as the tyrants created by the French Revolution. Unlike what occurred in the United States of America and, most especially, France, the revolution that took place in the German states was relatively mild. America had to shake off the greatest power on the planet—Britain—in a bloody revolutionary war. France unleashed all sorts of inner demons in its quest to overthrow the French monarchy and establish a republic.

The Prussians reformed their country at a much more even keel. For one thing, they never sought to overthrow their monarch. Frederick's reforms might have been great, but he was also still great. The people accepted him as their ultimate leader and patiently waited for the reforms that he enacted. They certainly were not rushing to send old Frederick off to the guillotine anytime soon. The same could also be said of the later reign of Maria Theresa. She was a mild reformer, and her own people—if not her neighbors—accepted the pace with which she governed.

It was precisely due to the non-radical nature of the reforms that the German states had a lack of unity and purpose. They also lacked any real assurance that any individual rights they had gained would continue. The rights of freedom of religion granted in the past had been arbitrarily rescinded by monarchs—who was to say that such a thing could not occur again?

In the late 1700s and early 1800s, when the upheaval in France was occurring, the French seemed to be showing the Germans a potential pathway to becoming a modern, enlightened civilization. This was not the first time that the French had intervened in German history. The French had played a major role in the Thirty Years' War during the struggles revolving around the Austrian succession.

After France was turned upside down by its own revolution and especially after the rise of general-turned-dictator Napoleon Bonaparte, the French began to forcibly interfere with the German states even more. In the aftermath of the French Revolution, French troops entered German lands, announcing themselves as enlightened liberators.

The French were eagerly playing the role of enlightened big brothers in the cultural march toward modernity. The French essentially promised to speed up the process of the slow reforms offered by Habsburg monarchs in Austria and the Hohenzollern monarchs (such as good old Frederick) in Prussia.

The Germans were already fairly experienced in the business of revolutionary tumult since the German states were centerstage during the Reformation. Although the Protestant Reformation centered around and was cloaked by religion, it was a call for social reform as well. Since most of these efforts did not turn out as planned by the chief reformers, the Germans had it burned into their consciousness to take calls to reconstruct social norms with a fair amount of caution.

The one big thing that the German reforms and the French Revolution had in common was the fact that they both sought to limit the power of the central government's intrusion in personal affairs. The Germans had fought a long, hard fight to allow them to have some freedom of religion. The French Revolution, likewise, quickly put an end to state-sanctioned religion. That is until the revolutionaries briefly (and quite bizarrely) reversed course and attempted to create their own universal state religion.

This was the design of the French revolutionary firebrand Maximilien Robespierre and would be exceedingly short-lived. Robespierre would eventually be executed. Ultimately, the French achieved a similar balance as the Germans, in which a limited amount of freedom of religion existed, free from the control of faraway religious leaders like the pope.

After the French Revolution erupted in 1789, the Germans began to wonder if perhaps they were not somehow behind when it came to the Enlightenment, which had swept across Western Europe. One person who seemed to ponder as much was the great German philosopher Immanuel Kant.

Kant looked toward the French and openly speculated. "Enlightenment is man's exodus from his self-incurred tutelage." In other words, enlightenment occurs when one seeks to leave the old pathways of tradition in order to discover new and more meaningful horizons.

Kant looked to his French brothers in philosophy, such as Voltaire and especially Jean-Jacques Rousseau. Rousseau was famous for stating his belief that "Everything is good when it leaves the hands of the [Creator], everything degenerates in the hands of man."[i]

Rousseau spoke of a very clear degeneration inherent in human civilization. French revolutionaries would need to correct this degeneration. French political intellectuals like Maximilien Robespierre agreed wholeheartedly that social institutions corrupted people and made otherwise good people bad. If those institutions were removed, humans could once again revert to their good, natural state.

However, back in Rousseau's day—and even today—the second the constructs of society, such as laws, a police force, and some sense of religious virtue, were removed, chaos was not far behind. Fans of Rousseau would learn the hard way that the institutions of society keep humans' worst inclinations in check, not the other way around.

Social rules and norms were created for a reason. Another great philosopher, Thomas Hobbes, was keen to point out that life would get pretty ugly, pretty fast, without laws. Rousseau thought that social institutions were the problem, but their removal would seemingly send humans back to the Stone Age. Whoever had the biggest club would be temporarily on top until someone with a bigger club came along. In short,

---

[i] Gibson, Andrew. *Modernity and the Political Fix.* 2019. Pg. 95.

such a society would not work. Without social institutions, the unchecked passions of the masses would run rampant.

Nevertheless, revolutionaries pointed to ideas spouted by Rousseau as gospel and their reasoning for doing what they did. The Bastille was stormed, and traditional leaders and representatives of society were put in chains.

Before things had turned quite so ugly, German philosophers were keen on borrowing ideas from French intellectuals. In the 1750s, under Frederick the Great, many in the Prussian court became Francophiles. Frederick loved all things French. He was fluent in both the language and the culture. Even so, Frederick believed that German culture was actually the better of the two. He believed that Germans had a tougher disposition and work ethic. They could make real and lasting change, whereas the French, as smart and ingenious as they were, were too weak-willed to really create anything of lasting importance.

Such things are noteworthy, considering Germany's later descent into madness under the Nazis, who also bragged about the strength of the German will. Even though the Nazis ran with this idea, it seems this had been a common theme in German society for many centuries. One could even argue that it dates back to the time of the Romans, who often cited the Germanic tribes they encountered as having a tenacious will.

Yet, the German barbarians of old worked hard to create society. Most of the leading lights of German society were not too thrilled in tearing society apart as the French revolutionaries suggested.

Frederick the Great was a free-thinking absolutist ruler, and he encouraged others to think for themselves. He even went as far as to have the Berlin Academy challenge its members to openly ponder the latest intrigues and philosophical musings. In 1780, just prior to his own passing, Frederick started a massive debate among the Germans over such complex concepts, such as whether it is useful to deceive people.

To many, such a question might seem wrong-footed from the start, but it is indeed a valid question for anyone interested in governing society. There are times when too much information, too soon, could cause more harm than benefit to the masses. Martin Luther famously opened up the floodgates by encouraging the laity to read the scriptures for themselves and find the truth of the Bible on their own. The results were cataclysmic. Without the Catholic Church handing down its own officially sanctioned interpretation, whole cities were fighting each other over their own perceived "truth" of the scripture. Considering all of this, one could rightfully argue and debate over just how much of the truth a government should tell its people.

We have examples of this approach actively in play today. If, for example, the United States military develops a cutting-edge stealth fighter that can maneuver in ways conventional aircraft could not, would they tell the public about it? Out of fears over national security, the public would be kept in the dark, especially in the initial stages of production, lest adversarial nations learn US secrets.

So, yes, as bad as it may seem at first glance, deceiving the public is often a matter of public policy.

German philosophical debate ultimately tended to side with solidarity with one's leader and one's nation. The notion of the "German nation" was a loose one since this was prior to the emergence of Germany as we know it today. However, the idea that society should ultimately defer to those in charge and show some sort of solidarity with the nation as a whole took hold among the German states in the aftermath of the French Revolution.

This could be viewed as the start of a kind of pseudo-German nationalism. The German states prized themselves for their cosmopolitan nature as the crossroads of Central Europe, but the threats from France caused a shift inward toward a more German nation.

The threat was enough to make the two leading lights of the German world, Frederick William II of Prussia and Austrian Habsburg ruler and Holy Roman Emperor Leopold II, join forces. This agreement to band together against the French occurred in 1790 at the Convention of Reichenback. The subsequent treaty was aimed at solidifying the budding coalition against revolutionary France.

A couple of years later, in 1792, the situation with France had reached a real tipping point, with French forces pushing right up to German borders. The German princes of the Rhine beefed up their previous agreement by entering into a mutual defense treaty with each other. France declared war on Austria in April 1792, and the French army subsequently rolled right into the Rhineland.

During this push, the French loudly proclaimed the liberation of several German cities, such as Worms, Mainz, and Speyer. A temporary wedge was made between the powers of Austria and Prussia, and the Prussians were convinced to remain neutral. The French continued to eat away at the Austrian side of the Holy Roman Empire, leading to a terrible defeat at Hohenlinden on December 3rd, 1800. This loss caused the Austrians to lose the western Rhineland.

By this point, Napoleon had already been declared emperor by the French and was determined to expand his imperial holdings. This unbridled ambition led to the stunning Battle of Austerlitz in 1805. Once again, Austria was delivered another terrible defeat.

The following year, in 1806, the Holy Roman Empire was dissolved. The reason for this dissolution was largely because Napoleon coerced the German princes of the Rhine to form the Confederation of the Rhine. After the Holy Roman Empire's dissolution, the Confederation of the Rhine came together even more. Prussia bore some guilt since it was a silent partner in all of this.

It did not take long for the Germans to realize just how terrible of a deal they had made. Some Germans likely felt they had made a deal with the devil, especially when it was realized in 1807 that Prussia, whose territory had already been gobbled up by the hungry French in the west, would end up losing even more. It was reduced to just its eastern holdings of Brandenburg, East Prussia, and Silesia.

Was this what Prussia was to be reduced to? Frederick the Great had fought hard to gain Silesia, but now, the Prussians had lost just about everything else. Prussia had been rendered into an ineffective rump state to serve French interests.

This situation would not stand for long. Germans were more determined than ever to stand together lest they fall prey to foreign depredations. The march toward German unification had just begun.

Chapter 8: Revolution to Unification

"German culture is above all the unity of artistic style in every expression of the life of a people."

-Frederich Nietzsche[i]

The French Revolution and its subsequent dictatorial conquest by Napoleon Bonaparte would end in disaster for the French. After running roughshod through Central Europe, the French dared to venture into the frigid depths of Russia. They arrived in Moscow in December 1812 only to find the city abandoned and everything burned to the ground.

The Russian army, which had relocated farther east, had set a trap for the unwary French. They had left a scorched and frozen earth behind them. The French tried to set up shop in the Russian capital but found that they were ill prepared for the winter. Without proper supplies and under constant attack by insurgents, they had to withdraw.

This led to a disastrous retreat across thousands of miles of snowy terrain that would leave Napoleon's army in shambles. The French were then dealt a terrible blow at the Battle of the Nations in Leipzig in 1813 by a combined force of British, Russians, and Prussians.

---

[i] Retallack, James. *Imperial Germany: 1871-1918.* 2008. Pg. 107.

The French were forced to negotiate the terms of their surrender at the Peace of Paris in 1814. Napoleon was arrested. He would briefly escape and cause trouble again in 1815, but it was a lost cause. He would once again be defeated, and this time, he remained in exile for the rest of his life.

Because of all this tumult, the German states had changed. They were now on a new trajectory toward unification. If anything, they knew that the more united they were, the less likely some outside force could shake them asunder. Other world powers were not so certain that a united Germany was in their best interests. They sought to confound or at least delay these developments. The great powers supported a much less robust version of the German Confederation of the Rhine. The legislative center for this new amalgamation of German states was Frankfurt. This divided realm was much more palatable to the great powers of Britain, France, and Russia.

The culture and society of the realm began to see a throwback to classic social structures. The postwar period of the 1820s has been ridiculed by some antagonists as the Biedermeier era. The Biedermeier era was really a mixed bag. It was an era that valued the upper middle class, but their status was not locked in. During this period, German society valued meritocracy and a strong work ethic. Those who were deemed to have worked hard enough could rise up to the middle class or beyond.

The Biedermeier era kept old societal values close to heart yet championed what historian Steven E. Ozment has described as an upwardly mobile society of innovative thinkers in which merit was prized over aristocratic heritage.[i] Yes, the Germans tried to have it both ways. They wished for strong law and order, conservative values, a love of king and country, and rapid mobility based upon meritocratic skill rather than birth. Anyone could be anything they wanted as long as they obeyed the king, worked hard, and proved their worth in whatever trade they applied themselves to.

Despite the disdain of its critics, the Biedermeier era proved to be immensely appealing to many, both inside and outside of Germany. Perhaps it is just human nature for people to eventually want more

---

[i] Ozment, Steven. *A Mighty Fortress*. 2004.

because those who benefited the most from this situation—the German middle class—ended up championing the revolutionary reforms that began in the 1830s.

In 1830, the July Revolution broke out in France. As we mentioned earlier, the French had greatly influenced German life and culture since the days of Roman Gaul and Germania. This sign of unrest in France led to the lands of Germany bracing themselves for homegrown unrest. Police in several states, including Saxony, Hannover, Bavaria, and Baden, put their officers on high alert.

They had good reason to be on their guard. Around this time, a new movement of German reformers, called the Young Germany movement, was getting ready to push their luck with the German government. Protesters mobilized in the 1840s, demanding changes such as open elections, universal voting for men, reform of the courts, and greater freedom of speech, press, and religion. These protests were fueled by further problems in 1846. A downturn in the economy and problems with certain crops vital to the vast bulk of Germans led to increasing levels of unrest.

Under this pressure, the loose confederation of German states began calling for a greater sense of unity by way of a national parliament and perhaps even a national constitution. This tumult had apparently reached a tipping point by March 1848. The disturbance became so great that the chief minister of affairs in Austria, Prince Metternich, fled to England, and Emperor Ferdinand I of Austria was run right out of Vienna.

In the meantime, King Frederick William IV of Prussia was in his palace as protests erupted all around him. Feeling decidedly backed into a corner, he began to make certain concessions to the protesters, but as is often the case, this acquiescence only added fuel to the fire. He soon found himself essentially under house arrest. While he was being confined in his palace, he was pressured by the reformers to approve the election of a brand-new parliament. The new national parliament first met on May 18th, 1848, in St. Paul's Church in the city of Frankfurt. The debates over the constitution continued into 1849 until what Steven E. Ozment describes as a kind of "rump parliament" was established in Stuttgart that June.[i] These gatherings typically consisted of 450 delegates

---

[i] Ozment, Steven. *A Mighty Fortress*. 2004.

from the middle class. This group clamored for reform but called for moderation. There was a balancing act at play between individual freedoms and the overarching authority of the state. Although the middle class was overrepresented, the members of parliament were cognizant of the lower classes and crafted legislation with them in mind.

These delegations became the voice of a proto-German state. This voice was seeking something akin to a constitutional monarchy in which the monarch had a more limited role than had been enjoyed in the past. But who would that monarch even be? A Habsburg? A Hohenzollern? Some believed that the best path forward would be to create a smaller state under the authority of Prussian King Frederick William IV.

However, Fredrick William was not thrilled about it. He remarked that any crown that the revolutionaries might give him would essentially be a dog collar. Rather than reigning, he would be reined in by the restraints placed on him by the revolutionaries.

At any rate, on April 3rd, 1849, when the assembly extended Frederick William an offer of a crown, he insisted that all of the kings, princes, and free cities of the empire be polled on how they felt about it first. Ultimately, he refused to accept their offer. Unable to convince Frederick William and unable to gain wider international recognition, the Frankfurt National Assembly fell apart. Its Prussian counterpart followed suit in May.

In the aftermath of all this, the dynamic figure of Otto von Bismarck began to rise to prominence. While no one can deny his importance to German history, the legacy of Bismarck has continued to divide the opinions of historians. It was under Bismarck that Germany first became a nation in its own right. Bismarck was crucial in Germany achieving this, but it is here that the political divide begins. Some argue that Bismarck stymied the modernization of Germany and the Enlightenment ideals that had begun many years before, while others argue that Bismarck was the steward of the Germans as they entered into the modern age.

Interestingly, if one were to look at Bismarck's personal background, one would see that his family life growing up was similarly divided. His dad lived the rather lackadaisical life of a Junker—that is, the relatively easy lifestyle of the property-holding elite of Prussia. His mother was more industrious. Living the life of a landlord was not fulfilling enough for her. Her ambition influenced her son to move away from the easy life of the aristocracy toward a life as an industrious civil servant for the bustling meritocracy.

Bismarck ended up at some of the top schools in Berlin. He graduated and succeeded in entering the civil service, but he initially did not take to it very well. Soon, he started to look fondly at the traditional aristocratic stylings of the Junkers.

While he kept one foot in the world of the aristocratic property owners of Prussia and the other in the world of civil service, his fortunes slowly but steadily began to rise. In 1848, Bismarck, from his post in the Prussian Diet, pushed back against the more radical reformers. His efforts were recognized by the Prussian powers, and from here on out, he was an in-demand pick for ministerial positions.

In 1851, Bismarck was made Prussia's official envoy to the German Confederation based out of Frankfurt. During his time in Frankfurt, Bismarck downplayed some of his previous rhetoric that had placed him in stiff opposition to much of the reforms. He became more of a pragmatist and began to adopt a moderate stance that he hoped would take Germany down a middle road somewhere between the two poles of conservative caution and liberal abandon.

Although Bismarck was initially opposed to German unification, he became more and more accepting—even encouraging—of the push toward it. Bismarck, true to his own pragmatic sense of realpolitik, which he would later make so famous, seemed to think that unification was inevitable and that it would be better served with the aristocratic Junker class at the helm rather than the most extreme revolutionaries.

Bismarck would become increasingly immersed in international politics. He —was an ambassador to Russia in 1859 and then an ambassador to France in 1862. During his time in France, he got a clear view of Napoleon III's government.

Napoleon III would later lead the French nation into a war with the Germans, just as his namesake, Napoleon I, had done several decades prior. Napoleon III had risen to power in France during the 1848 tumult that had rocked much of Europe. He had since eschewed democratic elections in favor of reigning as a popular despot and dictator over what was declared a new French Empire.

Perhaps this increasing threat of a reinvigorated France had Bismarck consider unification as not just a matter of reform but also of national security. Napoleon Bonaparte had thoroughly taken advantage of

German disunity and managed to destroy the Holy Roman Empire. He almost destroyed the Prussian and Austrian kingdoms as well. Germany needed to be unified to stand up to such threats, and it was likely with all of this in mind that Bismack went on the record in September of 1862 to state that Germany must be unified not by speeches and deliberation but by "blood and iron."

Strategic territorial changes were happening in the meantime. In November 1863, King Frederick VII of Denmark's passing instigated a dispute over the duchies of Holstein and Schleswig. Frederick VII's heir, Christian IX, was in the process of claiming them, but his claims were disputed by a Danish duke named Frederick von Augustenburg.

The Prussians came out on the side of the Danish duke, hoping to gain territory for themselves in the process. Bismarck was cautious about weighing in, but after Christian IX unilaterally annexed the territory, Prussia, with Austrian support, waged war against Denmark. The Prussian-Austrian coalition won and forced Christian IX to relinquish his claims.

Since the Prussians and Austrians were ostensibly supporting Danish Duke Augustenburg, one would think that the spoils would go to him as well. However, Prussia and Austria had other plans, which were made known by way of the Gastein Convention in 1865. Prussia was given control of Schleswig, and Austria gained control of Holstein.

Austria eventually went back on this treaty, which sparked a war between Prussia and Austria. The two sides came to a cataclysmic clash in Bohemia at the Battle of Königgrätz. The Austro-Prussian War ultimately ended with the 1866 Treaty of Prague, which led to the Austro-Hungarian Compromise the following year. The compromise saw the establishment of Austria-Hungary.

The year 1867 also saw the establishment of the North German Confederation. Bismarck played a big part in this new confederation of German states. He helped draft its constitution and would be appointed as its chancellor.

Prussia's western flank was significantly threatened by Napoleon III with the outbreak of the Franco-Prussian War in 1870. By this time, Otto von Bismarck had risen to the post of chancellor and had a front-row seat to all of the intrigue that led up to the war. France had been caught off guard by the stunning Prussian victory against Austria, and in many ways, it was itching for a fight. Bismarck, as astute as he was, realized as much.

It all started in 1870 when one of Prussian King William's family members—Prince Leopold of Hohenzollern-Sigmaringen—was asked to take over the Spanish throne, which had been empty since the tumult of the Glorious Revolution, which had taken place in Spain in 1868. Post-revolutionary Spain had limped along with a provisional government after deposing its Queen Isabella. But by 1870, the Spanish had begun sending invitations to Prince Leopold to see if he would take the helm of a constitutional monarchy.

This set off alarm bells in France since such a move would essentially have the French surrounded by German powers. The French complained about this to Prussia. At first, King William was conciliatory and considerate of France's concerns and was persuaded to discourage his relative from taking the Spanish up on their offer. However, when the French got a little too pushy and essentially demanded the Prussians pledge never to have any of their royal family members accept the crown for Spain, the Prussian king began to become agitated.

King William rejected this last request. The king's official missive fell into the lap of Bismarck to deliver, and he was crafty enough to take advantage of an explosive political situation. He knew that the French were saber-rattling, and Bismarck predicted that if a fight was to be had, the French would have to lose. So, he decided to do some last-minute revising of the king's letter to make it even more upsetting to the French to see if he could push them into war. He purposefully deleted any pleasantries and embellished any hints of aggression. He hoped that the harshness of the words would set the French off and make them want to fight. His letter revising scheme was a stunning success.

By July 1870, the French and the Prussians were fighting. The war did not go at all well for the French, and after months of bloody fighting, the Prussians were on the doorstep of Paris. French military units laid down their arms at Metz and Sedan, and the French were forced to capitulate. The French defeat resulted in the Prussians laying claim to the coveted regions of Lorraine and Alsace. Along with this land grab, the Prussian victors also made France fork over some five billion francs in reparations.

The French eventually made good on the terms of the treaty and paid back all that was demanded. The French would not forget this punitive measure and paid it back to the Germans a hundredfold when the Prussian successor state of Germany was defeated in World War One.

German nationalism had reached an undeniable high point after the victorious conclusion of the Franco-Prussian War. The lands of Germany, despite all odds, were coming together as one nation. Bismarck led the negotiations to make unification a reality. On January 18th, 1871, William (or Wilhelm) I of Prussia was made German emperor. Twenty-five German states united and saw the king of Prussia, now the German emperor, as their overlord. Bismarck was made the imperial chancellor of this new German Empire, or Reich as the Germans called it. Even so, Bismarck knew all too well that the international stage was quite precarious. There were still the dangers posed by a resentful France in the west, as well as the threat of intrigue from Russians in the east. Britain was unpredictable, as it freely entered into alliances with both powers.

A map of the German Reich.[81]

As such, Bismarck took a slow, cautious approach. His pragmatic caution irked Wilhelm I's successor, Wilhelm II, who rose to the throne of German emperor (or Kaiser) in 1888. Kaiser Wilhelm II had much greater ambition than his father and began to push for a more proactive German policy. This desire for more robust maneuvering on the world stage led him to force the aging Bismarck into retirement in 1890.

Kaiser Wilhelm II ramped up his aggressive imperial ambition by establishing colonies in Africa and Asia. Prior to this point in history, Germany had been largely left out of the colonial game that saw Britain, France, Spain, and even Italy seize extraterritorial possessions abroad. Kaiser Wilhelm was determined to establish what German colonies he could while he still had a chance.

During this scramble for colonies, the Kaiser made sure to beef up the German navy. This sparked a bit of an arms race with the British Empire; this arms race would continue all the way up until the outbreak of World War One.

The Kaiser's policies with its once reluctant ally, Austria-Hungary, would set the political stage on fire just enough to spark the conflagration of the First World War.

Chapter 9: The World Wars: Turmoil and Transformation

"Sir, this is Patton talking. The past fourteen days have been straight hell. Rains, snow, more rain, more snow—and I am beginning to wonder what's going on in your headquarters. Whose side are you on anyway?"

-General George S. Patton's prayer to God[i]

By the dawning of the 20th century, a resurgent Germany had much of the world worried. In the east, the Russians were concerned about what a more powerful and ever-expanding German state in the middle of Central Europe might mean for them. The British were locked in an arms race with the Germans, as both sought to dominate the high seas. The French had a long history of conflict with German states and had good reason to anticipate further aggression on the horizon.

These reservations led the three great powers of Russia, Britain, and France to forge a binding alliance to counterbalance the German Empire and its erstwhile ally, Austria-Hungary. Soon, mutual defense treaties were enacted that stated that an attack on one would be an attack on all.

Today, it seems easy to point out the folly of these treaties since we all know that this set the stage for World War One. However, at the same time, we are not that far removed from history. It could be argued that

---

[i] O'Reilly Bill. *Hitler's Last Days: The Death of the Nazi Regime and the World's Most Notorious Dictator.* 2015. Pg. 148.

NATO (the North Atlantic Treaty Organization) could lead to a similar entanglement. NATO's charter states that an attack on one is an attack on all. So, one could reasonably ask the question, how is that different from the entangled alliances that led to World War One?

In the years before World War One, many feared that some sort of armed confrontation would erupt. Many feared that it would occur between British and German ships. It was also feared that such an exchange would trigger a larger conflict.

Rather than a clash of arms between two antagonistic navies cruising through waters, World War One began in the Balkans in 1914. It was sparked by a terrorist act. Archduke Franz Ferdinand was visiting Austria-Hungary's holdings in Bosnia when he and his wife were assassinated by a Bosnian-Serb radical who was part of the Black Hand, a Serbian nationalist group. This event triggered the trap that would send the great powers on a collision course to war.

This was the trigger, but the factors that led the world to be on the brink of war are much more complicated. For decades (one could even argue centuries) prior to the assassination of Archduke Franz Ferdinand, unreasonable and entangling alliances had been put into place. There was also a resurgent sense of nationalism at work, which made the situation even more explosive.

Austria-Hungary had come into existence as a result of the Compromise of 1867, which bound the two crowns together. This compromise was made to avoid lingering territorial questions in the region between Austria and Hungary since Hungary, although within the Austrian Empire, was allowed to express its own nationalist ambitions by being granted a certain degree of autonomy. Hungary had its own parliament and oversaw its own internal affairs.

However, even though the merger of Austria and Hungary might have avoided a potential conflict between Austria and Hungary, more territorial questions would emerge in the following decades, the most pressing of which was centered around the Balkans.

Many parts of the Balkans had recently gained independence before the assassination. Prior to doing so, this part of the world had been dominated by the Islamic powerhouse known as the Ottoman Empire. The Ottomans originated from a Turkic tribe that fought its way into Asia Minor during the Middle Ages. They proved quite formidable and began skirmishing with the Greek Byzantines, who controlled much of the region. The Ottomans ultimately prevailed against the Greeks and captured the Byzantine capital of Constantinople in 1453, transforming it into modern-day Istanbul, Turkey. The Turks were not done, though. They marched right into the Balkans, taking control of Bulgaria, Albania, Macedonia, Serbia, Bosnia, Herzegovina, Montenegro, and even Greece itself.

It was not until the 1800s that these conquered nations began to shake the Ottomans off. Greece broke free of the Ottomans in 1823, and Bulgaria did the same in 1885. However, not every Balkan country enjoyed a clean-cut independence movement. Bosnia, for example, merely traded one empire for another. It was ripped from the Ottomans' grip in 1878, only to be placed directly under the control of the Austro-Hungarian Empire.

Many Bosnian Serbs were not happy with this arrangement. They were upset at being under the rule of the Austro-Hungarian monarchy. This discontent gave rise to strong feelings of nationalism. This resurgence of nationalism led to a Bosnian-Serb nationalist gunning down Archduke Franz Ferdinand.

After the archduke's assassination, the Austrians began to make increasingly draconian demands on Serbia. Serbia feared aggression and began mobilizing troops. Germany promised Austria its full support in any potential conflict. With Germany's backing, Austria declared war on Serbia after Serbia refused to submit to all of Austria's demands.

Shortly thereafter, Russia came to Serbia's aid. Germany made good on its pledge to support Austria and returned the favor by declaring war on Russia. Russia, Britain, and France all eventually declared war on Germany. Germany shored up its allies of Austria-Hungary and the Ottoman Empire, the latter of which joined the war in October 1914.

Western Europe quickly turned into the front lines of a battlefield. The Germans had long feared having to fight a two-front war, but now faced with Russians in the east and the British and the French in the west, they had no choice but to do so. German war planners enacted the Schlieffen Plan. The plan, named after its architect, Field Marshal Alfred von Schlieffen, had been conceived a decade prior, in 1905. Schlieffen died in 1913, a full year before the outbreak of World War One in 1914. Schlieffen's plan called for a concentrated drive of German armed forces through Belgium and then straight south to Paris in order to deal a knockout blow to the French. This would allow the Germans to concentrate all of their armed might against the Russians in the east.

The only problem with this was that it meant Germany would have to violate international norms by invading neutral Belgium. Prior to invading, the Germans petitioned the Belgian government to give them permission to move troops through its territory. Since Belgium was determined to remain neutral, the Belgians refused to concede to these demands. Not willing to take no for an answer, the German Army forced its way into Belgium.

The Schlieffen plan would not turn out as well as was hoped. Britain joined the war once Belgium was invaded. The German forces stalled and came to a stop in France, still quite far from the French capital of Paris. The German forces dug in their heels by literally digging trenches. The infamous trench warfare of the Western Front saw both sides locked in a bloody stalemate of endless fighting, with neither side giving much ground. The lines were clearly drawn by long trenches, which were topped off with barbed wire. Both sides made use of the latest industrial tools of death and destruction, such as machine guns, hand grenades, and even chemical weapons.

While the conflict on the Western Front stalled, the Germans made considerable gains on the Eastern Front. Led by German war hero Paul von Hindenburg, the German armed forces pounded away at an increasingly unstable and ill-equipped Russian Imperial Army. The Germans were further aided by political chaos in Russia. The Russian Revolution erupted in 1917 and was followed by a communist takeover. The communists had no interest in continuing to fight a war that had been launched by the now-deposed Russian tsar and sought to end it. This resulted in the Treaty of Brest-Litovsk in March 1918. This ended German fighting in the east and renewed hope among many Germans that the war could be won in the west.

However, this was not to be. The Americans joined the conflict, and the Western Allies continued to hammer the Germans on the Western Front. The German Army was low on both morale and supplies. The German government was forced to see the writing on the wall. The German high command capitulated, Wilhelm II abdicated, and the 1919 Treaty of Versailles went into effect.

The treaty that ended World War One is important because, in many ways, its harsh terms led to World War Two. The treaty led to painful territorial losses, such as the ceding of Alsace-Lorraine to France and the loss of Danzig (modern Gdansk). Allied forces actively continued to occupy the Rhineland that bordered Germany and France, a sight that would be a continuous eyesore for Germans in the years to come. The German military was forced into a state of disarmament. But even worse were the reparations that France demanded, which would essentially bankrupt the already struggling German economy. There was no consideration of these things at the end of the war; the Allied forces had lost a lot of men fighting the Germans, and they wanted punitive damages.

Germany was being made into a pariah, and there was not much hope of escaping the situation. Radical German politicians would use these feelings of desperation and anger to gain momentum among the disillusioned German masses.

However, it would take some time for these dark undercurrents to surface. The government that succeeded the toppled German Empire of Wilhelm II was far different from what these postwar malcontents would come up with. In 1919, on the heels of the Treaty of Versailles, a fairly liberal and forward-thinking republic, the Weimar Republic, was founded.

The Weimar Republic was a strange mix of socialism and conservatism. This socially conscious republic sought to aid its economically depressed citizens, while certain factions called for a return to the Germany of old.

In the middle of all this, the Communist Party of Germany was founded. The communists were inspired by the Russian Revolution of 1917 and attempted to spark something similar in Germany. They pushed to topple the Weimar Republic in 1919. They failed, but that same year, another disaffected German by the name of Adolf Hitler latched onto a radical group called the National Socialist German Workers' Party (better known as the Nazi Party today).

Hitler was a former artist-turned-soldier who had fought in World War One. He believed that Germany had been betrayed from the inside by conniving bureaucrats, and he sought to turn Jews into scapegoats. Jewish people had lived in Central Europe for centuries and had assimilated well into German society by the 20th century. Yet, Hitler was trying his best to paint them as both the ultimate outsiders and the ultimate insiders. They were outsiders in the sense that they were portrayed as not being true Germans, even if their families had roots that went all the way back to the days of the Holy Roman Empire. Hitler and his Nazi cronies also described the Jews as dastardly insiders. They said Jews were so well connected with the governmental machinery of Germany that they had stabbed Germany in the back during World War One by pulling the strings behind the scenes and pushing for an armistice.

Hitler, high on this vicious rhetoric, led his angry followers in the Beer Hall Pusch of 1923, which attempted to overthrow the Weimar Republic. This push, just like the communist attempt a few years prior, failed miserably, and Hitler and his henchmen were either arrested or driven into exile.

The conditions in the Weimar Republic deteriorated considerably after the stock market crash of 1929. The global economic depression is better known by Americans as the Great Depression. The Germans were discontent and desperate for something positive. In this backdrop, a recently pardoned Adolf Hitler made a surprising comeback. It is not often that someone could be thrown in prison for plotting a coup only to be pardoned and completely rehabilitated in the eyes of the public. However, this was what happened with Hitler. The man who had been previously tried as a traitor was now viewed by many as a patriot.

This time around, Hitler decided that he and the Nazi Party would not try to overthrow the government by force but through the ballot box. The Nazi Party ran for election and ended up winning big in the 1932 election. The Nazis won a third of the vote, making them a true power player in the Reichstag (the German Parliament).

Those who were most vulnerable to Nazi aggression—the Jews of Germany—watched these events in horror. For many, the writing on the wall was already quite clear. Many of those who were able to do so were already planning a possible exodus from Germany. Among them was an esteemed physicist by the name of Albert Einstein.

Germany had become a hub of great and profound scientific minds in the first few decades of the 20th century, with notable figures such as Max Planck, Werner Heisenberg, and Albert Einstein—just to name a few— coming to great prominence for their remarkable scientific findings. Einstein was of Jewish heritage, and he sensed what the rise of the Nazi Party might mean. He did not waste any time making arrangements to make his own exit from the country before it was too late. He and his wife Elsa left Germany on December 10th, 1932, and never looked back. Because of the intolerance of the Nazi Party, Albert Einstein never returned to the land of his birth.

On January 30th, 1933, Adolf Hitler became the chancellor of Germany. This made him the second-most powerful person in Germany after the aging president, Paul von Hindenburg. On February 27th, 1933, a young Dutchman by the name of Martin van der Lubbe attempted to set the Reichstag ablaze.

Although some historians have debated his motives, he was apparently a communist sympathizer. Whatever the case may be, Hitler used this terrorist attack as an excuse to declare a state of emergency and convinced Hindenburg to grant him emergency powers by way of the Enabling Act, which essentially made him dictator. Hindenburg would die the following year, and Hitler remained in complete control.

Hitler further cemented his grip on German society by silencing any opposition to his regime. In the summer of 1934, during what was termed the "Night of the Long Knives," there was an internal purge. Hitler and his subordinate Heinrich Himmler, who headed the SS (Schutzstaffel) and the Gestapo, began targeting another arm of Nazi enforcers known as the SA (Sturmabteilung). The SA was an older paramilitary group of the Nazi Party dating back to the 1920s. Its leader, Ernst Röhm, played a major role in helping Hitler's rise to power but had since fallen out of favor. Hitler was trying to gain the full support of Germany's armed forces at the time, and most of the top brass did not look too favorably on the SA, whose members were known to be disorderly, drunken thugs at best and all-out criminals at worst.

German generals and admirals wanted Hitler to get rid of them, and Hitler was willing to do so if it meant he gained the support of the German military. The SS took over the offices of the SA, and Henrich Himmler became Reichsführer of the SS, paving a path for his own rise to power within the Nazi hierarchy. The Nazis justified the purge by suggesting that Röhm and the SA were plotting to overthrow the government.

With the military on his side, Hitler began to rearm the German government. By 1935, Germany was in clear violation of the Treaty of Versailles, as German aircraft had been deployed in the skies over Germany. The following year, 1936, saw German troops head into the Rhineland. The Allied powers silently looked on.

This kickstarted a process of appeasement that would last until Germany invaded Poland in 1939. Although the world stood idly by for land grabs, the invasion of Poland could not be ignored. Britain and

France declared war on Germany, and Germany returned the favor. World War Two had officially begun.

Unlike World War One, this conflict did not begin as a two-front war for the Germans. In the first phase of World War Two, the Germans did not have to fight the Russians on the Eastern Front. On the contrary, the Russians were working with them. Before the invasion of Poland, the German government signed a non-aggression pact with Soviet Russia. Unbeknownst to the rest of the world, there was a secret provision in the pact that agreed to a division of Poland. As a result, Poland was divided in two; the Germans occupied western Poland, and the Soviets set up shop in eastern Poland.

With their eastern flank secure, in 1940, the German war machine rolled north into Denmark and Norway before heading west into the Netherlands and Belgium. Yes, the Germans were once again cutting through Belgium to get to France, but unlike World War One, the German war machine would not stall out in a wasteland of trenches. On the contrary, the German forces would deal France a knockout blow.

Right as France was on the verge of capitulation, Italy entered the war on the side of Germany, declaring war on an already practically defeated France on June 10th, 1940. On June 25th, 1940, the French capitulated to the Germans and signed an armistice.

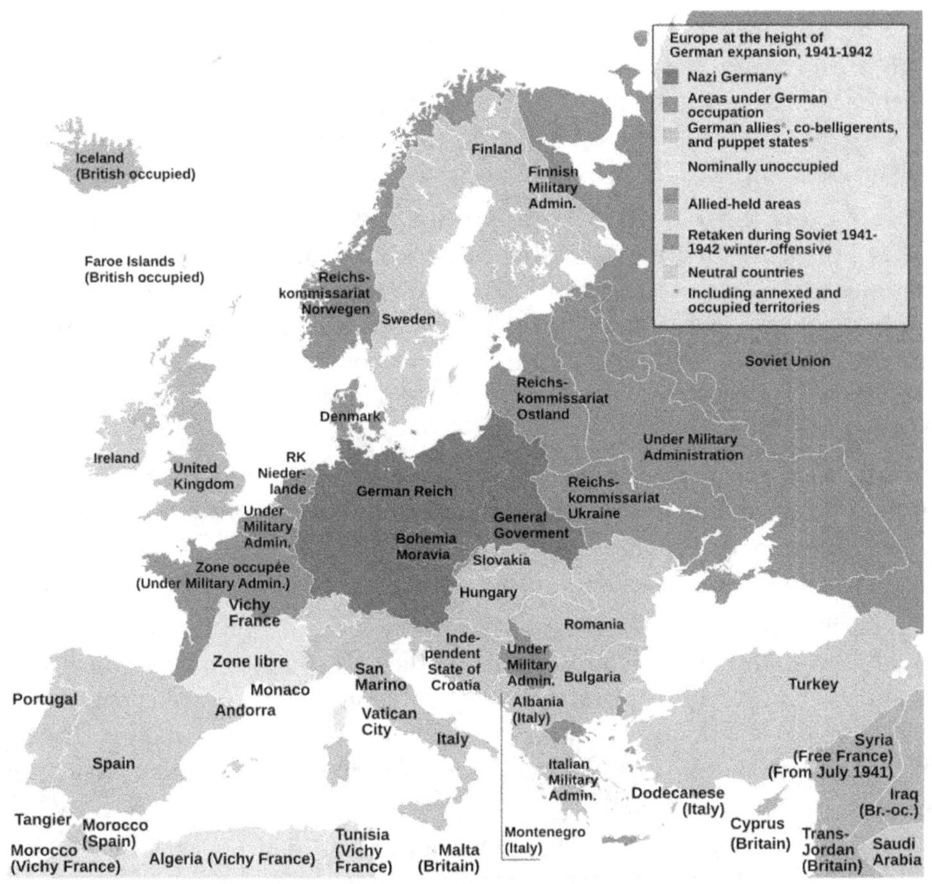

Height of German expansion in Europe.[82]

Britain became the only power left standing in the way of complete German domination of Western Europe. The Germans launched a brutal air war against Britain, which would become known as the Battle of Britain. However, British defenses proved surprisingly effective, and the Germans ultimately scrapped their plans to invade Britain. Frustrated with the British resistance, Hitler began looking east. In June of 1941, he did the unthinkable by double-crossing the Russians. Under the codename Operation Barbarossa, a war against Soviet Russia was unleashed. Initially, the Germans made tremendous gains. The Russians were caught by surprise and were pushed far back into the interior.

In the meantime, Germany's other ally, Japan, rocked the boat when it suddenly launched an unprovoked attack on a US naval base in Pearl Harbor, Hawaii. The attack occurred on December 7th, 1941. This incident finally dragged the United States into World War Two.

The Germans, in their push east, drove all the way to Moscow, but with supply lines stretched to their breaking point, they could go no further. In the summer of 1942, the Germans tried to drive farther south to seize the rich oilfields of the Russian Caucus. Doing so would have solved their supply line problem.

However, the German Army groups tasked with this feat would be smashed at Stalingrad. By this time, the United States had made significant inroads both against Japan and against German and Italian Axis forces in North Africa and the Mediterranean, further sealing Germany's doom. With the Germans making a slow, bloody retreat from the east, the Allies poured in from the west, landing in German-occupied Normandy, France, on June 6th, 1944.

The German forces would continue to get squeezed from both sides until they were finally forced to surrender in May 1945. Germany had been defeated in yet another world war, and the mad architect of this drama, Adolf Hitler, was dead in a Berlin bunker of an apparent suicide.

Hitler died alongside his newlywed wife, Eva Braun, on April 30th, 1945. He killed himself right as the Allies were closing in. True to his obstinate nature, he refused to take any blame for the catastrophe that had befallen Germany. In his so-called last will and testament, he did everything he could to try and remove any responsibility from his shoulders.

This final missive, penned by Hitler just one day prior to his suicide, was later found stuffed inside the bottom of a briefcase that had been tossed down a well. It had been apparently placed there by a man named Wilhelm Zander, who was one of the aides of Hitler's subordinate, Martin Bormann.[i]

Adolf Hitler's final will and testament contains his flat-out refusal to take responsibility for any of his actions. As Hitler put it, "I myself and my wife—in order to escape the disgrace of deposition or capitulation—choose death. It is our wish to be burnt immediately on the spot where I have carried out the greatest part of my daily work in the course of twelve years' service to my people."[ii]

---

[i] O'Reilly Bill. *Hitler's Last Days: The Death of the Nazi Regime and the World's Most Notorious Dictator.* 2015. Pgs. 453-454.

[ii] O'Reilly Bill. *Hitler's Last Days: The Death of the Nazi Regime and the World's Most Notorious Dictator.* 2015. Pg. 456.

Despite all of Hitler's denials, it was only after the war's end that the full horrors of the Holocaust would be made known. Prior to this, the outside world had only mere glimpses of the hostility that Hitler's regime had unleashed.

Although the full extent was not known, there had been some clear indicators that abusive measures had been taken against Jewish residents. Disturbing incidents such as Kristallnacht, or "Night of Broken Glass," in which Jewish businesses were destroyed and Jewish residents were harassed, had managed to make the international press.

This event occurred on November 9th, 1938. It was a heinous act of supposed collective punishment after a staff member of the German Embassy in Paris was murdered by a Jewish German. This first onslaught of hatred against the Jews actually did not go over as well as the Nazis had hoped. There were many Germans who were alarmed at what was happening. Perhaps they were not alarmed enough to really put a stop to it, but it was just enough to make the Nazis become a bit more discreet over how they conducted their persecution of people groups.

Once the Nazis had full control of their domain, they made sure to cover their tracks, and the full extent of what was happening was kept quiet. Jews were being loaded on train cars and sent to concentration camps. The average German did not quite understand what the fate of their Jewish neighbors actually was. This, of course, is no excuse for their silence, but most had no idea where the Jews were being taken and what the end result would be.

The Germans kept their insidious "Final Solution" secret. Adolf Hitler was hellbent on removing the Jews and other minorities, including Soviet prisoners of war. Initially, deportation was the proscribed method of getting rid of "undesirables." There was even talk of expelling Jews to faraway places like Siberia or Madagascar. When the concentration camps and ghettos that had been set up in Poland were being overloaded with detainees, the Nazis realized that mass deportations would be too costly. At the infamous Wannsee Conference on January 20th, 1942, the Nazis decided to employ their cynically titled "Final Solution."

They carried out a massive façade of carting Jewish people off to newly constructed concentration camps, where they were told they would work and live for the remainder of the war. The gates of Auschwitz even greeted them with the slogan "Arbeit Macht Frei" ("Work Makes One Free). These unfortunate souls were either sent to be gassed in the showers or forced to work under terrible conditions.

The Germans ordered Jewish camp inmates to take a "shower" for the purpose of delousing. The excuse was given that there was an outbreak of lice in the camps. The Jews were led into a room that looked like a large communal shower, complete with what looked like showerheads sticking out of the walls. They were made to stand under them, and the doors to the "shower room" (the gas chamber) were closed. The German guards outside would then turn on the gas. The victims were likely staring up at the faucets, fully expecting refreshing water to come out, only to be sprayed with poison gas. There was likely a terrible struggle as their lungs began to fail them, but it would not take long before the gas took its toll. Not all Jews perished in the gas chamber. Still, millions died in these horrible gas chambers.

The most glaring question of those who stumbled upon the aftermath of this horror show was, why? The answer is a complicated one, and it would likely take a whole book to even begin to come to grips with it.

First of all, one has to consider the historical precedents that existed before the Holocaust. The Jewish people have been historically persecuted for thousands of years. The Jews have often come into conflict with their neighbors over ideological differences. Judaism is a religion that calls for the nation of Israel to be holy and set apart.

When the Romans occupied the region, they found this stance a frustrating one. The Romans wished to spread the ideals of Greco-Roman culture over all the lands they occupied. When the Jews refused to act like the Romans, the two came into an ideological conflict.

After a series of Jewish revolts, the Roman legions poured in. The Romans destroyed the Jewish Temple in Jerusalem around the year 70 CE and dispersed the Jewish population. This was the start of the Jewish diaspora.

A Jewish sect known as Christians began spreading the gospel through the Roman Empire. The Roman Empire became Christian by the end of the 4th century. This spelled more problems for the Jewish diaspora, though, since Christians began to look at the Jews as not only heretics but as actively rejecting Christ.

One can only imagine the animosity that existed between Christians and Jews. Over the centuries, the Jewish diaspora in Christian Europe experienced both acceptance and hostility from their neighbors.

Adolf Hitler, for his part, hated both Jews and Christians. He kept his hatred of Christianity quiet since he knew that any move against the religion would not be feasible for him in the first phase of his plans for world domination. However, he went on the record with his associates to state that after the Jews were gone, he would come after the Christians next. In Hitler's mind, Christianity was an offshoot of Judaism, which weakened German morale. Hitler valued the Germanic values of the pagan past and preferred Odin, Thor, and Loki to the Father, the Son, and the Holy Spirit.

Hitler once stated, "Pure Christianity—the Christianity of the catacombs—is concerned with translating Christian doctrine into facts. It leads quite simply to the annihilation of mankind. It is wholehearted Bolshevism under a tinsel of metaphysics."[i] Hitler believed in survival of the fittest and despised anything that seemed to try to uplift the masses. He saw this as the "rotten branch of Christianity" at work.

Such things would have been shocking to everyday Germans, most of whom, despite their cowed silence, still considered themselves Christians. If known, it might have inspired them to stand up against Hitler and his Nazi henchmen. However, Hitler was crafty enough to keep these beliefs to himself. However, Hitler ultimately desired the eradication of anyone who did not share his views. To be clear, Adolf Hitler dreamed of a dystopian future in which everyone was firmly under the heel of the Nazi totalitarian boot. Fortunately for Germany and the rest of the world, that day never came.

[i] Spencer, Robert. *Religion of Peace?: Why Christianity Is and Islam Isn't.* 2007. Pg. 122.

Chapter 10: The Postwar and Cold War Era

"The smell of death overwhelmed us. More than 3,200 naked, emaciated bodies had been thrown into shallow graves. Others lay in the street where they had fallen. Lice crawled over the yellowed skin of their sharp, bony frames. I was too revolted to speak."

-General Omar Bradley[i]

On May 8th, 1945, the war in Europe officially came to an end. The United States and the Allies continued to fight Germany's former ally, Japan, for a few more months, but for Germany, it was over. And with the end of the war came quite a reckoning for the German people.

---

[i] O'Reilly Bill. *Hitler's Last Days: The Death of the Nazi Regime and the World's Most Notorious Dictator.* 2015. Pg. 292.

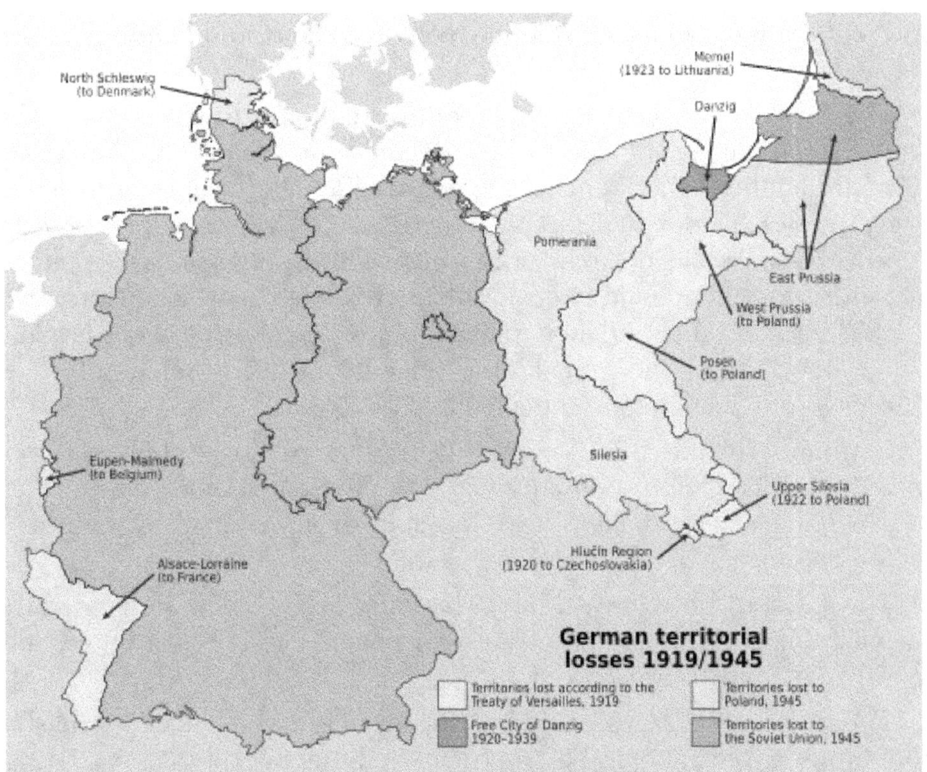

German territorial losses after both world wars.[88]

Germany was occupied by the Americans, British, and French in the west and the Russians in the east. Allied bombing in the later stages of the war had reduced most of Germany's cities to ruins and had killed an estimated 4.5 million Germans. Many of those Germans were civilians.

The defeated German survivors, as much as they had suffered, were in no position to condemn their conquerors. The vanquished had to look to those who had done the vanquishing for help as they clawed their way out of the wreckage that had been their homeland. They also had to come to grips with the fact that their nation was now a divided homeland.

The Germans found that some of the occupiers were more benign than others. The Soviets were more brutal. Fresh from the bloody and disturbing nightmare that had been the Eastern Front, the Russian troops were out for revenge. There are many accounts of Russians pouring into villages in East Germany, slaughtering men and raping women. The Russians also plundered and stole anything that might have been deemed valuable. Not all of this was spontaneous. Some of it was orchestrated. There were instances in which the Russians dismantled whole factories and sent them back east so that they could be repurposed and reinstalled in Russia.

The French, although not as bloodthirsty as the Russians, were also quite harsh, taking whatever they deemed fit. After the Americans admonished them, the French managed to stifle their feelings for revenge. The Americans reminded them of the Treaty of Versailles and let it be known that they did not want a repeat of the repercussions of punitive measures. No one wanted to deal with another world war. The Americans led the charge. They did not want to punish or destroy the Germans; rather, they wanted to rebuild the Allied-controlled sphere of West Germany so that it could eventually stand on its own.

Communism and the Western nations' increasingly chilly relations with the Soviet Union loomed large. The West realized it was in their own best interest to make West Germany strong enough to stand as a bulwark against encroaching communism.

The US led the way with this rebuilding of Germany by way of the Marshall Plan. This plan was a four-year initiative to inject resources into war-torn Western Europe.

The Soviets had plans of their own. In 1946, they helped establish a communist government in East Germany with the Socialist Union Party at the helm.

Both America and its allies, as well as the Soviets, had difficulty figuring out what to do with former Nazis. It seemed like common sense to just get rid of them all. However, upon further looking into the matter, the occupiers discovered there was a big difference between "nominal" Nazis and "real" Nazis. Toward the end of the Nazi regime, just about anyone who wanted to do anything by way of a professional career had to join the Nazi Party. These people did not necessarily join the party because they agreed with Nazi ideology; they only did so to get a job. It was for this reason that countless doctors, dentists, and construction workers were card-carrying Nazis. The occupiers had to learn not to worry so much about who was a party member (since most of the country was) but those who played a distinct role in the regime. After all, there was a big difference between a guy who worked every day of his life as a dentist and Heinrich Himmler, who was the head of the SS.

On May 23rd, 1949, the Western nations merged their three occupation zones together to establish the Federal Republic of West Germany. Germany was now clearly split between West and East.

The capital of West Germany was Bonn. Perhaps the most troubling part of this arrangement was the fact that the old German capital of Berlin, although well within the Soviet zone of influence, was split between the Allies and the Soviets. This created immense problems when the Soviets decided to shut off access to West Belin. Many retellings of this history give the impression that the Soviets did such a thing for no reason. It was as if they were just flexing their muscle and testing the resolve of the West. But what many retellings gloss over is the triggering event that led the Soviets to act.

The Western Allies had minted a new currency, German marks, in West Germany and West Berlin. The Soviets had created a different currency for the East Berliners. The trouble began when the Western-backed currency deposited in West Berlin began to circulate in East Berlin. This created a severe disruption among the East Berliners and outraged the Soviets, who viewed it as a trespass against previous agreements the West had made not to interfere with East Berlin. This incident led the Soviets to take the arguably drastic step of blockading the roads to West Berlin.

This act led to the Berlin Airlift, which was conducted between 1948 and 1949. This was an ingenious and daring air relief program in which the Americans and the British dropped packages of food, coal, and other necessities to the citizens of West Berlin from airplanes. The Soviets could shut down the roads, but they could not close the skies. They were unable to completely stop the flow of goods.

Germans watching a US plane fly in with supplies during the Berlin Airlift."

Realizing it was pointless, the Soviets agreed to lift the blockade. However, they would not give up on the idea of cutting East Berlin off from the West, and the Soviets continued to tighten their grip.

In 1955, East Germany was made an official part of the Warsaw Pact, which held the Eastern Bloc of communist states together. East Germany, which the communists had dubbed the German Democratic Republic, had become the front line in the Cold War. The lines were now clearly drawn between the Western and Eastern blocs. Adding to this was a menacing set of barbed wire that was placed across the border regions.

At this point, East and West Berlin were still open to traffic, but the obvious intention of making these border crossings more difficult led to an ever-increasing flood of East Berliners to the West. In 1961, in an effort to prevent Western meddling and to stave the flow of migrants from East Berlin to West Berlin, the communists began to construct a massive wall. The Berlin Wall, as it would be known, was a massive stretch of concrete. This wall was erected to effectively cut off East Berlin from West Berlin. There were several checkpoints along the wall, and armed soldiers watched to make sure no one tried to climb or otherwise penetrate this barrier.

On the other side of that wall, things were going far differently. In the late 1950s, West Germany experienced an economic boon known as the Wirtschaftswunder. The term roughly translates into English as "economic miracle." Why was it a miracle? Well, after being bombed during the war, West Germany was able to rebuild industrial plants, ramp up production, export products, and see huge economic growth. The year 1958 saw West Germany enter into the European Economic Community (the EEC), a precursor of what would ultimately become the European Union.

Those in charge of the German Democratic Republic (GDR) feared that East Germany might be left in West Germany's dust. Communist planners in 1963 enacted the New Economic System, a series of reforms designed to allow some decentralization from what had otherwise been a command economy. It also gave more control to the skilled technocrats, who were charged with running the most vital operations of the GDR.

These reforms improved the economy of the GDR for some time, with exceptional growth occurring by the 1970s. It was good while it lasted, but the bottom would eventually fall out.

Change was on its way. In 1971, German politician Erich Honecker rose to prominence as the general secretary of East Germany's communist party. Honecker wished to present himself as a party man, but he found himself being drawn into international unrest. In 1975, claims of human rights abuse led to the landmark Helsinki Declaration, which sought to give some basic guarantee of human rights in the Eastern Bloc—East Germany included. Such reforms stood in stark contrast to the Berlin Wall and the dreaded Stasi, the German secret police who watched everything that the East Germans did.

The East Germans increasingly longed to be reunited with the West. They embraced Western culture, just as they embraced news broadcasts that came from West Germany. As much as the communists wished to build walls and barriers, they could not stop broadcast TV signals!

In 1985, the new leader of the Soviet Union, Mikhail Gorbachev, began openly speaking of reform within the Soviet Union and its Eastern Bloc satellite states. He spoke of both glasnost ("openness") and perestroika ("reforming"). These were the two things that East Germans craved the most: governmental reform and the commitment to a more transparent and open society.

This openness allowed for more discussions about and even protests against the current conditions in East Germany. An increasingly bold public began to actively push back against the restrictions they had lived under, especially against the most visible symbol of their repression, the Berlin Wall.

Berliners greeted US President Ronald Reagan with cheers at the Brandenburg Gate in 1987. Reagan famously demanded, "Mr. Gorbachev, tear down this wall!" A couple of years later, the Germans helped Mr. Gorbachev do just that. On November 9th, 1989, both East and West Germans came together to dismantle the wall. This act was encouraged by guards who opened the gates and allowed citizens to pass back and forth. Even as an increasingly unruly crowd climbed and stood on top of the wall, the guards made it clear there would be no repercussions.

Seemingly given the green light, Germans began to use whatever they could, whether hammers or their bare hands, to tear down the Berlin Wall. The Soviets and their communist enforcers practically did nothing to stop this event from unfolding. Both the end of the Cold War and the reunification of Germany finally seemed near.

Chapter 11: Reunification and Beyond: Modern Germany

The Berlin Wall came crashing down in 1989. The following year, the country would officially come together as one. As cries of "Wir sind ein Volk!" (or as it would be rendered in English, "We are one people!") filled the air, Germans demanded that the previously fractured halves of their nation be put back together.

No one thought this would be an easy task, yet it was actually far easier than anyone imagined it would be. With just a stroke of a pen, on October 3rd, 1990, the reunification of Germany was made a reality. With this treaty, the German Democratic Republic was dismantled, and East Germany was absorbed into West Germany's federal republic. The capital of unified Germany would move from Bonn back to the traditional capital of Berlin.

These things were accomplished under West German Chancellor Helmut Kohl. Kohl was a charismatic and robust politician who set out on an ambitious ten-point program, which outlined the path forward for the full integration of the two halves of Germany into one nation.

Kohl was first elected in West Germany in 1982, and it was under his watch that the Berlin Wall fell in 1989 and the two halves were united in 1990. In fact, Kohl won his reelection in 1990 on the pledge to make sure that Germany was reunited sooner rather than later.

Once unification began, it was clear that East Germany had some catching up to do in order to match the industrial might and economic power of West Germany. Some outsiders voiced reservations about a united and stronger Germany. *Time* magazine even published a piece shortly after unification, openly asking if the world should be cautious in reviving a Germany that had previously instigated two global conflicts.

After the ecstatic joy of tearing down the wall and reunifying had died down, the Germans themselves began to question such things. Moreover, the Germans began to question their own identity. Who were they? And how could they rise above the guilt of their past? The West Germans had long ago begged for forgiveness for the past crimes of the Nazis. West Germany had been paying hefty reparations to Israel. It was a small consolation when compared to the horrors of the Holocaust, but it was at least an effort.

The East Germans had never really confronted their past. After the war, the communists, seeking to bolster East German morale against the West, twisted the narrative by insisting that the Nazis were an offshoot of capitalism. The East Germans were raised to believe that by becoming communists, they had distanced themselves from the Nazis. To this day, it is said that West Germans are more likely to be more apologetic about past atrocities even if they had not been born at the time they occurred than East Germans would. East Germans are also said to be more easygoing and more likely to fully embrace being German.

Helmut Kohl seemed eager to reassure the world that Germany had moved past the old sense of nationalism in favor of a more globalist stance. Germany's inroads in the nascent European Union (EU) seemed to back up such claims. In 1993, the EU as we know it today came into being through the Maastricht Treaty. This treaty sought to dissolve some aspects of national distinction in favor of universal citizenship within the EU. For many Germans eager to shed the guilt of the past and for those who felt too disconnected to even associate with it, this likely seemed to be the best and most logical step forward.

Kohl remained in office until 1998, when his successor, Gerhard Schröder, was elected. Gerhard positioned himself as a moderate. He was neither too liberal nor too conservative. Under Gerhard, Germany entered the Eurozone by officially adopting the EU currency (the euro) as legal tender. Gerhard stayed in office until 2005 when Angela Merkel was elected.

Merkel would have to deal with the Eurozone crisis that erupted during the Great Recession of 2008. While other EU countries faltered,

Germany remained strong. In fact, it was strong enough to repeatedly bail other EU members out. One of the newest additions to the EU, Greece, has been a major recipient of German aid.

The fact that Greece ended up owing Germany so much money in bailout loans would later create much resentment among the Greeks. This resentment came to a head in 2015 when Greece's prime minister, Alexis Tsipras, began to suggest that it should not be Greece paying Germany but rather Germany paying Greece. This was in light of a new push to get Germany to pay reparations for its part in invading and occupying Greece in the Second World War. Such things were not very popular with the German public, who felt as if they had already done more than enough since the war's end in 1945.

Such discussions were still underway when Germany and much of the rest of the world were rocked by a global pandemic. Germany experienced its first cases as early as January 2020.

Angela Merkel's response was to immediately send the nation into lockdown to prevent further spread of the disease. However, this had a dire effect on the economy since it meant no one was working. Disaffection with these results saw Angela Merkel make her exit after sixteen years of leadership. She was replaced by a more liberal politician, Olaf Scholz.

Since becoming chancellor, the greatest issue that Scholz has faced so far is the Russian invasion of Ukraine, which occurred in February 2022. Germany, along with the rest of the EU, Britain, and the United States, has been a strong supporter of Ukraine in its struggle against Russia.

Along with opening their wallets, Germans have also opened their doors, allowing over a million refugees from Ukraine, Syria, and other countries. During the first half of the 20th century, no one imagined Germany being such a welcoming place, but so far, the first few decades of the 21st century have changed that opinion considerably.

Conclusion

It is common for nations around the world to embrace some form of patriotism, some sense of nationalism. Americans sing the anthem "The Star-Spangled Banner" and the British proudly fly the Union Jack. Germans have long sought to have some sort of national identity. However, their quest for national recognition has been exceedingly difficult and is usually flummoxed by the preconceived notions of outsiders.

At the beginning of Germany's recorded history, the Romans noted a distinct culture and even attitude among the warring tribes of Central Europe. Roman observers admired not only the martial prowess of these warriors but also their sense of honor. The warriors seemed to have deep respect for family and tribal bonds. Such things, on a much smaller scale, form the very core of national identity. A nation of people could be said to be essentially one giant extended family of shared laws, customs, and values.

The Franks, which historians also link with French history, saw their warrior king, Clovis, attempt to make himself a new Roman emperor. Charlemagne the Great would prove successful at this task, being officially crowned as such in 800 CE by the pope. This kickstarted the Holy Roman Empire, a conglomeration of states in Central Europe so confusing and confounding that it provided excellent fodder for French satirist Voltaire. He joked that the realm was not really an empire. Roman, or holy!

After the Holy Roman Empire's dissolution, thanks to the actions of Napoleon Bonaparte, Prussia and Austria rose to prominence. These were both German-speaking realms, but the sense of nationalism in both were quite different. Rather than nationalism, both trended to embrace cosmopolitanism. However, when Prussia seized the rest of the German states in the west and forged its Reich (or empire), a long-dormant sense of German nationalism arose.

This sense of Germany's unique place in the world was nurtured during and after World War One. It then rose its ugly head in a horrific way during World War Two. After this nightmare came to a close, many, both outside and inside Germany, started saying, "Never again." And for most, the answer to never having such terrible things occur on German soil was to get rid of any sense of German identity.

It is for this reason that Germans today are more likely to shy away from the idea of nationalism. For them, the term "nationalist" is almost akin to a derogatory word. Germans, for the most part, want to embrace international globalism, multinational parties, and being part of supernational organizations like the European Union.

It has been a hard road for the denizens of Central Europe who aspire to take part in what amounts to a post-German society. But hopefully, as they travel down this difficult, winding path, this nation will find a much brighter and more meaningful future.

Here's another book by Enthralling History that you might like

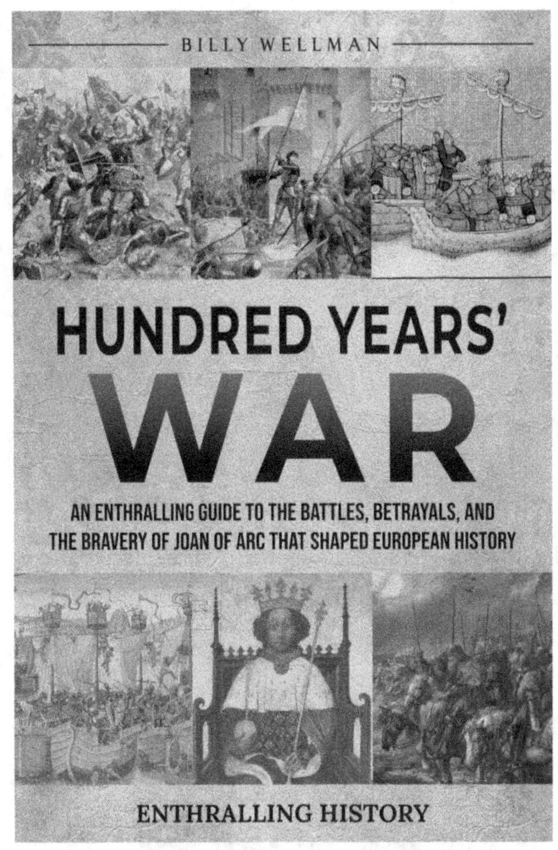

Free limited time bonus

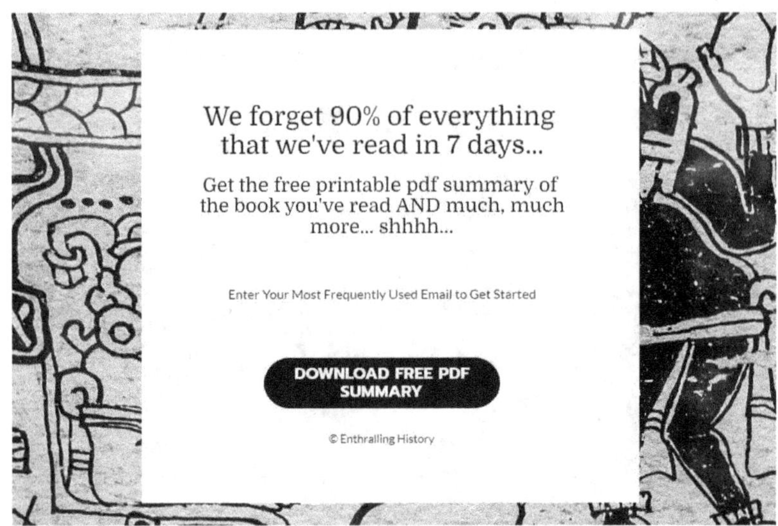

Stop for a moment. We have a free bonus set up for you. The problem is this: we forget 90% of everything that we read after 7 days. Crazy fact, right? Here's the solution: we've created a printable, 1-page pdf summary for this book that you're reading now. All you have to do to get your free pdf summary is to go to the following website:

https://livetolearn.lpages.co/enthrallinghistory/

Or, Scan the QR code!

Once you do, it will be intuitive. Enjoy, and thank you!

Bibliography

Part 1: The Holy Roman Empire

Heather, Peter. Empires and barbarians: The fall of Rome and the birth of Europe. Oxford University Press, 2010.

Contreni, John J. "Introduction:" The Merovingian Kingdoms", 450-751." French Historical Studies 19, no. 3 (1996): 755.

Barbero, Alessandro. Charlemagne: Father of a continent. University of California Press, 2018.

Joranson, Einar. "The Dissolution of the Carolingian Fisc in the Ninth Century." (1936): 545-547.

Merlo, Brian. "Pope John X and the End of the Formosan Dispute in Rome." PhD diss., Saint Louis University, 2018.

Ganshof, François Louis. Feudalism. Vol. 34. University of Toronto Press, 1996.

MacLean, Simon. "History and politics in late Carolingian and Ottonian Europe: the Chronicle of Regino of Prüm and Adalbert of Magdeburg." In History and politics in late Carolingian and Ottonian Europe. Manchester University Press, 2013.

HAUFF, Andrea. The Kingdom of Upper Burgundy and the East Frankish Kingdom at the beginning of the 10th century. *History Compass*, 2017, 15.8: e12396.

BACHRACH, David Stewart. Milites and Warfare in Pre-Crusade Germany. *War in History*, 2015, 22.3: 298-343.

BACHRACH, David. Exercise of royal power in early medieval Europe: the case of Otto the Great 936–73. *Early Medieval Europe*, 2009, 17.4: 389-419.

BACHRACH, David S. Early Ottonian Warfare: The Perspective from Corvey. *Journal of Military History*, 2011, 75.2.

WILSON, Joseph. Holy Anointment and Realpolitik in the Age of Otto I. 2015.

Robbie, Steven. "Can silence speak volumes? Widukind's Res Gestae Saxonicae and the coronation of Otto I reconsidered." Early Medieval Europe 20, no. 3 (2012): 333-362.

Poole, Reginald L. "The names and numbers of medieval popes." The English Historical Review 32, no. 128 (1917): 465-478.

Grabowski, Antoni. "Liudprand of Cremona's papa monstrum: The Image of Pope John XII in the Historia Ottonis." Early Medieval Europe 23, no. 1 (2015): 67-92.

Brook, Lindsay. "Popes and Pornocrats: Rome in the early middle ages." Foundations 1, no. 1 (2003): 5-21.

Roach, Levi. "The Ottonians and Italy." German History 36, no. 3 (2018): 349-364.

Osborne, John. "The dower charter of Otto II and Theophanu, and the Roman scriptorium at Santi Apostoli." Papers of the British School at Rome 89 (2021): 137-157.

Welton, Megan, and Sarah Greer. "Establishing Just Rule: The Diplomatic Negotiations of the Dominae Imperiales in the Ottonian Succession Crisis of 983–985." Frühmittelalterliche Studien 55, no. 1 (2021): 315-342.

Zeller, Jules. L'empire germanique et l'Eglise au Moyen-Age: les Henri. Vol. 3. Didier, 1876.

Morrison, Karl F. "Canossa: A Revision." Traditio 18 (1962): 121-148.

De Mesquita, Bruce Bueno. "Popes, Kings, and endogenous institutions: The Concordat of Worms and the origins of sovereignty." International Studies Review 2, no. 2 (2000): 93-118.

Roche, Jason T. "King Conrad III in the Byzantine Empire: a foil for native imperial virtue." (2015).

Weiler, B. (2009). The King as judge: Henry II and Frederick Barbarossa as seen by their contemporaries. In Challenging the boundaries of medieval history: the legacy of Timothy Reuter (pp. 115-140).

Velov, Ivana. Literary and Historical Interpretation of Frederick Barbarossa's Conquest of the Italian Communes: Analysis of the Events and Personalities Described in the Novel "Baudolino" by Umberto Eco. *ДИПЛОМАТИЈА И БЕЗБЕДНОСТ*, 249.

FRANKE, Daniel. From Defeat to Victory in Northern Italy: Comparing Staufen Strategy and Operations at Legnano and Cortenuova, 1176-1237. *Nuova Antologia Militare*, 2021, 2.5: 27.

Friederich A. Warlord or Financial Strategist: Frederick Barbarossa. Johns Hopkins University. 2022 Nov 10;3(1).

Frederick I. The crusade of Frederick Barbarossa: The history of the expedition of the Emperor Frederick and related texts. Ashgate Publishing, Ltd.; 2010.

Bryce, James, *The Holy Roman Empire,* MacMillan and Company, 1866. 232

Painter, Sidney, *A History of the Middle Ages 284-1500,* The MacMillan press LTD, 1973. 326

Holmes, George, *The Oxford History of Medieval Europe,* Oxford University press, 1988. 225

Wilson, Peter H. *Heart of Europe: A History of the Holy Roman Empire.* Harvard University Press, 2016, 557

Grand Larousse encyclopedia, Vuk Karadzic, 1971-1973. 372

Febvre, Lucien, *Martin Luther: A Destiny,* LDI, 1996. 77

Wilson PH. The Causes of the Thirty Years War 1618–48. The English Historical Review. 2008 Jun 1;123(502):554-86.

Mortimer G. The Origins of the Thirty Years War and the Revolt in Bohemia, 1618. Springer; 2015 Aug 11.

POLIŠENSKÝ, Josef V. The Thirty Years' War. Past & Present, 1954, 6: 31-43.

LOCKHART, Paul Douglas. Political Language and Wartime Propaganda in Denmark, 1625–1629. European History Quarterly, 2001, 31.1: 5-42.

Davis TM. The Swedish Intervention: How the Thirty Years War Became International. The Alexandrian. 2017;6(1).

Nicklisch N, Ramsthaler F, Meller H, Friederich S, Alt KW. The face of war: Trauma analysis of a mass grave from the Battle of Lützen (1632). PLoS One. 2017 May 22;12(5):e0178252.

Rehman I. Raison d'Etat: Richelieu's Grand Strategy During the Thirty Years' War (May 2019). Texas National Security Review. 2019.

GROSS, Leo. The peace of Westphalia, 1648–1948. *American Journal of International Law,* 1948, 42.1: 20-41.

EVANS, Robert; WILSON, Peter (ed.). The Holy Roman Empire, 1495-1806: A European Perspective. Brill, 2012.

Part 2: The Habsburgs

History's Women. (2023, November 8). Maria Theresa. Retrieved from History's Women: https://historyswomen.com/women-who-ruled/maria-theresa/.

Abernethy, S. (2013, May 3). Charles the Bold, Duke of Burgundy. Retrieved from The Freelance History Writer: https://thefreelancehistorywriter.com/2013/05/03/charles-the-bold-duke-of-burgundy/.

Biography.com. (2021, October 21). Maria Theresa. Retrieved from Biography.com: https://www.biography.com/royalty/maria-theresa.

Britannica.com. (2023, November 8). Conflicts with Revolutionary France, 1790-1805. Retrieved from Britannica.com: https://www.britannica.com/place/Austria/Conflicts-with-revolutionary-France-1790-1805.

Britannica.com. (2023, October 26). Mature Career of Tycho Brahe. Retrieved from Britannica.com: https://www.britannica.com/biography/Tycho-Brahe-Danish-astronomer/Mature-career.

Britannica.com. (2023, October 17). Partitions of Poland. Retrieved from Britannica.com: https://www.britannica.com/event/Partitions-of-Poland.

Britannica.com. (2023, October 28). War of the Spanish Succession. Retrieved from Britannica.com: https://www.britannica.com/event/War-of-the-Spanish-Succession.

BritishBattles.com. (2023, October 28). Battle of Blenheim. Retrieved from Britishbattles.com: https://www.britishbattles.com/war-of-the-spanish-succession/battle-of-blenheim/.

Canun, N. (2022, March 21). 5 Most Brutal Conquistadors of the New World. Retrieved from Spanish Academy: https://www.spanish.academy/blog/5-most-brutal-conquistadors-of-the-new-world/.

Cavendish, R. (2007, November). Spanish Bankruptcy. Retrieved from History Today: https://www.historytoday.com/archive/spanish-bankruptcy.

Christopher Marx, C. B. (2017, September 17). Talking Cure Models: A Framework of Analysis. Retrieved from National Library of Medicine: https://www.ncbi.nlm.nih.gov/pmc/articles/PMC5601393/#:~:text=The%20%E2%80%9Ctalking%20cure%2C%E2%80%9D%20then,the%20patient%20from%20hysteric%20symptoms.

Classicfm.com. (2023, October 31). Johann Strauss II: A Life. Retrieved from Classicfm.com: https://www.classicfm.com/composers/strauss-ii/guides/johann-strauss-ii-life/.

Classicfm.com. (2023, October 31). Johannes Brahms. Retrieved from Classicfm.com: https://www.classicfm.com/composers/brahms/.

DailyHistory.org. (2023, October 28). How Did the Peace of Augsburg (1555) Lead to the Thirty Years' War (1618-1648). Retrieved from DailyHistory.org: https://dailyhistory.org/How_did_the_Peace_of_Augsburg_(1555)_lead_to_the_Thirty_Years_War_(1618-1648).

DBpedia.org. (2023, October 30). Austro-Hungarian Compromise of 1867. Retrieved from DBpedia.org: https://dbpedia.org/page/Austro-Hungarian_Compromise_of_1867.

Encyclopedia.com. (2023, October 25). Mining, The Americas. Retrieved from Encyclopedia.com: https://www.encyclopedia.com/history/encyclopedias-almanacs-transcripts-and-maps/mining-americas.

Famous Scientists. (2023, October 26). Johannes Kepler. Retrieved from Famousscientists.org: https://www.famousscientists.org/johannes-kepler/.

Ferdinand, M. d. (2023, September 17). Charles V Holy Roman Emperor. Retrieved from Britannica.com: https://www.britannica.com/biography/Charles-V-Holy-Roman-emperor.

Flantzer, S. (2023, May 29). Mary, Duchess of Burgundy, Archduchess of Austria. Retrieved from Unofficial Royalty: https://www.unofficialroyalty.com/mary-duchess-of-burgundy-archduchess-of-austria/.

Friehs, J. T. (2023, October 25). Working at Court I: Pro and Contra. Retrieved from The World of the Habsburgs: https://www.habsburger.net/en/chapter/working-court-i-pro-and-contra.

Getlen, L. (2015, July 26). Meet the World's Richest Man Who Changed Christianity. Retrieved from New York Post.com: https://nypost.com/2015/07/26/meet-historys-richest-man-who-changed-christianity/.

Gruber, S. (2023, November 8). Maria Theresa: The "Great Reformer." Retrieved from The World of the Habsburgs: https://www.habsburger.net/en/chapter/maria-theresa-great-reformer.

Gruber, S. (2023, October 28). Wallenstein: Death by Murder. Retrieved from The World of the Habsburgs: https://www.habsburger.net/en/chapter/wallenstein-death-murder.

Hall, R. C. (2018, April 4). War in the Balkans. Retrieved from International Encyclopedia of the First World War: https://encyclopedia.1914-1918-online.net/article/war_in_the_balkans.

Heath, R. (2023, October 21). Emperor Charles V and the Fugger Family. Retrieved from Emperor Charles V: https://www.emperorcharlesv.com/charles-v-fugger-family/.

Heritage History. (2023, October 30). Hungarian Revolution. Retrieved from Heritage-History.com: https://www.heritage-history.com/index.php?c=resources&s=war-dir&f=wars_hungarian.

History. (2021, June 25). Austria's Archduke Ferdinand Assassinated. Retrieved from History.com: https://www.history.com/this-day-in-history/archduke-ferdinand-assassinated.

History Guild. (2023, November 11). The Congress of Vienna. Retrieved from Historyguid.org: https://historyguild.org/the-congress-of-vienna/.

History Learning. (2023, October 28). The Edict of Restitution. Retrieved from History Learning: https://historylearning.com/the-thirty-years-war0/edict-of-restitution/.

History Skills. (2023, September 14). The Valladolid Debate: When Europeans Argued About Whether Indigenous People Were Human. Retrieved from Historyskills.com: https://www.historyskills.com/classroom/year-8/valladolid-debate/.

Holy Roman Empire Association. (2023, October 21). Holy Roman Emperor Frederick III-1440-1493. Retrieved from Holy Roman Empire Association: http://www.holyromanempireassociation.com/holy-roman-emperor-frederick-iii-.html.

Infoplease. (2023, October 28). Thirty Years' War: The Danish Period. Retrieved from Infoplease.com: https://www.infoplease.com/encyclopedia/history/modern-europe/wars-battles/thirty-years-war/the-danish-period.

Keithly, D. M. (2008, April 3). Maria Theresa. Retrieved from Enlightenment-revolution.org: https://enlightenment-revolution.org/index.php?title=Maria_Theresa.

Kilroy-Ewbank, D. L. (2023, October 25). El Escorial, Spain. Retrieved from Khan Academy: https://www.khanacademy.org/humanities/renaissance-reformation/xa6688040:spain-portugal-15th-16th-century/xa6688040:16th-century-spain/a/el-escorial-spain.

Lumen Learning. (2023, October 28). The Peace of Westphalia and Sovereignty. Retrieved from Lumenlearning.com: https://courses.lumenlearning.com/atd-herkimer-westerncivilization/chapter/the-peace-of-westphalia-and-sovereignty/.

Lumen Learning. (2023, October 28). War of Spanish Succession. Retrieved from Lumenlearning.com: https://courses.lumenlearning.com/suny-fmcc-boundless-worldhistory/chapter/war-of-spanish-succession/.

Macgregory History. (2023, October 31). July Crisis 1914. Retrieved from Macgregoryhistory.com: https://www.macgregorishistory.com/wp-content/uploads/2020/12/WWI-July-Crisis-1914.pdf

Mark, H. W. (2023, July 13). Battle of Austerlitz. Retrieved from World History Encyclopedia: https://www.worldhistory.org/article/2253/battle-of-austerlitz/.

Mark, H. W. (2023, September 4). War of the Sixth Coalition. Retrieved from World History Encyclopedia: https://www.worldhistory.org/War_of_the_Sixth_Coalition/.

Maxwell, K. (2020, December 30). The Beginnings of Globalization: The Spanish Silver Trade Routes. Retrieved from Defense.info: https://defense.info/global-dynamics/2020/12/the-beginnings-of-globalization-the-spanish-silver-trade-routes/.

Mediakron.bc.edu. (2023, October 25). Turkish Bombard. Retrieved from Mediakron.bc.edu: https://mediakron.bc.edu/ottomans/turkish-bombard/siege-of-vienna.

Munoz, J. A. (2019, September 20). Profit vs. Usury: Difference from the Point of View of Saint Thomas Aquinas. Retrieved from The Tseconomist: https://thetseconomist.wordpress.com/2019/09/20/profit-vs-usury-difference-from-the-point-of-view-of-saint-thomas-aquinas/.

Musee Protestant. (2023, October 21). The Augsburg Confession (1530). Retrieved from Museeprotestant.org: https://museeprotestant.org/en/notice/the-augsburg-confession-1530/.

New Advent. (2023, October 28). German (Catholic) League. Retrieved from New Advent: https://www.newadvent.org/cathen/09100a.htm

New Advent. (2023, October 23). Johannes Tserclaes, County of Tilly. Retrieved from New Advent: https://www.newadvent.org/cathen/14724c.htm.

New Advent. (2023, November 8). Wenzel Anton Kaunitz. Retrieved from NewAdvent.org: https://www.newadvent.org/cathen/08611b.htm.

OAW. (2023, October 25). Music at the Courts of the House of Habsburg. Retrieved from OAW: https://www.oeaw.ac.at/acdh/projects/music-at-the-courts-of-the-house-of-habsburg.

Officeapp.live.com. (2023, October 25). Born with a Silve Spoon The Origin of World Trade in 1571. Retrieved from Officeapp.live.com: https://view.officeapps.live.com/op/view.aspx?src=https%3A%2F%2Fwww.birdvilleschools.net%2Fcms%2Flib2%2FTX01000797%2FCentricity%2FDomain%2F3775%2FBorn_with_a_Silver_SpoonThe_Origin_of_World_Trade_in_1571.doc&wdOrigin=BROWSELINK

Palffy, G. (2002). The Border Defense System in Hungary in the Sixteenth and Seventeenth Centuries. Retrieved from Academia.edu: https://www.academia.edu/539595/The_Border_Defense_System_in_Hungary_in_the_Sixteenth_and_Seventeenth_Centuries_In_A_Millennium_of_Hungarian_Military_History_Ed_L%C3%A1szl%C3%B3_Veszpr%C3%A9my_B%C3%A9la_K_Kir%C3%A1ly_New_York_Social_Science_Monographs_Bro.

Parry, V. (2023, October 25). Suleyman the Magnificent. Retrieved from Britannica.com: https://www.britannica.com/biography/Suleyman-the-Magnificent.

PBS.org. (2023, February 10). The Ulm-Austerlitz Campaign, 1805. Retrieved from PBS.org: https://www.pbs.org/empires/napoleon/n_war/campaign/page_6.html.

Radioswissclassic. (2023, October 25). Cornelius Canis. Retrieved from Radioswissclassic: https://www.radioswissclassic.ch/en/music-database/musician/54261523c37de6c3eba58ffec69f05ab13193d/biography?app =true.

Redazione. (2018, August 21). Tycho Brahe, Astronomer and Alchemist at the Court of Rudolf II. Retrieved from Progretto: http://www.progetto.cz/tycho-brahe-astronomo-e-alchimista-alla-corte-di-rodolfo-ii/?lang=en.

Robertson, Angus. The Crossroads of Civilization: A History of Vienna. 2022.

Royal Museums Greenwich. (2023, November 8). Queen Elizabeth I's Speech to the Troops at Tilbury. Retrieved from Rmg.co.uk: https://www.rmg.co.uk/stories/topics/queen-elizabeth-speech-troops-tilbury.

Schloss Schonbrunn. (2023, October 25). Architectural History: 17th and 18th Century. Retrieved from Schoenbrunn.at: https://www.schoenbrunn.at/en/about-schoenbrunn/the-palace/history/architectural-history-17th-and-early-18th-century.

Sellers, W. (2023, March 13). Opinion: The Forgotten Hungarian Revolution. Retrieved from Alabama Political Reporter: https://www.alreporter.com/2023/03/13/opinion-the-forgotten-hungarian-revolution/.

Serlin, D. (2014, May 1). Turning the Tide: Venetian Contributions to the Battle of Lepanto. Retrieved from Vtuhr.org: https://vtuhr.org/articles/10.21061/vtuhr.v3i0.21.

Smith, S. S. (2015, August 18). Gustavus Adolphus Revolutionized European Warfare. Retrieved from Investors.com: https://www.investors.com/news/management/leaders-and-success/gustavus-adolphus-father-of-modern-warfare/.

Sorkin, A. D. (2015, September 11). How to Finance an Emperor's Election. Retrieved from The New Yorker: https://www.newyorker.com/news/amy-davidson/how-to-finance-an-emperors-election.

Study.com. (2023, October 30). The Dual Monarchy of Austria-Hungary. Retrieved from Study.com: https://study.com/learn/lesson/hungarian-austrian-dual-monarchy-ausgleich.html#:~:text=The%20Ausgleich%2C%20or%20the%20formal,Ferenc%20Deak%2C%20and%20other%20delegates.

Sun, L. (2020, Fall). Late Imperial China, Silver, and Global Trade Routes. Retrieved from Association for Asian Studies: https://www.asianstudies.org/publications/eaa/archives/late-imperial-china-silver-and-global-trade-routes/.

The Art Story. (20232, October 31). Summary of the Vienna Secession. Retrieved from Theartsotry.org: https://www.theartstory.org/movement/vienna-secession/.

The Art Story. (2023, October 25). Diego Velazquez. Retrieved from Theartstory.org: https://www.theartstory.org/artist/velazquez-diego/.

The Bohemian Religious Peace (July 1609). (2023, October 28). Retrieved from GHDI: https://ghdi.ghi-dc.org/sub_document.cfm?document_id=4501.

The Economist. (2016, December 24). How Vienna Produced Ideas That Shaped the West. Retrieved from Economist.com: https://www.economist.com/christmas-specials/2016/12/24/how-vienna-produced-ideas-that-shaped-the-west.

The Museum of Fine Arts, Houston. (2023, October 25). "Habsburg Splendor: Masterpieces from Vienna's Imperial Collections". Retrieved from MFAH.org: https://www.mfah.org/press/major-traveling-exhibition-masterpieces-austrian-habsburg-dynasty-brings.

The Royal Hampshire Regiment. (2023, October 28). The War of the Spanish Succession. Retrieved from Royalhampshirereiment.org: https://www.royalhampshireregiment.org/about-the-museum/timeline/war-spanish-succession/.

The World of the Habsburgs. (2023, October 21). Rudolf I of Habsburgs: From "Poor Count" to King of the Romans. Retrieved from The World of the Habsburgs: https://www.habsburger.net/en/chapter/rudolf-i-habsburg-poor-count-king-romans.

The World of the Habsburgs. (2023, October 21). The Habsburgs' Origins as a Swiss Noble Family. Retrieved from The World of the Habsburgs: https://www.habsburger.net/en/chapter/habsburgs-origins-swiss-noble-family.

Visiting Vienna. (2023, June 7). Prince Eugene: What You Need to Know. Retrieved from Visitingvienna.com: https://www.visitingvienna.com/culture/prince-eugene-savoy/.

Wethey, H. E. (2023, September 23). El Greco. Retrieved from Britannica.com: https://www.britannica.com/biography/El-Greco.

Wilson, D. (2020, May 23). The 1618 Defenestration of Prague Explained. Retrieved from History Extra: https://www.historyextra.com/period/stuart/1618-defenestration-prague-facts-history-explained-what-happened-why-castle-protestant-catholic/.

Woods, A. (2005, July 19). The 400th Anniversary of Don Quixote: Spain in the Age of Cervantes. Retrieved from Marxist.com: https://www.marxist.com/don-quixote-cervantes150705.htm.

Part 3: History of Prussia

Bach, Thomas Parnell. "Throne and Altar: Pietism and the Hohenzollerns." PhD diss., University of South Carolina, 1995.

Clark, Christopher. *Iron Kingdom: The Rise and Downfall of Prussia, 1600–1947*. Cambridge, MA: Belknap Press of Harvard University Press, 2006.

Colla, Marcus. "Constructing the Prussia-Myth in East Germany, 1945–61." *Journal of Contemporary History* 54, no. 3 (2019): 557–581.

Duffy, Christopher. *The Army of Frederick the Great.* New York: Hippocrene Books, 1974.

Dwyer, Philip G., ed. *Modern Prussian History, 1830–1947.* Cambridge: Cambridge University Press, 2014.

Friedrich, Karin. *The Other Prussia: Royal Prussia, Poland and Liberty, 1569–1772.* Cambridge: Cambridge University Press, 2000.

Haffner, Sebastian. *The Rise and Fall of Prussia.* Translated by Terence Prittie. London: Weidenfeld & Nicolson, 1981.

Jeroschin, Nikolaus von. *The Chronicle of Prussia.* Translated and edited by Mary Fischer. Farnham: Ashgate, 2012.

Koch, H. W. *A History of Prussia.* London: Longman, 1978.

McKay, Derek. The Great Elector: Frederick William of Brandenburg-Prussia. London: Longman, 2001.

Murray, Scott W. "The Origins of an Illusion: British Policy and Opinion, and the Development of Prussian Liberalism, 1848–1871." PhD diss., University of Oxford, 2004.

Shennan, Margaret. *The Rise of Brandenburg-Prussia 1618–1740.* London: Routledge, 1995.

Part 4: History of Germany

Coy, Jason Philip. *A Brief History of Germany.* 2010.

Detwiler, Donald. *Germany: A Short History.* 1976.

Ozment, Steven. *A Mighty Fortress.* 2004.

Benjamin G., Craig. *The Big History of Civilizations.* 2016.

Murray, V. *The Crusades: An Encyclopedia.* 2006.

McGiffert, Cushman. *Martin Luther: The Man and His Work.* 1911.

Gibson, Andrew. *Modernity and the Political Fix.* 2019.

Spencer, Robert. *Religion of Peace?: Why Christianity Is and Islam Isn't.* 2007.

McCabe, Joseph. *A History of the Popes.* 1939.

Middleton, John. *World Monarchies and Dynasties.* 2005.

Pelican, Jaroslav. *Credo: Historical and Theological Guide to Creeds and Confessions of Faith.* 2014.

O'Reilly Bill. *Hitler's Last Days: The Death of the Nazi Regime and the World's Most Notorious Dictator.* 2015.

Retallack, James. *Imperial Germany: 1871-1918.* 2008.

The New English Bible with the Apocrypha. 1970.

Image Sources

1   User:MapMaster, CC BY-SA 2.5 <https://creativecommons.org/licenses/by-sa/2.5>, via Wikimedia Commons, https://commons.wikimedia.org/w/index.php?curid=1234669

2   Kairom13, CC BY-SA 4.0 <https://creativecommons.org/licenses/by-sa/4.0>, via Wikimedia Commons, https://commons.wikimedia.org/w/index.php?curid=112316299

3   https://commons.wikimedia.org/w/index.php?curid=198993

4   https://commons.wikimedia.org/w/index.php?curid=2009655

5   https://commons.wikimedia.org/w/index.php?curid=7849382

6   https://commons.wikimedia.org/w/index.php?curid=1668262

7   https://commons.wikimedia.org/w/index.php?curid=54691316

8   https://commons.wikimedia.org/w/index.php?curid=80912

9   https://commons.wikimedia.org/w/index.php?curid=3108659

10 https://commons.wikimedia.org/w/index.php?curid=228070

11 Kandi, CC BY-SA 4.0 <https://creativecommons.org/licenses/by-sa/4.0>, via Wikimedia Commons https://commons.wikimedia.org/w/index.php?curid=56789387

12 https://commons.wikimedia.org/w/index.php?curid=6433070

13 By User:Ssolbergj, CC BY-SA 4.0 <https://creativecommons.org/licenses/by-sa/4.0>, via Wikimedia Commons; https://commons.wikimedia.org/wiki/File:Or_three_leopards_sable.svg

14 By Medhelan, CC BY-SA 4.0 <https://creativecommons.org/licenses/by-sa/4.0>, via Wikimedia Commons, https://commons.wikimedia.org/wiki/File: Member_Cities_of_the_Lombard_Leagues.png

15 https://commons.wikimedia.org/wiki/File:Balduineum_Wahl_Heinrich_VII.jpg

16 https://commons.wikimedia.org/wiki/File:Das_Interregnum_Drei_M% C3%A4nner_am_Grab_eines_Kaisers.jpg

17 This file is licensed under the Creative Commons Attribution-Share Alike 2.0 Germany license. https://commons.wikimedia.org/wiki/File:Rudolf_Speyerer_Dom.JPG

18 By User:Captain Blood, CC BY-SA 3.0 <http://creativecommons.org/licenses/by-sa/3.0/>, via Wikimedia Commons, https://commons.wikimedia.org/wiki/File:HRR_14Jh.jpg

19 TribalDragon1, CC BY-SA 4.0 <https://creativecommons.org/licenses/by-sa/4.0>, via Wikimedia Commons https://commons.wikimedia.org/wiki/File:Frederick_III_Coronation_Tapestry.jpg

20 https://commons.wikimedia.org/wiki/File:Maarten_van_Heemskerck_-_Santa_Maria_della_Febbre,_Vatican_Obelisk,_Saint_Peter%27s_Basilica_in_const ruction_(1532).jpg

21 https://commons.wikimedia.org/wiki/File:Schlosskirche_Wittenberg.jpg

22 https://commons.wikimedia.org/wiki/File:Deutschland_im_XVI._ Jahrhundert_(Putzger).jpg

23 https://commons.wikimedia.org/wiki/File:Peace-of-augsburg_1555.jpg

24 https://commons.wikimedia.org/w/index.php?curid=1431443

25 https://commons.wikimedia.org/w/index.php?curid=21330817

26 https://commons.wikimedia.org/w/index.php?curid=93172350

27 Astrokey44, CC BY-SA 3.0 <http://creativecommons.org/licenses/by-sa/3.0/>, via Wikimedia Commons https://commons.wikimedia.org/w/index.php?curid=1612601

28 https://commons.wikimedia.org/wiki/File:AlbrechtI.jpg

29 https://commons.wikimedia.org/wiki/File:Albrecht_II_as_Roman-German_king.jpg

30 https://commons.wikimedia.org/wiki/File:Portrait_of_Charles_V,_Holy_ Roman_Emperor,_seated_(1500%E2%80%931558),_formerly_attributed_to_Titian _(Alte_Pinakothek,_Munich).jpg

31 https://commons.wikimedia.org/wiki/File:Albrecht_D%C3%BCrer_080.jpg

32 https://commons.wikimedia.org/wiki/File:Lucas_Cranach_d.%C3%84._-_Martin_Luther,_1528_(Veste_Coburg).jpg

33 https://commons.wikimedia.org/wiki/File:Map_of_New_Spain_by_ Abraham_Ortelius.jpeg

34 https://commons.wikimedia.org/wiki/File:Matteo_Perez_d%27_Aleccio_(1547-1616)_-_The_Siege_of_Malta,_Attack_on_the_Post_of_the_Castilian_Knights,_ 21_August_1565_-_BHC0257_-_Royal_Museums_Greenwich.jpg

35 https://commons.wikimedia.org/wiki/File:El_Greco_-
_The_Burial_of_the_Count_of_Orgaz.JPG

36 https://commons.wikimedia.org/wiki/File:Las_Meninas,_by_Diego_
Vel%C3%A1zquez,_from_Prado_in_Google_Earth.jpg

37 Jebulon, CC0, via Wikimedia Commons;
https://commons.wikimedia.org/wiki/File:Facade_monastery_San_Lorenzo_de_El_
Escorial_Spain.jpg

38 https://commons.wikimedia.org/wiki/File:Vertumnus_%C3%A5rstidernas_
gud_m%C3%A5lad_av_Giuseppe_Arcimboldo_1591_-_Skoklosters_slott_-
_91503.jpg

39 https://commons.wikimedia.org/wiki/File:Los_horrores_de_la_guerra.jpg

40 Map_Thirty_Years_War-fr.svg: historicairderivative work: P. S. Burton, CC BY-SA
2.5 <https://creativecommons.org/licenses/by-sa/2.5>, via Wikimedia Commons;
https://commons.wikimedia.org/wiki/File:Map_Thirty_Years_War-en.svg

41 https://commons.wikimedia.org/wiki/File:Juan_de_Miranda_Carreno_002.jpg

42 https://commons.wikimedia.org/wiki/File:Prinz_Eugene_of_Savoy.PNG

43 https://commons.wikimedia.org/wiki/File:Europe,_1714.png

44 https://commons.wikimedia.org/wiki/File:Kaiserin_Maria_Theresia_(HRR).jpg

45 https://commons.wikimedia.org/wiki/File:Jean-Etienne_Liotard_12.jpg

46 https://commons.wikimedia.org/wiki/File:Peace_of_Basel.png

47 https://commons.wikimedia.org/wiki/File:Napoleon_Marie_Louise_Marriage1.jpeg

48 Alexander Altenhof, CC BY-SA 4.0 <https://creativecommons.org/licenses/by-
sa/4.0>, via Wikimedia Commons;
https://commons.wikimedia.org/wiki/File:Europe_1815_map_en.png

49 https://commons.wikimedia.org/wiki/File:Kollarz_Kossuth_Cegl%C3%A9den
_1848.JPG

50 https://commons.wikimedia.org/wiki/File:Emperor_Francis_Joseph.jpg

51 https://en.wikipedia.org/wiki/File:The_Kiss_-_Gustav_Klimt_-
_Google_Cultural_Institute.jpg

52 Österreich-Ungarns_Ende.png: AlphaCentauri / derivative work: P. S. Burton, CC
BY-SA 3.0 <http://creativecommons.org/licenses/by-sa/3.0/>, via Wikimedia
Commons; https://commons.wikimedia.org/wiki/File:Dissolution_of_Austria-
Hungary.png

53 MapMaster, CC BY-SA 3.0 <http://creativecommons.org/licenses/by-sa/3.0/>, via
Wikimedia Commons, https://commons.wikimedia.org
/wiki/File:Baltic_Tribes_c_1200.svg

54 S. Bollmann, CC BY-SA 3.0 <https://creativecommons.org/licenses/by-sa/3.0>, via
Wikimedia Commons, https://commons.wikimedia.org/wiki/File:
Teutonic_Order_1410.png

55 https://commons.wikimedia.org/wiki/File:Frans_Luycx_-_Frederick_William,_Elector_of_Brandenburg,_at_three-quarter-length.jpg

56 https://commons.wikimedia.org/wiki/File:Adolph-von-Menzel-Tafelrunde2.jpg

57 https://commons.wikimedia.org/wiki/File:Christian_Wolff.jpg

58 Rijksmuseum, CC0, via Wikimedia Commons, https://commons.wikimedia.org/wiki/File:Portret_van_Pierre_Louis_Maupertuis,_RP-P-1910-4953.jpg

59 https://commons.wikimedia.org/wiki/File:D%27apr%C3%A8s_Nicolas_de_Largilli%C3%A8re,_portrait_de_Voltaire_(Institut_et_Mus%C3%A9e_Voltaire)_-001.jpg

60 https://commons.wikimedia.org/wiki/File:BachC.P.E-739858.jpg

61 https://commons.wikimedia.org/wiki/File:Jean-Baptiste_de_Boyer_Marquis_d%27Argens.jpg

62 https://commons.wikimedia.org/wiki/File:Portrait_de_Julien_Offray_de_La_Mettrie.jpg

63 https://commons.wikimedia.org/wiki/File:Francesco_Algarotti_(Liotard).jpg

64 https://commons.wikimedia.org/wiki/File:Immanuel_Kant_portrait_c1790.jpg

65 Bryan Rutherford, CC BY-SA 4.0 <https://creativecommons.org/licenses/by-sa/4.0>, via Wikimedia Commons, https://commons.wikimedia.org/wiki/File:Europe_1740_en.png

66 Bryan Rutherford, CC BY-SA 4.0 <https://creativecommons.org/licenses/by-sa/4.0>, via Wikimedia Commons, https://commons.wikimedia.org/wiki/File:Europe_1783-1792_en.png

67 https://commons.wikimedia.org/wiki/File:Antoine_Pesne_-_Frederick_the_Great_as_Crown_Prince_-_WGA17377.jpg

68 Arthur Kampf, CC BY-SA 4.0 <https://creativecommons.org/licenses/by-sa/4.0>, via Wikimedia Commons, https://commons.wikimedia.org/wiki/File:Frederick_the_Great_as_standard-bearer_at_the_battlefield.jpg

69 Thomas Wolf, www.foto-tw.de, CC BY-SA 3.0 <https://creativecommons.org/licenses/by-sa/3.0>, via Wikimedia Commons, https://commons.wikimedia.org/wiki/File:Brandenburger_Tor_abends.jpg

70 https://commons.wikimedia.org/wiki/File:Bust_of_Queen_Louise_asleep,_by_Christian_Daniel_Rauch,_1817,_marble_-_Germanisches_Nationalmuseum_-_Nuremberg,_Germany_-_DSC03377.jpg

71 https://commons.wikimedia.org/wiki/File:Kaiser_Wilhelm_II_of_Germany_-_1902_(cropped).jpg

72 Bullenwächter, CC BY 3.0 <https://creativecommons.org/licenses/by/3.0>, via Wikimedia Commons; https://commons.wikimedia.org/wiki/File:Bronze_figure_of_a_German_Biblioth%C3%A8que_Nationale.jpg

73 User:MapMaster, CC BY-SA 2.5 <https://creativecommons.org/licenses/by-sa/2.5>, via Wikimedia Commons; https://commons.wikimedia.org/wiki/File:Invasions_of_the_Roman_Empire_1.png

74 Blank map of Europe.svg: maix¿?derivative work: Alphathon, CC BY-SA 4.0 <https://creativecommons.org/licenses/by-sa/4.0>, via Wikimedia Commons; https://commons.wikimedia.org/wiki/File:Francia_814.svg

75 Holy Roman Empire 1000 map-fr.svg: Sémhurderivative work: OwenBlacker | Discussion, CC BY-SA 3.0 <https://creativecommons.org/licenses/by-sa/3.0>, via Wikimedia Commons; https://commons.wikimedia.org/wiki/File:Holy_Roman_Empire_11th_century_map-en.svg

76 https://commons.wikimedia.org/wiki/File:Friedrich_I._Barbarossa.jpg

77 https://commons.wikimedia.org/wiki/File:Peter_Janssen,_Kaiser_Friedrich_II.jpg

78 https://commons.wikimedia.org/wiki/File:Luther_at_the_Diet_of_Worms.jpg

79 Map_Thirty_Years_War-fr.svg: historicairderivative work: P. S. Burton, CC BY-SA 2.5 <https://creativecommons.org/licenses/by-sa/2.5>, via Wikimedia Commons; https://commons.wikimedia.org/wiki/File:Map_Thirty_Years_War-en.svg

80 https://commons.wikimedia.org/wiki/File:Friedrich_der_Gro%C3%9Fe_(1781_or_1786)_-_Google_Art_Project.jpg

81 Deutsches_Reich1.png: kgbergerderivative work: Wiggy!, CC BY-SA 2.5 <https://creativecommons.org/licenses/by-sa/2.5>, via Wikimedia Commons; https://commons.wikimedia.org/wiki/File:Deutsches_Reich_(1871-1918)-en.png

82 Goran tek-en, CC BY-SA 4.0 <https://creativecommons.org/licenses/by-sa/4.0>, via Wikimedia Commons; https://commons.wikimedia.org/wiki/File:World_War_II_in_Europe,_1942.svg

83 Aeroid, CC BY-SA 4.0 <https://creativecommons.org/licenses/by-sa/4.0>, via Wikimedia Commons; https://commons.wikimedia.org/wiki/File:German_territorial_losses_1919_and_1945.svg

84 https://commons.wikimedia.org/wiki/File:C-54landingattemplehof.jpg